JON LEWIS is the editor of *The Mammoth Book of On the Edge*, *The Mammoth Book of Endurance & Adventure* and *The Mammoth Book of How It Happened: Everest*. He lives in Herefordshire with his wife and two children.

THE MAMMOTH BOOK OF

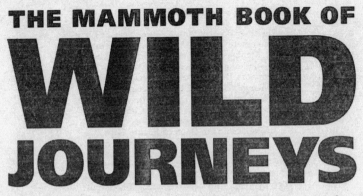

WILD JOURNEYS

45 heart-stopping accounts of adventure travel

Edited by
Jon E. Lewis

ROBINSON
London

Constable & Robinson Ltd
3 The Lanchesters
162 Fulham Palace Road
London W6 9ER
www.constablerobinson.com

First published by Robinson,
an imprint of Constable & Robinson Ltd 2005

A copy of the British Library Cataloguing in
Publication Data is available from the British Library

ISBN 1–84529–153–0

Printed and bound in the EU

1 3 5 7 9 10 8 6 4 2

CONTENTS

INTRODUCTION

Introductions to anthologies are always a little like inviting people to a wine-tasting and then giving them a pep talk. They would infinitely prefer to start sampling the product straightaway. That said, some words of welcome are called for.

The "Wild" in the *Wild Journeys* collected here is largely the Wild-erness of the last remote places on the globe – the Himalayas, Antarctica, the Syrian Desert, the Amazon, the Congo, the Atlantic. But sometimes it is not where you go that counts, but how you go. Tom Fremantle's walk through post-9/11 America with a mule was a "Wild" – in the colloquial sense of unusual – journey, as was Hunter S. Thompson's drug-fuelled road trip through the same country twenty years before. Christina Dodwell's microlight flight across West Africa falls into the same eccentric category.

The "Wild" of the far corner of the world and the "Wild" of the unconventional are not so poles apart as they seem. It is usually forgotten that "Travel" comes from the same etymological root as "Travail". The travellers' tales in this anthology of Wild Journeys are all about what the dictionary defines as "painful effort", be that effort the moral one of risking derision for a travelling style or the physical one of placing oneself in hardship, even danger. Both senses of "Wild" allow the art of

travel-writing to flourish – which is to follow the byways
in the mind which unfamiliar external sights and experiences produce. It is a paradox, but the best – the truest –
travel-writing reveals as much about the human condition
as it does of the outside scenery. The title of Laurens van
der Post's travelogue *Venture to the Interior* might stand
as the generic title for all travel literature.

It has become fashionable to dismiss van der Post as a
fantasist, yet he understood the essence of travel. In searching for the lost bushmen of the Kalahari, van der Post noted:
"With our twentieth-century selves we have forgotten the
importance of being truly and openly primitive . . . We need
primitive nature the First Man in ourselves, it seems, as the
lungs need air and the body water . . . I thought finally that of
all the nostalgias that haunt the human heart the greatest of
them all for me, is an everlasting longing to bring what is
youngest home to what is oldest, in us all."

When we step outside the safety and the routine of the
modern context, then we enter our own Wildness. We
make a pilgrimage back to our primitive selves. We
connect with Nature.

Of course, sometimes it is only possible to travel vicar-
iously and sit in the armchair and read of others' daring
and do. The near fifty writers represented here move that
armchair in all the right directions. When we cannot make
the pilgrimage ourselves, they will go for us.

By definition, these pilgrims are intentional voyagers.
Their troubles are of their own making. And what troubles
they've seen: Apsley Cherry-Garrard's mid-winter trek
across the Antarctic waste to Cape Crozier sets the bench-
mark, although Umberto Nobile's airship flight to the North
Pole, Redmond O'Hanlon's dugout canoe trip in the Amazon,
Bertram Thomas's camel voyage across the Empty Quarter,
F.A. Worsley's open-boat crossing of the South Atlantic
might also claim to be "The Worst Journey in the World".

They are certainly reminders of the truism that the
more travail in the travel, the more worthwhile is the trip.

THE WORST JOURNEY IN THE WORLD

Apsley Cherry-Garrard

Born in Bedford, England, in 1886, Apsley Cherry-Garrard was the second-youngest member of Scott's doomed 1910–13 Antarctic expedition. Everything Cherry-Garrard did thereafter – and he lived until 1959 – was an anti-climax, even service in the First World War. "Talk of ex-soldiers," he later wrote, "give me ex-antarcticists, unsoured and with their ideals intact: they could sweep the world." Cherry-Garrard paid due homage to his fellow "antarcticists" in his only book, The Worst Journey in the World, *his account of the Scott expedition. First published in 1922* The Worst Journey in the World *has attracted many plaudits;* Outside *magazine once ranked it as the best travel book in the world. The "Worst Journey" of the title was not Scott's final push on the Pole, or even the subsequent hunt for the team's corpses, but the 1911 "Winter Journey" undertaken by Bowers, Wilson and the myopic Cherry-Garrard to Cape Crozier in search of the nesting place of the emperor penguin. Here "Cherry" describes the return leg:*

But this I know: we on this journey were already beginning to think of death as a friend. As we groped our way back that night, sleepless, icy, and dog-tired in the dark and the wind and the drift, a crevasse seemed almost a friendly gift.

"Things must improve," said Bill next day, "I think we reached bed-rock last night." We hadn't, by a long way.

It was like this.

We moved into the igloo for the first time, for we had to save oil by using our blubber stove if we were to have any left to travel home with, and we did not wish to cover our tent with the oily black filth which the use of blubber necessitates. The blizzard blew all night, and we were covered with drift which came in through hundreds of leaks: in this wind-swept place we had found no soft snow with which we could pack our hard snow blocks. As we flensed some rubber from one of our penguin skins the powdery drift covered everything we had.

Though uncomfortable this was nothing to worry about overmuch. Some of the drift which the blizzard was bringing would collect to leeward of our hut and the rocks below which it was built, and they could be used to make our hut more weather-proof. Then with great difficulty we got the blubber stove to start, and it spouted a blob of boiling oil into Bill's eye. For the rest of the night he lay, quite unable to stifle his groans, obviously in very great pain: he told us afterwards that he thought his eye was gone. We managed to cook a meal somehow, and Birdie got the stove going afterwards, but it was quite useless to try and warm the place. I got out and cut the green canvas outside the door, so as to get the roof cloth in under the stones, and then packed it down as well as I could with snow, and so blocked most of the drift coming in.

It is extraordinary how often angels and fools do the same thing in this life, and I have never been able to settle which we were on this journey. I never heard an angry word: once only (when this same day I could not pull Bill up the cliff out of the penguin rookery) I heard an impatient one: and these groans were the nearest approach to complaint. Most men would have howled. "I think we reached bed-rock last night," was strong language for Bill. "I was incapacitated for a short time," he says in his report to Scott. Endurance was tested on this journey under unique circumstances, and always these two men, with all the burden of responsibility which did not fall upon myself, displayed that quality which is perhaps the only one which may be said with certainty to make for success, self-control.

We spent the next day – it was 21 July – in collecting every scrap of soft snow we could find and packing it into the crevices between our hard snow blocks. It was a pitifully small amount but we could see no cracks when we had finished. To counteract the lifting tendency the wind had on our roof we cut some great flat hard snow blocks and laid them on the canvas top to steady it against the sledge which formed the ridge support. We also pitched our tent outside the igloo door. Both tent and igloo were therefore eight or nine hundred feet up Terror: both were below an outcrop of rocks from which the mountain fell steeply to the Barrier behind us, and from this direction came the blizzards. In front of us the slope fell for a mile or more down to the ice-cliffs, so wind-swept that we had to wear crampons to walk upon it. Most of the tent was in the lee of the igloo, but the cap of it came over the igloo roof, while a segment of the tent itself jutted out beyond the igloo wall.

That night we took much of our gear into the tent and lighted the blubber stove. I always mistrusted that stove, and every moment I expected it to flare up and burn the tent. But the heat it gave, as it burned furiously, with the double lining of the tent to contain it, was considerable.

It did not matter, except for a routine which we never managed to keep, whether we started to thaw our way into our frozen sleeping-bags at four in the morning or four in the afternoon. I think we must have turned in during the afternoon of that Friday, leaving the cooker, our finnesko, a deal of our foot-gear, Bowers's bag of personal gear, and many other things in the tent. I expect we left the blubber stove there too, for it was quite useless at present to try and warm the igloo. The tent floor-cloth was under our sleeping-bags in the igloo.

"Things must improve," said Bill. After all there was much for which to be thankful. I don't think anybody could have made a better igloo with the hard snow blocks and rocks which were all we had: we would get it air-tight by degrees. The blubber stove was working, and we had fuel for it: we had also found a way down to the penguins and had three complete, though frozen eggs: the two which had been in my mitts smashed when I fell about because I could not wear spectacles. Also the twilight given by the sun below the horizon at noon was getting longer.

But already we had been out twice as long in winter as the longest previous journeys in spring. The men who made those journeys had daylight where we had darkness, they had never had such low temperatures, generally nothing approaching them, and they had seldom worked in such difficult country. The nearest approach to healthy sleep we had had for nearly a month was when during blizzards the temperature allowed the warmth of our bodies to thaw some of the ice in our clothing and sleeping-bags into water. The wear and tear on our minds was very great. We were certainly weaker. We had a little more than a tin of oil to get back on, and we knew the conditions we had to face on that journey across the Barrier: even with fresh men and fresh gear it had been almost unendurable.

And so we spent half an hour or more getting into our bags. Cirrus cloud was moving across the face of the stars from the north; it looked rather hazy and thick to the south, but it is always difficult to judge weather in the dark. There was little wind and the temperature was in the minus twenties. We felt no particular uneasiness. Our tent was well dug in, and was also held down by rocks and the heavy tank off the sledge which were placed on the skirting as additional security. We felt that no power on earth could move the thick walls of our igloo, nor drag the canvas roof from the middle of the embankment into which it was packed and lashed.

"Things must improve," said Bill.

I do not know what time it was when I woke up. It was calm, with that absolute silence which can be so soothing or so terrible as circumstances dictate. Then there came a sob of wind, and all was still again. Ten minutes and it was blowing as though the world was having a fit of hysterics. The earth was torn in pieces: the indescribable fury and roar of it all cannot be imagined.

"Bill, Bill, the tent has gone," was the next I remember – from Bowers shouting at us again and again through the door. It is always these early morning shocks which hit one hardest: our slow minds suggested that this might mean a peculiarly lingering form of death. Journey after journey Birdie and I fought our way across the few yards which had separated the tent from the igloo door. I have never understood why so much of our gear which was in the tent remained, even in the lee of the igloo. The place where the tent had been was littered with gear, and when we came to reckon up afterwards we had everything except the bottom piece of the cooker, and the top of the outer cooker. We never saw these again. The most wonderful thing of all was that our finnesko were lying where they were left, which happened to be on the ground in the part of the tent which was under the lee of the igloo. Also Birdie's bag of personal gear was there, and a tin of sweets.

Birdie brought two tins of sweets away with him. One we had to celebrate our arrival at the Knoll: this was the second, of which we knew nothing, and which was for Bill's birthday, the next day. We started eating them on Saturday, however, and the tin came in useful to Bill afterwards.

To get that gear in we fought against solid walls of black snow which flowed past us and tried to hurl us down the slope. Once started nothing could have stopped us. I saw Birdie knocked over once, but he clawed his way back just in time. Having passed everything we could find in to Bill, we got back into the igloo, and started to collect things together, including our very dishevelled minds.

There was no doubt that we were in the devil of a mess, and it was not altogether our fault. We had had to put our igloo more or less where we could get rocks with which to build it. Very naturally we had given both our tent and igloo all the shelter we could from the full force of the wind, and now it seemed we were in danger, not because they were in the wind, but because they were not sufficiently in it. The main force of the hurricane, deflected by the ridge behind, fled over our heads and appeared to form by suction a vacuum below. Our tent had either been sucked upwards into this, or had been blown away because some of it was in the wind while some of it was not. The roof of our igloo was being wrenched upwards and then dropped back with great crashes: the drift was spouting in, not it seemed because it was blown in from outside, but because it was sucked in from within: the lee, not the weather, wall was the worst. Already everything was six or eight inches under snow.

Very soon we began to be alarmed about the igloo. For some time the heavy snow blocks we had heaved up on to the canvas roof kept it weighted down. But it seemed that they were being gradually moved off by the hurricane. The tension became well-nigh unendurable: the waiting in all that welter of noise was maddening. Minute after minute, hour after hour – those snow blocks were off now anyway, and the roof was smashed up and down – no canvas ever made could stand it indefinitely.

We got a meal that Saturday morning, our last for a very long time as it happened. Oil being of such importance to us we tried to use the blubber stove, but after several preliminary spasms it came to pieces in our hands, some solder having melted; and a very good thing too, I thought, for it was more dangerous than useful. We finished cooking our meal on the primus. Two bits of the cooker having been blown away we had to balance it on the primus as best we could. We then settled that in view of the shortage of oil we would not have another meal for as long as possible. As a matter of fact God settled that for us.

We did all we could to stop up the places where the drift was coming in, plugging the holes with our socks, mitts and other clothing. But it was no real good. Our igloo was a vacuum which was filling itself up as soon as possible: and when snow was not coming in a fine black moraine dust took its place, covering us and everything. For twenty-four hours we waited for the roof to go: things were so bad now that we dare not unlash the door.

Many hours ago Bill had told us that if the roof went he considered that our best chance would be to roll over in our sleeping-bags until we were lying on the openings, and get frozen and drifted in.

Gradually the situation got more desperate. The distance between the taut-sucked canvas and the sledge on which it should have been resting became greater, and this must have been due to the stretching of the canvas itself and the loss of the snow blocks on the top: it was not drawing out of the walls. The crashes as it dropped and banged out again were louder. There was more snow coming through the walls, though all our loose mitts, socks and smaller clothing were stuffed into the worst places: our pyjama jackets were stuffed between the roof and the rocks over the door. The rocks were lifting and shaking here till we thought they would fall.

We talked by shouting, and long before this one of us proposed to try and get the Alpine rope lashed down over the roof from outside. But Bowers said it was an absolute impossibility in that wind. "You could never ask men at

sea to try such a thing," he said. He was up and out of his
bag continually, stopping up holes, pressing against bits
of roof to try and prevent the flapping and so forth. He
was magnificent.

And then it went.

Birdie was over by the door, where the canvas which
was bent over the lintel board was working worse than
anywhere else. Bill was practically out of his bag pressing
against some part with a long stick of some kind. I don't
know what I was doing but I was half out of and half in my
bag.

The top of the door opened in little slits and that green
Willesden canvas flapped into hundreds of little fragments in fewer seconds than it takes to read this. The
uproar of it all was indescribable. Even above the savage
thunder of that great wind on the mountain came the lash
of the canvas as it was whipped to little tiny strips. The
highest rocks which we had built into our walls fell upon
us, and a sheet of drift came in.

Birdie dived for his sleeping-bag and eventually got in,
together with a terrible lot of drift. Bill also – but he was
better off: I was already half into mine and all right, so I
turned to help Bill. "Get into your own," he shouted, and
when I continued to try and help him, he leaned over until
his mouth was against my ear. "*Please*, Cherry," he said,
and his voice was terribly anxious. I know he felt responsible: feared it was he who had brought us to this ghastly
end.

The next I knew was Bowers's head across Bill's body.
"We're all right," he yelled, and we answered in the
affirmative. Despite the fact that we knew we only said
so because we knew we were all wrong, this statement was
helpful. Then we turned our bags over as far as possible,
so that the bottom of the bag was uppermost and the flaps
were more or less beneath us. And we lay and thought,
and sometimes we sang.

I suppose, wrote Wilson, we were all revolving plans to

get back without a tent: and the one thing we had left was the floor-cloth upon which we were actually lying. Of course we could not speak at present, but later after the blizzard had stopped we discussed the possibility of digging a hole in the snow each night and covering it over with the floor-cloth. I do not think we had any idea that we could really get back in those temperatures in our present state of ice by such means, but no one ever hinted at such a thing. Birdie and Bill sang quite a lot of songs and hymns, snatches of which reached me every now and then, and I chimed in, somewhat feebly I suspect. Of course we were getting pretty badly drifted up. "I was resolved to keep warm," wrote Bowers, "and beneath my debris covering I paddled my feet and sang all the songs and hymns I knew to pass the time. I would occasionally thump Bill, and as he still moved I knew he was alive all right – what a birthday for him!" Birdie was more drifted up than we, but at times we all had to hummock ourselves up to heave the snow off our bags. By opening the flaps of our bags we could get small pinches of soft drift which we pressed together and put into our mouths to melt. When our hands warmed up again we got some more; so we did not get very thirsty. A few ribbons of canvas still remained in the wall over our heads, and these produced volleys of cracks like pistol shots hour after hour. The canvas never drew out from the walls, not an inch. The wind made just the same noise as an express train running fast through a tunnel if you have both the windows down.

I can well believe that neither of my companions gave up hope for an instant. They must have been frightened, but they were never disturbed. As for me I never had any hope at all; and when the roof went I felt that this was the end. What else could I think? We had spent days in reaching this place through the darkness in cold such as had never been experienced by human beings. We had been out for four weeks under conditions in which no man had existed previously for more than a few days, if that.

During this time we had seldom slept except from sheer physical exhaustion, as men sleep on the rack; and every minute of it we had been fighting for the bed-rock necessaries of bare existence, and always in the dark. We had kept ourselves going by enormous care of our feet and hands and bodies, by burning oil, and by having plenty of hot fatty food. Now we had no tent, one tin of oil left out of six, and only part of our cooker. When we were lucky and not too cold we could almost wring water from our clothes, and directly we got out of our sleeping-bags we were frozen into solid sheets of armoured ice. In cold temperatures with all the advantages of a tent over our heads we were already taking more than an hour of fierce struggling and cramp to get into our sleeping-bags – so frozen were they and so long did it take us to thaw our way in. No! Without the tent we were dead men.

And there seemed not one chance in a million that we should ever see our tent again. We were 900 feet up on the mountain side, and the wind blew about as hard as a wind can blow straight out to sea. First there was a steep slope, so hard that a pick made little impression upon it, so slippery that if you started down in finnesko you never could stop: this ended in a great ice-cliff some hundreds of feet high, and then came miles of pressure ridges, cre-vassed and tumbled, in which you might as well look for a daisy as a tent: and after that the open sea. The chances, however, were that the tent had just been taken up into the air and dropped somewhere in this sea well on the way to New Zealand. Obviously the tent was gone.

Face to face with real death one does not think of the things that torment the bad people in the tracts, and fill the good people with bliss. I might have speculated on my chances of going to Heaven; but candidly I did not care. I could not have wept if I had tried. I had no wish to review the evils of my past. But the past did seem to have been a bit wasted. The road to Hell may be paved with good inten-tions: the road to Heaven is paved with lost opportunities.

I wanted those years over again. What fun I would have with them: what glorious fun! It was a pity. Well has the Persian said that when we come to die we, remembering that God is merciful, will gnaw our elbows with remorse for thinking of the things we have not done for fear of the Day of Judgement.

And I wanted peaches and syrup – badly. We had them at the hut, sweeter and more luscious than you can imagine. And we have been without sugar for a month. Yes – especially the syrup.

Thus impiously I set out to die, making up my mind that I was not going to try and keep warm, that it might not take too long, and thinking I would try and get some morphia from the medical case if it got very bad. Not a bit heroic, and entirely true! Yes! comfortable, warm reader. Men do not fear death, they fear the pain of dying.

And then quite naturally and no doubt disappointingly to those who would like to read of my last agonies (for who would not give pleasure by his death?) I fell asleep. I expect the temperature was pretty high during this great blizzard, and anything near zero was very high to us. That and the snow which drifted over us made a pleasant wet kind of snipe marsh inside our sleeping-bags, and I am sure we all dozed a good bit. There was so much to worry about that there was not the least use in worrying: and we were so *very* tired. We were hungry, for the last meal we had had was in the morning of the day before, but hunger was not very pressing.

And so we lay, wet and quite fairly warm, hour after hour while the wind roared round us, blowing storm force continually and rising in the gusts to something inde-scribable. Storm force is force 11, and force 12 is the biggest wind which can be logged: Bowers logged it force 11, but he was always so afraid of overestimating that he was inclined to underrate. I think it was blowing a full hurricane. Sometimes awake, sometimes dozing, we had not a very uncomfortable time so far as I can remember. I knew that parties which had come to Cape Crozier in the spring had experienced blizzards which lasted eight or ten days. But this did not worry us as much as I think it did Bill: I was numb. I vaguely called to mind that Peary had survived a blizzard in the open: but wasn't that in the summer?

It was in the early morning of Saturday (22 July) that we discovered the loss of the tent. Some time during that morning we had had our last meal. The roof went about noon on Sunday and we had had no meal in the interval because our supply of oil was so low; nor could we move out of our bags except as a last necessity. By Sunday night we had been without a meal for some thirty-six hours.

The rocks which fell upon us when the roof went did no damage, and though we could not get out of our bags to move them, we could fit ourselves into them without difficulty. More serious was the drift which began to pile up all round and over us. It helped to keep us warm of course, but at the same time in these comparatively high temperatures it saturated our bags even worse than they were before. If we did not find the tent (and its recovery would be a miracle) these bags and the floor-cloth of the tent on which we were lying were all we had in that fight back across the Barrier which could, I suppose, have only had one end.

Meanwhile we had to wait. It was nearly 70 miles home and it had taken us the best part of three weeks to come. In our less miserable moments we tried to think out ways of getting back, but I do not remember very much about that time. Sunday morning faded into Sunday afternoon – into Sunday night – into Monday morning. Till then the blizzard had raged with monstrous fury; the winds of the world were there, and they had all gone mad. We had bad winds at Cape Evans this year, and we had far worse the next winter when the open water was at our doors. But I have never heard or felt or seen a wind like this. I wondered why it did not carry away the earth.

In the early hours of Monday there was an occasional hint of a lull. Ordinarily in a big winter blizzard, when you have lived for several days and nights with that turmoil in your ears, the lulls are more trying than the noise: "the feel of not to feel it". I do not remember noticing that now. Seven or eight more hours passed, and though it was still blowing we could make ourselves heard to one another without great difficulty. It was two days and two nights since we had had a meal.

We decided to get out of our bags and make a search for the tent. We did so, bitterly cold and utterly miserable, though I do not think any of us showed it. In the darkness we could see very little, and no trace whatever of the tent. We returned against the wind, nursing our faces and hands, and settled that we must try and cook a meal somehow. We managed about the weirdest meal eaten north or south. We got the floor-cloth wedged under our bags, then got into our bags and drew the floor-cloth over our heads. Between us we got the primus alight somehow, and by hand we balanced the cooker on top of it, minus the two members which had been blown away. The flame flickered in the draughts. Very slowly the snow in the cooker melted, we threw in a plentiful supply of pemmican, and the smell of it was better than anything on earth. In time we got both tea and pemmican, which was full of hairs from our bags, penguin feathers, dirt and debris, but delicious. The blubber left in the cooker got burnt and gave the tea a burnt taste. None of us ever forgot that meal: I enjoyed it as much as such a meal could be enjoyed, and that burnt taste will always bring back the memory.

It was still dark and we lay down in our bags again, but soon a little glow of light began to come up, and we turned out to have a further search for the tent. Birdie went off before Bill and me. Clumsily I dragged my eider-down out of my bag on my feet, all sopping wet: it was impossible to get it back and I let it freeze: it was soon just like a rock. The sky to the south was as black and sinister as it could possibly be. It looked as though the blizzard would be on us again in a moment.

I followed Bill down the slope. We could find nothing. But, as we searched, we heard a shout somewhere below and to the right. We got on a slope, slipped, and went sliding down quite unable to stop ourselves, and came upon Birdie with the tent, the outer lining still on the bamboos. Our lives had been taken away and given back to us.

We were so thankful we said nothing.

The tent must have been gripped up into the air, shutting as it rose. The bamboos, with the inner lining lashed to them, had entangled the outer cover, and the whole went up together like a shut umbrella. This was our salvation. If it had opened in the air nothing could have prevented its destruction. As it was, with all the accumulated ice upon it, it must have weighed the best part of 100 lbs. It had been dropped about half a mile away, at the bottom of a steep slope: and it fell in a hollow, still shut up. The main force of the wind had passed over it, and there it was, with the bamboos and fastenings wrenched and strained, and the ends of two of the poles broken, but the silk untorn.

If that tent went again we were going with it. We made our way back up the slope with it, carrying it solemnly and reverently, precious as though it were something not quite of the earth. And we dug it in as tent was never dug in before; not by the igloo, but in the old place farther down where we had first arrived. And while Bill was doing this Birdie and I went back to the igloo and dug and scratched and shook away the drift inside until we had found nearly all our gear. It is wonderful how little we lost when the roof went. Most of our gear was hung on the sledge, which was part of the roof, or was packed into the holes of the hut to try and make it drift-proof, and the things must have been blown inwards into the bottom of the hut by the wind from the south and the back draught from the north. Then they were all drifted up. Of course a certain number of mitts and socks were blown away and lost, but the only important things were Bill's fur mitts, which were stuffed into a hole in the rocks of the hut. We loaded up the sledge and pushed it down the slope. I don't know how Birdie was feeling, but I felt so weak that it was the greatest labour. The blizzard looked right on top of us.

We had another meal, and we wanted it: and as the good hoosh ran down into our feet and hands, and up into our cheeks and ears and brains, we discussed what we would do next. Birdie was all for another go at the Emperor penguins. Dear Birdie, he never would admit that he was beaten – I don't know that he ever really was! "I think he [Wilson] thought he had landed us in a bad corner and was determined to go straight home, though I was for one other tap at the Rookery. However, I had placed myself under his orders for this trip voluntarily, and so we started the next day for home."* There could really be no common-sense doubt: we had to go back, and we were already very doubtful whether we should ever manage to get into our sleeping-bags in very low temperature, so ghastly had they become.

I don't know when it was, but I remember walking down that slope – I don't know why, perhaps to try and find the bottom of the cooker – and thinking that there was nothing on earth that a man under such circumstances would not give for a good warm sleep. He would give everything he possessed: he would give – how many – years of his life. One or two at any rate – perhaps five? Yes – I would give five. I remember the sastrugi, the view of the Knoll, the dim hazy black smudge of the sea far away below: the tiny bits of green canvas that twittered in the wind on the surface of the snow: the cold misery of it all, and the weakness which was biting into my heart.

* Bowers

For days Birdie had been urging me to use his eider-down lining – his beautiful dry bag of the finest down – which he had never slipped into his own fur bag. I had refused: I felt that I should be a beast to take it.

We packed the tank ready for a start back in the morning and turned in, utterly worn out. It was only –12° that night, but my left big-toe was frost-bitten in my bag which I was trying to use without an eider-down lining, and my bag was always too big for me. It must have taken several hours to get it back, by beating one foot against the other. When we got up, as soon as we could, as we did every night, for our bags were nearly impossible, it was blowing fairly hard and looked like blizzing. We had a lot to do, two or three hours' work, packing sledges and making a depot of what we did not want, in a corner of the igloo. We left the second sledge, and a note tied to the handle of the pickaxe.

We started down the slope in a wind which was rising all the time and –15°. My job was to balance the sledge behind: I was so utterly done I don't believe I could have pulled effectively. Birdie was much the strongest of us. The strain and want of sleep was getting me in the neck, and Bill looked very bad. At the bottom we turned our faces to the Barrier, our backs to the penguins, but after doing about a mile it looked so threatening in the south that we camped in a big wind, our hands going one after the other. We had nothing but the hardest wind-swept sastrugi, and it was a long business: there was only the smallest amount of drift, and we were afraid the icy snow blocks would chafe the tent. Birdie lashed the full biscuit tin to the door to prevent its flapping, and also got what he called the tent downhaul round the cap and then tied it about himself outside his bag: if the tent went he was going too.

I was feeling as if I should crack, and accepted Birdie's eider-down. It was wonderfully self-sacrificing of him: more than I can write. I felt a brute to take it, but I was getting useless unless I got some sleep which my big bag would not allow. Bill and Birdie kept on telling me to do less: that I was doing more than my share of the work: but I think that I was getting more and more weak. Birdie kept wonderfully strong: he slept most of the night: the difficulty for him was to get into his bag without going to sleep. He kept the meteorological log untiringly, but some of these nights he had to give it up for the time because he could not keep awake. He used to fall asleep with his pannikin in his hand and let it fall: and sometimes he had the primus.

Bill's bag was getting hopeless: it was really too small for an eider-down and was splitting all over the place: great long holes. He never consciously slept for nights: he did sleep a bit, for we heard him. Except for this night, and the next when Birdie's eider-down was still fairly dry, I never consciously slept; except that I used to wake for five or six nights running with the same nightmare – that we were drifted up, and that Bill and Birdie were passing the gear into my bag, cutting it open to do so, or some other variation – I did not know that I had been asleep at all:

"We had hardly reached the pit," wrote Bowers,

when a furious wind came on again and we had to camp. All that night the tent flapped like the noise of musketry, owing to two poles having been broken at the ends and the fit spoilt. I thought it would end matters by going altogether and lashed it down as much as I could, attaching the apex to a line round my own bag. The wind abated after $1\frac{1}{2}$ days and we set out, doing five or six miles before we found ourselves among crevasses.

We had plugged ahead all that day (26 July) in a terrible light, blundering in among pressure and up on to the slopes of Terror. The temperature dropped from $-21°$ to $-45°$.

Several times [we] stepped into rotten-lidded crevasses in smooth wind-swept ice. We continued,
however, feeling our way along by keeping always
off hard ice-slopes and on the crustier deeper snow
which characterizes the hollows of the pressure
ridges, which I believed we had once more fouled
in the dark. We had no light, and no landmarks to
guide us, except vague and indistinct silhouetted
slopes ahead, which were always altering and whose
distance and character it was impossible to judge.
We never knew whether we were approaching a
steep slope at close quarters or a long slope of Terror,
miles away, and eventually we travelled on by the
ear, and by the feel of the snow under our feet, for
both the sound and the touch told one much of the
chances of crevasses or of safe going. We continued
thus in the dark in the hope that we were at any rate
in the right direction.*

And then we camped after getting into a bunch of
crevasses, completely lost. Bill said, "At any rate I think
we are well clear of the pressure." But there were pressure
pops all night, as though someone was whacking an empty
tub.

It was Birdie's picture hat which made the trouble next
day. "What do you think of *that* for a hat, sir?" I heard
him say to Scott a few days before we started, holding it
out much as Lucille displays her latest Paris model. Scott
looked at it quietly for a time: "I'll tell you when you come
back, Birdie," he said. It was a complicated affair with all
kinds of nose-guards and buttons and lanyards: he
thought he was going to set it to suit the wind much as
he would set the sails of a ship. We spent a long time with
our housewifes before this and other trips, for everybody
has their own ideas as to how to alter their clothing for the

* Wilson in *Scott's Last Expedition*, vol. ii, p. 58.

best. When finished some looked neat, like Bill: others baggy, like Scott or Seaman Evans: others rough than ready, like Oates and Bowers: a few perhaps more rough than ready, and I will not mention names. Anyway Birdie's hat became improper immediately it was well iced up.

When we got a little light in the morning we found we were a little north of the two patches of moraine on Terror. Though we did not know it, we were on the point where the pressure runs up against Terror, and we could dimly see that we were right up against something. We started to try and clear it, but soon had an enormous ridge, blotting out the moraine and half Terror, rising like a great hill on our right. Bill said the only thing was to go right on and hope it would lower; all the time, however, there was a bad feeling that we might be putting any number of ridges between us and the mountain. After a while we tried to cross this one, but had to turn back for crevasses, both Bill and I putting a leg down. We went on for about twenty minutes and found a lower place, and turned to rise up it diagonally, and reached the top. Just over the top Birdie went right down a crevasse, which was about wide enough to take him. He was out of sight and out of reach from the surface, hanging in his harness. Bill went for his harness, I went for the bow of the sledge: Bill told me to get the Alpine rope and Birdie directed from below what we could do. We could not possibly haul him up as he was, for the sides of the crevasse were soft and he could not help himself.

"My helmet was so frozen up," wrote Bowers,

that my head was encased in a solid block of ice, and I could not look down without inclining my whole body. As a result Bill stumbled one foot into a crevasse and I landed in it with both mine [even as I shouted a warning], the bridge gave way and down I went. Fortunately our sledge harness is made with a view to resisting this sort of thing, and there I hung with the bottomless pit below and the ice-crusted sides alongside, so narrow that to step over it would have been quite easy had I been able to see it. Bill said, "What do you want?" I asked for an Alpine rope with a bowline for my foot: and taking up first the bowline and then my harness they got me out.

Meanwhile on the surface I lay over the crevasse and gave Birdie the bowline: he put it on his foot: then he raised his foot, giving me some slack: I held the rope while he raised himself on his foot, thus giving Bill some slack on the harness: Bill then held the harness, allowing Birdie to raise his foot and give me some slack again. We got him up inch by inch, our fingers getting bitten, for the temperature was –46°. Afterwards we often used this way of getting people out of crevasses, and it was a wonderful piece of presence of mind that it was invented, so far as I know, on the spur of the moment by a frozen man hanging in one himself.

In front of us we could see another ridge, and we did not know how many lay beyond that. Things looked pretty bad. Bill took a long lead on the Alpine rope and we got down our present difficulty all right. This method of the leader being on a long trace in front we all agreed to be very useful. From this moment our luck changed and everything went for us to the end. When we went out on the sea-ice the whole experience was over in a few days, Hut Point was always in sight, and there was daylight. I always had the feeling that the whole series of events had been brought about by an extraordinary run of accidents, and that after a certain stage it was quite beyond our power to guide the course of them. When on the way to Cape Crozier the moon suddenly came out of the cloud to show us a great crevasse which would have taken us all with our sledge without any difficulty, I felt that we were not to go under this trip after such a deliverance. When we had lost our tent, and there was a very great balance of probability that we should never find it again, and we were lying out the blizzard in our bags, I saw that we were face to face with a long fight against cold which we could not have survived. I cannot write how helpless I believed we were to help ourselves, and how we were brought out of a very terrible series of experiences. When we started back I had a feeling that things were going to change for the better, and this day I had a distinct idea that we were to have one more bad experience and that after that we could hope for better things.

By running along the hollow we cleared the pressure ridges, and continued all day up and down, but met no crevasses. Indeed, we met no more crevasses and no more pressure. I think it was upon this day that a wonderful glow stretched over the Barrier edge from Cape Crozier: at the base it was the most vivid crimson it is possible to imagine, shading upwards through every shade of red to light green, and so into a deep blue sky. It is the most vivid red I have ever seen in the sky.

It was −49° in the night and we were away early in −47°. By midday we were rising Terror Point, opening Erebus rapidly, and got the first really light day, though the sun would not appear over the horizon for another month. I cannot describe what a relief the light was to us. We crossed the point outside our former track, and saw inside us the ridges where we had been blizzed for three days on our outward journey.

The minimum was −66° the next night and we were now back in the windless bight of Barrier with its soft snow, low temperatures, fogs and mists, and lingering settlements of the inside crusts. Saturday and Sunday, the 29th and 30th, we plugged on across this waste, iced up as usual but always with Castle Rock getting bigger. Sometimes it looked like fog or wind, but it always cleared away. We were getting weak, how weak we can only realize now, but we got in good marches, though slow

– days when we did $4\frac{1}{2}$, $7\frac{1}{4}$, $6\frac{3}{4}$, $6\frac{1}{2}$, $7\frac{1}{2}$ miles. On our outward journey we had been relaying and getting forward about $1\frac{1}{2}$ miles a day at this point. The surface which we had dreaded so much was not so sandy or soft as when we had come out, and the settlements were more marked. These are caused by a crust falling under your feet. Generally the area involved is some twenty yards or so round you, and the surface falls through an air space for two or three inches with a soft "crush" which may at first make you think there are crevasses about. In the region where we now travelled they were much more pronounced than elsewhere, and one day, when Bill was inside the tent lighting the primus, I put my foot into a hole that I had dug. This started a big settlement: sledge, tent and all of us dropped about a foot, and the noise of it ran away for miles and miles: we listened to it until we began to get too cold. It must have lasted a full three minutes.

In the pauses of our marching we halted in our harness, the ropes of which lay slack in the powdery snow. We stood panting with our backs against the mountainous mass of frozen gear which was our load. There was no wind, at any rate no more than light airs: our breath crackled as it froze. There was no unnecessary conversation: I don't know why our tongues never got frozen, but all my teeth, the nerves of which had been killed, split to pieces. We had been going perhaps three hours since lunch.

"How are your feet, Cherry?" from Bill.

"Very cold."

"That's all right; so are mine." We didn't worry to ask Birdie: he never had a frost-bitten foot from start to finish.

Half an hour later, as we marched, Bill would ask the same question. I tell him that all feeling has gone: Bill still has some feeling in one of his but the other is lost. He settled we had better camp: another ghastly night ahead.

We started to get out of our harnesses, while Bill, before doing anything else, would take the fur mitts from his hands, carefully shape any soft parts as they froze (generally, however, our mitts did not thaw on our hands), and lay them on the snow in front of him – two dark dots. His proper fur mitts were lost when the igloo roof went: these were the delicate dog-skin linings we had in addition, beautiful things to look at and to feel when new, excellent when dry to turn the screws of a theodolite, but too dainty for straps and lanyards. Just now I don't know what he could have done without them.

Working with our woollen half-mitts and mitts on our hands all the time, and our fur mitts over them when possible, we gradually got the buckles undone, and spread the green canvas floor-cloth on the snow. This was also fitted to be used as a sail, but we never could have rigged a sail on this journey. The shovel and the bamboos, with a lining, itself lined with ice, lashed to them, were packed on the top of the load and were now put on the snow until wanted. Our next job was to lift our three sleeping-bags one by one on to the floor-cloth: they covered it, bulging over the sides – those obstinate coffins which were all our life to us . . . One of us is off by now to nurse his fingers back. The cooker was unlashed from the top of the instrument box; some parts of it were put on the bags with the primus, methylated spirit can, matches and so forth; others left to be filled with snow later. Taking a pole in each hand we three spread the bamboos over the whole. "All right? Down!" from Bill; and we lowered them gently on to the soft snow, that they might not sink too far. The ice on the inner lining of the tent was formed mostly from the steam of the cooker. This we had been unable to beat or chip off in the past, and we were now, truth to tell, past worrying about it. The little ventilator in the top, made to let out this steam, had been tied up in order to keep in all possible heat. Then over the outer cover, and for one of us the third worst job of the day was to begin. The worst job was to get into our bags: the second or equal worst was to lie in them for six hours (we had brought it down to six): this third worst was to get the primus lighted and a meal on the way.

As cook of the day you took the broken metal frame-work, all that remained of our candlestick, and got your-self with difficulty into the funnel which formed the door. The enclosed space of the tent seemed much colder than the outside air: you tried three or four match-boxes and no match would strike: almost desperate, you asked for a new box to be given you from the sledge and got a light from this because it had not yet been in the warmth, so called, of the tent. The candle hung by a wire from the cap of the tent. It would be tedious to tell of the times we had getting the primus alight, and the lanyards of the weekly food bag unlashed. Probably by now the other two men have dug in the tent; squared up outside; filled and passed in the cooker; set the thermometer under the sledge and so forth. There were always one or two odd jobs which wanted doing as well: but you may be sure they came in as soon as possible when they heard the primus hissing, and saw the glow of light inside. Birdie made a bottom for the cooker out of an empty biscuit tin to take the place of the part which was blown away. On the whole this was a success, but we had to hold it steady – on Bill's sleeping-bag, for the flat frozen bags spread all over the floor space. Cooking was a longer business now. Someone whacked out the biscuit, and the cook put the ration of pemmican into the inner cooker which was by now half full of water. As opportunity offered we got out of our day, and into our night foot-gear – fleecy camel-hair stockings and fur boots. In the dim light we examined our feet for frost-bite.

I do not think it took us less than an hour to get a hot meal to our lips: pemmican followed by hot water in which we soaked our biscuits. For lunch we had tea and biscuits: for breakfast, pemmican, biscuits and tea.

We could not have managed more food bags – three were bad enough, and the lashings of everything were like wire. The lashing of the tent door, however, was the worst, and it *had* to be tied tightly, especially if it was blowing. In the early days we took great pains to brush rime from the tent before packing it up, but we were long past that now.

The hoosh got down into our feet: we nursed back frost-bites: and we were all the warmer for having got our dry foot-gear on before supper. Then we started to get into our bags.

Birdie's bag fitted him beautifully, though perhaps it would have been a little small with an eider-down inside. He must have had a greater heat supply than other men; for he never had serious trouble with his feet, while ours were constantly frost-bitten: he slept, I should be afraid to say how much, longer than we did, even in these last days: it was a pleasure, lying awake practically all night, to hear his snores. He turned his bag inside out from fur to skin, and skin to fur, many times during the journey, and thus got rid of a lot of moisture which came out as snow or actual knobs of ice. When we did turn our bags the only way was to do so directly we turned out, and even then you had to be quick before the bag froze. Getting out of the tent at night it was quite a race to get back to your bag before it hardened. Of course this was in the lowest temperatures.

We could not burn our bags and we tried putting the lighted primus into them to thaw them out, but this was not very successful. Before this time, when it was very cold, we lighted the primus in the morning while we were still in our bags: and in the evening we kept it going until we were just getting or had got the mouths of our bags levered open. But returning we had no oil for such luxuries, until the last day or two.

I do not believe that any man, however sick he is, has a much worse time than we had in those bags, shaking with cold until our backs would almost break. One of the added troubles which came to us on our return was the sodden condition of our hands in our bags at night. We had to wear our mitts and half-mitts, and they were as wet as they could be: when we got up in the morning we had washer-women's hands – white, crinkled, sodden. That was an unhealthy way to start the day's work. We really wanted some bags of saennegrass for hands as well as feet; one of the blessings of that kind of bag being that you can shake the moisture from it: but we only had enough for our wretched feet.

The horrors of that return journey are blurred to my memory and I know they were blurred to my body at the time. I think this applies to all of us, for we were much weakened and callous. The day we got down to the penguins I had not cared whether I fell into a crevasse or not. We had been through a great deal since then. I know that we slept on the march; for I woke up when I bumped against Birdie, and Birdie woke when he bumped against me. I think Bill steering out in front managed to keep awake. I know we fell asleep if we waited in the comparatively warm tent when the primus was alight – with our pannikins or the primus in our hands. I know that our sleeping-bags were so full of ice that we did not worry if we spilt water or hoosh over them as they lay on the floor-cloth, when we cooked on them with our maimed cooker. They were so bad that we never rolled them up in the usual way when we got out of them in the morning: we opened their mouths as much as possible before they froze, and hoisted them more or less flat on to the sledge. All three of us helped to raise each bag, which looked rather like a squashed coffin and was probably a good deal harder. I know that if it was only –40° when we camped for the night we considered quite seriously that we were going to have a warm one, and that when we got up in the morning if the temperature was in the minus sixties we did not inquire what it was. The day's march was bliss compared to the night's rest, and both were awful. We were about as bad as men can be and do good travelling: but I never heard a word of complaint, nor, I believe, an oath, and I saw self-sacrifice standing every test.

Always we were getting nearer home: and we were doing good marches. We were going to pull through; it was only a matter of sticking this for a few more days; six, five, four . . . three perhaps now, if we were not blizzed. Our main hut was behind that ridge where the mist was always forming and blowing away, and there was Castle Rock: we might even see Observation Hill tomorrow, and the *Discovery* Hut furnished and trim was behind it, and they would have sent some dry sleeping-bags from Cape Evans to greet us there. We reckoned our troubles over at the Barrier edge, and assuredly it was not far away. "You've got it in the neck, stick it, you've got it in the neck" – it was always running in my head.

And we *did* stick it. How good the memories of those days are. With jokes about Birdie's picture hat: with songs we remembered off the gramophone: with ready words of sympathy for frost-bitten feet: with generous smiles for poor jests: with suggestions of happy beds to come. We did not forget the Please and Thank You, which means much in such circumstances, and all the little links with decent civilization which we could still keep going. I'll swear there was still a grace about us when we staggered in. And we kept our tempers – even with God.

We *might* reach Hut Point tonight: we were burning more oil now, that one-gallon tin had lasted us well: and burning more candle too; at one time we feared they would give out. A hell of a morning we had: –57° in our present state. But it was calm, and the Barrier edge could not be much farther now. The surface was getting harder: there were a few wind-blown furrows, the crust was coming up to us. The sledge was dragging easier: we always suspected the Barrier sloped downwards here-abouts. Now the hard snow was on the surface, peeping out like great inverted basins on which we slipped, and our feet became warmer for not sinking into soft snow. Suddenly we saw a gleam of light in the line of darkness running across our course. It was the Barrier edge: we were all right now.

We ran the sledge off a snow-drift on to the sea-ice, with the same cold stream of air flowing down it which wrecked my hands five weeks ago: pushed out of this, camped and had a meal: the temperature had already risen to −43°. We could almost feel it getting warmer as we went round Cape Armitage on the last three miles. We managed to haul our sledge up the ice foot, and dug the drift away from the door. The old hut struck us as fairly warm.

Bill was convinced that we ought not to go into the warm hut at Cape Evans when we arrived there – tomorrow night! We ought to get back to warmth gradually, live in a tent outside, or in the annexe for a day or two. But I'm sure we never meant to do it. Just now Hut Point did not prejudice us in favour of such abstinence. It was just as we had left it: there was nothing sent down for us there – no sleeping-bags, nor sugar: but there was plenty of oil. Inside the hut we pitched a dry tent left there since Depot Journey days, set two primuses going in it; sat dozing on our bags; and drank cocoa without sugar so thick that next morning we were gorged with it. We were very happy, falling asleep between each mouthful, and after several hours discussed schemes of not getting into our bags at all. But someone would have to keep the primus going to prevent frost-bite, and we could not trust ourselves to keep awake. Bill and I tried to sing a part-song. Finally we sopped our way into our bags. We only stuck *them* three hours, and thankfully turned out at 3 a.m., and were ready to pack up when we heard the wind come away. It was no good, so we sat in our tent and dozed again. The wind dropped at 9.30: we were off at 11. We walked out into what seemed to us a blaze of light. It was not until the following year that I understood that a great part of such twilight as there is in the latter part of the winter was cut off from us by the mountains under which we travelled. Now, with nothing between us and the northern horizon below which lay the sun, we saw as we had not seen for months, and the iridescent clouds that day were beautiful.

We just pulled for all we were worth and did nearly two miles an hour: for two miles a baddish salt surface, then big undulating hard sastrugi and good going. We slept as we walked. We had done eight miles by 4 p.m. and were past Glacier Tongue. We lunched there.

As we began to gather our gear together to pack up for the last time, Bill said quietly, "I want to thank you two for what you have done. I couldn't have found two better companions – and what is more I never shall."

I am proud of that.

Antarctic exploration is seldom as bad as you imagine, seldom as bad as it sounds. But this journey had beggared our language: no words could express its horror.

We trudged on for several more hours and it grew very dark. There was a discussion as to where Cape Evans lay. We rounded it at last: it must have been ten or eleven o'clock, and it was possible that someone might see us as we pulled towards the hut. "Spread out well," said Bill, "and they will be able to see that there are three men." But we pulled along the cape, over the tide-crack, up the bank to the very door of the hut without a sound. No noise from the stable, nor the bark of a dog from the snow drifts above us. We halted and stood there trying to get ourselves and one another out of our frozen harnesses – the usual long job. The door opened – "Good God! here is the Crozier Party," said a voice, and disappeared.

Thus ended the worst journey in the world.

BEAUTY AND THE BADLANDS

Bill Donahue

Donahue writes for Outside *and* Mother Jones; *he lives in Portland, Oregon.*

Just beyond Bismarck, as the train chugged west over the prairie, spitting little black clouds of soot into the sky, the land suddenly changed. On the east side of the Missouri River, the Dakota plains had been unbroken – green and dull and flat as a pool table. Now there were sharp ravines and barren gray slopes and narrow red spires looming above a clay basin that had, for 600 millennia, been eroded by rivers and wind. The badlands: here was that infamous swath of dry terrain that encompasses both prairie flats and jagged gulches as it stretches through the westernmost reaches of Nebraska and the Dakotas.

One can imagine the young Harvard grad on the train – the slight, bespectacled fellow in the black derby – peering out at the rough land with apprehension, and with such awe that the little hairs in his mustache quavered. In 1883, Theodore Roosevelt was not yet the hearty, monocle-wearing honcho we have immortalized as "TR." No, at 24, he was rather a green New York state assemblyman who was still recovering from a childhood plagued by cholera morbus, and he'd come out to the Dakota Territory with boyish notions of shooting a buffalo.

Over the next month in what is today North Dakota, Roosevelt was to experience all the Wild West thrills he craved. He rode horseback through rolling hills of silver sage. He hunted deer in the pelting rain, got tangled up in a cactus, and then shot his buffalo and, in gleeful celebration, performed an Indian war dance over the carcass. By the end of the month, Roosevelt was so enchanted with the badlands that he bought 500 head of cattle to graze by the banks of the Little Missouri River.

And then he began coming west whenever his legislature wasn't in session, spending a week, maybe two weeks at a time in the Territory and living in robust blue-blood splendor. Roosevelt had some locals build him a cabin. He helped his ranchhands herd cattle through the plains' swirling dust, and as his holdings grew to include two ranches and 5,000 head, he slowly transformed from a blind romantic into a seasoned outdoorsman who loves the land because he knows it. He sat before a crackling fire, atop a bearskin rug, and wrote of the great out-of-doors – of, for instance, the "immensity and mystery" of the wilderness and of the Little Missouri, which, "in times of freshets runs a muddy torrent that neither man nor beast can pass."

Such words, recorded in six books that Roosevelt wrote about the Dakota Territory, would become a sort of soundtrack to his presidency, which lasted from 1901 to 1909. The first conservationist to occupy the Oval Office, TR established the Forest Service, placed vast quantities of coal and mineral deposits under federal control, created 16 national monuments, and doubled the number of national parks, adding among others Mesa Verde and Crater Lake. All the while, he remembered his time in the Territory as formative, character building. "I never would have become president," he once said, "if it had not been for my experiences in North Dakota." The Territory was the place where he first established his own empire, 1,500 miles removed from his aristocratic clan in Manhattan, and it was the place where he learned to lasso a bull.

Roosevelt's stint as a Dakota cattleman lasted only four years (he called it quits after the brutal winter of 1886–87 killed hundreds in his herd), but today, if you visit the Little Missouri National Grasslands, a Delaware-size swath of North Dakota badlands that is managed by the Forest Service, it's as though TR never left. The 70,000-acre Theodore Roosevelt National Park adjoins the Grasslands, and in the tourist town of Medora, the play *Bully*, a hagiographic drama about TR, is staged in his honor daily.

The myth is that western North Dakota is still the rugged, unvanquished place that shaped our most rugged president. But the truth is that Teddy Roosevelt's old stomping ground is in trouble – threatened by both cattle ranching and oil drilling.

Fifty-four thousand cows now graze on the Little Missouri National Grasslands on an average summer day. They chew the range, often, until the grass is little more than stubble, and all around them are roads, many of them built by the oil industry. In 1950 oil was discovered under the Grasslands, which sit atop a relict seabed, and tankers and servicemen have been rumbling into the backcountry ever since. There are 3,000 miles of roads on the Grasslands now, and 600 operational wells. Amerada Hess, Burlington Resources, and myriad smaller oil companies are collectively extracting 30,000 barrels a day. And if the current administration gets its way, the Grasslands will soon see more oil production, more roads, more gravel drilling pads, and more oil trucks.

President Bush's energy plan is premised on the assumption that America "faces the most serious energy shortage since the oil embargoes of the 1970s." It eschews conservation and calls instead for the development of new oil fields. Bush is most intent on tapping a potential 600,000 barrels of crude a day from the Arctic National Wildlife Refuge. But as our relations with Saudi Arabia and other oil-producing nations become more tenuous, he's turning with increased thirst toward lower-profile sources of fuel: the Gulf of Mexico, the Rocky Mountain Front, and the Little Missouri Grasslands.

The Forest Service estimates that an unfettered oil industry could plant up to 600 new wells on the Little Missouri National Grasslands over the next decade, and the agency now seems poised to help make that prospect a reality. Last August, after completing the usual public-input process, which resulted in a Grasslands plan that banned roadbuilding on 130,000 acres and limited grazing, the Forest Service made a rare gesture: It gave the public six additional months to comment on the final document. The move was a boon to North Dakota's oilmen and ranchers. The 200-page plan crafted during the last eco-friendly days of the Clinton administration was suddenly open to revision by the aides of President Bush.

The Forest Service is expected to produce the final management plan this spring. And even if the new document still designates 130,000 acres as roadless, an unlikely outcome, it will only protect the land until a new management plan is enacted 10 to 15 years hence.

Wayde Schafer, the conservation organizer for the Sierra Club in North Dakota, is concerned. "The grass-lands," he explains, "were once unbroken from Canada to Texas. The great cattle drives came up through the grasslands of Texas, all the way to the Dakotas, and the Oregon Trail went through here, and the trail to the California gold rush. But today roads, cities, and agricultural fields have fragmented the grasslands almost beyond recognition. Just a few large tracts remain."

This spring, the Sierra Club, along with North Dakota

Wildlife and the North Dakota-based Badlands Conservation Alliance, will publish a report urging that 218,000 acres of the Little Missouri National Grasslands be designated as wilderness and thereby permanently protected from roadbuilding. The report will also suggest that 15 miles of the Little Missouri River be protected as "wild" and 6 as "scenic."

The proposals face an uphill battle. While 87 percent of all North Dakotans want wilderness on the Grasslands (according to an independent poll commissioned by the Sierra Club in 1999), the state's two senators – Democrats Kent Conrad and Byron Dorgan – are beholden to the ranch vote. They're loath to recommend the Grasslands for such a set-aside.

"Getting wilderness designation won't be easy," Schafer concedes, "but that doesn't make it any less worthy a goal. People need to have refuges they can visit to re-create their sense of place. They need to be able to go out onto the Grasslands, into rough country, and experience what Roosevelt did: the strong wind, the sun, a test of one's mettle."

Ah yes, a test! I knew what that word meant, precisely, on the evening I landed in western North Dakota. It was raining. Indeed, the region was in the midst of one of its wettest Junes on record. The dirt roads leading northwest from Medora were at times a slippery gumbo, but I pressed on, through darkness, until I came to an absurdly slick hill and began fishtailing down, toward a cluster of juniper bushes. I parked and shouldered my backpack. Then I walked barefoot across the Little Missouri. The muddy water tore at my shins and chunks of junipers gushed in the current; I anchored my feet on the bottom and made it to the other side.

Here I was, at last, at the site of Theodore Roosevelt's Elkhorn Ranch. The old cabin was gone, thanks to a circa-1900 fire, but the wind's wild rustling of the cottonwoods conjured a sentence from TR's *Hunting Trips of a Ranch-*

man: "From [Elkhorn's] low, long verandah, shaded by leafy cottonwoods, one looks across sandbars and shallows to a strip of meadowlands."

I warmed a tin of Dinty Moore beef stew (the most Rooseveltian meal I could muster under the circumstances) and then went to sleep.

In the morning, I set off on a walk beside the Little Missouri. On the hillside above, there was an oil-drilling rig: a 100-foot-high tower affixed with lights that pulsed silver.

Beneath me as I hiked was a 60-foot-wide current that was vital now in the rain – flooding sandy bottoms, babbling over small stones, and lapping at tree trunks as it bore a brown cloud of silt away. I watched the river. It looked, I imagined, more or less like the river Roosevelt saw each spring when he arrived from New York. As I sloshed along, shivering (it was 50 degrees out, and so windy the rain hit my face at an angle), I remembered how TR, whose cattle drank from the river, saw the Little Missouri as central. "The river flows in long sigmoid curves," he wrote, "through an alluvial valley of no great width. From the edges of the valley, the land rises abruptly in steep high buttes. This broken country extends back from the river for many miles. Every few miles, it is crossed by creeks that open into the Little Missouri, some of them having in their beds here and there a never-failing spring or muddy alkaline-water hole. From these creeks run coulees, or narrow, winding valleys, through which water flows when the snow melts; their bottoms contain patches of brush, and they lead back into the heart of the Bad Lands."

Roosevelt apprehended the river as a geological force – the same force I watched carving the ravine a little bit deeper as I stood there, getting drenched. On the hillside, lights flashed and men in yellow slickers hurried about the base of the drill, checking its progress.

Just as I was leaving the Elkhorn, the rain stopped. I

cracked the car window and the smell of wet sage wafted in as I drove east 20 miles, to the town of Grassy Butte, to meet with the man who is arguably the most stalwart advocate for wilderness on the Grasslands, John Heiser.

Heiser, 51, is a fourth-generation Dakota rancher; he founded the Badlands Conservation Alliance three years ago. Just before I got to North Dakota, Heiser had defended his campaign for wilderness by telling the Associated Press, "There are things that need to be said, and I've said them, and now my neighbours won't talk to me." In the picture that ran next to the quote, Heiser was lean with a rough, wind-weathered face and cool blue eyes that were piercing in their conviction. I felt like I was paying a visit to a sort of grasslands Thoreau.

The first thing Heiser wanted to show me, once I rattled into his driveway, was the pasture where the vesper sparrows had built their nest and laid eggs early that spring. The eggs were still there – brown-speckled, oblong little things in the wheat grass – and Heiser expected them to fledge in a couple of weeks. "I never drive in here," he said, striding beside me in worn denim coveralls. "I don't like to drive on wild grass."

Heiser's voice was deep and unfaltering and he seemed to revel in making absolute statements. I guessed that he probably never fit in too well with North Dakota's rock-ribbed mainstream. "No," he said, "when I was a kid and my dad cut down green ash to make fence posts, I felt sad for the dead trees." Heiser deepened his ecological ethic after college when he took a job herding bison for Theodore Roosevelt National Park. "I chased them on horseback," he said, "sometimes for twenty miles at a dead run. I grew to respect them. Bison are independent. They have fire in their eyes. They resist being tamed."

We walked on and Heiser pointed out the western wallflowers underfoot, and the prairie smoke, a flower whose thin, hairlike fruits look, collectively, like a red mist. Heiser's cows plodded nearby in the blue grama grass. He has 95 head on his 760 acres, and caring for them is hard work. Heiser doesn't use a backhoe to muck out the corral where he winters his yearlings; he uses a wheelbarrow. He doesn't use a pickup to check on his cattle either. Instead, he goes from pasture to pasture on horseback or, more frequently, on foot.

Heiser's whole ranch is ribboned with thin paths he's beaten into the soil, and as we walked one along the edge of a Forest Service-managed pond, Heiser told me about "an incredible evening. I sat by the shore here the other night," he said, "and I saw two beavers – half-grown, the size of footballs – building a dam. One kept diving and bringing up mud, and the other would bring sticks from across the water in his mouth. I watched for an hour, and then I told my neighbor about it. A few days later, I found one of the beavers floating head-down in the pond, shot."

We climbed to the top of a hill, and Heiser kept talking. "This is where I grew up, from the time I was zero," he said. "It's where my connections to nature were formed. It's where I saw bighorn sheep come in from the cold and prairie fires burn. You have experiences like that, when you are young, and you acquire a deep topophilia, a love of place, that you can't escape. It leads you to defend that place."

Since starting the Badlands Conservation Alliance, Heiser has helped defeat an oil company that sought to drill within sight of the national park, and has led nature walks into the badlands' backcountry springs. He is typical of North Dakota environmentalists, who tend to be homegrown and take action because they've seen the idyllic places of their childhood whittled away. But he is also possessed of a singular focus. One winter, he told me as we meandered back toward his barn, he went 30 straight days without ever driving away from his ranch. He just holed up, cooked frozen beef, and kept notes on the black-tailed deer that fed on the hay outside his window. Many other winters, he's conducted backcountry poetry hikes. "If the windchill drops below zero," he said, "I try to cancel, but otherwise we go out a few miles and find shelter and there, beneath a juniper tree or in the lee of a sandstone ledge, we read for maybe half an hour: Gary Snyder, Walt Whitman, Mary Oliver. Poetry fits the badlands. It's life distilled to its bare essentials."

After I left John Heiser's ranch, I drove north to the badlands' only sizable community – Watford City, population 1,500. Watford, which calls itself "the REAL West," is a rarity: a small town almost devoid of chain stores. On its main drag, there is Larsen's Service Drugs, the City Bar, Bob's Bar, Tubby's Auto Sales, Heggen Farm Equipment, and the Four Eyes Motel, whose fluorescent sign bears a drawing of a rather cherubic-looking TR. The soul of the town, though, is just off Main Street in the McKenzie County Bank, where the lobby is appointed with mounted trophies – a moose, a cougar, an elk – and where Vice President Dale Patten can usually be found, fretting.

Patten, a tall, bony man with a balding dome of a forehead, makes his living loaning money to ranchers. He is a commissioner for McKenzie County and he is dead set against the Sierra Club's call for wilderness on the Grasslands. But he and his allies – the commissioners in nearby Billings, Golden Valley, and Slope Counties – have yet to mobilize against wilderness, focusing instead on the Forest Service's Grasslands plan. On the morning I visited Patten at seven, he was underlining the legalese in the Forest Service plan. "This could be apocalyptic," he told me, peering up from his desk. "This plan could have a bigger impact on our way of life than anything since the droughts of the thirties."

Patten was a font of statistics. Citing a report commissioned by the Heritage Association of North Dakota, a group he co-chairs, he argued that the state could lose a billion dollars over the next decade – $500 million in ranching revenues and $500 million in oil revenues. These dire figures were based on a draft of the Grasslands plan that's since been supplanted by a newer, oil-and ranch-friendly version. They were also speculative, and I was not inclined to believe them.

The plan does not enjoin ranchers from grazing cattle – or even driving – in roadless areas. These regions abound with two-track "prairie trails," auto routes too insubstantial to meet the Forest Service's arcane definition of "road," and ranchers can drive on them. Indeed, nationwide, ranchers (and only ranchers) are allowed to drive into federally designated wilderness. If they fill out the requisite paperwork, they can even drive off the two-tracks in wilderness – to rescue a hurt cow, say, or mend a torn fence. The Forest Service predicts that enacting its Grasslands plan would cause, at most, a 9 per cent decrease in grazing and would annually cost the ten counties closest to the Grasslands a total of $2.8 million in lost income. The agency's literature also suggests that, if grazing and oil are curtailed, more and more hikers and mountain bikers will come to the Grasslands, along with their tourist dollars.

But the word "billion" transfixed Patten and he and I spent half a day driving around in his Ford Explorer, surveying a country that is, he insisted, "placed on the brink of economic peril by the Forest Service." We drove by some oil wells, and Patten told me that McKenzie County gets a million or so dollars a year in royalties from drilling on the Grasslands.

Patten and I also visited a tiny elementary school whose student body had dwindled to four. We talked about what Wal-Marts have done to disintegrate small towns on the plains. After a while, we crossed a dry gulch, Horse Creek, and turned off into a patch of Grasslands the Forest Service proposes to keep roadless. We crunched a few miles down a scoria two-track, passing a deer and a few cows, and then Patten pointed toward something in the far distance: a line of white rocks cleared long ago, to the side of a crop field, by homesteaders. The homesteaders had vanished, probably after a string of dry years that crushed North Dakota 60-odd years ago, and now the rocks were surrounded by a sea of grass. They were a sad sight. Someone had failed here.

The truth is that thousands and thousands of people have failed on the badlands. It is an aptly named place: cold, hot, lonely, steep, and underlain with dusty soil that some years gets no more than five inches of rain. It is a place where the prospect of failure is a somber, everyday reality. The Forest Service plan is, on such a landscape, just another black cloud. The cloud probably carries no hail, but folks in McKenzie County do not even want to find out. "Trying to make a living here is hard enough as it is," Patten said. We drove on.

Over the next couple of days, I drove around some more on the Grasslands. All told, I drove over 800 miles in reporting this story and, as I bought all of my fuel in North Dakota, it's a fairly safe bet that I burned up a bit of the Grasslands. This realization made me ask some questions: Should I have skipped driving deep into and around the backcountry? Should I have hiked in? Do all of us drive too much? Are there other alternatives?

I can see Theodore Roosevelt rolling his eyes at such queries. It is quite possible that TR, were he alive today, would be the proud owner of a gargantuan SUV with a custom interior made out of ocelot hide. But perhaps not, for he was a visionary, a radical in Brooks Brothers clothing, and if I squint now, I can see him motoring about in a stylish Honda Insight, his brow furrowed as he glides toward the nirvana of 70 miles per gallon.

The Grasslands cannot, in the long run, withstand the drilling that a consumptive America demands of it. Short of sacrificing the land so loved by Roosevelt, or reverting to horseback as a way to get around, is it possible to devise an energy policy – one that emphasizes higher gas mileage for cars, better transportation systems, and more energy-efficient buildings and appliances? What would a far-sighted president like TR propose?

One can only speculate, and I was doing just that – gnawing on a make-believe historical bone – when I decided, at last, to end my stay in the badlands with a hike. I walked – first over the Buckhorn Trail in the national park and then off this trail and through a broad, grassy plain scattered with juniper and on up the bare brown slope of a butte. It was hot and the sun glared, but the dried mud was soft like pine needles under my feet. I kept going and the hillside got steeper and rocky and a couple of times I had to throw my hands out in front of me and grab at a crag. I pulled my way onto the top, finally, and then stood there in the strong wind and felt my shirt flap at my ribs and the sweat cool and dry on my skin.

Beneath me, there were no people, no sounds, no signs of civilization. Only a gray rock, a cluster of cottonwoods, a green hillside, a sandstone cliff that was yellow and bright in the sun. The land seemed endless, and endowed with a pattern that surpassed logic. I wanted it to stay that way forever.

IN TROUBLE AGAIN

Redmond O'Hanlon

Born in 1947, Redmond O'Hanlon is a former lecturer in English Literature at Oxford University. His first travel book was Into the Heart of Borneo, *which narrated an expedition to the mountains of Batu Tiban with James Fenton. The extract below is from Redmond's second travel volume,* In Trouble Again: A Journey Between the Orinoco and the Amazon.

The dugout came to a standstill. I looked up. Culimacaré had run the bow into the bank. Chimo was resting on his punt pole, staring ahead. Simon suddenly clasped his arms to his head and bowed his body right forward between his knees.

"Oh god, oh god," he said, beginning to rock himself back and forth, "dear god."

We had come out into another channel. But there were axe marks everywhere. It had been cleared. The vegetation had been cleared right down the stream. Someone had come here before us. We had been forestalled. It was all too late. I felt cold down my back, dull and blank in the head, weary, old.

"Who is it?" I said.

"Who is it?" repeated Simon with a strangled chuckle. "Who is it? It's us, you idiot. *We did it.*"

A little way down to the left I recognized the bole of a big red hardwood.

"It's all right," I said, "we've just come in a circle. We'll go back and try again."

Simon flung himself back against the tarpaulin.

"We're lost," he said, pounding his pack with his fist, "it'll take months. *We're lost.*"

The second dugout came up. Galvis shouted his habitual formulaic greeting.

"Simon! No problema!"

"Bloody big problem," muttered Simon, unsmiling. He stared at the duckboards, plucking at his forehead with his right hand, as if he were scraping a cobweb off his face. "You've got to let me go, Redmond. I don't trust myself. *I shall do something terrible.* You've got to let me have their dugout and get back to San Carlos. Galvis will come. He can't stand it either. And Valentine – he's so old he should never have come in the first place."

"Pull yourself together," I said, at once feeling absurd. "You'd never make it without Chimo. And anyway, we must have two boats to get through the Maturaca. What if we smash a boat on these logs?"

Simon shut his eyes, lay back on the tarpaulin, and turned away.

Refusing to speak, Simon sat and looked at the water slipping past the gunwale. We poled quickly and silently down our old track: we drew almost level with a young otter eating something at the bank edge before he looked round, thickset on his short legs, considered us and then scampered off between the thin trees. Culimacaré punted the bow in and picked up a dead paca. A large fruit-eating rodent, about two and a half feet long, it had rat-like front teeth, long whiskers, long toes, and an orange-brown furry coat covered in white spots and lines like a baby

fallow deer. Its belly and chest were white; there were two
teats between the front legs and two between the back.
The broad nose and mouth were covered in foam: the paca
had obviously died by drowning, the otter catching it
from the river and keeping its face underwater. The otter
had begun to eat at the back of the neck.

"It's a gift from God," said Chimo, "and bad luck on
the perro de agua."

We stopped early at one of our own old campsites, an
island at a junction of two narrow, deep channels. We
started a fire, placed water on to boil for scalding the paca
skin, and put up our shelters and hammocks from the
ready-made posts and cross-pieces. Pablo took Chimo's
gun and paddled off on a hunt in the curiara.

Simon retired to his hammock. Down to his last two
cigarettes, he had nearly finished the stock of paperbacks,
too; tonight of all nights, I noticed, he was finally going to
confront *Heart of Darkness*.

Frogs peeped like chaffinches, quacked like mallard,
cawed like rooks. I had a swim, fully dressed, in the cold
water, washing myself and my clothes at the same time. I
then dried myself under my mosquito net; dusted my
crutch in zinc-talc anti-fungus powder (Juan, who had
spurned such an un-macho indulgence, now had difficulty walking); put Anthisan on the bites of the day,
Savlon on the cuts, Canesten cream on my badly rotted
feet. I re-covered myself in sticky Jungle Formula every-
thing-repellent and thought with admiration of Humboldt and Wallace and Spruce who had had none of
these fetishistic comforts.

There was a shot from some way off – although it was
difficult to judge the distance of a noise in such a landscape where even the sound waves from an explosion were
broken up, stilled and smothered almost at once. Valentine and Chimo laid the paca on a bed of palm leaves,
poured boiling water over it, scraped off the fur, slit open
the stomach, threw the guts in the water and jointed the

meat. The bladder drifted slowly away, bobbing up and down, pulled from below by piranhas.

I took out my maps again: CODESUR thought the entrance to the Maturaca was to the north-west of us: Charlie's diagram thought we were in the right place; the Operational Navigational Chart I had bought in London made a wild guess in heavy blue, put a large swamp to the north, but had sound advice for pilots flying to the east of Neblina: "ABRUPT CLIFFS REPORTED IN THIS AREA – HAZARDOUS FLYING UNDER 13,000 FEET."

I was saved from my perplexity by a happy shout. Pablo appeared, the little canoe half swamped by the weight of a huge cayman. We hauled it out and measured it: almost exactly six feet long. Its back, knobbed and ridged, was the exact colour of the brown-black water, its tail was mottled with light patches like dim spots of filtered sunlight. We laid it down on the muddy ground, white belly uppermost. Chimo felt about in the middle just up from its back legs and pulled a slim white penis out of an armoured pouch flush with the curve of the underside. Personally, said Chimo, he could do with an arrangement like that himself round here. It would make life a lot easier. It would make swimming a pleasure. We all agreed. Chimo pointed to the cayman's front right foot: he'd lost all his claws, probably in a fight with an otter when he was a young man. Really big caymans were more likely to go for you than an alligator was, said Chimo, and they were much quicker in the water.

Valentine began to build a platform for smoking the meat; Galvis had almost finished preparing the paca soup. Pablo and the otter had temporarily dispelled the perpetual anxiety about finding food: maybe we could still find the Maturaca, despite everything. Perhaps Simon would recover in a week or two. We turned the cayman over and Pablo opened it up with axe blows along its backbone: unlike alligators and crocodiles, caymans possess an interlocking series of bony plates which protect their sto-

machs. We cut out the dense flesh in sections and laid it on
Valentine's platform: Charlie's knife no longer seemed
quite such an excessive instrument. I slit open the distended stomach and released an appalling stench.

"Jesus," said Simon, who, unnoticed, had come to
watch.

I peeled back the lining and pulled out something that
was covered in fur and slime. It was a small monkey with
big circular eyes; it was intact apart from its tail, its little
hands and feet still in place.

"No, no," said Simon, stepping against a tree, holding
the back of his hand to his nose. "Just promise me, Redmond. Just promise me *you're not going to eat that as well*."

"Mono de las noches," said Chimo.

It was a Nocturnal or Owl monkey – first described by
Humboldt – the only truly night-living monkey in the
world, which comes out fifteen minutes after sunset, safe
from every predator except the great horned owl and, it
seemed, the cayman. It is monogamous: mother and
father and the babies (one a year, and they leave home
when they are two and a half years old) move about
together foraging for fruits, insects, nectar and suitable
leaves. A lonely male searching for a mate will hoot like an
owl, but only when the moon is full. What had happened?
Had a two-year-old fluffed its jump? I threw the tightly
furred little body into the water.

Galvis announced that paca soup was ready. And he
had also cooked Simon's rice and put out a tin of Spam.

"Come on, Galvis," said Simon, banging his mess-tin
with his spoon, "it's the eighth day – where's my tomato
ketchup?"

Juan translated.

"Galvis says it is in the boat," said Juan. "And it is only
the seventh day. You divided the stores. It is your rule.
You must stick to it."

"It's the eighth day," said Simon, doggedly, still banging his tin, "and I want Galvis to get my tomato ketchup."

"Why don't *you* get it?" I said.

"Just keep out of this," said Simon.

"It's only a bottle of tomato ketchup." I said.

"*Precisely*," said Simon.

"You listen," said Juan, shaking with rage, his sharp chin and beard thrust forward, "here we are, lost in this swamp. Everyone is trying to be cheerful, even when we are all afraid. We are lost. We have no food but the paca and the cayman and your rice and tins of meat which were meant to be for all of us to stop us from starvation, but which now are almost gone – and you complain about your sauces."

"Steady," I said.

Simon turned on me, his eyes wild, his face taut.

"I'm going to kill this little shit," he said, "I warn you. I'm going to bust his teeth in."

"Not here," I said, suddenly exhausted. "Fight anywhere else if you must, but not here. Just for my sake."

"Dear god," said Simon, throwing his mess tin and spoon to the ground and bringing his right fist down on the side of his thigh with a convulsive spasm.

Hunched forward, he walked to the edge of the island, by the black, still-rising water, and he looked up into the dark overhang of trees. Then he threw his head up and back, like a dog.

"Where's-my-tom-ato-ketch-up?" he screamed into six million square kilometres of jungle.

There was no echo from the soft leaves.

CROSSING THE EMPTY QUARTER

Bertram Thomas

The Englishman Bertram Thomas (1892–1950) made the first crossing of the "Abode of Emptiness" or Rub 'al Khali in Arabia. He was accompanied on his venture, which lasted 67 days over the winter of 1930–1, by a party of Rashid Bedouin who had sworn loyalty to him.

Never before had the great South Arabian desert of Rub 'al Khali been crossed by white man, and the ambition to be its pioneer seized me as it had seized every adventurous Englishman whose lot has been cast in Arabia. But before I tell of the manner of my camel crossing and of the things that befell, I must briefly introduce the reader who is uninitiated in matters Arabian to the lie of the land.

"The World," said the medieval Moslem geographer, "is in shape like a ball, and it floats in the circumambient ocean like an egg in water, half in and half out. Of the exposed portion one half constitutes the Inhabited Quarter, while the remaining half is the Empty Quarter, the Rub 'al Khali placed in the barren wastes of Arabia."

An extravagant estimate, this, of the place of our wanderings; yet it is no mean desert that approaches an area as big as England and France together. That it should

have remained *terra incognita* till after the icy Polar
regions, the tropic sources of the Amazon, and the vast
interior spaces of Asia and Africa had been made to yield
up their secrets to Western curiosity, is strange. An
Arabian explanation was given to the traveller Charles
Doughty, by his genial companion Zayed as Shaykhan,
that worthy, with his finger upon a page of Arab script,
declaring the matter in this wise: "God has given two of
the four parts of the earth to the children of Adam, the
third part He has given to Gog and Magog, the fourth is
the Rub 'al Khali void of the breath of life."

Lack of rain and merciless heat indeed make of this a
place where the Persian poet would have us believe "the
panting sinner receives a foretaste of his future destiny."
Certainly human life can be but spasmodically supported,
and then mostly round the desert's fringes, where, among
semi-barbarous nomadic tribes, hunger and the raid are
Nature's pruning-hooks.

Native suspicion and an insular outlook combine with
insecurity of life to keep the infidel intruder at arm's
length, and he who would travel hopefully and usefully
requires some apprenticeship and acclimatisation: needs
must he speak the tongue, know the mind, grow a beard,
dress and act like his desert companions, betraying, for
instance, no squeamishness over drinking water, pestifer-
ous though it might be, drawn from unsampled waterholes come upon in the burning sands, and not improved
by churning in strong-smelling animal-skins carried on
the march. But to our story!

On the 5th October, 1931, the S.S. *British Grenadier*,
homeward bound from Persia, arrived off Muscat harbour at dawn, and there picked me up, by arrangement,
from a small boat. Two nights later I was dropped,
clothed in native dress, into an Arab dhow we sighted
riding at anchor off the central-south Arabian shore.
Landing, I made my way to the rendezvous where I
had expected a trusted Arab chieftain who had served

me on an earlier desert expedition, but I found neither him nor his promised string of riding camels.

Experience had taught me the need of not disclosing my plans to anyone in a land where secrecy of movement at the outset is imperative. My hopes of even making a start were thus dashed, and, sick at my bad luck, I turned up into the Qara Mountains to think and to scheme, while I explored and hunted their forested slopes. More than two impatient months passed before despair gave way to reviving hope.

It was the 10th December when at last I set out from Dhufar with a party of desert Arabs that included the famous Sheikh Salih, of the Rashid (Kathir) tribe, 26 warriors – nearly all of whom could show the scars of wounds, none of whom had I set eyes on before – and 40 camels. The first day's march was as usual cut short, some of the men returning to the booths to buy a trifling gimcrack with which to gladden the eyes of their beauties far away in the black tents, some for a final watering at the sweet well of the mosque, while skins in which we carried our water were oiled and made watertight, and crude, improvised sacks, which did for pack-saddles, were given a final look over.

Our northerly course, on the morrow, led upward through the dense jungles of the Qara escarpment, where I had reaped a bountiful harvest for the Museum – hyenas, wolves, and coneys, snakes and lizards, chameleons, birds, and butterflies; and at Qatan I looked back for a last glimpse of the blue Indian Ocean 3,000 feet below. Waving yellow meadows that crowned the uplands gave place to libaniferous shrubs as we wended our way down the far side, amid red and rugged rocks wherein were groves of the frankincense and myrrh trees that gave rise to the fame of the Arabia of antiquity, of which we gain echoes in the Bible. Never could camp-fires have been more luxuriantly fragrant.

Soon we were to bid farewell to this pleasant countryside of rippling brooks and gay bird life, the decorative stork by day and the eerie sound of the tree-bat by night. The pebbly gorge of Dauka, by which we descended, grew shallower as we went, and became but a sandy, serpentine depression in the arid wilderness beyond. In such ancient dried-up river-beds as this is the secret of life, for the night dews that here collect give rise to an arterial way of desert flora across the barren plain and the route of the caravan.

The foothills of the southern mountains soon sank below our horizon in rear, and the vast clean spaces of a flint-strewn steppe stretched northward before us. Sand-devils, slender columns of whirling sand, sometimes swept hither and thither; sometimes the skyline danced before us in a hot, shimmering mirage, distorting a far-away bush into an expansive copse, an antelope into some monstrous creature, and generally playing tricks with lakes of illusory water.

For the next two months the stars were my only roof, for I travelled, like my companions, without a tent; and as the thermometer almost immediately fell to 45° fahrenheit at night, one felt bitterly cold after the hot days in the saddle, wearing the same clothes day and night. The luxury of a tent had to be eschewed, in order to keep camel-loads at a minimum, for there were certain indispensable things to carry – rations of rice, sugar, native fat, and dates; mapping instruments: a compass, sextant, artificial horizon, chronometers, barometers, and hydrometer; natural-history skinning instruments, killing-bottles, and preserving chests; a rifle, for none goes unarmed in these parts, it being held neither safe nor respectable; and to pay my way, gunnybags stuffed with 3,000 Maria Theresa dollars, which I kept under my saddle by day and my pillow by night.

I had to be careful to conceal my sextant and keep my star observations unobserved, lest I be suspected of magic or worse, and to this end I always contrived to sleep some thirty or forty yards away from the camp and wait till my companions had settled down for the night. This they did after prayers and hobbling their camels over the best pastures available, lying sprawling around the flickering camp-fires with their rifle as their only bedding.

A few days' march northward across the gently declining steppe brought us to the waterhole of Shisur, where we dallied for two days to rest our camels preparatory to a nine-days' waterless and hungry stretch westward. This was to be the most dangerous part of my journey, for it is a no-man's-land with a bloody reputation for raiding and counter-raiding between the various tribes of these southern borderlands; and as I was moving with Rashidi tribesmen, I was particularly apprehensive of a collision with a party of the Sa'ar tribe, their hereditary enemies, for whom, moreover, the money I carried would doubtless have acted as a magnet.

Yellow sand-dunes rose tier upon tier, backing the western reaches of Umm al Hait, the mighty, dried-up river-system I had discovered and mapped on an earlier journey; and hummocky summits were crowned with tamarisk, which in these hungry marches brought our camels running up at the glad sight. It is impossible to carry fodder over these long trails, and camels have to fend for themselves, or rather, a small, well-mounted reconnaissance party goes off to discover the best pastures in the neighbourhood before a general move.

Hence the route taken by the desert traveller cannot with certainty be determined; his course will most likely not be the straightest and shortest one between two points, as with an aeroplane in the air or a ship at sea. And thus it came about that although my plan was to cross the sands northward from sea to sea, I here found myself travelling from east to west along the southern bulwark of the sands.

The full force of the tropical afternoon sun in our faces made me appreciate the Beduin headdress, the long kerchief which can be wound round the face being merciful indeed as a protection from the sun's burning rays, though my lips and nostrils rarely escaped. Glare glasses I never used, for the reason of possible queer effects on my companions' unaccustomed minds.

"Look, sahib!" said the Arabs riding at my side, one afternoon, and pointing to the ground. "There is the road to Ubar. Ubar was a great city that our fathers have told us existed in olden times; a city that possessed much treasure and had date gardens and a fort of red silver (gold); it now lies buried beneath the sands, men say in the Rumlait Shu'ait, maybe a few days to the north."

I had heard of Ubar, an ancient Atlantis of the sands, as it were, from Arab companions of an earlier expedition in the eastern desert, but none could tell of its location. Where my notice was now directed there were deep impressions as of ancient caravan tracks in the hard steppe surface, leading away only to be lost under a wall of sand.

Desiccation of climate through the ages and the extension of the sands, ever encroaching southward, could have brought about its disuse, for it can have led to nowhere worth leading to in historic times, and is now good for nothing. If this local tradition is well founded, Ubar may preserve a memory of the famed land of Ophir, long since lost in the mists of antiquity.

Our course, now trending more to the south, past the dunes of Yibaila and Yadila, was interesting for large, silvery patches in the hollows suggesting a dried-up sea, but which turned out to be sheets of gypsum; though, curiously enough, all along this borderland between sand and steppe, 1,000 feet and more above sea-level and to-day more than 100 miles from the coast, the surface was strewn with oyster and other shell fossils, suggesting that this desert was once an ocean bed.

Beyond Yadila I was next to experience what is extremely rare even for an Arabian explorer, and that was singing sands. As we were floundering along through heavy dune country, the silence was suddenly broken and I was startled for a moment, not knowing what the interruption was or whence it came. "Listen to that ridge bellowing," said a Badu at my side, and looking to where he pointed I saw away on our right hand a steepish sand-cliff about a hundred feet high.

I was too deeply absorbed in the sound to talk, and there was nothing unusual to the eye. The hour was 4.15, and a slight northerly wind blew from the rear of the cliff. I must often have observed similar conditions, but never before heard any accompanying bellowing, only the spec-tacle of a film of sand smoking over the sand-ridges to build up a shape recalling a centurion's helmet. But here the leeward side of the cliff, facing us, was a fairly steep sloping wall, and maybe the surface sands were sliding; certainly some mysterious friction was in progress on a vast scale to produce such startling loud booming. The noise was comparable to a deep pedal-note of an organ, or the siren of a ship heard, say, from a couple of cables distant. It continued for about two minutes and then ended as abruptly as it had begun.

The term "singing sands" seems hardly the most sat-isfactory one to describe a loud and single note, but it is too firmly established to cavil over, for singing sands are mentioned by quite early Chinese writers, and Marco Polo, who crossed the Great Gobi Desert in the thirteenth century, wrote: "Sometimes you shall hear the sound of musical instruments and still more commonly the sound of drums."

We bade adieu to hungry and shivering steppe border-lands, and, turning northward, struck into the body of the sands. The scene before us was magnificent. The sands became almost Alpine in architectural structure, towering mountainously above us, and from the summits we were rewarded with the most glorious panoramas of purest rose-red colour. This Uruq region of the central south must surely be the loftiest throughout all the great ocean of sands.

Our camels climbed arduously the soft slopes, and, slithering knee-deep, made slow progress. No one remained mounted. Indeed, there were places where we had to dig footholds in the sands to enable our animals to climb, other places where we turned back to find an easier way. No horse could have negotiated these southern sands, even if brought here, and the waterless marches behind us, with many consecutive days of ten hours in the saddle, would have made the bringing impossible. A motor-car, too, would surely have charged these slopes in vain.

"The gift of God" – that is the illuminating name by which the Arab nomad knows the camel; and how great is his consideration for her! Time and time again I found myself the only member of our party in the saddle, the Arabs preferring to walk and so spare their mounts, running hither and thither to collect a juicy tuft of camel-thorn with which to feed the hungry brutes as we marched along. In the deserts, halts are called, not in accordance with a European watch, but where Nature has, for the nonce, blessed the site with camel pastures. The great ungainly beasts, which you start by despising and learn greatly to admire, are the only means by which you move forward to success or back and out to safety. If camels perish in the remoter waterless wastes, their masters must perish with them.

Christmas Eve was to be a night of excitement and false alarm. We had arrived late in camp, camels had been hobbled and shooed off to the scant bushes, from behind some of which came the brisk noises of merry camp-fire parties. There was a sudden scream. To me it was like the hooting of an owl or the whining of some wild beast.

"*Gom! Gom!* – Raiders! Raiders!" shouted the excitable Beduin, leaping to their feet, their rifles at the ready; and my Arab servant came running across to me with my Winchester and ammunition. Our *rabias* (safe-escorts) of the Awamir and Karab tribes rushed out in different directions into the night, shouting – "We are alert! We are alert! We are So-and-so (giving their names) of such-and-such tribes. These are our party and are under our protection."*

The object of this was to save us from raiders of their own particular tribes, if such they were, for these would then stay their hand. The cry, I gathered, is never abused: certainly in 1928 I had owed my life, during a journey through the south-eastern borderlands, to my Harsusi *rabia*, who saved us from ambush by members of his own tribe after these had already opened fire at short range.

Our camels were now played out. Their humps, plump and large at the outset, told a story; for the hump is the barometer of the camel's condition, and ours had fallen miserably away. To move onwards involved raising fresh camels, a contingency that had been foreseen, and Sheikh Salih sent ahead to search the Rashidi habitat. He and I had at the outset counted on the need of four relays, but in the event three proved sufficient.

Propitious rains (over great areas rain does not fall throughout the year) of last season in the sands of Dakaka had given rise to superior pastures, and to that area, therefore, the herds had this year gravitated. At the waterhole of Khor Dhahiyah we acquired a new caravan and pushed leisurely westward towards where our third caravan for the final northward dash across the sands was to assemble.

My companions scanned the sands for sign of friend or foe. "Look, sahib! that's So-and-so," my men said, pointing to a camel's foot impression that looked, to me, like any other. "See! she is gone with calf: look how deep are the impressions of her tracks!" And so, following these in the sands, we came up with the object of our quest.

The accuracy of their divination was fascinating. Reading sand-imprints recalled finger-print identifying in the

---

* The night's vigil proved to have been unnecessary, for at dawn the tracks of a sand-wolf were traced near by; its whoop had been mistaken for the war-cry of raiders in the final act.

West, except that it is far less laborious and slow, and not at all the technical job of a highly trained specialist. In fact, every Badu bred in these sands reads the sand-imprints with the readiest facility, for all creation goes unshod, except on an occasion when a Badu wears socks against extreme heat or cold – this being rare, because it is considered effeminate.

The sands are thus an open diary, and he who runs may read. Every one of my companions not only knew at a glance the foot impression of every man and every camel in my caravan, but claimed to know every one of his tribe and not a few of his enemies. No bird may alight, no wild beast or insect pass but needs must leave its history in the sands, and the record lasts until the next wind rises and obliterates it. To tell-tale sand-tracks a sand-fox and many snakes, hares, and lizards, which I added to my collection, owed their undoing, for their hiding-places were in vain.

Whenever, in future, we halted for the night, generally just before sunset, Hamad, my Murra *rabia*, would slink back over our tracks for a few miles with my telescope to ensure that we were not being tracked by an enemy, and return just after nightfall with the good news that camp-fires could now be safely lighted.

I picked up fragments of ostrich eggs, often in a semi-petrified condition, and members of my party had shot ostriches hereabouts in their youth, though these birds appear now to be extinct. So also the *rim* or white gazelle is becoming rare, though I saw horns lying about, while the common red gazelle and the larger edible lizards are inhabitants of the bordering steppe rather than of the sands, as is the antelope, specimens of which I shot, besides bringing home a young live one.

It is the antelope whose long, straight horns occasionally appear to be a single spear when she runs across your front, thus giving rise, as some suppose, to the ancient myth of the unicorn. This legendary guardian of chastity

allowed none but virtuous maidens to approach it, when
its anger turned to joy; and, singularly, to-day in these
southern marches the only musical instrument known is a
pipe made of antelope horn, which the Arab maiden plays
on the joyful occasions of marriage and circumcision.

Of animal life in the sands, a small sand-coloured wolf
is said to be met with in parts where subsoil water,
however brackish, can be reached by pawing; a sand-
coloured fox and a lynx – relatively non-drinking varieties
– are commoner; and the hare, the most widespread
mammal, is hunted by the Beduin's *salugi* dog (familiar
to British breeders as the Salukhi hound). Of birds I saw
very few – bustards, sand-larks, sand-grouse, owls, and
the most common, a black raven, while old eggs in a
gigantic nest show that the Abyssinian tawny eagle comes
on important visits.

The full moon before the fast month of Ramadhan
found us at the waterhole of Shanna, where my third,
last, and much-reduced caravan (13 men and 5 pack
animals) was to rendezvous. One of our old camels was
ailing, and there is only one way with a worn-out camel in
the desert – namely, to kill and eat it. The law of Leviticus
is also the law of Islam: flesh not lawfully slaughtered is
sinful to eat; wherefore the hats went round, and 56
dollars, plus her earnings due from me, satisfied the
owner of the almost blind 40-year-old Fatira. The beast
was slaughtered, jointed, and divided into heaps after the
Arabs had all had a good swig at the contents of her
bladder – they had done the same to the antelope's
bladder – and for the joints the Beduin now cast lots.

In the steppe, where stones availed, they would have
grilled the carcass on a heap of heated stones with a fire
beneath – the Stone Age manner, surely! Here as much as
sufficed for a meal was boiled in brackish water, and the
rest they allowed to remain uncooked, and so carried it
exposed on their saddles, where all the cooking that it
received was drying from the heat of the sun. These

saddle-dainties the Beduin were to nibble with great relish in the marches ahead, and to declare to be very good. My own view, I confess, was one to be concealed!

The zero hour for the dash northward had arrived. Star sights and traverse-plotting showed my position on the 10th January, 1932, to be lat. 19° N., long. 50° 45' E. My objective, Qatar, on the Persian Gulf, was thus bearing slightly to the east of north, about 330 miles in a straight line across the mysterious sands. Two only of my thirteen Beduin – the Murras – claimed to have been over this line of desert before. I had rations left for but twenty-five days.

Clearly, no one could afford to fall ill. A hold-up for ten days, an insufficient rate of progress, a meeting with a party of raiders outnumbering us – any of these might spell disaster. Throughout my journey I was screened from any Arab encampments, that, for all I knew, might have been just over the skyline, the single exception being a tiny encampment of Murra, kinsmen of my guide, where an old man lay dying.

It was made up of one or two miserably small tents, roughly spun – doubtless by the womenfolk – of brown and white camel's hair; tent-pegs that once had been the horns of an antelope; a hammer and a leathern bucket or two – these perhaps typical of the belongings of poor nomadic folk, among whom wealth is counted, primarily, in the noble possessions of camel herds and firearms.

Marching north, the character of the desert sands changed; from the sweeping red landscapes of Dakaka we passed through the region of Suwahib, of lighter hue and characteristic parallel ridges in echelon formation; then the white ocean calms of the central sands, succeeded by a rolling swell of redder colour; and with these changing belts the desert flora changed too, the height above sea-level falling progressively.

Contrary to expectation, the great central sand-ocean was found to be not waterless. We dug down to water at quite shallow depths – a fathom and a half or so; but it was so brackish as to be almost undrinkable – not unlike Epsom-salt both in taste and in its effect on man and beast. There are places where even the camel cannot drink the water, though normally when pastures bring nomads to these parts their camels play the part of distillers, for they drink the water and their masters drink their milk.

The shallow waterholes of the southern sands are sometimes filled in, after water, to hinder a possible pursuer, but in the low, shallowing sands of the north, where patches of hard floor made their first appearance, the waterholes were regular wells, sometimes seventeen fathoms and more deep. They are rare and precious, too, apart from their sweeter contents, for great labour and skill have gone to their making. Both making and cleaning out, which must be done periodically, exact a toll of life, for the soft sides are prone to slip in and entomb the miners, and all that avails for revetment is the branches of dwarf sand-bushes.

Onwards through these great silent wastes my little party moved ever northwards, and my bones no longer ached at the daily demand of eight hours in the saddle. On setting out in the morning the Badu with his first foot forward would mumble some pious invocation – a constant reminder of the great uncertainty and insecurity which shadows him:

In the name of God the Merciful, the
   Compassionate,
Reliance is upon Thee.
There is none other and none equal to Thee.
In the name of God the Merciful.
Deliverance from the slinking devil;
And on Him we rely.

Their inborn philosophy of life is strictly fatalistic, holding that whatever comes to pass is according to a

Divine and inscrutable Will. Their attitude to me, at first sullen and suspicious, changed with growing intimacy as the days passed, and they could be, with a few exceptions, cheerful and friendly companions. Under the stimulating effects of a juicy patch of camel pasture come upon unexpectedly, they would break forth into merry chanting, while around the night camp-fire they never tired of telling me stories from their entrancing folklore.

January 22nd brought the first of a series of sandstorms, and I passed many fitful nights. The hissing of the sand-laden wind, the rattling of pack-cordage, and icy cold feet – for the night temperature often fell to within five degrees of freezing point – made sleeping out-of-doors, without a roof over one's head, intolerable.

Eagerly one waited for the dawn. The wind then dropped, and camp-fires were the scene of huddled, shivering Beduin who now roused their camels that had been rounded up overnight for safety, and the wretched beasts shuffled off to graze and feel the warmth of the rising sun. For me the nights had tragic results, the sand-drifts having buried my instruments, making some of them of little further use.

But I was on the last lap. And though for many days sweeping, stinging, blinding winds enveloped us in a blanket of yellow mist, a fine morning came when, climbing the towering sand-hill of Nakhala, I beheld before me a silver streak of sea along the faraway sky-line. Success was in sight. Keeping the coast a day's march, by report, on our right hand, our northerly course carried us through quarry-like country abounding in fossil shells, the aneroid recording below sea-level readings.

And here we came upon an interesting discovery – a lake in this wilderness. For several miles we marched along its western shore. The Beduin, walking to the edge, brought away large chunks of rock salt that for a width of twenty feet lined its border. There along the water's edge, too, was a line of dead-white locusts, desiccated specimens of the large red variety which, collected and thrown alive on to the hot ash of the camp-fire, sizzles into one of the few delicacies of the Beduin. Wretched creatures, these locusts, for they seem to delight in swarming out from the thirsty desert in spring-time, only to take a suicidal plunge into the first water they come to.

Our lake behind us, we trekked on through bleak stony country, the haunt of owl and wolf, that proved to be the base of the Qatar peninsula. A Gulf *shamal* was blowing, but its attendant cold and drizzling rain were powerless to damp the enthusiasm of my poor companions on the eve of a rare pay-day. They chanted the water-chants which, alas! I should be hearing for the last time, and our thirsty camels pricked up their ears with eager knowingness. And so, at last, we came to the fort of Qatar's ruler standing bold and beckoning on the rim of the sea. The dim luxury of a bath and a square meal was at hand. I had lost a stone and a half in weight on my 650-mile camel journey, but the great south Arabian desert, hitherto a blank on our maps, had ceased to be an enigma and a reproach.

WALKABOUT

Ffyona Campbell

Called by Sir Ranulph Fiennes the "greatest walker of them all", Ffyona Campbell began her walk around the world in 1983, aged sixteen. Eleven years and 20,000 miles later she returned to her start point, John O'Groats. Below is an extract from the Australian leg of Campbell's world walking tour, undertaken with the aid of driver-factotum David Richard and the "Wombat", a Toyota campervan.

Day 45

Another blister had become infected. It was blue and bruised around the edges and oozing pus, but my pain threshold had risen after the previous infection and, popping an antibiotic, I managed to hobble along.

It was so hot that the thermometer shaft shattered on the outside of the Wombat and the mercury was gone. My ears thumped and the soles of my shoes stuck to the melting bitumen. I had felt that kind of heat in America, pushed hard through its barriers but never quite reached breaking point. I was curious about these "walls"; what did dehydration feel like? I was searching for my limits – deserts are perfect places to find them.

The sun sapped my energy. I was sluggish. Birds

nodded off in the thrumming heat as everything slowed around me. Discarded snake skins lay drying in the verges like parchment scrolls and the flesh of rotting roos curled away from bones and stank. All around me the blur of scrub, blue bush, sky and sun. There were mirages and I must have sweated enough to look like one myself to the two road-trains that thundered past. They were the first I had seen – trucks hauling at least two container trailers, and I had been warned – they move over for no one. Their whiplash tailwinds belched the stench of burning rubber, heating the mirages. I was thirsty and lightheaded. The Wombat was like an oven when I reached it.

"No more," I gasped. "I will walk only at night." I had to increase my daily distance and night was the only solution to avoid the sun.

We marked the road and drove ahead to Iron Knob where we knew there was a campground with a space for the afternoon. The park was a patch of cleared scrub where two gums stood, twisted and wizened as though they had squirmed over the years to find shelter from the sun. A 1960s caravan, of a type we endearingly referred to as a "mouldy shower curtain", was parked under one; we stopped under the other. The sun was directly overhead.

Desperate to sleep, I tried to count sheep, tried to count flies, but only slept lightly. David tried to sleep cramped up in the front and I felt guilty. I had not asked him to, but the heat of two people on the bed, sweating and bumping into each other was not conducive to any kind of rest.

It was 7.30 p.m. by the time I stepped again on to the road. It was cooler now the sun had gone, but the wind that had crossed the northern deserts was still hot. The moon was so bright that if I had been walking the other way I would have needed to wear sunglasses.

Beyond Iron Knob lay the source of its name; a massive mountain of iron ore which is the principal source of raw material for the Australian steel industry. The lights from the mine could be seen across the desert for hours; I felt I was getting nowhere. David was tired and went ahead to sleep leaving me alone. I could hear my breathing and the even fall of my feet. The lights of a car extended my shadow in front of me. It slowed.

"You trying to get somewhere?"

"I'm on a charity walk."

"S'truth. Good on ya, mate. Where ya walkin'?"

"Perth."

"You've got a long way to go."

"I've come a long way too."

"Where?"

"I've walked from Scotland." I liked to shock sometimes, and alone in the desert in the dead of night seemed the perfect opportunity.

He told me he was from Kalgoorlie.

"When will you get there?"

"Late tomorrow night, what about you?"

"I do sixty to seventy kilometres a day."

"Well, I'll buy you a beer when you get there. That'll be about a month from now. Sure you don't want a lift?"

"Thanks, but I'm earning that beer." A month and I still wouldn't be in Perth.

A fresh kill was sprawled across my path. A fox was eating it. He didn't run as I passed, but hissed and flashed possessive yellow eyes in the light of my torch. I put up my hands and spoke softly. "It's OK, I've already eaten, thank you." It was so still, so quiet the stars beamed above and the Half-Heart was there, guiding me to the west. The Seven Sisters pulled Jupiter across the sky in a formation I named the Chariot, racing the ancient planets to the west. To walk the other way would have been like swimming against the tide.

I passed a rest area where the dark form of a road-train loomed and then another. The drivers lay sleeping, oblivious to a small person walking by. Then one of them awoke, the engine started, the lights flooded across the land, so brightly that my shadow was fierce. The truck slowed as it reached me, but instead of seeing a friendly

face looking down from the lighted cab, I could see
nothing but an arm.

"I don't need a lift thanks!" I shouted up at the light
and suddenly the arm threw something. Catching a shaft
of light it looked like a cigarette butt; I dodged. It was an
apple. I picked it up and waved after them. I rubbed it on
my T-shirt and walked on, munching quietly.

Then there was no noise except for me. The skulls of
roos lay white on the verge. A mouse scurried out from
the desert, ran a full circle around me and then fled back
into the scrub. Shooting stars ripped across the dome.
How big everything is in the desert.

I reached the Wombat at 2.15 a.m. We tucked into a feast
and I finished a cigarette. It was time to go. My feet were
painful, the air was sleepy. "Just one more, and I'll be off." I
lit another and supped my tea. Each movement sounded so
loud in the desert. But there was nobody to hear a cry for help.

"You OK?"

"Yeah, I'm fine. Don't worry about me." But David
was my lifeline and I did worry about him. He was
beginning to look drawn and grey around the eyes. He
looked older.

I stubbed out the cigarette and stepped out into the
night. It took a while for the light-headed nicotine effect
to be replaced by easy breathing in the clean night air.
Those bloody "stink things". I did try to give up but
there were no other rewards at the end of the day worth
walking for. I couldn't get fired up for a whisky because
we didn't have any and the food was so unpalatable that I
wouldn't have walked as far as the fridge for it.

During the fourth quarter the dawn came rippling
through the scrub behind me with a luxuriously light
breeze and Venus shone bright in its midst. I felt very sick
as I walked the last six kilometres, perhaps from drinking
coffee but perhaps, more probably, I was not used to
feeling so tired at this time in the morning; my mind was
saying, "Oh God another day."

WEST WITH THE NIGHT

Beryl Markham

Beryl Markham was born in England in 1902, although she spent most of her childhood in East Africa, where her father farmed and bred horses. Aged twenty-nine Markham determined to become a pilot, and made headlines in 1936 when she became the first person to fly solo across the Atlantic from east to west. Her only book, West with the Night, *a volume of autobiography, was published in 1942. She died in 1989.*

I have seldom dreamed a dream worth dreaming again, or at least none worth recording. Mine are not enigmatic dreams; they are peopled with characters who are plausible and who do plausible things, and I am the most plausible amongst them. All the characters in my dreams have quiet voices like the voice of the man who telephoned me at Elstree one morning in September of 1936 and told me that there was rain and strong head winds over the west of England and over the Irish Sea, and that there were variable winds and clear skies in mid-Atlantic and fog off the coast of Newfoundland.

"If you are still determined to fly the Atlantic this late in the year," the voice said, "the Air Ministry suggests that the weather it is able to forecast for tonight, and for tomorrow morning, will be about the best you can expect."

The voice had a few other things to say, but not many, and then it was gone, and I lay in bed half-suspecting that the telephone call and the man who made it were only parts of the mediocre dream I had been dreaming. I felt that if I closed my eyes the unreal quality of the message would be re-established, and that, when I opened them again, this would be another ordinary day with its usual beginning and its usual routine.

But of course I could not close my eyes, nor my mind, nor my memory. I could lie there for a few moments – remembering how it had begun, and telling myself, with senseless repetition, that by tomorrow morning I should either have flown the Atlantic to America – or I should not have flown it. In either case this was the day I would try.

I could stare up at the ceiling of my bedroom in Aldenham House, which was a ceiling undistinguished as ceilings go, and feel less resolute than anxious, much less brave than foolhardy. I could say to myself, "You needn't do it, of course," knowing at the same time that nothing is so inexorable as a promise to your pride.

I could ask, "Why risk it?" as I have been asked since, and I could answer, "Each to his element." By his nature a sailor must sail, by his nature a flyer must fly. I could compute that I had flown a quarter of a million miles; and I could foresee that, so long as I had a plane and the sky was there, I should go on flying more miles.

There was nothing extraordinary in this. I had learned a craft and had worked hard learning it. My hands had been taught to seek the controls of a plane. Usage had taught them. They were at ease clinging to a stick, as a cobbler's fingers are in repose grasping an awl. No human pursuit achieves dignity until it can be called work, and when you can experience a physical loneliness for the tools of your trade, you see that the other things – the experiments, the irrelevant vocations, the vanities you used to hold – were false to you.

Record flights had actually never interested me very

much for myself. There were people who thought that such flights were done for admiration and publicity, and worse. But of all the records – from Louis Blériot's first crossing of the English Channel in 1909, through and beyond Kingsford Smith's flight from San Francisco to Sydney, Australia – none had been made by amateurs, nor by novices, nor by men or women less than hardened to failure, or less than masters of their trade. None of these was false. They were a company that simple respect and simple ambition made it worth more than an effort to follow.

The Carberrys (of Seramai) were in London and I could remember everything about their dinner party – even the menu. I could remember June Carberry and all her guests, and the man named McCarthy, who lived in Zanzibar, leaning across the table and saying, "J. C., why don't you finance Beryl for a record flight?"

I could lie there staring lazily at the ceiling and recall J. C.'s dry answer: "A number of pilots have flown the North Atlantic, west to east. Only Jim Mollison has done it alone the other way – from Ireland. Nobody has done it alone from England – man or woman. I'd be interested in that, but nothing else. If you want to try it, Burl, I'll back you. I think Edgar Percival could build a plane that would do it, provided you can fly it. Want to chance it?"

"Yes."

I could remember saying that better than I could remember anything – except J. C.'s almost ghoulish grin, and his remark that sealed the agreement: "It's a deal, Burl. I'll furnish the plane and you fly the Atlantic – but, gee, I wouldn't tackle it for a million. Think of all that black water! Think how cold it is!"

And I had thought of both.

I had thought of both for a while, and then there had been other things to think about. I had moved to Elstree, half-hour's flight from the Percival Aircraft Works at Gravesend, and almost daily for three months now I had flown down to the factory in a hired plane and

watched the Vega Gull they were making for me. I had
watched her birth and watched her growth. I had watched
her wings take shape, and seen wood and fabric moulded
to her ribs to form her long, sleek belly, and I had seen her
engine cradled into her frame, and made fast.

The Gull had a turquoise-blue body and silver wings.
Edgar Percival had made her with care, with skill, and
with worry – the care of a veteran flyer, the skill of a
master designer, and the worry of a friend. Actually the
plane was a standard sport model with a range of only six
hundred and sixty miles. But she had a special under-
carriage built to carry the weight of her extra oil and
petrol tanks. The tanks were fixed into the wings, into the
centre section, and into the cabin itself. In the cabin they
formed a wall around my seat, and each tank had a petcock
of its own. The petcocks were important.

"If you open one," said Percival, "without shutting the
other first, you may get an airlock. You know the tanks in
the cabin have no gauges, so it may be best to let one run
completely dry before opening the next. Your motor
might go dead in the interval – but she'll start again.
She's a De Havilland Gipsy – and Gipsys never stop."

I had talked to Tom. We had spent hours going over the
Atlantic chart, and I had realized that the tinker of Molo,
now one of England's great pilots, had traded his dreams
and had got in return a better thing. Tom had grown older
too; he had jettisoned a deadweight of irrelevant hopes
and wonders, and had left himself a realistic code that had
no room for temporizing or easy sentiment.

"I'm glad you're going to do it, Beryl. It won't be
simple. If you can get off the ground in the first place,
with such an immense load of fuel, you'll be alone in that
plane about a night and a day – mostly night. Doing it east
to west, the wind's against you. In September, so is the
weather. You won't have a radio. If you misjudge your
course only a few degrees, you'll end up in Labrador or in
the sea – so don't misjudge anything."

Tom could still grin. He had grinned; he had said: "Anyway, it ought to amuse you to think that your financial backer lives on a farm called 'Place of Death' and your plane is being built at 'Gravesend.' If you were consistent, you'd christen the Gull 'The Flying Tombstone.'"

I hadn't been that consistent. I had watched the building of the plane and I had trained for the flight like an athlete. And now, as I lay in bed, fully awake, I could still hear the quiet voice of the man from the Air Ministry intoning, like the voice of a dispassionate court clerk: ". . . the weather for tonight and tomorrow . . . will be about the best you can expect." I should have liked to discuss the flight once more with Tom before I took off, but he was on a special job up north. I got out of bed and bathed and put on my flying clothes and took some cold chicken packed in a cardboard box and flew over to the military field at Abingdon, where the Vega Gull waited for me under the care of the R.A.F. I remember that the weather was clear and still.

Jim Mollison lent me his watch. He said: "This is not a gift. I wouldn't part with it for anything. It got me across the North Atlantic and the South Atlantic too. Don't lose it – and, for God's sake, don't get it wet. Salt water would ruin the works."

Brian Lewis gave me a life-saving jacket. Brian owned the plane I had been using between Elstree and Gravesend, and he had thought a long time about a farewell gift. What could be more practical than a pneumatic jacket that could be inflated through a rubber tube?

"You could float around in it for days," said Brian. But I had to decide between the life-saver and warm clothes. I couldn't have both, because of their bulk, and I hate the cold, so I left the jacket.

And Jock Cameron, Brian's mechanic, gave me a sprig of heather. If it had been a whole bush of heather, complete with roots growing in an earthen jar, I think

I should have taken it, bulky or not. The blessing of Scotland, bestowed by a Scotsman, is not to be dismissed. Nor is the well-wishing of a ground mechanic to be taken lightly, for these men are the pilot's contact with reality.

It is too much that with all those pedestrian centuries behind us we should, in a few decades, have learned to fly; it is too heady a thought, too proud a boast. Only the dirt on a mechanic's hands, the straining vise, the splintered bolt of steel underfoot on the hangar floor – only these and such anxiety as the face of a Jock Cameron can hold for a pilot and his plane before a flight, serve to remind us that, not unlike the heather, we too are earthbound. We fly, but we have not "conquered" the air. Nature presides in all her dignity, permitting us the study and the use of such of her forces as we may understand. It is when we presume to intimacy, having been granted only tolerance, that the harsh stick falls across our impudent knuckles and we rub the pain, staring upward, startled by our ignorance.

"Here is a sprig of heather," said Jock, and I took it and pinned it into a pocket of my flying jacket.

There were press cars parked outside the field at Abingdon, and several press planes and photographers, but the R.A.F. kept everyone away from the grounds except technicians and a few of my friends.

The Carberrys had sailed for New York a month ago to wait for me there. Tom was still out of reach with no knowledge of my decision to leave, but that didn't matter so much, I thought. It didn't matter because Tom was unchanging – neither a fairweather pilot nor a fairweather friend. If for a month, or a year, or two years we sometimes had not seen each other, it still hadn't mattered. Nor did this. Tom would never say, "You should have let me know." He assumed that I had learned all that he had tried to teach me, and for my part, I thought of him, even then, as the merest student must think of his mentor. I could sit in a cabin overcrowded with petrol tanks and set my course for North America, but the knowledge of my hands on the controls would be Tom's knowledge. His words of caution and words of guidance, spoken so long ago, so many times, on bright mornings over the veldt or over a forest, or with a far mountain visible at the tip of our wing, would be spoken again, if I asked.

So it didn't matter, I thought. It was silly to think about.

You can live a lifetime and, at the end of it, know more about other people than you know about yourself. You learn to watch other people, but you never watch yourself because you strive against loneliness. If you read a book, or shuffle a deck of cards, or care for a dog, you are avoiding yourself. The abhorrence of loneliness is as natural as wanting to live at all. If it were otherwise, men would never have bothered to make an alphabet, nor to have fashioned words out of what were only animal sounds, nor to have crossed continents – each man to see what the other looked like.

Being alone in an aeroplane for even so short a time as a night and a day, irrevocably alone, with nothing to observe but your instruments and your own hands in semi-darkness, nothing to contemplate but the size of your small courage, nothing to wonder about but the beliefs, the faces, and the hopes rooted in your mind – such an experience can be as startling as the first awareness of a stranger walking by your side at night. You are the stranger.

It is dark already and I am over the south of Ireland. There are the lights of Cork and the lights are wet; they are drenched in Irish rain, and I am above them and dry. I am above them and the plane roars in a sobbing world, but it imparts no sadness to me. I feel the security of solitude, the exhilaration of escape. So long as I can see the lights and imagine the people walking under them, I feel selfishly triumphant, as if I have eluded care and left even the small sorrow of rain in other hands.

It is a little over an hour now since I left Abingdon. England, Wales, and the Irish Sea are behind me like so much time used up. On a long flight distance and time are the same. But there had been a moment when Time stopped – and Distance too. It was the moment I lifted the blue-and-silver Gull from the aerodrome, the moment the photographers aimed their cameras, the moment I felt the craft refuse its burden and strain toward the earth in sullen rebellion, only to listen at last to the persuasion of stick and elevators, the dogmatic argument of blueprints that said she *had* to fly because the figures proved it.

So she had flown, and once airborne, once she had yielded to the sophistry of a draughtsman's board, she had said, "There: I have lifted the weight. Now, where are we bound?" – and the question had frightened me.

"We are bound for a place thirty-six hundred miles from here – two thousand miles of it unbroken ocean. Most of the way it will be night. We are flying west with the night."

So there behind me is Cork; and ahead of me is Berehaven Lighthouse. It is the last light, standing on the last land. I watch it, counting the frequency of its flashes – so many to the minute. Then I pass it and fly out to sea.

The fear is gone now – not overcome nor reasoned away. It is gone because something else has taken its place; the confidence and the trust, the inherent belief in the security of land underfoot – now this faith is transferred to my plane, because the land has vanished and there is no other tangible thing to fix faith upon. Flight is but momentary escape from the eternal custody of earth.

Rain continues to fall, and outside the cabin it is totally dark. My altimeter says that the Atlantic is two thousand feet below me, my Sperry Artificial Horizon says that I am flying level. I judge my drift at three degrees more than my weather chart suggests, and fly accordingly. I am flying blind. A beam to follow would help. So would a radio – but then, so would clear weather. The voice of the man at the Air Ministry had not promised storm.

I feel the wind rising and the rain falls hard. The smell

of petrol in the cabin is so strong and the roar of the plane so loud that my senses are almost deadened. Gradually it becomes unthinkable that existence was ever otherwise.

At ten o'clock p.m. I am flying along the Great Circle Course for Harbour Grace, Newfoundland, into a forty-mile headwind at a speed of 130 miles an hour. Because of the weather, I cannot be sure of how many more hours I have to fly, but I think it must be between sixteen and eighteen.

At ten-thirty I am still flying on the large cabin tank of petrol, hoping to use it up and put an end to the liquid swirl that has rocked the plane since my take-off. The tank has no gauge, but written on its side is the assurance: "This tank is good for four hours."

There is nothing ambiguous about such a guaranty. I believe it, but at twenty-five minutes to eleven, my motor coughs and dies, and the Gull is powerless above the sea.

I realize that the heavy drone of the plane has been, until this moment, complete and comforting silence. It is the actual silence following the last splutter of the engine that stuns me. I can't feel any fear; I can't feel anything. I can only observe with a kind of stupid disinterest that my hands are violently active and know that, while they move, I am being hypnotized by the needle of my altimeter.

I suppose that the denial of natural impulse is what is meant by "keeping calm," but impulse has reason in it. If it is night and you are sitting in an aeroplane with a stalled motor, and there are two thousand feet between you and the sea, nothing can be more reasonable than the impulse to pull back your stick in the hope of adding to that two thousand, if only by a little. The thought, the knowledge, the law that tells you that your hope lies not in this, but in a contrary act – the act of directing your impotent craft toward the water – seems a terrifying abandonment, not only of reason, but of sanity. Your mind and your heart reject it. It is your hands – your stranger's hands – that follow with unfeeling precision the letter of the law.

I sit there and watch my hands push forward on the stick and feel the Gull respond and begin its dive to the sea. Of course it is a simple thing; surely the cabin tank has run dry too soon. I need only to turn another petcock . . .

But it is dark in the cabin. It is easy to see the luminous dial of the altimeter and to note that my height is now eleven hundred feet, but it is not easy to see a petcock that is somewhere near the floor of the plane. A hand gropes and reappears with an electric torch, and fingers, moving with agonizing composure, find the petcock and turn it; and I wait.

At three hundred feet the motor is still dead, and I am conscious that the needle of my altimeter seems to whirl like the spoke of a spindle winding up the remaining distance between the plane and the water. There is some lightning, but the quick flash only serves to emphasize the darkness. How high can waves reach – twenty feet, perhaps? Thirty?

It is impossible to avoid the thought that this is the end of my flight, but my reactions are not orthodox; the various incidents of my entire life do not run through my mind like a motion-picture film gone mad. I only feel that all this has happened before – and it has. It has all happened a hundred times in my mind, in my sleep, so that now I am not really caught in terror; I recognize a familiar scene, a familiar story with its climax dulled by too much telling.

I do not know how close to the waves I am when the motor explodes to life again. But the sound is almost meaningless. I see my hand easing back on the stick, and I feel the Gull climb up into the storm, and I see the altimeter whirl like a spindle again, paying out the distance between myself and the sea.

The storm is strong. It is comforting. It is like a friend shaking me and saying, "Wake up! You were only dreaming."

But soon I am thinking. By simple calculation I find that my motor had been silent for perhaps an instant more than thirty seconds.

I ought to thank God – and I do, though indirectly. I thank Geoffrey De Havilland who designed the indomitable Gipsy, and who, after all, must have been designed by God in the first place.

A lighted ship – the daybreak – some steep cliffs standing in the sea. The meaning of these will never change for pilots. If one day an ocean can be flown within an hour, if men can build a plane that so masters time, the sight of land will be no less welcome to the steersman of that fantastic craft. He will have cheated laws that the cunning of science has taught him how to cheat, and he will feel his guilt and be eager for the sanctuary of the soil.

I saw the ship and the daybreak, and then I saw the cliffs of Newfoundland wound in ribbons of fog. I felt the elation I had so long imagined, and I felt the happy guilt of having circumvented the stern authority of the weather and the sea. But mine was a minor triumph; my swift Gull was not so swift as to have escaped unnoticed. The night and the storm had caught her and we had flown blind for nineteen hours.

I was tired now, and cold. Ice began to film the glass of the cabin windows and the fog played a magician's game with the land. But the land was there. I could not see it, but I had seen it. I could not afford to believe that it was any land but the land I wanted. I could not afford to believe that my navigation was at fault, because there was no time for doubt.

South to Cape Race, west to Sydney on Cape Breton Island. With my protractor, my map, and my compass, I set my new course, humming the ditty that Tom had taught me: "Variation West – magnetic best. Variation East – magnetic least." A silly rhyme, but it served to placate, for the moment, two warring poles – the magnetic

and the true. I flew south and found the lighthouse of
Cape Race protruding from the fog like a warning finger.
I circled twice and went on over the Gulf of Saint
Lawrence.

After a while there would be New Brunswick, and then
Maine – and then New York. I could anticipate. I could
almost say, "Well, if you stay awake, you'll find it's only a
matter of time now" – but there was no question of
staying awake. I was tired and I had not moved an inch
since that uncertain moment at Abingdon when the Gull
had elected to rise with her load and fly, but I could not
have closed my eyes. I could sit there in the cabin, walled
in glass and petrol tanks, and be grateful for the sun and
the light, and the fact that I could see the water under me.
They were almost the last waves I had to pass. Four
hundred miles of water, but then the land again – Cape
Breton. I would stop at Sydney to refuel and go on. It was
easy now. It would be like stopping at Kisumu and going
on.

Success breeds confidence. But who has a right to
confidence except the Gods? I had a following wind,
my last tank of petrol was more than three-quarters full,
and the world was as bright to me as if it were a new
world, never touched. If I had been wiser, I might have
known that such moments are, like innocence, short-
lived. My engine began to shudder before I saw the land.
It died, it spluttered, it started again and limped along. It
coughed and spat black exhaust toward the sea.

There are words for everything. There was a word for
this – airlock, I thought. This had to be an airlock because
there was petrol enough. I thought I might clear it by
turning on and turning off all the empty tanks, and so I
did that. The handles of the petcocks were sharp little
pins of metal, and when I had opened and closed them a
dozen times, I saw that my hands were bleeding and that
the blood was dropping on my maps and on my clothes,
but the effort wasn't any good. I coasted along on a sick

and halting engine. The oil pressure and the oil temperature gauges were normal, the magnetos working, and yet I
lost altitude slowly while the realization of failure seeped
into my heart. If I made the land, I should have been the
first to fly the North Atlantic from England, but from my
point of view, from a pilot's point of view, a forced
landing was failure because New York was my goal. If
only I could land and then take off, I would make it still
. . . if only, if only . . .

The engine cuts again, and then catches, and each time it
spurts to life I climb as high as I can get, and then it splutters
and stops and I glide once more toward the water, to rise
again and descend again, like a hunting sea bird.

I find the land. Visibility is perfect now and I see land
forty or fifty miles ahead. If I am on my course, that will
be Cape Breton. Minute after minute goes by. The
minutes almost materialize; they pass before my eyes like
links in a long slow-moving chain, and each time the
engine cuts, I see a broken link in the chain and catch my
breath until it passes.

The land is under me. I snatch my map and stare at it to
confirm my whereabouts. I am, even at my present
crippled speed, only twelve minutes from Sydney Airport, where I can land for repairs and then go on.

The engine cuts once more and I begin to glide, but
now I am not worried; she will start again, as she has done,
and I will gain altitude and fly into Sydney.

But she doesn't start. This time she's dead as death; the
Gull settles earthward and it isn't any earth I know. It is
black earth stuck with boulders and I hang above it, on
hope and on a motionless propeller. Only I cannot hang
above it long. The earth hurries to meet me, I bank, turn,
and sideslip to dodge the boulders, my wheels touch, and
I feel them submerge. The nose of the plane is engulfed
in mud, and I go forward striking my head on the glass
of the cabin front, hearing it shatter, feeling blood pour
over my face.

I stumble out of the plane and sink to my knees in muck and stand there foolishly staring, not at the lifeless land, but at my watch.

Twenty-one hours and twenty-five minutes.

Atlantic flight. Abingdon, England, to a nameless swamp – nonstop.

A Cape Breton Islander found me – a fisherman trudging over the bog saw the Gull with her tail in the air and her nose buried, and then he saw me floundering in the embracing soil of his native land. I had been wandering for an hour and the black mud had got up to my waist and the blood from the cut in my head had met the mud halfway.

From a distance, the fisherman directed me with his arms and with shouts toward the firm places in the bog, and for another hour I walked on them and came toward him like a citizen of Hades blinded by the sun, but it wasn't the sun; I hadn't slept for forty hours.

He took me to his hut on the edge of the coast and I found that built upon the rocks there was a little cubicle that housed an ancient telephone – put there in case of shipwrecks.

I telephoned to Sydney Airport to say that I was safe and to prevent a needless search being made. On the following morning I did step out of a plane at Floyd Bennett Field and there was a crowd of people still waiting there to greet me, but the plane I stepped from was not the Gull, and for days while I was in New York I kept thinking about that and wishing over and over again that it had been the Gull, until the wish lost its significance, and time moved on, overcoming many things it met on the way.

THE CROSSING

Nick Danziger

Nick Danziger, born in 1958, is an Anglo-American travel writer and artist. In the extract below, from Danziger's Travels, *he relates his 1984 escape from Soviet-occupied Afghanistan with a mujahedin jeep convoy bound for Pakistan.*

The journey, as we bucked and bumped our way across the desert, was quite backbreaking, but I felt that I could take it pretty uncomplainingly, for after all it would only be another couple of nights, and then . . . Then, goodbye helicopters, MiGs, RPGs and barren desert. Why, in 72 hours' time I would be relaxing in the swimming pool of a sumptuous hotel.

My daydreams were abruptly overwhelmed by the sight of another burnt-out Symorgh. It was the fifth wreck we had passed. How many dead, I wondered, just in this little struggle for control of the road. Clearly it was not firmly back in mujahedin hands.

We were going to have to travel for a short stretch along the main road that links Kabul and Kandahar, and we had sent scouts ahead to check if it was clear. Now, we pulled over to await their return. It was a tense time, and I found myself having to breathe deeply and regularly to contain my excitement. I did not think I could bear it if they were to return and say "*Ra band*" – the way is closed.

"When can we expect them?" I asked one of my companions – a rather better-off young man, who had feigned sickness off and on in the hope of getting me to give him some pills, which I think he took to be like sweets.

"Two hours," he said promptly. I decided to expect them in four. In fact, they returned in precisely two hours, and you could tell by their faces what they were going to say.

"*Ra band*."

We spent the rest of that night and the whole of the next day holed up tensely at an oasis, marking time under the shadow of the trees, while the scouts were dispatched yet again to keep an eye on the situation. Restlessly, we once again discussed alternative possibilities. As we did so, Abdul Mohmy, his usual tireless self, went to bake bread for us at a nearby hamlet.

"Could we walk?" I asked.

"It would take five days – if we could get through."

"No water," said Abdul Rahman. He was more restless than anyone else, and clearly couldn't relax.

"What's the matter with him? Is he ill?" I asked Zahir, my minder.

"I think he must be afraid," replied Zahir.

With two hours of daylight left the scouts returned, this time with the heartening but almost unbelievable news that the road was once again "*ra azad*". I hoped it would still be so by the time we reached it. We headed off at once.

We had only just cleared the first hill and begun to travel along a dry river bed when someone near me began to scream, "*Tiare!*"

The panicky word caught on, and soon they were all yelling it, craning for a sight of the sky from the packed jeep. They had spotted a plane.

The jeep slowed violently, and we struggled to bail out, but there were many unable to jump when the jeep decided to take off at full speed. We were the middle jeep. The leader had carried on apparently unaware; the last one had seen the panic ahead and reversed up a hill. Ours had come to a halt some way off and the driver and the mechanic were throwing a tarpaulin over it. We had all rushed up a steep incline and now crouched huddled together, taking refuge in whatever crevice we could find – all, that is, except for one man who had taken off in the other direction – into the open – where, to my total disbelief, he now knelt and proceeded to pray. We strained our ears for the noise of the returning jet, but we must have been just in time to get out of its way, for the sound of its engine faded and finally died.

Once the danger was over, the whole group settled down to pray – I have to say that I found this vexing, given how urgent our situation was. Our driver seemed to pray for an inordinately long time.

We caught up with the first jeep. They, too, had heard the plane, and had rounded a bend and pulled up close to the cliff-wall of the valley we had been passing through.

"Thank God for that valley," the mechanic said.

"Thank God we weren't five minutes further along the track," said the driver. "Then we would have been in open desert."

During the long days of marching before Nouzad, I had learned to tell the time by measuring the length of my shadow cast by the sun. Now I tried to teach myself how to get my bearings by the stars. I always kept an eye on where the nearest mountains were, and remembered the location of the last oasis we had visited. This wasn't easy. We never took a direct route, but were forever weaving around the desert. I was most impressed by our drivers' uncanny sense of direction, but perhaps the close brush with the aeroplane had disconcerted them more than somewhat, for all at once the three jeeps pulled up

together and the drivers announced that they were lost. It
was by now dark, and to go on without a guide would have
been foolhardy. Luckily, and as always happens in the
Afghan desert, other life appeared within a matter of
moments, in the form of a tractor and its driver.

Immediately our drivers started to argue with our
commanders about who was going to pay this guide for
his services. Each side was trying to outdo the other, of
course, and there was lot of lip-curling and "Call yourselves Muslims?" going on. Meantime valuable minutes
ticked by, and my nerves were becoming frayed.

"How much are you arguing about?" I asked.

"He wants 1,000 *Afghanis*."

About £7! I was about to pull out the money in
Afghanis, thinking, to hell with this, I'll pay, but then
I stopped. I knew that such a gesture would be hopeless.
It would also betray me and endanger my companions. So
I sat and seethed until the argument was resolved, trying
to calm myself with the thought that for an Afghan, £7 is a
considerable sum.

The tractor-driver guided us down a dirt track to a
village where dozens and dozens of children milled about,
despite the fact that by now it was the middle of the night.
We stopped for the mechanics to overhaul the jeeps as far
as they could, and for our drivers to find out how far we
were still from the Kabul–Kandahar road.

"Three hours," came the inevitable reply. Gloomily,
we refuelled the jeeps from the oildrums they carried and
set off again – but at snail's pace, for the track ahead was
full of pitfalls, and we had to send two mujahedin ahead of
each vehicle to guide us. However, at length we reached
the road. Our tractor-driving guide left us, and I was
about to breathe a sigh of relief. Then one of the jeeps
broke down. It took half an hour to repair it, by which
time I estimated that we had a bare hour of darkness left to
travel in. But now, instead of taking to the road, our
drivers took off along a track to the left of it.

The track led us to a bowl-shaped area surrounded on three sides by precipitous mountains.

"What are we doing here?" I asked Abdul Rahman as calmly as I could.

Abdul Rahman had recovered quite a lot of his composure. "We will camp here tonight, and then in the morning we will climb to the guerrilla stronghold at the top of that hill," he said.

During all my time in Afghanistan, I tried to place my faith in the people in whose hands my safety lay. I had had no difficulty in doing this with Ismail Khan, but I felt doubtful about Abdul Rahman. I decided that I would try to panic him. Fortuitously, high overhead, a large plane flew by. It was still dark enough to see its red landing light flashing clearly.

"Do you see that?" I asked him.

"Yes."

"That light is a camera. The Russians are taking photographs of us every time it flashes."

I had hoped that he would order an immediate evacuation. Instead he looked rather pleased and wandered off. I was nonplussed but a few minutes later I was surrounded by delighted mujahedin.

"Did you see that plane?" they chorused.

"Yes."

"It was taking pictures of us. Isn't that something?" they announced proudly. "Abdul Rahman told us. Truly, he is a great commander, to know such things."

I did discover that the mujahedin stronghold we had invited ourselves to belonged to a group called Jabhe. In the freezing dawn of 13 September we threw tarpaulins over the jeeps, parked, as I now saw, among several other similarly shrouded vehicles. Then, wrapped in our patous, we climbed the path uphill. We hadn't gone far when,

"Halt! Who goes there?" demanded a young mujahed, popping up from behind a rock, complete with Kalashnikov, which he proceeded to fire, once, into the air. We were frisked and disarmed, and only then allowed to proceed. We were told not to stray from the path, which was clearly marked with black flags, and on either side of which drivers and passengers lay sleeping in niches and crevices in the rocks. We came to a halt at the top of an improvised waiting area-cum-mosque. The holy *mirhab* of the mosque was simply marked out in a semi-circle of stones. Here, Abdul Mohmy spent several hours in prayer – an action which gave me serious and grave concern. Mohmy was highly intelligent and genuinely tough. He would not pray so long and so earnestly without good reason. I noticed too that high morale and good humour had somehow evaporated overnight. To my horror, it looked as though the trip to Pakistan had finally been abandoned, though I could not fathom why.

Later the reason became clear. There had been a report on the BBC the night before that the Russians intended to seal the border once and for all. Most of the day was spent brooding, or in *sotto voce* discussion, but by late afternoon a decision appeared to have been reached, and we all trooped down to the jeeps. Hope rose in me before I could suppress it.

"What's happening?" I asked Aminullah, a brazen commander who had joined us on the road.

"Tonight we will try for the border," he said. "Tonight it will be make or break."

Our party was joined by eight heavily armed Jabhe mujahedin in their own Symorgh. They were mean-looking characters, and one of them still sported his sunglasses, though the light had long since faded; but any demonstration of extra support was reassuring, as we would have to join the main road at a junction by a village where a Russian garrison was situated. We left after a lengthy prayer meeting, but finally the engines roared, beards were wiped, Allah was invoked, and off we went.

The extra Symorgh carrying the eight guerrillas took up the rear. We never saw them again.

On reaching the Kabul–Kandahar road we were confronted by a tumult. Our headlights caught a crowd of mujahedin running hither and thither, brandishing their guns and shouting frantically. Not far beyond them loomed the sinister shapes of buildings. The first jeep roared off down the road, and the second jeep and ours followed closely, while we passengers either kept a lookout for mines or bent our heads in prayer. We could in fact have been travelling faster, but we dared not, for fear of not being able to brake in time to avoid a pothole or a mine. I wondered if we could have avoided a mine anyway, but then I realised that the local mujahedin had sent scouts up ahead and these had lit signal flares to tell us that a particular stretch of road was clear. Proceeding like this, from signal to signal, we travelled some way. After a time, we braked hard and swerved off the road down a steep bank to the right. Lights ablaze, we headed for the foothills, but we paused briefly with a group of mujahedin who proudly showed us the mines they had collected. Mines are simply placed on the tarmac by the army, and the same technique is employed by the mujahedin when they manage to collect them, rather than being blown up by them. But I hadn't got time to try to make sense out of this, for I was worrying now about why we still had our lights on as we headed across country. What if the Russians had landed heli-borne troops ahead to ambush us? Sometimes I wished I hadn't such a vivid imagination.

Soon the track we were following petered out, and several mujahedin with torches were dispatched to find it again in the darkness ahead. This was done amid several arguments about the relative correctness of the route we'd chosen. We made slow progress, but soon it became evident that the route was impassable.

But impassable or not, there was no turning back now. We all left the vehicles to walk. Maybe with no load, the drivers could coax the jeeps through the slippery uphill scree. This they did, but we had to gather rocks to build some kind of grippable surface for the tyres ahead, and progress became agonisingly slow. Sometimes a jeep would get stuck and we would have to construct a winch to haul it forwards – a process that took several hours. Our hands and feet were bleeding from the rocks, and we were covered with dust.

This went on for two despairing days, but just as our water was running out, the terrain eased. We made a relatively trouble-free descent to a dry river bed, gratefully climbed into the jeeps again and roared off. The river bed was as good as a motorway after what we'd been through, but still better was to come: a village had been sighted ahead.

"Afghanistan! Afghanistan!" my companions all shouted in relieved triumph.

The only obligatory halts were those made for prayers, though even then only a few people descended – most of us were too impatient. Our driver took ages, and grated on everyone's nerves.

"Do it later," people shouted at him. "We're nearly there!"

Placidly, he completed his prayers. Then and not before did we head off again. We were the last jeep. The others had already disappeared from view and we were on our way at speed to catch up. It was dawn, and soon we could be easily spotted by enemy aircraft.

"Never mind – we'll be in Pakistan in an hour," someone said confidently.

I was still doubtful, but the mujahedin could hardly contain their jubilation. Another village had appeared on the horizon. Could it be that that village was in Pakistan? It seemed likely, people thought. Closer and closer we came to it. Then our engine seized.

The order was quickly given to make a run for the village, while the driver and mechanic stayed with the vehicle to see what was wrong. The village was soon reached. No, this wasn't Pakistan, they told us. Pakistan was an hour away.

At least we were sheltered and reunited with the other two vehicles. Ours limped into the village soon after, and all three were covered to prevent them from being spotted from the air. There was nothing to do now but kill time until nightfall, so we spent the day either in prayer or eating pomegranates. I'd never eaten one in my life before I travelled to Afghanistan. Now I was developing quite a taste for them. Kandahar airport was to our west, and we could see in the distance the ominous roving of helicopters and MiGs. The area we were in, however, seemed to have been untouched by the violence of the war. This may have been due to the policies of the local Russian commander.

As usual, estimates varied about how long it would actually take us to reach the border. One hour was the most optimistic, six hours the most pessimistic, but the general consensus was that we would have to spend an hour and a half driving through a narrow gorge, mined by the Russians, and here an additional danger existed. Here indeed the Russians sometimes landed heli-borne troops to ambush those entering or leaving the country by the strip of road that threaded it.

A village scout had been sent ahead to spy out the land but by late afternoon he still hadn't returned.

"He'll be back," Abdul Rahman said.

"I hope so. If he doesn't return, it'll mean he's been either killed or captured – and both those things mean the enemy is around," I said. I thought about what Rahman had said to me when I'd broached the possibility of walking across – "They'll either catch you in the open or you'll die of thirst" – he was probably right. I had better stick with the jeep, come what may, I thought.

We were all exhausted by now, after all the struggles and dashed hopes, but we still felt anxious and everyone prayed vigorously. Dusk fell, and there was still no sign of the scout. They decided to leave it in God's hands – "*Insha Allah*" – and piled into the jeeps.

Our jeep hadn't gone a hundred yards before the engine stalled again. They'd obviously made a botched job of the repair – what was needed was a new starter motor, of which we carried a spare – and now – when we had least time – they would have to do the job properly.

As they worked I watched them in exasperation. Then an old man appeared wraith-like out of the darkness.

"The tanks are coming," he announced.

My heart stopped. But he had spoken Pashtu, of which I only understood a little, and perhaps I had misheard him.

"Did he say the tanks are coming?" I asked Abdul Rahman.

"No," replied Rahman. "He said the tanks *aren't* coming." But it seemed to me unlikely that the old man would have gone to the effort of following us out into the darkness to impart such non-news. Besides, one of the drivers' little boys had started to wail bitterly.

"How's the starter motor going?"

"Nearly there," came a muffled and frantic reply, which might have meant anything.

I looked around desperately. I couldn't believe our bad luck. Everyone was crowding round the open bonnet to conceal as far as possible the torchlight which was illuminating the mechanic's work. Our armed escort, bringing his rifle to the ready, ordered some of our men to prime the grenades for the RPG, but then it transpired that no one knew how to. What a way to perish, I thought bitterly. By now we could hear the ominous rumble of tanks quite clearly. The little boy whimpered. The rest of us were silent, gazing fearfully into the night behind us.

And then the engine fired. I think that the noise of that engine will remain the sweetest sound I shall ever hear. We piled in before you could say "Allah" and, praying that nothing else would go wrong, bolted down the road after our companion jeeps.

Incredibly, the other jeeps had waited for us. Irrespective of danger and the possibility of escaping, I noticed that no one was ever abandoned. A frenzied search now began among the other mechanics to find the requisite nuts and bolts from their own toolkits to bolt our new starter motor securely into place. We were in open desert, and a kilometre away we could see the faint glimmer of the lights of the tanks. Oh, God, I thought . . . so near and yet so far . . . please don't let them get us now . . . All at once I found myself repeating the *kalimeh*, and it comforted me.

The two little boys clung to each other and wept, while the mujahedin awkwardly tried to comfort them. I watched the tanks. Surely they could see us with their nightsights?

And then I realised that they were not heading towards us, but away from us. The patrol hadn't seen us. All of a sudden a red tracer bullet soared high into the air to the south. We couldn't make out what, was going on, but one thing was certain: the Russians' attention was focused elsewhere.

An hour later we reached the mouth of the gorge. We switched our headlights off, and the jeeps filled with the murmur of prayers. I, too, cupped my hands and repeated "*Bismillah Rahman-i-Rahim . . .*" once again. The tension was overpowering as we gazed up at the looming sides of the gorge, soon lost in the thick darkness.

Allah must have been with us. This last part of the journey was a kind of summation of all that was Afghanistan for me: whether the scout had actually come this far, whether he had returned or gone off somewhere else, I would never know. We had allies though: the goats and sheep gently foraging for food, and with them – a shepherd. Where the terrain was so rough that apart from this strip of road the only access troops could find to it was by helicopter, a shepherd stood alone somewhere above us on the walls of the gorge. We could not see him – indeed, we never saw him – but his voice drifted down to us like a god's – and it provided, as all Afghans do, information. After the usual formal exchange of greetings, he told us that another vehicle had passed safely through not two hours earlier. There had been no activity since. Therefore there were probably no mines, and there could be no ambush. Our hearts leapt.

Further on there was a grim reminder that others had not been so lucky. The wreck of a burnt-out jeep lay by the side of the road.

We emerged from the gorge feeling that truly nothing could stop us now. And as if to confirm our confidence, there on the horizon we could see the twinkling electric lights of Chaman, just inside the Pakistan border. It had been two months since I had seen electric light, and even at this distance it seemed strangely miraculous, and bright.

HEART OF DARKNESS

Helen Winternitz

Winternitz, an American journalist, journeyed up the Congo River in 1985. She travelled aboard a four-deck riverboat named the Major Mudimbi.

Being less gregarious than I, Tim liked to sit at the prow of the *Mudimbi*'s leading barge and gaze at the river unfolding. This barge was comparatively peaceful. On its flat expanse, neighborhoods of makeshift tents had sprung up in the spaces between pieces of heavy cargo, which included a Volkswagen, barrels of gasoline and diesel fuel, bales of used clothes, and Simon Kepe's red furniture. It was almost quiet up there, far enough away from the straining engines so that it rode smoothly across the water as if pushed by some giant and benevolent hand.

Tim found a spot where he could lean against a low bulkhead and study the river that was wider with each mile we traveled in from the mountains that had choked its passage near Kinshasa. In the mornings the river still was brown, a uniform brown; it had no red tinge, no green hint, no blue possibility, nothing to proclaim it Africa's greatest river. But the rising sun changed its countenance.

Under the bombarding light it took on a silvery sheen, and by noontime it gleamed like dirty sheet metal.

The farther we traveled upriver, the more difficult it was to tell where we were and where we had been. The river had become a skein of channels that split and merged and split again around island after island. Some four thousand of these islands interrupt the river, disguising its size, slicing its currents into mere insinuations of the greater watercourse. Each reach of the river looked the same, bend after bend, hour after hour, mile after mile. The only apprehensible change in the scenery was with the forest, which was getting thicker, always thicker. From the mass of foliage, an occasional palm or an old giant of the forest would thrust itself free, shooting straight up into the air and then blossoming into a lofty crown.

Sometimes, villages slid by, insignificant clearings in the greenery, a patch of rubiginous dirt and houses built of sticks and thatch. Sometimes, a few raggedly dressed people would look up from their chores to stare, startled, at the churning riverboat. Naked children ran along the banks, pursuing the *Mudimbi* as if to catch it, and then waving until the boat labored beyond their sight around some bend in the river or curve of an island.

Young men hung out on the foredeck, trading and smoking marijuana, and bathing in the patch of privacy provided by the bulkhead. Dunking buckets into the river water, they sloshed themselves mostly clean with the muddy water, bending and stretching and letting the water run down their lean bodies to the deck where it evaporated in minutes. Once they had washed, they, too, leaned back and watched the river.

The prow was the place to watch the pirogues coming in. Against the silver immensity of the river, the canoes that lay in wait for the riverboat formed a pattern of dark curves, chiseled to points at the ends like uncertain smiles. They were no different from those crafted by the early

Bantu settlers who swept through the Congo Basin in a great migration before the time of Christ. The dugouts, the largest of them wide enough to hold a hippopotamus and long enough to carry forty people, were made to look impossibly delicate by the sheer size of the river rocking them down its currents. Warned of the riverboat's approach by a system of drum signals passed along the banks, the river people paddled out to the edge of the main boat channel, a pathway up the river that zigzagged around sandbars, muddy shallows, and islands. They waited then for the boat to draw abreast, standing with their long paddles still.

At an exactly figured moment, they flashed their paddles, bending from their waists and balancing with a grace practised down through generations, shooting their canoes toward the boat. As a dugout came sliding toward the side of the boat, veering and slithering in the turbulent water at the boat's side, the front paddler grabbed for a railing or another canoe, anything more stable than the rushing water. The riverboat plowed ahead, paying no heed to the struggling paddlers, not even when an occasional canoe bounced off its side or overturned in the turbulence.

The river people, some of whom travel for days from villages on the Congo's tributaries, came with the bottoms of their pirogues laden with fish, eels, oranges, and other fruits. Dying fish flapped and writhed on the lower decks, making it difficult to walk without stepping on the tail of some giant fish whose penny-sized eyes stared, glazing, toward death. A hundred varieties of fish were hauled from the muddy depths of the river to the muddy decks of the riverboat, from the placid carp whose meat is succulently plentiful to the slimy eels that are common riverine fare. The Congo breeds startlingly ugly fish, including a catfish that grows up to six feet long with a be-whiskered snout like that of a pig, and wonderfully delicate fishes, including an almost round variety with lustrous yellow scales that resembles an oversized gold piece.

The canoes served up a widening bounty of forest produce. We could buy fresh fruit like bananas, oranges, or papayas; mammoth snails, chewy and served in hot pepper sauce; the charcoaled caterpillars that tasted like Fritos; roasted crocodile, a delicacy; flying squirrel; antelope killed that same day in the forest; fat tree grubs, the larvae of beetles that are sauteed in curry sauce and are a prized source of protein; and monkey.

Dead monkeys, whose meat is highly regarded fare, began piling up all over the boat after we left Mbandaka. Canoe after canoe arrived at the *Mudimbi*'s side heaped with monkey carcasses, little green monkeys, brown furred monkeys, and rufous monkeys with elegant tails. The hunters wrapped the tails forward around the necks of the freshly killed creatures and then carried the trussed monkeys in bunches by the improvised handles of their tails. It reminded me of the way an American woman carries a bulky handbag by its strap, holding it out stiffly so that it won't bang against her thighs.

Besides the fresh monkeys, blackened carcasses of smoked monkeys were heaped in nearly every corner. They were smoked in the indelicate Zairian sense, which means roasted until charred into a state of long-term preservation. Unfortunately, the smoked carcasses still resembled monkeys. The high heat of the roasting had curled the monkeys' little hands into fists and locked their mouths open, the thinner flesh of their lips burned away so that their teeth grimaced nakedly, transfixed forever in silent screams.

We ate some monkey ourselves, not the smoked kind but some fresh meat stewed in a gravy. Gustatory pleasure was not our aim in this meal and, in fact, we were perturbed at the idea of eating an animal that was so close to being humanly intelligent. But I thought it my duty as a journalist, as a student of the river, to try it when the Germans asked us if we wanted to share a monkey with them. They had persuaded one of the cooks to stew up a monkey that Gunther had bought, a beautiful one with a long tail and delicate face. Andrew and Elly came up from the barges to have some of it with us in the dining room.

The stew arrived in a big bowl. I had expected the meat to be cut away from the bone and its true nature disguised, but the limbs and various parts of the monkey's trunk were clearly represented among the chunks of meat floating in the gravy – a leg here, ribs there, a socketed hip bone. The waiter served it on piles of rice and, to my disgust, dished out on my plate one of the very identifiable hind legs, intact from hip to anklebone. Mustering my bravery, I took a couple of bites, enough to note that the meat tasted fine, gamy like a rabbit, if a little stringy. Not far from the table, the little green monkeys were running back and forth on the dining room bar.

I donated the remainder of my leg meat to Andrew, who ate prodigiously, taking three helpings and spooning up the last strands of meat. Then he sucked on the bones. Andrew was always hungry, always trying to eke out his money, living mostly off boiled manioc, which sold cheaply on the barges. For a couple of pennies you could buy a lump of the starchy vegetable, which comes out tasting like gluey tapioca pudding. One lump was enough to make you feel full for a few hours.

Even when he had eaten, Andrew looked hungry. He never looked quite healthy. His clothes were worn and dirty and his hair hung down lankly across his forehead. The tops of his feet were blistered by a case of scabies he had picked up sleeping on some filthy blankets on Mount Cameroon and were so raw that he could not bear to lace his sneakers closed. Andrew seemed unable to find the place in the world he was seeking, a place where his being no longer chafed and suffered.

One morning, a pair of fishermen hauled aboard several strings of the gold-piece fish and a jug of homemade palm wine. They swung their strings of fish in the air, making them look like glittering necklaces, and quickly sold them to one of the *commerçants*.

When the fishermen set the jug of wine out on the deck, a circle of passengers gathered around them. This wine is made from the juice of the generous raffia palms, whose fruits provide oil and whose fronds provide thatch, and it is a favorite drink in central Africa. The fishermen ladled out the wine with two plastic cups, charging six cents a cup. Among the drinkers were some soldiers in camouflage uniforms who quaffed down cup after cup and then moved off from the others, muttering and joking among themselves. They made me nervous, for they seemed to have no officer and no purpose other than to amuse themselves. I edged around to the other side of the wine pot, nearer to the fishermen, who took this as a signal that I wanted some of the drink, too. I did want to try it for the sake of curiosity, but I was afraid of it because of the possibility that it had been diluted with river water infested with any number of virulent diseases, such as schistosomiasis, which attacks your bladder and intestines, and amoebic infections that give you terrible dysentery. The fishermen held out a cup of their wine.

"Go ahead. Drink it. It is free. They want you to try it," one of the drinkers advised. I did not want to try to explain my qualms so I took the cup and drank, praying that I wasn't drinking down any vicious bugs. The wine tasted like old lemonade.

I decided to follow these two fishermen and talk to them. They spoke only Lingala and a smattering of French, but they tried politely to answer my questions, bizarre as my interest in them must have seemed. They let me follow along, this pair of friendly men who undoubtedly could harpoon a hippopotamus and whose ancestors may well have been among the warriors who, with good reason, tried to kill Stanley.

Immediately after finishing with the wine, the fishermen bought some bread and wolfed it down, swallowing it without chewing. They had been paddling out from their village for more than a day, moving down their tributary through the night, steering a course through marshes and around islands whose geography they knew by heart, by daylight or by starlight. They could read the river by deciphering its bends and ripples as easily as I could read street signs back home.

They also bought two cigarettes, one each, which they puffed down to the smallest smokable stub almost without pause. Few people in Zaire are rich enough to buy a whole pack of cigarettes at once and smoke any time they want. The merchants who sold cigarettes on the *Mudimbi* doled them out, collecting a few pennies for each one. A sure dividing mark between the rich and poor nations is the way cigarettes are sold and possessions treated. In countries where material life is hard, everything a person owns is distinct. An enamel bowl, a cooking pot, a piece of cloth, a pair of shoes, a bar of soap, all these items are valued for their considerable worth.

The fishermen were brothers-in-law and neither was particularly prosperous. They wore no shoes and their hands were as heavily calloused as their feet. They wore cheap patterned shirts, the kind made in Hong Kong or Taiwan and sold everywhere in Africa, and their polyester pants were shiny with wear.

Most of the river people dressed up, if they could, for the excursion to the riverboat, wearing shoes if they had them. The women kept to the traditional patterned cloths that they wrapped and knotted around themselves, but the men liked to look modern. The height of Congo fashion was the jogging suit. Despite the heat and the humidity, an outfit of matching warm-up pants and jacket was the equivalent of the Sunday-best suit. Bright pastel suits – aquamarine, canary yellow, rose pink – were popular, and the sharpest male dressers added a further touch of exuberance by painting their thumbnails with red polish.

The fishermen held the money they had earned from the fish and wine in their fists and began touring the *Mudimbi*'s markets. Maneuvering through the crowded passageways, they compared prices, fingered bolts of cloth, examined the soles of plastic sandals, inquired about the freshness of manioc, and looked over baskets of medicines. This was their prelude to buying a few things. They bought a bar of yellow soap for washing clothes, two razorblades, seven unlabeled medicine capsules for "fevers," and another plastic cup. They also bought two notepads for their children, who studied at a school near their village run by a local teacher.

With the remainder of their earnings, the fishermen splurged. They climbed up to an upper tier and found a bar, where they bought beers, one each. The music was loud, scratchy, and insistently melodic. The fishermen sipped from their bottles, listened, and looked down at their feet. But as the music took hold and they finished their beer, they began dancing, really dancing. Zairians dance as if they have problems no longer, as if the poverty and the struggling have ended, as if their history were filled with triumph. The people at the beer parlor were dancing effervescently, men with men, women with women, men with women.

I joined in, dancing with the fishermen and letting myself go, as surprised to be dancing with them as they were with me, and as delighted. The people around us were moving for the sake of the music, their feet gliding from step to step, back and forth, their arms and their backs undulating toward their moving feet. The riverbanks were gliding past, the canoes gliding in, the feet gliding, as the barge was gliding, across the smoothly opaque water, going upriver in time, in tune with the pulse of the music, in time to a beat born in the Congo and reverberating across the Congo, dancing their way upriver, the rock music blaring and rasping and bare feet slapping out the rhythm on the metal deck.

The longer the fishermen stayed aboard the *Mudimbi*, the farther they had to paddle home, so after a while they had to leave the music. Before they untied their pirogue, I talked to them as best I could within the narrow territory of words we all understood.

They asked me if there was a river like the Congo from where I came in the United States. I told them what I could about the Mississippi and about the catfish from that river, that the fish are smaller and the river has few canoes and fewer islands, but still it is the biggest river the United States boasts. I explained also that if the Mississippi has fewer canoes, it has more boats and many more cities, many more people. They wanted to know how people caught fish on the Mississippi and I told them with hooks and nets, similar to what they used, but in bigger and more comfortable boats so that the work is not as difficult.

"We work very hard. We must fish under the sun when it is very hot," one of them said.

"It is getting harder to live," the other joined in with a complaint about the rottenness of the economy that we had heard from others and would hear again on our trip across Zaire. "The prices are going higher. The money is getting smaller."

It was late afternoon when the fishermen pushed away from the *Mudimbi*, standing at each end of their canoe, paddling toward their village somewhere in a clearing isolated in the green splendor of the forest.

THE BRENDAN VOYAGE

Tim Severin

Like Heyerdahl's Kon-Tiki *voyage, Tim Severin's* Brendan *expedition was a modern-day attempt to prove an historical legend: in this case that sixth-century Irish priest St Brendan had crossed the Atlantic to America in a skin boat. In the extract from* The Brendan Voyage *below, Severin's reconstructed medieval leather-and-wood craft has reached midway between Iceland and Greenland.*

At 6:20 a.m. on May 20, we picked up a faint signal from Prins Christianssund which gave the weather forecast I had been dreading: we were due for a southwest gale, force 8 rising to force 9 of about forty-five miles an hour, precisely from the direction in which we were headed. We scarcely needed the warning. The ugly look of the cloudy wrack ahead of us was enough to advise us that we were in for heavy weather. Sure enough, within an hour, we were struggling first to reef the mainsail, then to lower it altogether and lash it down. Only the tiny headsail was left up to draw us away downwind and give the helmsman a chance to jockey the boat among the ever-larger seas which now began to tumble and break around us. Even as we worked to belay the mainsail, it was clear that we had left one precaution too late; the heavy leeboard should have been taken in earlier. Now the weight of water had jammed it solidly against the hull. Each time the boat heeled to the pressure of the wind, the leading edge of the leeboard dipped into the sea and, like a ploughshare, carved a great slice of water from the ocean, over the gunwale, to pour solidly into the bilges. In ten minutes the water inside the boat was swirling above the level of the floorboards, and the watch – George and I – could feel *Brendan* growing more and more sluggish. This was dangerous, because she was no longer rising properly to the seas; and the loose water was heaving back and forth, unbalancing her. *Brendan* squirmed like a gaffed salmon and began to level off. Water bubbled and gushed out of the floorboards beneath me. Frantically, I re-doubled the speed of pumping, and heard the thump, thump, thump of George briskly operating the bilge pump near the helmsman. Trondur emerged from his shelter, crawled to the starboard midship's pump, and aided in emptying the boat. When the water level was under control I climbed back and peered into the shelter.

There I saw Arthur sitting, disconsolate. On all sides he was surrounded by sodden clothing. His sleeping bag was sopping wet and his hair plastered to his scalp. "I'm afraid half the shelter is soaked, and my cameras have been drenched," he said.

"A big wave broke over the stern and traveled up the boat. It pushed in the rear flap of the shelter and poured on top of him," George explained. "Did it drown the radios?" I asked anxiously. "I don't think so," Arthur replied, "though there's spray all over them." I removed my wet oilskins, crawled into the shelter and dabbed carefully at the sets with a strip of dry cloth. Then I tentatively flicked on the power. To my relief the radios came to life. "Better sponge up the puddles as best you can," I advised Arthur. "There's a spare dry sleeping bag which Edan was using. Meanwhile, I think I'd better put extra plastic bags around the radios in case we get pooped by another wave."

It was lucky I did so. When the watches changed, George and I peeled off our oilskins, crawled inside, and lay down in our sleeping bags. Trondur and Arthur took it in twenty-minute spells to nurse *Brendan* through the seas.

George and I were half asleep, when out of nowhere there came a thunderous roar, an almighty crash, and a solid sheet of water cascaded into the cabin. It brushed aside the rear flap, slammed over the thwart, and hit with such force that water sprayed onto the shelter roof lining. The water was icy, straight from the East Greenland current. Underneath us in our sleeping bags, the sheep-skin mattresses literally floated off the cabin floor. A moment later, there was the frigid shock as the water soaked through the sleeping bags. "Pump her! Quick, pump her! She's heavy!" somebody shouted. Frantically, George clawed out of his sleeping bag and raced out of the shelter, wearing only his underwear. In the same move-ment he had scooped up his immersion suit, which was hanging on the steering frame, zipped himself into it, and was swarming forward to get to the bilge pumps. At the helm Arthur was desperately wrestling with the steering paddle, trying to keep *Brendan* straight to the waves. Trondur, his oilskins glistening, was peeling back the small awning over the cooker and getting ready to bail. For want of a bucket, he had grabbed up the largest saucepan.

Ankle-deep in water in the cabin, I took a quick look around to see if anything could be saved from the water. Virtually all our gear was saturated. A book floated forlornly across the floor; the sleeping bags lay like half-submerged corpses. Water was sloshing everywhere. Quickly I jotted our last estimated position, tore the leaf from the message pad, and stuffed it in my pocket. If *Brendan* filled and sank, our only chance was to broadcast

a MAYDAY with an accurate position advice. I thrust the
small VHF transmitter, spare batteries, and a microphone
into a satchel which I placed, ready to be grabbed, on top
of the radio board. Then I, too, clambered into my
immersion suit and went forward to help George, who
was ratcheting away, flat out, at the port midship's pump.
As I passed Trondur, I could see what a shambles the
steering area had become. He was standing up to his knees
in water, steadily scooping away, while around his legs
bobbed pots and pans, jars of food, empty sea-boots, and
wet rags. This was a full emergency.

Pump, pump, pump. The two of us heaved back and
forth at the pump handles, sending two feeble little
squirts of water back into the ocean. Curled up in the
wet darkness beneath the tarpaulin, one had a heightened
sense of the crippled motion of the boat. *Brendan* lay
almost stopped in the water, dead and sluggish, while the
water inside her swirled ominously back and forth. She
was so low in the sea that even the smaller waves lapped
over the gunwale and added more water to the bilges. It
was a race against the distinctive rhythm of the sea. As I
heaved frantically at the pump handle, I wondered if there
was another wave waiting to break and fill her. Would she
stay afloat? And what a Godforsaken place for this emergency to happen – halfway between Iceland and Greenland. What had the experts said? Survival time in this
near-freezing water was five minutes or less.

Pump, pump, pump. A glance through a chink of the
tarpaulin revealed the cause of our distress. The full
strength of the Atlantic was showing itself. Whipped
up by the gale racing clear from Greenland, the waters
were thrashing in wild frenzy. The main motion was the
steady pounding of huge waves from the south-west,
overtoppling their crests in a welter of foam. Flickering
across the surface as far as the eye could see were spume
streaks drawn out by the gale across the skin of the water.
Here and there cross waves slid athwart the main wave

direction, and collided. When they met, they burst upward as though cannon shells were landing. It was an
awesome sight.

Pump, pump, pump. It took forty-five minutes of non-
stop work with pumps and Trondur's saucepan to reduce
the water in the boat to a safer level, and lighten *Brendan*.
Then we could assess the damage. Structurally *Brendan*
seemed as tight as ever. The steering frame was still in
place, and the seams of stitching had held. It was easy to
see where the wave had struck. It had come aboard at the
unprotected flank of the boat, through the open gap
beside the steering paddle. Right in the wave's path stood
the metal cooker box. It had taken the full brunt of the
wave. One side of the box was stove in and completely
twisted. The retaining clip had been smashed open, and
its rivets sheared off cleanly by the force of the blow.

The scene inside the cabin was heartbreaking. Everything on floor level, which was most of our equipment,
was awash in water trapped on top of the plastic sheet we
used as a base for our living quarters. We opened the flap
that led forward beneath the central tarpaulin, and one by
one I handed through to George the dripping floor mats,
sodden sleeping bags, sheepskins oozing water, soaked
clothing. Everything was saturated in icy, salt water. Only
the radios and equipment perched above floor level had
been saved, together with the contents of our personal kit
bags, which, thank heavens, had remained waterproof.
Our spare clothes, at least, were dry.

George was shivering with cold and pulled on proper
clothing at last. "Christ," he muttered as he struggled
into a sweater, "I hope your theory is right that body heat
will dry out our sleeping bags. I don't fancy being this wet
for the rest of the voyage." As soon as the shelter was clear
of gear, I concentrated on trying to get rid of the water on
the floor, mopping up puddles and stabbing drain holes in
the plastic floor with a knife. After half an hour's work it
was obvious we would have to be content with the

glistening wet interior. The shelter would never become any drier. Back from the tarpaulin tunnel, George passed everything we had evacuated, except the three sheepskins and one sleeping bag. These were so saturated that even after we had tried to squeeze them dry, the water poured out in rivulets.

Exhausted, George and I crawled back into the remaining two sleeping bags, trying to ignore the fact that we were drenched to the skin and the sleeping bags lay clammy upon us. For nearly thirty-six hours we'd been working with scarcely any sleep.

Boom! Again a heavy wave came toppling over the stern, smashed aside the shelter door and poured in, slopping over my face as I lay head-to-stern. We sprang up and tried to save the sleeping bags from the flood. But it was too late. In a split second the situation had returned to exactly where it had been before. Water was everywhere. The bilges were full, and the cabin was awash. *Brendan* was near-stationary before the breaking seas, and George and I were wading around the cabin floor with icy water soaking through our stockinged feet.

Once again it was back to the pumps for an hour, rocking back and forth at the pump handles, hoping silently that another wave would not add to the damage while *Brendan* was handicapped. Then back to the same chore of stripping out the cabin contents, squeezing out the sodden items, mopping up and returning everything to its place. I flicked on the radio. There was a heart-stopping moment of silence before I realized that the radio had been knocked off-tune in the hectic scramble. As soon as I had corrected the fault, I put out a call to try to report our position in case of disaster. But no one was listening. We were many miles off any shipping lanes, and with the radio's tuning unit drenched with water and the waves over-topping the aerial more than half the time, I thought it was very doubtful that we were putting out a readable signal. The little VHF set had fared even worse.

Water had got into it, and it would only squeak and click in frustration. I switched the set off before it did itself an electrical injury.

"We've got to do something about those big waves," I said. "We're exhausting ourselves pumping and working the boat. This can't go on. The cabin will soon be unlivable."

The crew looked at me with eyes raw-rimmed from exhaustion and the constant salt spray. The wind buffeted the mast and plucked at the tarpaulin: the waves kept up their ceaseless rumble and roar: and for a moment I seriously wondered what on earth the four of us were doing here in this lonely, half-frozen part of the Atlantic; cold, drenched, and very tired, and out of touch with the outside world.

"I propose we put up an oar as a mizzen-mast," I went on. "Rig a mizzen staysail and put out the sea anchor so that she rides nose up to the waves. It means taking a risk when we peel back the tarpaulin to dig out the oar – a wave might catch and fill her – and it will be a dangerous maneuver trying to turn the boat around. She could be caught broadside. But the curragh men of Aran ride out heavy weather, head to wind, hanging onto their salmon nets as sea anchors."

I saw Trondur was looking very doubtful. "What do you think, Trondur?" Of all of us, Trondur had by far the most experience in these heavy northern seas.

"What we are doing now is right," he said. "It is better that *Brendan* is this way to the waves. Now she can move with them." He twisted his hands to imitate *Brendan* zig-zagging down the combers. "If we have sea anchor." Trondur continued, "*Brendan* cannot move. When big wave hits the bow, I think tarpaulin will break and we have very much water in the boat. Water in stern of *Brendan* is not so much problem. Water in bow, I think, is big problem. Now we must stop water in stern and in cabin."

But how? What we needed was some way of closing the large gap between the cabin and the helmsman's position. But even if we cut up a sail as an awning, or used some of the forward tarpaulin, which we could ill afford to do, I doubted if they would withstand the pressure if we rigged them over the gap. We needed something extremely strong, yet something which we could erect at once in the teeth of the gale.

Then I had it. Leather! Under the cabin floor lay a spare oxhide and several slightly smaller sheets of spare leather. They were intended as patches if *Brendan* sprang a leak or was gashed. Now they could be used to plug a far more dangerous hole in our defenses. At the same moment I remembered, absolutely vividly, an encyclopedia illustration of the Roman army *Testudo*, the "tortoise" under which the Roman legionnaires advanced against a town rampart, holding leather shields overlapping above their heads to ward off missiles thrown by the defenders. Why hadn't I thought of it before?

For the third time, I began emptying out the contents of the cabin, peeled back the floor sheet with a sticky ripping sound, and prized up the leather sheets where they had lain on the deck boards. "Get a fistful of thongs," I told George. "I want to lace the hides together." He crawled forward.

I shoved the leather sheets out of the cabin door. They were stiff and unwieldy in the cold. So much the better, I thought, they will be like armor plate.

Quickly I pointed out to Trondur what needed to be done. Immediately he grasped the principle, nodded his understanding, and gave a quick grin of approval.

Then he was off, knife in hand, scrambling up onto *Brendan*'s unprotected stern where the waves washed over the camber of the stern deck. It was a very treacherous spot, but it was the only place where the job could be done properly. With one hand Trondur held onto his perch, and with the other he worked on the leather sheets we passed up to him. Every now and then, the roar of an oncoming breaker warned him to drop his work, and hold on with both hands while *Brendan* bucked and shuddered and the wave crest swirled over the stern. Meanwhile, Arthur at the helm kept *Brendan* as steady as he could, and George, balancing on the port gunwale, pinned down each sheet of leather to prevent it being swept away by the gale. Trondur's job was to cut a line of holes along the edge of the oxhide in the right place for the leather thongs to lash down and join together the tortoise. With the full power of his trained sculptor's hand, Trondur drove his knife point again and again through the quarter-inch-thick leather, twisted and sawed, and carved out neat hole after neat hole like a machine. It was an impressive display of strength. Then George fed the leather thongs through the holes, tied down the corner of the main hide, and laced on the overlapping plates.

In less than fifteen minutes the job was done. A leather apron covered the larger part of *Brendan*'s open stern, leaving just enough room for the helmsman to stand upright, his torso projecting up through the tortoise. Leather cheek plates guarded the flanks.

Boom! Another breaker crashed over the stern, but this time caromed safely off the tortoise and poured harm-lessly back into the Atlantic; only in one spot did it penetrate in quantity, where I had plugged a gap beneath the leather apron with my spare oilskin trousers. So great was the force of the water that the trousers shot out from the gap, flying across the cockpit on the head of a spout of water.

The tortoise won the battle for us that night. Several more potentially destructive waves curled over *Brendan*, broke, and shattered themselves harmlessly against our leather defenses. Only a fraction of that water entered the bilges, and was easily pumped back into the sea. Poking up through his hole in the leather plating, the helmsman had a hard and bitter time of it. Facing aft and steering to ride the waves, he was battered achingly in the ribs by the sharp edge of the tortoise while the wind scoured his face. From time to time a breaker would flail his chest, and it was so uncomfortable that each man stayed only fifteen minutes at the helm before he had to be replaced, his hands and face numb in the biting cold.

But it was worth it. Even if we were losing the distance we had made and were being blown back in our tracks, we had survived the encounter with our first major Greenland gale. We had made *Brendan* seaworthy to face the unusual conditions of those hostile seas, and we had done so with our own ingenuity and skills. Above all, we had succeeded by using the same basic materials which had been available to Saint Brendan and the Irish seagoing monks. It was cause for genuine satisfaction.

The Brendan *reached Newfoundland on 26 June 1977.*

DEN OF THIEVES

Kevin Rushby

Kevin Rushby is the author of the books Eating the Flowers of Paradise, Chasing the Mountain of Light *and* Hunting Pirate Heaven. *Travelling through India researching the Thuggee cult, Rushby encountered bandits of a more modern type, as recounted in his* Children of Kali.

The temple of Kali at Kali Ghat is on the south side of Kolkata. I dropped off the tram and walked past the line of stalls and shops selling all kinds of souvenirs: postcards, masks, balloons, votive trays, handkerchiefs to cover the offerings – yes, the rumal was there still – and huge trays of hibiscus flowers, Kali's blood-red favourite.

The temple itself was in the centre of a large paved square, almost entirely hidden by the stalls and shops clustered around. Crowds of excited people swarmed in carrying garlands of hibiscus, a queue came out of the gate and wound around the building like a cobra's tail. Guides and pundits were grabbing anyone they could – help with your devotions, for a fee. But I did not enter immediately. I walked past the temple, turned the corner where the Little Sisters of Mercy have their hospital, then took a narrow paved lane down towards the river.

It was a residential area, densely populated: women washing clothes, buffaloes strolling and naked children scampering around. Towards the end, a few yards before a low archway, was a temple. Not a huge one like that back up the lane, this was a simple room with a tiled floor, a Shiva lingam, a brass snake, a brass urn full of ashes and a couple of grass mats. There was no one here, however, the open frontage was sealed off with one of those cantilevered barred gates.

"Is it the Baba you are wanting?" a voice asked and I turned to find a tall elderly man wrapped in brown shawls.

"Yes."

He indicated that I should follow him and led me on through several alleyways, each narrower than the last. A man taking a bath in an aluminium tray had to stop soaping himself to let us past; scabrous dogs and bold cockerels were driven before us. Finally we came to a tall building that had been divided into apartments. The division was clear because a concrete wall had been built in the middle of the front door, splitting the entrance hall neatly into two narrow squeezes. We entered, sideways, to avoid touching the walls which were dripping with water and green algal gunk. There were sounds all around – the high chatter of women, bangs and clatters, the sizzle and spark of an electrical fault – but there was little light. My guide took my wrist and led me through a maze of dishevelled concrete.

It was almost impossible to see where the original building had been in this morass of shoddy additions. Mezzanine levels that were not level grabbed space from corridors, forcing us to bend double; random supporting pillars rose like crusty stalagmites from the floor; cock-eyed beams were balanced on breeze-blocks. In one place it opened up into what passed for a light well, and I looked up, past the forlorn washing line with its threadbare sarong and a home-knitted balaclava (in this heat?), past concrete lintels and projecting rusty reinforcing rods, all the way to the little square of sky. This was certainly the bottom of the well: a place for the people thrown down by modern life, as surely as any thug ever threw down a strangled corpse.

We moved on, squeezed between two pipes and came to a low plywood door where my guide knocked. There was a shout from within, then some conversation about "the British man" and "the Baba". The door opened and my guide showed me in, around a tatty curtain of sackcloth. He did not follow and the door was rapidly closed behind me, then bolted by a slim young man in a sarong. The damp heat and the smell of ganja fell over my face like a warm wet flannel.

I'll admit to a stab of nervous energy at that moment, some fear even. It was a room so low that I had to bend my head, it was at most ten feet wide and as many deep, lit by a naked low-wattage bulb that hung low down one side on a tattered cable. There were no windows and just one item of furniture, a huge high bed that occupied the full width of the room and came within a yard of the door. It was covered in a patchwork of blankets and shawls, several overflowing ashtrays, a pile of playing cards, perhaps three dozen empty beer cans and nine half-naked men.

I think they must have been as surprised to find me there as I was. They stared in disbelief, check sarongs around their waists and torsoes bare and glistening with sweat, playing cards in their hands. One had a huge ramshackle spliff in his mouth. Their faces were villainous, no doubt, especially lit from below like that: the dim golden light cutting up through grizzled chins and moustaches to hooded wary eyes.

"*Kamon achew*," I said, my first attempt at Bengali. Nobody moved.

The one with the spliff was older than the others. He now slowly took the smoking giant from his mouth and spoke.

"English," he said, nodding gently, then added something in quick Bengali.

One of the others jumped down off the bed and took my bag from me – I let it go feebly – then he bent down and removed my shoes.

"Come," said the older man, patting the bed next to him.

I crawled across the covers, weaving my way around the remains of a fish curry and all the other things, then sat cross-legged next to him.

Almost simultaneously I heard the wall say something. Just a whisper, but it came from the scabby top corner of the room. The older man leaned around me and, taking hold of a tab on the wall, he yanked open a small duct. I could see a tiny smudge of daylight. It can hardly have been more than five or ten minutes since I had left the sunshine outside, but I had that feeling you get as a child when you leave the cinema after a thrilling film and are shocked to find night has not yet come.

One of the other men rummaged under the bed covers, then put a small package in the duct and shut it.

"Ganja," said the older man to me without being asked. "We selling ganja and charas – good one – from Bangladesh and Assam."

"You're a gang?"

He showed a glint of gold tooth. "No, we are gangsters."

I don't suffer from claustrophobia. In fact, I quite like confined spaces: my writing room has always been a den or a cave. Once I made the mistake of trying an attic with a lovely window overlooking a pleasant rural scene, but I ended up in the walk-in wardrobe. Lack of air, however, is another thing and that room was hot and suffocating.

"The Baba?" I asked. "Is he coming?"

They shared a joke at that.

"Baba not here," said the boss, the only one who appeared to speak anything but Bengali. He gave some orders and a beer can was pressed into my hand, then the spliff into my mouth. It was so acrid I choked and passed it on. They gathered around in a circle with eager faces.

"Fish curry?" asked Boss. I pressed my hand to my heart and shook my head. The fish glared.

Silence fell as if we were waiting a signal. The youths were watchful, most with one knee drawn up, one cross-legged.

"OK, English," said Boss, slipping me an evil, sidelong grin. "Time to play gin rummy."

The packs of cards were the cleanest items in that room. He shuffled with casual dexterity, drawing out a series of great slithering arcs, then violently smacking them back together into his palm before dealing.

It was quite some time since I had lain on the bed in Hogenakkal with Jayapalani and learned gin rummy with all its originals and duplicates. Now I had some Bengali variations and a little pressure, yet I won the first round. My deal.

I was clumsy and smiled too much. When I picked up my hand, I could see instantly that my shuffling had been cursory, but no one complained and I had a great hand. I won again.

Losing the third was clearly an imperative and I started with an unpromising set of cards, but I got some breaks. Initially there were wry smiles and some laughter, then frowns and sharp intakes of breath. Eye contact ended. I wiped a bead of sweat from my nose and wished I had not given up smoking, at least I could have offered them nicotine. The third came my way, a narrow victory from Boss in second place again.

I knew I had to lose the fourth. It was probably compulsory in Bengali gang law. I picked up and saw nine of clubs, eight and seven. They might make me eat the fish curry.

And ten. They might make me smoke the compost heap again. We started and I was throwing away good cards and making Boss frown. But it worked, I managed to come last with a huge points tally. On the next hand Boss took the lead and I wondered if perhaps I was playing only as well as the other men. By the fifth and Boss's victory I knew I was not the only one who had snatched a great defeat. We were all very happy then and the smiles returned.

I was handed another beer and let off the fish curry and compost heap. Things seemed pretty relaxed now so I ventured some enquiries about their business. Boss was happy to talk.

"These two boys go to Bangladesh for ganja."

"Is it difficult?"

"Oh!" He translated and they all laughed. "Very dangerous. Policemen searching."

"And if they find it?"

"No. Never finding. Maybe jail, maybe pay money."

"You go with a passport?" I had to explain a bit before he understood.

"No, no passport, no papers. Secret business."

"And you sell it in Kolkata – who to?"

"We sell to all peoples. Workers, students, businessmen."

"Holy men – sadhus and sannyasis?"

Boss smiled. "For sadhu we give freely."

It's one of those paradoxes India has: everyone knows that holy men smoke ganja and they need it to be holy, but those who bring ganja to holy men are criminals and must be locked up for long periods.

"Do you live here because of the temple of Kali?"

"Kali is our mother. If you neglect your mother, what kind of man are you?"

The younger gangsters wanted me to learn some Bengali.

"*Tumi kotai jave?*"

"*Kali ghat jachhi.*"

They fell about laughing, upsetting some beer cans.

I was wondering how I was to get out when a telephone rang. They hauled it out from under the bed and handed it to Boss, a huge blue plastic thing with a grubby white dial. He spoke briefly then replaced the receiver and gave some orders.

I was ushered off the bed and told to put on my shoes. Then, after some heartfelt goodbyes and promises to visit again, I was led by one of their number back out into the world of daylight.

When we reached the temple there was a small crowd of people outside who parted to let us through. Inside, reclined on the grass mat, was the Baba. He was a tiny man, very old, but with a bright mischievous look in his eye.

"Ah! British fella. I am so sorry I was not here when you arrived."

He moved to let me come and sit beside him. His hair was grey and straggled halfway down the loose purple waistcoat that he wore along with a dhoti.

"That's no problem," I said. "This young man and his friends looked after me."

The Baba grinned. "Oh, they are very good boys though they are undoubtedly miscreants! They look after me." He translated for the benefit of the crowd who all smiled indulgently. The young gangster came and touched the Baba's feet, then settled himself there like a contented dog. At the same time a small package of ganja was passed up to a helper who began to prepare a pipe.

"You came to see the Mother?"

I nodded.

The Baba touched my arm. "Wait until tomorrow and come early morning. There will be a great ceremony tomorrow."

"You live here because of the Mother?"

"Yes. Thirty-three years ago I gave up my possessions to devote myself."

"What did you do before that?"

"I had many positions: government service for some years, then I had an engineering business. That developed into a successful thing – offices all over India, but I handed it to my sons and retired. Now I am ninety-one and I have no regrets."

"Did you wander?"

"I am not sannyasi. To be sannyasi one must never stay more than three days in a place. I went to live in the smashan – you understand? The burning ground. I stayed seven years there."

I thought how wonderful India was, that a businessman could throw it all up and live as a destitute in a crematorium without anyone raising as much as an eyebrow.

The pipe had been carefully prepared, all rough pieces removed and the leaves shredded. Now it was lit and passed to him.

"Why the smashan?"

"It is a place to concentrate and forget the trivial things of life."

He put his hands together and pressing his mouth to the space between finger and thumb, pulled hard twice, then handed the pipe to me. I drew a mouthful of smoke.

"I am not aghori," he continued. "I have no special teachings to give, no secrets. I have need of nothing. I just do my japa [his mantra]."

I told him about the thugs and what the aghori in Varanasi had said about them being blessed. He smiled.

"According to their system, they were correct."

"But murderers?"

"Miscreants." He passed the pipe to the gangster and watched him smoke. "This boy is a miscreant, but he is good to me. I look in his heart and see a good boy. I don't ask him what he does, I suppose he smuggles ganja and sells it and according to our law that means he is a criminal. In the British time, you know, abortion was a serious crime, punished by seven years in prison, and now

the government pay people money to do it. Night for day.
In the old times we looked for a husband for our daughters: a boy with many brothers and strong parents – that
was enough. Now they search for a boy who knows
computers, without brothers and parents deceased. Night
for day."

"Things change – even morals?"

Another pipe was being prepared.

"All you need to know is that if you put padi, you will
get padi – not wheat. As you sow, so you reap. In Gujarat
they burned down the churches of Christians and now
they have had a terrible earthquake. Is there a connection?
By science, no. But I think if there is something bad in
your heart, bad things will come to you. And good will
bring good. It is very simple – no secrets, no special
teachings. Thirty-three years ago I gave everything away
and walked from the house with empty hands. Since then
I never use money and yet I am never hungry. How is
that?"

He took the second pipe and, leaning forward, drew on
it. As he did so, a lock of his grey hair came across and
dangled in the burning ganja. Seeing this, the gangster
put out his hand and, with great tenderness, gently
pushed the lock away, behind the Baba's ear.

ACROSS THE SYRIAN DESERT

Gertrude Bell

It was of the Englishwoman Gertrude Bell (1868–1926)
that an Arab chief remarked, "And if this is one of their
women! Allah, what must their men be like!" Bell was a
writer, spy, mountaineer, archaeologist and traveller; among
her most remarkable journeys was a fourteen-day crossing of
the Syrian Desert in 1911.

DUMEIR
February 9th [1911]

We're off. And now I must tell you the course of the
negotiations which preceded this journey. First as you
know I went to the sons of Abdul Kadir and they called up
Sheikh Muhammad Bassam and asked him to help me. I
called on him the following evening. He said it was too
early, the desert camels had not come in to Damascus,
there was not a dulul (riding camel) to be had and I must
send out to a village a few hours away and buy. This was
discouraging, as I could not hope to get them for less than
£15 apiece. I wanted five, and I should probably have to
sell them for an old song at Hit. Next day Fattuh went
down into the bazaar and came back with the news that he
and Bassam between them had found an owner of camels

ready to hire for £7 apiece. It was dear, but I closed with the offer. All the arrangements were made and I dispatched the caravan by the Palmyra road. Then followed misfortune. The snow closed down upon us, the desert post did not come in for three weeks, and till it came we were without a guide. Then Bassam invented another scheme. The old sheikh of Kubeisa near Hit (you know the place) was in Damascus and wanted to return home; he would journey with us and guide us. So all was settled again.

But the Sheikh Muhammad en Nawan made continuous delays; we were helpless, for we could not cross the Syrian desert without a guide and still the post did not come in. The snow in the desert had been without parallel. At last Muhammad en Nawan was ready. I sent off my camels to Dumeir yesterday (it is the frontier village of the desert) and went myself to sleep at the English hospital, whence it was easier to slip off unobserved. For I am supposed to be travelling by Palmyra and Deir with four zaptiehs. This morning Fattuh and I drove here, it took us four hours, and the sheikh came on his dulul. The whole party is assembled in the house of a native of Kubeisa, I am lodged in a large, windowless room spread with felts, a camel is stabled at my door and over the way Fattuh is cooking my dinner. One has to put on clogs to walk across the yard, so inconceivably muddy it is, and in the village one can't walk at all, one must ride. I got in about one and lunched, after which I mounted my mare and went out to see some ruins a mile or two away. It was a big Roman fortified camp. And beyond it the desert stretched away to the horizon. That is where we go to-morrow. It's too heavenly to be back in all this again, Roman forts and Arab tents and the wide desert . . . We have got for a guide the last desert postman who came in three days ago, having been delayed nine days by the snow. His name is Ali.

SYRIAN DESERT
February 10th

There is in Dumeir a very beautiful temple, rather like one of the temples at Baalbek. As soon as the sun was up I went out and took some photographs of it, but I was ready long before our camels were loaded; the first day's packing is always a long business. Finally we got off soon after nine, a party of fifteen, myself, the sheikh, Fattuh, Ali and my four camel men, and the other seven merchants who are going across to the Euphrates to buy sheep. In half an hour we passed the little Turkish guard house which is the last outpost of civilisation and plunged into the wilderness. Our road lay before us over a flat expanse bounded to the N. by the range of barren hills that trend away to the N.E. and divide us from the Palmyran desert, and to the S. by a number of distant tells, volcanic I should think. I rode my mare all day, for I can come and go more easily upon her, but when we get into the heart of the desert I shall ride a camel. It's less tiring. Three hours from Dumeir we came to some water pools, which are dry in summer, and here we filled our skins, for where we are camping there is no water. There was a keen wind, rising sometimes into a violent storm which brought gusts of hail upon us, but fortunately it was behind us so that it did not do us much harm. Late in the afternoon another hailstorm broke over us and clearing away left the distant hills white with snow. We had come to a place where there was a little scrub which would serve as firewood, and here we camped under the lee of some rising ground. Our companions have three big Arab tents, open in front, and we our two English tents, and oddly enough we are quite warm in spite of the rain and cold wind. I don't know why it is that one seldom feels cold in the desert; perhaps because of the absence of damp. The stony, sandy ground never becomes muddy. A little grass is beginning to grow and as you look over the wide expanse in front of you it is almost green. The old sheikh is lamenting that we are not

in a house in Damsacus (but I think one's first camp in the
Hamar is worth a street full of houses). "By the head of
your father!" he said, "how can you leave the garden of
the world and come out into this wilderness?" Perhaps it
does require explanation.

February 11th

But to-day's experiences will not serve to justify my
attitude. When I went to bed a hurricane was blowing.
I woke from time to time and heard the good Fattuh
hammering in the tent pegs, and wondered if any tent
would stand up in that gale and also what was going to
happen next. About an hour before dawn Fattuh called
me and asked whether I was cold. I woke in surprise and
putting my hand out felt the waterproof valise that covered me wet with snow. "It is like the sea," cried Fattuh.
Therefore I lighted a candle and saw that it had drifted
into my tent a foot deep. I dug down, found my boots and
hat and put them under the Wolsey valise; I had gone to
bed as I stood, and put all my extra clothing under the
valise for warmth, so that nothing had come to harm. At
dawn Fattuh dragged out the waterproof sheet that covers
the ground and with it most of the snow. The snow was
lying in great drifts where the wind had blown it, it was
banked up against our tents and those of the Arabs and
every hour or so the wind brought a fresh storm upon us.
We cleared it out of our tents and settled down to a day as
little uncomfortable as we could manage to make it . . .

February 12th

We have got into smooth waters at last. You can imagine
what I felt like when I looked out of my tent before dawn
and saw a clear sky and the snow almost vanished. But the
cold! Everything in my tent was frozen stiff – yesterday's
damp skirt was like a board, my gloves like iron, my
sponges – well, I'll draw a veil over my sponges – I did
not use them much . . . I spent an hour trudging back-

wards and forwards over the frozen desert trying to pretend I was warm while the camels were loaded. The frozen tents took a world of time to pack – with frozen fingers too. We were off soon after eight, but for the first hour the wet desert was like a sheet of glass and the camels slipped about and fell down with much groaning and moaning. They are singularly unfitted to cope with emergencies. For the next hour we plodded over a slippery melting surface, for which they are scarcely better suited, then suddenly we got out of the snow zone and all was well. I got on to my camel and rode her for the rest of the day. She is the most charming of animals. You ride a camel with only a halter which you mostly tie loosely round the peak of your saddle. A tap with your camel switch on one side of her neck or the other tells her the direction you want her to go, a touch with your heels sends her on, but when you wish her to sit down you have to hit her lightly and often on the neck saying at the same time: "Kh kh kh kh," that's as near as I can spell it. The big soft saddle, the *shedad*, is so easy and comfortable that you never tire. You loll about and eat your lunch and observe the landscape through your glasses: you might almost sleep. So we swung on through an absolutely flat plain till past five, when we came to a shallow valley with low banks on either side, and here we camped. The name of the place is Aitha, there is a full moon and it is absolutely still except for the sound of the pounding of coffee beans in the tents of my travelling companions. I could desire nothing pleasanter.

February 13th

We were off soon after six. The sun rose gloriously half an hour later and we began to unfreeze. It is very cold riding on a camel, I don't know why unless it has to do with her extreme height. We rode on talking cheerfully of our various adventures till after ten which is the time when my companions lunch, so I lunch too. The camels were going rather languidly for they were thirsty, not having drunk since they left Damascus. They won't drink when it is very cold. But our guide, Ali, promised us some pools ahead, good water, he said. When we got there we found that some Arabs had camped not far off and nothing remained of the pools but trampled mud . . . So we had to go searching round for another pool and at last we found one about a mile away with a very little water in it, but enough for the riding camels, my mare and our water skins. It is exceedingly muddy however. We got into camp about four not far from some Arab tents . . . It is a wonderfully interesting experience this. Last night they all sat up half the night because my mare pricked her ears and they thought she heard robbers. They ran up the banks and cried out, "Don't come near! we have soldiers with us and camels." It seemed to me when I heard of it (I was asleep at the time) a very open deceit, but it seems to have served the purpose for the thief retired. As we rode this morning Ali detected hoof marks on the hard ground and was satisfied that it was the mare of our enemy.

February 14th

What I accuse them of is not that they choose to live differently from us: for my part I like that; but that they do their own job so very badly . . . Everybody in the desert knows that camels frequently stray away while feeding, yet it occurs to no one to put a man to watch over them. No, when we get into camp they are just turned off to feed where they like and go where they will. Consequently yesterday at dusk four of our baggage camels were missing and a riding camel belonging to one of the Damascene sheep merchants and everyone had to turn out to look for them. I could not do anything so I did not bother and while I was dining the sheikh looked in and said our camels had come back – let us thank God! It is certain that no one else could claim any credit. But the riding camel was not to be found, nor had she

come back when I was ready to start at 4.30 this morning.
We decided to wait till dawn and that being two hours off
and the temperature 30° I went to bed again and to sleep.
At dawn there was no news of her, so we started, leaving
word with some Arabs where we were gone. She has not
yet appeared, nor do I think she will. I was very sorry for
the merchant, who now goes afoot, and very much bored
by the delay. For we can't make it up at the other end
because the camels have to eat for at least two hours before
sunset. They eat shik; so does my little mare, she being a
native of the desert. At ten o'clock we came to some big
water pools, carefully hollowed out "in the first days,"
said Ali, with the earth banked up high round them, but
now half-filled with mud and the banks broken. Still they
hold a good deal a water in the winter and the inhabitants
of the desert for miles around were driving their sheep
and camels there to drink. We too filled our water skins.
We got into camp at three, near some Arab tents. The
sheikh, a charming old man, has just paid us a long visit.
We sat round Muhammad's coffee fire and talked. It was
all the more cheerful because the temperature is now 46° –
a blessed change from 26°. My sponges have unfrozen for
the first time. We have got up into the high, flat plain
which is the true Hamad, the Smooth, and the horizon
from my tent door is as round as the horizon of the sea.
The sharp, dry air is wonderfully delicious: I think every
day of the Syrian desert must prolong your life by two
years. Sheikh Muhammad had confided to me that he had
three wives, one in Damascus, one in Kubeisa, and one in
Bagdad, but the last he has not seen for twenty-three
years. "She has grown old, oh lady – by the truth of God!
and she never bore but one daughter."

February 15th

We were off at five this morning in bitter frost. Can you
picture the singular beauty of these moonlit departures?
The frail Arab tents falling one by one, leaving the camp-

fires blazing into the night; the dark masses of the kneeling camels; the shrouded figures binding up the loads, shaking the ice from the water skins, or crouched over the hearth for a moment's warmth before mounting. "Yallah, yallah, oh, children!" cries the old sheikh, knocking the ashes out of his narghileh. "Are we ready?" So we set out across the dim wilderness, Sheikh Muhammad leading on his white dulul. The sky ahead reddens, and fades, the moon pales and in sudden splendour the sun rushes up over the rim of the world. To see with the eyes is good, but while I wonder and rejoice to look upon this primeval existence, it does not seem to be a new thing; it is familiar, it is a part of inherited memory. After an hour and a half of marching we came to the pool of Khafiyeh, and since there is no water for three days ahead we had to fill all our empty skins. But the pool was a sheet of ice, the water skins were frozen and needed careful handling – for if you unfold them they crack and break – and we lighted a fire and set to work to thaw them and ourselves. I sent the slow baggage camels on, and with much labour we softened the skins and contrived to fill them. The sun was now up and a more barren prospect than it revealed you cannot imagine. The Hamad stretched in front of us, flat and almost absolutely bare; for several hours we rode over a wilderness of flints on which nothing grew. It was also the coldest day we have had, for the keen frosty wind blew straight into our faces. We stopped once to wait for the baggage camels and warmed ourselves at a bonfire meanwhile, and again we stopped for half an hour to lunch. We watched our shadows catch us up and march ahead of us as the sun sank westward and at three o'clock we pitched camp in the stony waste. Yet I can only tell you that we have spent a very pleasant day. The old sheikh never stops talking, bless him, he orders us all about when we pitch and break up camp, but as Fattuh and I know much more about the pitching of our tents than he does, we pay no attention. "Oh Fattuh," said I this evening when he had given us endless advice, "do you pity the wife in Bagdad?" "Effendim," said Fattuh, "she must be exceedingly at rest." Still, for my part I should be sorry not to see Sheikh Muhammad for twenty-three years.

February 16th

After I had gone to bed last night I heard Ali shouting to all whom it might concern: "We are English soldiers! English soldiers!" But there was no one to hear and the desert would have received with equal indifference the information that we were Roman legionaries. We came to the end of the inhospitable Hamad to-day, and the desert is once more diversified by a slight rise and fall of the ground. It is still entirely waterless, so waterless that in the spring when the grass grows thick the Arabs cannot camp here. All along our way there is proof of former water storage – I should think Early Moslem, marking the Abbassid post road. The pools have been dug out and banked up, but they are now full of earth and there is very little water in them. We are camped to-night in what is called a valley. It takes a practised eye to distinguish the valley from the mountain, the one is so shallow and the other so low. The valleys are often two miles wide and you can distinguish them best by the fact that there are generally more "trees" in them than on the heights. I have made great friends with one of the sheep merchants. His name is Muhiyyed Din. He is coming back in the spring over this road with his lambs. They eat as they go and travel four hours a day. "It must be a dull job," said I. "Eh wallah!" he replied, "but if the spring grass is good the master of the lambs rejoices to see them grow fat." He travels over the whole desert, here and in Mesopotamia, buying sheep and camels; to Nejd too, and to Egypt, and he tells me delightful tales of his adventures. What with one thing and another the eight or nine hours of camel riding a day are never dull. But Truth of God! the cold!

February 17th

We were running short of water this morning. The water difficulty has been enhanced by the cold. The standing pools are exceedingly shallow so that when there is an inch of ice over them little remains but mud; what the water is like that you scrape up under these conditions I leave to the imagination. Besides the mud it has a sharp acrid taste of skins after forty-eight hours in them – not unhealthy I believe, but neither is it pleasant. So it happened that we had to cut down rather to the south to-day instead of going to the well of Kara which we could not have reached this evening. Sheikh Muhammad was much agitated at this programme. He expected to find the camps of the tribes whom he knew at and near the well, and he feared that by coming to the south of them we might find ourselves upon the path of a possible raiding party of Arabs whom he did not know coming up from the south. Ali tried to reassure him, saying that the chances were against raiding parties (good, please God!) and that we were relying upon God. But the sheikh was not to be comforted. "Life of God! what is this talk! To God is the command! we are in the Shamuyyeh where no one is safe – Face of God!" He is master of a wonderful variety of pious ejaculations. So we rode for an hour or two (until we forgot about it) carefully scanning the horizon for ghazus; it was just as well that we had this to occupy us, for the whole day's march was over ground as flat as a board. It had been excruciatingly cold in the early morning – but about midday the wind shifted round to the south and we began to feel the warmth of the sun. For the first time we shed our fur coats, and the lizards came out of their holes. Also the horizon was decorated with fantastic mirages which greatly added to the enjoyment of looking for ghazus. An almost imperceptible rise in the ground would from afar stand up above the solid earth as if it were the high back of a camel. We saw tents with men beside them pitched on the edge of mirage lakes and when at last we actually did come to a stretch of shallow water, it was a long time before I could believe that it was not imaginary. I saw how the atmospheric delusion worked by watching some gazelles. They galloped away over the plain just like ordinary gazelles, but when they came to the mirage they suddenly got up on to stilts and looked the size of camels. It is excessively bewildering to be deprived of the use of one's eyes in this way. We had a ten hours' march to reach the water by which we are camped. It lies in a wide shallow basin of mud, most of it is dried up, but a few pools remain in the deeper parts. The Arabs use some sort of white chalky stone – is it chalk? – to precipitate the mud. We have got some with us. We boil the water, powder the chalk and put it in and it takes nearly all the mud down to the bottom. Then we pour off the water.

February 18th

We were pursued all day by a mad wind which ended by bringing a shower of sleet upon us while we were getting into camp. In consequence of the inclemency of the weather I had the greatest difficulty in getting the sheikh and the camel drivers to leave their tents and they were still sitting over the coffee fire when we and the Damascene merchants were ready to start. Inspired of God I pulled out their tent pegs and brought their roof about their ears – to the great joy of all except those who were sitting under it. So we got off half an hour before dawn and after about an hour's riding dropped down off the smooth plain into an endless succession of hills and deep valleys – when I say *deep* they are about 200 feet deep and they all run north into the hollow plain of Kara. I much prefer this sort of country to the endless flat and it is quite interesting sitting a camel down a stony descent. The unspeakable devilish wind was fortunately behind us – Call upon the Prophet! but it did blow!

February 20th

We marched yesterday thirteen and a half hours without
getting anywhere. We set off at five in a delicious still
night with a temperature of 36 – it felt quite balmy. The
sun rose clear and beautiful as we passed through the gates
of our valley into a wide low plain – we were to reach the
Wady Hauran, which is the father of all valleys in this
desert, in ten hours, and the little ruin of Muheiwir in half
an hour more and there was to be plentiful clear water. We
were in good spirits, as you may imagine; the sheikh sang
songs of Nejd and Ali instructed me in all the desert roads.
We rode on and on. At two o'clock I asked Ali whether it
were two hours to Muheiwir? "More," said he. "Three?"
said I. "Oh, lady, more." "Four?" I asked with a little
sinking of heart. "Wallahi, not so much." We rode on over
low hills and hollow plains. At five we dropped into the
second of the valleys el Ud. By this time Fattuh and I were
on ahead and Ali was anxiously scanning the landscape
from every high rock. The sheikh had sat down to smoke a
narghileh while the baggage camels came up. "My lady,"
said Fattuh, "I do not think we shall reach water tonight." And the whole supply of water which we had was
about a cupful in my flask. We went on for another half-
hour down the valley and finally, in concert with Ali,
selected a spot for a camp. It was waterless, but, said he,
the water was not more than two hours off: he would take
skins and fetch some, and meantime the starving camels
would eat trees. But when the others came up, the Father
of Camels, Abdullah, he from whom we hired our beasts,
protested that he must have water to mix the camel meal
that night (they eat a kind of dough), and rather against
our better judgment we went on. We rode an hour farther,
by which time it was pitch dark. Then Muhiyyed Din
came up to me and said that if by chance we were to meet a
ghazu in the dark night it might go ill with us. That there
was reason in this was admitted by all; we dumped down
where we stood, in spite of the darkness Fattuh had my

tent up before you could wink, while I hobbled my mare and hunted among the camel loads for my bed. No one else put up a tent; they drew the camels together and under the shelter they gave made a fire of what trees they could find. Fattuh and I divided the water in my flask into two parts; with half we made some tea which he and I shared over some tinned meat and some bread; the other half we kept for the next morning when I shared it with the sheikh. We were none of us thirsty really; this weather does not make you thirsty. But my poor little mare had not drunk for two days, and she whinnied to everyone she saw. The last thing I heard before I went to sleep was the good Fattuh reasoning with her. "There is no water," he was saying. "There is none. Ma fi, ma fi." Soon after five he woke me up. I put on my boots, drank the tea he brought (having sent half to the poor old sheikh, who had passed the night under the lee of his camel) and went out into a cheerless daybreak. The sky was heavy with low-hanging clouds, the thermometer stood at 34, as we mounted our camels a faint and rather dismal glow in the east told us that the sun was rising. It was as well that we had not tried to reach water the night before. We rode to-day for six and a half hours before we got to rain pools in the Wady Hauran, and an hour more to Muheiwir and a couple of good wells in the valley bed. For the first four hours our way lay across barren levels; after a time we saw innumerable camels pasturing near the bare horizon and realized that we must be nearing the valley: there is no water anywhere but in the Hauran and all the tents of the Deleim are gathered near it. Then we began to descend through dry and stony water-courses and at midday found ourselves at the bottom of the great valley, and marched along the edge of a river of stones with a few rain pools lying in it. So we came to Muheiwir which is a small mined fort, and here we found two men of the Deleim with a flock of sheep – the first men we have seen for four days. Their camp is about three miles away. Under the ruined fort there are some deep springs in the bed of the stream and by them we camped, feeling that we needed a few hours' rest after all our exertions. The sheikh had lighted his coffee fire while I was taking a first cursory view of the ruin. "Oh, lady," he cried, "honour us!" I sat down and drank a cup of coffee. "Where," said he, looking at me critically, "where is thy face in Damascus, and where thy face here?" And I am bound to say that his remark was not without justification. But after ten days of frost and wind and sun what would you have? The clouds have all cleared away – sun and water and ruins, the heart of man can desire no more. The sheikh salutes you.

February 21st

We got off at four this morning and made a twelve hours' stage. It was freezing a little when we started, the moon rode high upon the shoulder of the Scorpion and was not strong enough to extinguish him – this waning moon has done us great service. It took us two hours to climb up out of the Wady Hauran. I was talking to Muhiyyed Din when the sheikh came up, and said "Oh, lady, speech before dawn is not good." He was afraid of raising some hidden foe. Reckless courage is not his characteristic. We have camped under a low bank, selecting carefully the east side of it so that our camp fires can be seen only by the friendly Deleim to the east of us. We are nowhere to-night – just out in the open wilderness which has come to feel so homelike. Four of the sheep merchants left us yesterday hearing that the sheikhs with whom they deal were camped near at hand, for each man deals every year with the same sheikh. If you could see the western sky with the evening star burning in it, you would give thanks – as I do.

February 22nd

An hour's ride from our camp this morning brought us to the small desert fortress of Amej . . . But Muhiyyed Din and the other sheep merchants found that their sheikhs were close at hand and we parted with much regret and a plentiful exchange of blessings. So we rode on till at four o'clock we reached the fortress of Khubbaz and here we have camped beneath the walls where Fattuh and I camped two years ago. It feels almost like returning home. It blew all day; I must own that the desert would be nicer if it were not so plagued with wind. The sheikh and Ali and one of the camel drivers sang trios for part of the afternoon to beguile the way. I have written down some of the sheikh's songs. They are not by him, however, but by the most famous of modern desert poets, the late Emir of Nejd.

February 23rd

The morning came grey and cheerless with an occasional scud of rain. We set off about six and took the familiar path across barren watercourses to Ain Zaza. The rain fell upon us and made heavy and sticky going, but it cleared before we reached the Ain and we lunched there and waited for the baggage camels till eleven. Kubeisa was only an hour and a half away, and it being so early I determined to refuse all the sheikh's pressing invitations that we should spend the night with him, and push on to Hit, three and a half hours farther. The baggage camels were informed of the change of plan and Fattuh and I rode on in high spirits at the thought of rejoining our caravan that evening. For you remember the caravan which we despatched from Damascus was to wait for us at Hit. But before we reached Kubeisa the rain came down again in torrents. Now the ground here is what the Arabs called *sabkha*, soft, crumbly salt marsh, sandy when it is dry and ready at a moment's notice to turn into a world of glutinous paste. This is what it did, and since camels cannot walk in mud I was presently aware of a stupendous downfall and found myself and my camel prostrate in the sticky glue. It feels like the end of the universe when your camel falls down. However we both rolled up unhurt and made the best of our way to the gates of Kubeisa. And here another misfortune awaited us. The rain was still falling, heavily. Abdullah, Father of Camels, declared that his beasts could not go on to Hit across a road all *sabkha*, and even Fattuh admitted that, tired and hungry as they were, it would be impossible. So in great triumph and with much praising of God, the sheikh conducted us to his house where I was seized by a pack of beautiful and very inquisitive women ("They are shameless!" said Fattuh indignantly) and conducted into the pitch-dark room on the ground floor which is the living-room. But the sheikh rescued me and took me upstairs to the reception room on the roof. Everyone we met fell on his neck and greeted him with a kiss on either cheek, and no sooner were we seated upstairs and a bonfire of trees lighted in the middle of the room, than all the worthies of Kubeisa began to assemble to greet him and hear the news. At the end they numbered at least fifty. Now this was the room in which I was supposed to eat and sleep – there was no other. I took Fattuh aside – or rather outside, for the room was packed to overflowing – and said "The night will be troublesome." Fattuh knitted his brows and without a word strode down the stairs. I returned to the company and when the room grew too smoky with trees and tobacco sat outside talking to the sheikh's charming son, Namân. The rain had stopped. My old acquaintances in Kubeisa had all been up to salute me and I sat by the fire and listened to the talk and prayed that Fattuh might find some means of escape. He was as resourceful as usual. After a couple of hours he returned and said, "With your permission, oh, Muhammad. We are ready." He had found a couple of camels and a donkey and we were off. So we took a most affectionate leave of the sheikh and left him to his narghileh. Half the town of Kubeisa, the female half, followed us through the streets, and we turned our faces to Hit. The two camels carried our diminished loads, Fattuh rode the donkey (it was so small that his feet touched the ground and he presently abandoned it in favour of one of the baggage camels and sent it back) and I was supposed to ride my mare. But she had a sore heel, poor little thing, and kept stumbling in the mud, so I walked most of the way. We left at 2.30 and had two and a half hours before sunset. The first part of our way was hard and dry; presently we saw the smoke of the Hit pitch fires upon the horizon and when we had passed between some low hills, there was the great mound of Hit and its single minaret in front of us. There remained an hour and a half of journey, the sun had set and our road was all *sabkha*. The camels slipped and slithered and tumbled down: "Their legs are like soap," explained the camel boy. If the rain had fallen again we should have been done. But it kept off till just as we reached Hit. The mound still loomed through the night and we could just see enough to keep more or less to our road – less rather than more – but not enough to make out whether stone or mud or sulphur pools lay in front of us. So we three great travellers, Fattuh, the mare and I, came into Hit, wet and weary, trudging through the dark, and looking, I make no doubt, like so many vagabonds, and thus ingloriously ended our fine adventure. The khan stands outside the town; the khanji is an old friend. "Ya Abud!" shouted Fattuh, "the caravan, our caravan, is it here?" "Kinship and welcome and may the earth be wide to you! They are here!" The muleteers hurried out, seized my bridle, seized my hand in theirs and laid it upon their forehead. All was safe and well, we and they and the animals and the packs. Praise God! there is no other but He. The khanji brought me tea, and various friends came to call, I dined and washed and went to bed.

And so you see, we have crossed the Syrian Desert as easily as if it had been the Sultan's highroad, and we have made many friends and seen the ruins we went out to see, and over and above all I have conceived quite a new theory about the mediæval roads through the desert which I will prove some day by another journey.

A LONG CLIMB IN THE HINDU KUSH

Eric Newby

Born in London in 1919, Newby served with the Special Boat Section during the Second World War until captured off the coast of Sicily. After the war he engaged in several careers, but was foremost a traveller; his travel books include Slowly Down the Ganges, Love and War in the Appenines *and* The Big Red Train Ride. A Short Walk in the Hindu Kush *recounts Newby's amateur climbing adventures around Asia, undertaken with his friend, Hugh Carless.*

First we tackled the castlelike knob to our left, going up the north side. It had all the attributes of an exposed face, together with a truly awe-inspiring drop of three thousand feet to the east glacier, and it was bitterly cold; like everywhere else we had so far been on this aggravating mountain there were no good belays. Up to now in the most difficult circumstances we had managed a few grim little jokes, but now on the face of this abominable castle our capacity for humour finally deserted us.

From the top of the castle there was the choice of the north side which was cold and grim or the south, a labyrinthine chaos of rock, fitted with clefts and chimneys too narrow to admit the human frame without pain. In one of these clefts that split a great boulder twenty feet long, we both became wedged and only extricated ourselves with difficulty. Sometimes exasperated with this lunatic place we would force a way over the ridge through the soft snow only to find ourselves, with no way of going on, forced to return by the way we had come.

But as we advanced, the ridge became more and more narrow and eventually we emerged on to a perfect knife edge. Ahead, but separated from us by two formidable buttresses, was the summit, a simple cone of snow as high as Box Hill.

We dug ourselves a hole in the snow and considered our position. The view was colossal. Below us on every side mountains surged away it seemed for ever; we looked down on glaciers and snow-covered peaks that perhaps no one has ever seen before, except from the air. To the west and north we could see the great axis of the Hindu Kush and its southward curve, from the Anjuman Pass around the northern marches of Nuristan. Away to the east-north-east was the great snow-covered mountain we had seen from the wall of the east glacier, Tirich Mir, the 25,000-foot giant on the Chitral border, and to the south-west the mountains that separated Nuristan from Paryshir.

Our own immediate situation was no less impressive. A stone dropped from one hand would have landed on one of the upper glaciers of the Chamar Valley, while from the other it would have landed on the east glacier. Hugh, having determined the altitude to be 19,100 feet, now gave a practical demonstration of this by dropping the aneroid, which fell with only one bounce into the Chamar Valley.

"Bloody thing," said Hugh gloomily. "I don't think it was much use anyway." Above us choughs circled uttering melancholy croaking noises. "We've got to make a decision about going on," he said. "And we've got to be absolutely certain it's the right one, because our lives are going to depend on it."

Anywhere else such a remark would have sounded over dramatic. Here it seemed no more than an accurate statement of fact.

"How long do you think it will take to get to the top?"

"All of four hours and then only if we don't go any slower."

It was now one-thirty; we had been climbing for nine hours.

"That means five-thirty at the summit. Going down, four hours at least to the Castle, and then twenty minutes to the *col* on the ridge. It'll be nine o'clock. Then there's the ice slope. Do you think we can manage the *col* to the camp in the dark?"

"The only alternative is to sleep on the ridge. We haven't got any sleeping-bags. I'm afraid we wouldn't last out. We can try if you like."

For a moment we were dotty enough to consider going on. It was a terrific temptation: we were only seven hundred feet below the summit. Then we decided to give up. Both of us were nearly in tears. Sadly we ate our nougat and drank our cold coffee.

The descent was terrible. With the stimulus of the summit gone, we suddenly realized how tired we were. But, although our strength and morale were ebbing, we both agreed to take every possible precaution. There was no mountain rescue service on this mountain. If anything happened to one of us, a bad sprain would be enough, it would be the end for both. As we went down I found myself mumbling to myself again and again, "One man's death diminishes mee, one man's death diminishes mee."

Yet, though we were exhausted, we felt an immense sense of companionship. At this difficult moment the sense of dependence on one another, engendered perhaps by the fact that we were roped together and had one another's lives in our hands, produced in me a feeling of great affection for Hugh, this tiresome character who had led me to such a spot.

At six we were at the *col* below the Castle, exactly as he had prophesied. The conditions were very bad. All the way down from the Castle a tremendous wind had been blowing and the mountainside was flooded in a ghastly yellow light as the sun went down. As the clouds came up the wind became a blizzard, a howling gale with hail and snow battering us. We had come down from the Castle without crampons. Now to cross the head of the *col* in this wind on the frozen snow, we had to put them on again. Still wearing them, we lowered ourselves one by one over the overhanging crest into a gully on the south face.

The south face was a grey desolation and the gully was the wrong one. It was too wide for an easy descent and was smooth ice the whole way for two hundred feet.

Twice we had to take off and put on our crampons, almost blubbering with fatigue and vexation, as the straps were frozen and adjusting them seemed to take an eternity. Worst of all the wind on the ridge was blowing snow into the gully, half blinding us and sending down big chunks of rock. One of these hit Hugh on the shoulder, hurting him badly, and I thought he was going to faint. The gully was succeeded by a minute chimney full of ice, down which I glissaded on my behind for twenty feet until Hugh pulled me up. Very stupidly I was wearing my crampons attached to a sling round my middle and I sat on them for the full distance, so that they went in to the full length of the spikes, scarring me for life in a most interesting manner.

By now it was quite dark. We had an hour on the rocks, now covered with a fresh sheet of ice, that I shall remember for the rest of my life. Then we were home. "Home" was just the ledge with the two sleeping bags, some food and the stoves, but we had thought of nothing else for hours.

As we stumbled on to it, a great dark shape rose up and struck a match, illuminating an ugly, well-known face with a wart on its forehead. It was Shir Muhammad, most feckless and brutal of drivers, come up to find us.

"I was worried about you," he said simply, "so I came."

It was nine o'clock; we had been climbing for seventeen hours.

By now we were beyond speech. After a long hour the contents of both cooking pots boiled simultaneously, so we drank tea and ate tomato soup at the same time. It was a disagreeable mixture, which we followed with a pot of neat jam and two formidable-looking sleeping-pills that from their size seemed more suitable for horses than human beings.

"I don't approve of drugs," were Hugh's last words before we both sank into a coma, "but I think that under the circumstances we're justified."

We woke at five. My first thought as I came to was that I had been operated on, an illusion heightened by the sight of Hugh's bloody bandaged hands gripping the mouth of his sleeping bag. Mine were now in the same condition as Hugh's had been two days previously; his were worse than ever.

It took us both a long time to dress and Shir Muhammad had to button our trousers, which was a difficult operation for someone who had never had fly buttons of his own. It was the only time I ever saw him laugh. Then he laced our boots.

As soon as I started to move I realized that my feet were beyond boots, so I decided to wear rubber shoes.

By the time we left the platform it was like a hot plate. Shir Muhammad went first, skipping downhill like a goat bearing a great load. Soon he became impatient with our funereal progress and left us far behind.

At the head of the glacier Hugh stopped and took off his pack.

"What's the matter?"

"Rope," he croaked. "Left a rope. Got to go back."

"Don't be an ass."

"Might need it . . . another try."

"Not this year."

It was useless to argue with him. He was already crawling uphill. My return to fetch the karabiner on the other glacier had created an impossible precedent.

The glare of the small snowfield was appalling. My goggles were somewhere in my rucksack, but I had not the will-power to stop and look for them. Soon I developed a splitting headache. With my rubber shoes on I fell continuously. I found myself becoming very grumpy.

At the top of the *moraine* Abdul Ghiyas was waiting for us. He had passed Shir Muhammad without seeing him, somewhere in the labyrinth on the lower slopes of this provoking mountain, and was clucking to himself anxiously.

"Where is Carless *Seb*?"

"Up."

"He is dead?"

"No, he is coming."

"You have climbed the mountain?"

"No."

"Why is Carless *Seb* not with you?"

It was only after much pantomime that I was able to convince him that Hugh was not dead, sacrificed to my own ambition, and he consented to follow me down, carrying my load.

But at the camp we waited an hour, two hours for Hugh; there was no sign of him. I began to be worried and reproached myself for not having waited. The three drivers, huddled over the fire preparing a great secret mess in honour of our arrival, were mumbling, "Carless *Seb*, Carless *Seb*, where is Carless *Seb*?" droning on and on.

Finally Hugh appeared. With his beard full of glacial cream and his cracked lips, he looked like what he in fact was, the survivor of a spectacular disaster.

"Where have you been? We've been worried stiff."

"I got the rope," he said, "then I went to sleep under a rock."

ICE BIRD

David Lewis

David Lewis was born in New Zealand in 1919. At the age of forty-five he gave up his London medical practice to sail around the world with his wife and two small daughters, an adventure related in the books Daughters of the Wind *and* Children of Three Oceans. *His other travel books include* Ice Bird, *an account of his 1972–3 single-handed boat journey to and from Antarctica. The many awards accorded Lewis include the Gold Medal of the Royal Institute of Navigation and the Royal Yacht Squadron's 1974 Chichester award for a single-handed cruise.*

It was midnight when I awoke. Ranks of misty bergs ringed us around in a deceptively innocent-seeming amphitheatre. Gentle snow flakes flickered down. Somewhat rested, I got under way. *Ice Bird* stole silently across the floor of that mighty amphitheatre into a dawn that for once was clear save for snow showers, skirting ever and anon glistening white symbols of beauty – and fear. The very biggest, I noticed with awe, were reflecting their own individual ice blink on to the patch of sky directly above them. But before the day was ended we would be sailing through a different world.

That evening saw *Ice Bird* dashing along through the
misty darkness amid cascades of spray before a rising
westerly gale. My warm quilted clothing was soaked
through before ever I thought to exchange the heavy
parka and fur-lined mitts for waterproof Marlin jacket
and rubber gloves.

The steadily increasing strength of the wind and the
need for a vigilant ice watch kept me fully awake right
through that night and the following day, 14 January. I
could not have kept going so long, of course, had not the
wind-vane been handling the steering. By 4.30 p.m. the
gale had increased to force nine and *Ice Bird*, even under
her little storm jib, was beginning to yaw and steer wildly
as she ran down the face of the towering seas. I deemed it
prudent, while retaining the jib, to stream a sea anchor
astern to steady her.

This was in line with the "gale technique" I had
worked out in the light of last season's experiences. *Ice
Bird* would be steered before gales under storm jib as
previously, and again at an angle for ease of control, rather
than dead down-wind. But this time I would trail a sea
anchor behind to hold the stern up to the seas and to help
prevent the yacht from slewing round broadside on.
Steering would be the job of the Aries vane gear, whose
power in strong winds far outstripped my own strength.
It possessed the added advantage of being impervious to
fatigue. (Experience has generally confirmed my reasoning. The sea anchor's warp would have to be prevented
from fouling anything. It is true the device failed to
prevent, though I believe it mitigated, the final disaster,
but then I was steering with the less efficient tiller lines.)

My own sea anchor, prepared in advance at Palmer, was
made up of two tyres weighted with a small anchor,
streamed at the end of thirty fathoms of two-inch nylon.
The warp was coiled ready on the afterdeck and parcelled
against chafe with the last of the kangaroo skin coat. The
tyres and anchor were lashed to the stern rail.

All that was necessary on the afternoon of the 14th was to cut the securing cord, lower the contraption over the side and pay out the warp. The drag was appreciable and *Ice Bird* ran far more steadily with the vane in complete control. Evening drew on, bringing with it no abatement of the gale. Worse, now we had to run the gauntlet of the bergs through squalls of blinding snow. Any contact with substantial ice would be instantly fatal in the seas that were running. The spray was being dashed a hundred feet into the air each time a wave smashed against one of the rock-like monsters. "Keeping desperate lookout for ice – the lethal factor in this near whiteout," I wrote fearfully.

To my unutterable relief, the snow showers ceased before midnight, but the temperature was well below zero and, in the early morning hours of 15 January, a freezing mist began to reduce visibility again to danger level. Then at long last the gale began to moderate. The risk of being rolled over by the still dangerous seas if I took in sail and let the yacht lie a-hull, seemed preferable to further risking collision with ice. After all, a capsize could be survived, being smashed to pieces against a berg could not.

Lowering the jib and leaving the sea anchor still trailing and the yacht to its own devices, I crawled, wet and shivering, into my sleeping bag. Periodically I looked out to make sure that no large ice was near, but I altered nothing for the rest of the night and on through the following day, while the gale slowly eased.

The cause of the disastrous misadventure that now occurred is uncertain. It probably was impact with ice, gone unnoticed in the slamming swell, or perhaps the sea anchor warp snagged the casing and somehow caused it to shear. At any rate, when I looked out at 4 p.m. the precious self-steering gear was in ruins, broken beyond any possibility of repair.

A sizeable segment of the main supporting frame was gone, and of the system of levers and gears there remained not a trace. The sea had swallowed them all. Only a well-equipped engineering factory could replace the lost parts and repair the shattered frame.

Profoundly depressed by this heavy blow, I remained miserably hove-to until the next day, 16 January, when I hauled the sea anchor back aboard, hoisted sail and took my place at the tiller lines, which were henceforth to occupy the major portion of my waking hours. We were exactly a week out from Signy and the moment was opportune for a review of strategy.

A disappointing 325 miles had been made good to the eastward. The options as to course remained open, since the South Sandwich Islands were still 200 miles ahead. A route going north in "Australian" latitudes would, because of the earth's curvature, be twice as long as one through the southern sixties. But the ice conditions made survival, rather than distance, the prime consideration; and there was a limit to the number of narrow escapes I could hope to get away with. The immediate problem was how best to escape from the icebergs into waters where I could keep sailing in safety day and night. I decided to start tentatively working northwards and see what happened.

The probable lengthening of the voyage emphasized the importance of conserving drinking water. So far, the log showed I had been using less than two pints a day: an acceptable figure.

The prospect of hand steering to Australia was daunting. But I had done it last year for two months, so could do it again. There was the comforting knowledge that, with head or beam winds, the helm could be adjusted so that *Ice Bird* would look after herself. Down-wind she demanded continuous attention and the nearer a dead run the course, the more the care needed to prevent her from broaching-to. Thus the favourable west winds I had so longed for, and which would generally prevail, would exact their toll in soul-destroying hours of monotonous concentration.

The first twenty-four hours without the vane were encouraging, the run from noon on the 16th to noon on the 17th being 76 miles. But this ground was won at the expense of a whole night's exhausting vigil and was only made possible by clear weather. I counted bergs to pass the time and before I tired of the game we had passed fifty in seven hours, the concentration showing no signs of diminishing. Hot drinks were at a premium, being prepared by a process of hurried dashes to stove and lockers. A major preoccupation was how to keep my fur-lined and quilted mitts from becoming soaked, through contact with the wet steering lines, for the only drying agent was my own body heat. I found no real solution and the mitts remained damp.

Whenever the outlook ahead was reasonably clear I would thankfully get out of the bitter wind and steer from the edge of a bunk by the compass mounted on the cabin table – now a boon beyond price. Frequent trips to the hatchway to scan the sea were, of course, necessary. The chill of early morning found me shivering in the companionway, easing myself into the least uncomfortable position. The concentration of decaying bergs through which we were sailing was for the moment so dense as to preclude even a visit to the heads. My notes in the log grew understandably scrappy.

I had to give in eventually and lower sail to sleep. When I awoke it was evening and a heavy fog effectively ruled out another night under way. Instead I spent it dozing fitfully, lying fully clothed on top of my sleeping bag, and was not sorry when morning came. A "friendly neighbourhood berg", in the log's words, and a party of chinstrap penguins welcomed me back on deck when, still in heavy fog, I sleepily hoisted sail.

Thirty-nine hours later the fog had not lifted. *Ice Bird* floated becalmed on a polished ebony sea. It was eleven o'clock at night and very dark. All at once I became aware of the rumble of breakers somewhere off in the mist. I

listened tensely, trying to decide the direction. Then it
came again, but this time much louder, through some
acoustic rift in the fog – the crash of surf. The illusion that
the current was sweeping us down upon it was very
strong. I well knew this could not be so, since, in the
absence of wind, yacht and unseen berg would drift at
exactly the same rate; but I was frightened. I had been
tinkering with the motor earlier and it started at once.
Ice Bird began to glide rapidly through the darkness.
But which way had she turned while I was busy with the
engine? The exhaust effectively covered the noise of the
breakers. Could we be circling back into danger? I lost all
sense of direction and, for a moment, became prey to
absurd panic. Then, pulling myself together, I switched
off the motor until I had located the sound again (we *had*
curved back towards it) and, holding a torch to light the
compass, set off again in the opposite direction until I
judged we had gone a safe distance.

Nor did I ever catch a glimpse of the berg that had
caused so much worry, for the fog was still as thick as ever
when I hoisted sail to a light south-easter in the morning.

Such a very dense fog I classified as "one page fog".
The system was this: I would sit reading in the cabin, if
necessary steering by the inside compass; after finishing
each page (or two, in "two page fog") I would put the
book down, step up into the hatchway and peer intently
ahead. I grew to detest this monotonous routine, but
could think of no better way of keeping a regular lookout
and remaining warm in the interim. I found that a continuous watch of more than half an hour in the companionway left me chilled to the bone. Assessing the fog's
density was difficult and only reliable when confirmed by
an actual ice sighting. I was to have a sighting that
particular morning with a vengeance.

First I stared out and saw nothing. Then something
unreal in the texture of the fog made me look again, and
there it was, a pale, ghostly monster dead ahead, no more

than two hundred yards off. I reached down and slammed the tiller hard over. *Ice Bird* pivoted on her heel and ran down-wind past the face of the berg and rounded a corner into its lee, to be promptly becalmed in the wind shadow. There she rocked helplessly to and fro among the small ice debris for ten minutes, before a series of savage little squalls, plummeting down from the hidden crest, laid the yacht over and drove her clear.

A welcome change from fog to light mist in the afternoon brought relief from the constant watchfulness. I was happy for the moment to have left behind the grey confines of fog. But the absurd delusion persisted, that the place where we had fled the unseen berg in the darkness would remain forever intact and unchanged, like some gloomy forest, from which we had escaped.

Largely to bolster my own morale I shaved (my beard is normally confined to my chin), a painful process, as I did not feel justified in using more than half a mug of hot water. My first intention, to re-use the shaving water for coffee, was abandoned after one glance at the mixture of stubble and lather. I could not stomach it. Not long after this praiseworthy effort the wind changed, so that I had to take over the tiller lines until 10 p.m., when the presence of some very large bergs and the increasing darkness caused me to lower sail for the night.

This practice of taking down the sails at nightfall was now becoming routine, though visibility was not often good enough to permit me to keep on so late. A few anxious nights spent staring blindly into the blackness soon convinced me of the wisdom of choosing an open space in which to spend the night in good time, while the bergs were still visible and their distance away could be judged. The plan paid off in security. True, a nocturnal wind change did once set the yacht uncomfortably close to a pair of bergs that had earlier been to windward but this was an exception. Unfortunately eight hours, the average time spent motionless, was a sizeable chunk to lose out of the twenty-four.

At first light on 21 January, I managed to overcome my extreme reluctance to leave the warm sleeping bag and drag myself awake and on deck into the bitter 5 a.m. cold. Once the sails were up and sheeted and before taking the helm to head down-wind, I confided my plaint to the log. "Jesus! What an effort," I wrote. The next entry was at half-past four in the afternoon and I underlined it: "Hand steering all day."

Those eleven hours of steering (by no means an exceptional stretch) left little time for anything else apart from reading, snatching hurried snacks and taking and working out the only sun sight the roof of stratus allowed. The food was limited to what I could reach from the box under the table without letting go of the tyrannical tiller line: corned beef, from which I cut slabs with my knife; biscuits eaten butterless; chocolate – all garnished with .little balls of fluff from my woollen gloves (my fingers and fragile nails, still tender from last year's frostbite, had to be protected even when I was below).

This sun sight was typical enough to serve as an example of the two I usually shot (each sight gave one position line, their intersection was needed for a fix). The appearance of shadows in the cabin first alerted me. Sure enough, a pale disc was discernible behind thin overcast.

I hastily collected together the sight form, a biro, my glasses and some toilet paper and heaped them on the lee bunk where they could not roll off. Lifting the sextant out of its box, I scrambled up into the cockpit, clipping on the safety line as I went. Wedging myself as securely as possible and steering with one foot on the tiller, I snatched the sight as the yacht rose to the crest of a wave and immediately checked the time. Or tried to – the sleeve of my parka had, as usual, slipped over the wrist watch and I had to count the seconds while I prized back the sleeve.

Repeating the time of the sight to myself, I slid back into the cabin and scribbled down the figures before I forgot them. But I had to wipe my glasses with toilet paper, remove them and wipe them again, before I could read the sextant scale. The next operation, after replacing the instrument in its locker and putting the yacht back on course, was to work out the sight. Holding the tiller line in my left hand, I turned over the pages of the nautical almanac with the gloved fingers of my right and, equally clumsily, entered the figures on the sight form. Only at the final stage of plotting on the chart, did I abandon all attempts at steering and concentrate on angles and intercepts. This afternoon sight put us in 34° 10′ West longitude and, coupled with dead reckoning, made our run for the past twenty-four hours (including the seven spent hove-to) a better than average seventy-seven miles.

To my relief, the wind soon backed after this. The helm could be left to itself until dusk and bergs suggested the advisability of taking in sail.

How dramatically the face of the sea could change! In the evening a score of rather featureless hummocked bergs had littered the horizon. I awoke next day surrounded by shapes of unreality – turreted gothic castles, a "bugs bunny" (christened for the ears) and one soaring ice tower, breathtaking in its purity. Making sure a camera was loaded, I sailed up to them – narrowly avoiding a collision, in my photographic over-enthusiasm! Somewhat deflated, I squared away towards the north-east.

RIVER OF DOUBT

Theodore Roosevelt

"TR" was born in 1858, and served as the twenty-fifth President of the United States of America. On retiring from politics he made, in 1914, the first descent of a previously unknown tributary of the Amazon, which was subsequently named Rio Roosevelt. He was accompanied on the descent by his son, Kermit, and the Brazilian explorer, Candido Rondon.

On the morning of March 22 we started in our six canoes. We made ten kilometres. Twenty minutes after starting we came to the first rapids. Here everyone walked except the three best paddlers, who took the canoes down in succession – an hour's job. Soon after this we struck a bees' nest in the top of a tree overhanging the river; our steersman climbed out and robbed it, but, alas! lost the honey on the way back. We came to a small steep fall, which we did not dare run in our overladen, clumsy, and cranky dugouts. Fortunately we were able to follow a deep canal which led off for a kilometre, returning just below the falls, fifty yards from where it had started. Then, having been in the boats and in motion only one hour and a half, we came to a long stretch of rapids which it took us six hours to descend, and we camped at the foot. Everything was taken out of the canoes, and they were run down in succession. At one difficult and perilous place they were let down by ropes; and even thus we almost lost one.

We went down the right bank. On the opposite bank was an Indian village, evidently inhabited only during the dry season. The marks on the stumps of trees showed that these Indians had axes and knives; and there were old fields in which maize, beans, and cotton had been grown. The forest dripped and steamed. Rubber-trees were plentiful. At one point the tops of a group of tall trees were covered with yellow-white blossoms. Others bore red blossoms. Many of the big trees, of different kinds, were buttressed at the base with great thin walls of wood. Others, including both palms and ordinary trees, showed an even stranger peculiarity. The trunk, near the base, but sometimes six or eight feet from the ground, was split into a dozen or twenty branches or small trunks which sloped outward in tent-like shape, each becoming a root. The larger trees of this type looked as if their trunks were seated on the tops of the pole-frames of Indian tepees. At one point in the stream, to our great surprise, we saw a flying-fish. It skimmed the water like a swallow for over twenty yards.

Although we made only ten kilometres we worked hard all day. The last canoes were brought down and moored to the bank at nightfall. Our tents were pitched in the darkness.

Next day we made thirteen kilometres. We ran, all told, a little over an hour and three-quarters. Seven hours were spent in getting past a series of rapids at which the portage, over rocky and difficult ground, was a kilometre long. The canoes were run down empty – a hazardous run, in which one of them upset.

Yet while we were actually on the river, paddling and floating down-stream along the reaches of swift, smooth water, it was very lovely. When we started in the morning, the day was overcast and the air was heavy with vapour.

Ahead of us the shrouded river stretched between dim walls of forest, half-seen in the mist. Then the sun burned up the fog, and loomed through it in a red splendour that changed first to gold and then to molten white. In the dazzling light, under the brilliant blue of the sky, every detail of the magnificent forest was vivid to the eye: the great trees, the network of bush-ropes, the caverns of greenery, where thick-leaved vines covered all things else. Wherever there was a hidden boulder the surface of the current was broken by waves. In one place in mid-stream, a pyramidal rock thrust itself six feet above the surface of the river. On the banks we found fresh Indian sign.

In the morning, just before leaving this camp, a tapir swam across stream a little way above us; but unfortunately we could not get a shot at it. An ample supply of tapir beef would have meant much to us. We had started with fifty days' rations; but this by no means meant full rations, in the sense of giving every man all he wanted to eat. We had two meals a day, and were on rather short commons – both our mess and the camaradas' – except when we got plenty of palm-tops. For our mess we had the boxes chosen by Fiala, each containing a day's rations for six men, our number. But we made each box last a day and a half, or at times two days, and in addition we gave some of the food to the camaradas. It was only on the rare occasions when we had killed some monkeys or curássows, or caught some fish, that everybody had enough. We would have welcomed that tapir. So far the game, fish, and fruit had been too scarce to be an element of weight in our food supply. In an exploring trip like ours, through a difficult and utterly unknown country, especially if densely forested, there is little time to halt, and game cannot be counted on. It is only in lands like our own West thirty years ago, like South Africa in the middle of the last century, like East Africa today, that game can be made the chief food supply. On this trip our only substantial food supply from the country hitherto had been that furnished by the palm-tops. Two men were detailed every day to cut down palms for food.

A kilometre and a half after leaving this camp we came on a stretch of big rapids. The river here twists in loops, and we had heard the roaring of these rapids the previous afternoon. Then we passed out of earshot of them; but Antonio Correa, our best waterman, insisted all along that the roaring meant rapids worse than any we had encountered for some days. "I was brought up in the water, and I know it like a fish, and all its sounds," said he. He was right. We had to carry the loads nearly a kilometre that afternoon, and the canoes were pulled out on the bank so that they might be in readiness to be dragged overland next day. Rondon, Lyra, Kermit, and Antonio Correa explored both sides of the river. On the opposite or left bank they found the mouth of a considerable river, bigger than the Rio Kermit, flowing in from the west and making its entrance in the middle of the rapids. This river we christened the Taunay, in honour of a distinguished Brazilian, an explorer, a soldier, a senator, who was also a writer of note. Kermit had with him two of his novels, and I had read one of his books dealing with a disastrous retreat during the Paraguayan war.

Next morning, the 25th, the canoes were brought down. A path was chopped for them and rollers laid; and half-way down the rapids Lyra and Kermit, who were overseeing the work as well as doing their share of the pushing and hauling, got them into a canal of smooth water, which saved much severe labour. As our food supply lowered we were constantly more desirous of economizing the strength of the men. One day more would complete a month since we had embarked on the Dúvida – as we had started in February, the lunar and calendar months coincided. We had used up over half our provisions. We had come only a trifle over 160 kilometres, thanks to the character and number of the rapids. We believed we had three or four times the distance yet to go before coming to a part of the river where we might hope to meet assistance, either from rubber-gatherers or from Pyrineus, if he were really coming up the river which we were going down. If the rapids continued to be as they had been it could not be much more than three weeks before we were in straits for food, aside from the ever-present danger of accident in the rapids; and if our progress were no faster than it had been – and we were straining to do our best – we would in such event still have several hundreds of kilometres of unknown river before us. We could not even hazard a guess at what *was in front* . . .

Two of our men were down with fever. Another man, Julio, a fellow of powerful frame, was utterly worthless, being an inborn, lazy shirker with the heart of a ferocious cur in the body of a bullock. The others were good men, some of them very good indeed. They were under the immediate supervision of Pedrinho Craveiro, who was *first-class in every way* . . .

In mid-afternoon we were once more in the canoes; but we had paddled with the current only a few minutes, we had gone only a kilometre, when the roar of rapids in front again forced us to haul up to the bank. As usual, Rondon, Lyra, and Kermit, with Antonio Correa, explored both sides while camp was being pitched. The rapids were longer and of steeper descent than the last, but on the opposite or western side there was a passage down which we thought we could get the empty dugouts at the cost of dragging them only a few yards at one spot. The loads were to be carried down the hither bank, for a kilometre, to the smooth water. The river foamed between great rounded masses of rock, and at one point there was a sheer fall of six or eight feet. We found and ate wild pineapples. Wild beans were in flower. At dinner we had a toucan and a couple of parrots, which were very good.

All next day was spent by Lyra in superintending our three best watermen as they took the canoes down the west side of the rapids, to the foot, at the spot to which the

camp had meantime been shifted. In the forest some of
the huge sipas, or rope vines, which were as big as cables,
bore clusters of fragrant flowers. The men found several
honey-trees, and fruits of various kinds, and small cocoa-
nuts; they chopped down an ample number of palms for
the palm-cabbage; and most important of all, they gathered a quantity of big Brazil-nuts, which when roasted
tasted like the best of chestnuts, and are nutritious; and
they caught a number of big piranhas, which were good
eating. So we all had a feast, and everybody had enough to
eat and was happy . . .

Next morning we went about three kilometres before
coming to some steep hills, beautiful to look upon, clad as
they were in dense, tall, tropical forest, but ominous of
new rapids. Sure enough, at their foot we had to haul up
and prepare for a long portage. The canoes we ran down
empty. Even so, we were within an ace of losing two, the
lashed couple in which I ordinarily journeyed. In a sharp
bend of the rapids, between two big curls, they were
swept among the boulders and under the matted branches
which stretched out from the bank. They filled, and the
racing current pinned them where they were, one partly
on the other. All of us had to help get them clear. Their
fastenings were chopped asunder with axes. Kermit and
half a dozen of the men, stripped to the skin, made their
way to a small rock island in the little falls just above the
canoes, and let down a rope which we tied to the outer
most canoe. The rest of us, up to our armpits and barely
able to keep our footing as we slipped and stumbled
among the boulders in the swift current, lifted and
shoved, while Kermit and his men pulled the rope and
fastened the slack to a half-submerged tree. Each canoe in
succession was hauled up the little rock island, baled, and
then taken down in safety by two paddlers. It was nearly
four o'clock before we were again ready to start, having
been delayed by a rain storm so heavy that we could not
see across the river. Ten minutes' run took us to the head

of another series of rapids; the exploring party returned
with the news that we had an all day's job ahead of us; and
we made camp in the rain, which did not matter much, as
we were already drenched through. It was impossible
with the wet wood, to make a fire sufficiently hot to
dry all our soggy things, for the rain was still falling. A
tapir was seen from our boat, but, as at the moment we
were being whisked round in a complete circle by a
whirlpool, I did not myself see it in time to shoot.

Next morning we went down a kilometre, and then
landed on the other side of the river. The canoes were run
down, and the loads carried to the other side of a little
river coming in from the west, which Colonel Rondon
christened Cherrie River. Across this we went on a bridge
consisting of a huge tree felled by Macario, one of our best
men. Here we camped, while Rondon, Lyra, Kermit, and
Antonio Correa explored what was ahead. They were
absent until mid-afternoon. Then they returned with
the news that we were among ranges of low mountains,
utterly different in formation from the high plateau region
to which the first rapids, those we had come to on March
2, belonged. Through the first range of these mountains
the river ran in a gorge, some three kilometres long,
immediately ahead of us. The ground was so rough
and steep that it would be impossible to drag the canoes
over it and difficult enough to carry the loads; and the
rapids were so bad, containing several falls, one of at least
ten metres in height, that it was doubtful how many of the
canoes we could get down them. Kermit, who was the
only man with much experience of rope work, was the
only man who believed we could get the canoes down at
all; and it was, of course, possible that we should have to
build new ones at the foot to supply the place of any that
were lost or left behind. In view of the length and
character of the portage, and of all the unpleasant possibilities that were ahead, and of the need of keeping every
pound of food, it was necessary to reduce weight in every

possible way and to throw away everything except the barest necessities.

We thought we had reduced our baggage before, but now we cut to the bone. We kept the fly for all six of us to sleep under. Kermit's shoes had gone, thanks to the amount of work in the water which he had been doing; and he took the pair I had been wearing, while I put on my spare pair. In addition to the clothes I wore, I kept one set of pyjamas, a spare pair of drawers, a spare pair of socks, half a dozen handkerchiefs, my washkit, my pocket medicine-case, and a little bag containing my spare spectacles, gun-grease, some adhesive plaster, some needles and thread, the "fly-dope", and my purse and letter of credit, to be used at Manaos. All of these went into the bag containing my cot, blanket, and mosquito-net. I also carried a cartridge-bag containing my cartridges, head-net, and gauntlets. Kermit cut down even closer, and the others about as close.

The last three days of March we spent in getting to the foot of the rapids in this gorge. Lyra and Kermit, with four of the best watermen, handled the empty canoes. The work was not only difficult and laborious, in the extreme, but hazardous; for the walls of the gorge were so sheer that at the worst places they had to cling to narrow shelves on the face of the rock, while letting the canoes down with ropes. Meanwhile Rondon surveyed and cut a trail for the burden-bearers, and superintended the portage of the loads. The rocky sides of the gorge were too steep for laden men to attempt to traverse them. Accordingly the trail had to go over the top of the mountain, both the ascent and the descent of the rock-strewn, forest-clad slopes being very steep. It was hard work to carry loads over such a trail. From the top of the mountain, through an opening in the trees on the edge of a cliff, there was a beautiful view of the country ahead. All around and in front of us there were ranges of low mountains about the height of the lower ridges of the Alleghanies. Their sides

were steep and they were covered with the matted growth
of the tropical forest. Our next camping-place at the foot
of the gorge was almost beneath us, and from thence the
river ran in a straight line, flecked with white water, for
about a kilometre. Then it disappeared behind and between mountain ridges, which we supposed meant further
rapids. It was a view well worth seeing; but, beautiful
although the country ahead of us was, its character was
such as to promise further hardships, difficulty, and
exhausting labour, and especially further delay; and delay
was a serious matter to men whose food supply was
beginning to run short, whose equipment was reduced
to the minimum, who for a month, with the utmost toil,
had made very slow progress, and who had no idea of
either the distance or the difficulties of the route in front
of them . . .

During this portage the weather favoured us. We were
coming toward the close of the rainy season. On the last
day of the month, when we moved camp to the foot of the
gorge, there was a thunder-storm; but on the whole we
were not bothered by rain until the last night when it
rained heavily, driving under the fly so as to wet my cot
and bedding. However, I slept comfortably enough,
rolled in the damp blanket. Without the blanket I should
have been uncomfortable; a blanket is a necessity for
health. On the third day Lyra and Kermit, with their
daring and hard-working watermen after wearing labour,
succeeded in getting five canoes through the worst of the
rapids to the chief fall. The sixth, which was frail and
weak, had its bottom beaten out on the jagged rocks of the
broken water. On this night, although I thought I had put
my clothes out of reach, both the termites and the carre-
gadores ants got at them, ate holes in one boot, ate one leg
of my drawers, and riddled my handkerchief; and I now
had nothing to replace anything that was destroyed.

Next day Lyra, Kermit, and their camaradas brought
the five canoes that were left down to camp. They had in

four days accomplished a work of incredible labour and of
the utmost importance; for at the first glance it had
seemed an absolute impossibility to avoid abandoning
the canoes when we found that the river sank into a
cataract-broken torrent at the bottom of a canyon-like
gorge between steep mountains. On April 2 we once more
started, wondering how soon we should strike other
rapids in the mountains ahead, and whether in any reasonable time we should, as the aneroid indicated, be so
low down that we should necessarily be in a plain where
we could make a journey of at least a few days without
rapids. We had been exactly a month going through an
uninterrupted succession of rapids. During that month
we had come only about 110 kilometres, and had descended nearly 150 metres – the figures are approximate
but fairly accurate. We had lost four of the canoes with
which we started, and one other, which we had built, and
the life of one man; and the life of a dog which by its death
had, in all probability, saved the life of Colonel Rondon.
In a straight line northward, toward our supposed destination, we had not made more than a mile and a quarter a
day; at the cost of bitter toil for most of the party, of much
risk for some of the party, and of some risk and some
hardship for all the party. Most of the camaradas were
down-hearted, naturally enough, and occasionally asked
one of us if we really believed that we should ever get out
alive; and we had to cheer them up as best we could.

There was no change in our work for the time being.
We made but three kilometres that day. Most of the party
walked all the time; but the dugouts carried the luggage
until we struck the head of the series of rapids which were
to take up the next two or three days. The river rushed
through a wild gorge, a chasm or canyon, between two
mountains. Its sides were very steep, mere rock walls,
although in most places so covered with the luxuriant
growth of the trees and bushes that clung in the crevices,
and with green moss, that the naked rock was hardly seen.

Rondon, Lyra, and Kermit, who were in front, found a small level spot with a beach of sand, and sent back word to camp there while they spent several hours in exploring the country ahead. The canoes were run down empty, and the loads carried painfully along the face of the cliffs; so bad was the trail that I found it rather hard to follow although carrying nothing but my rifle and cartridge bag. The explorers returned with the information that the mountains stretched ahead of us, and that there were rapids as far as they had gone. We could only hope that the aneroid was not hopelessly out of kilter and that we should, therefore, fairly soon find ourselves in comparatively level country. The severe toil, on a rather limited food supply, was telling on the strength as well as on the spirits of the men; Lyra and Kermit in addition to their other work, performed as much actual physical labour as any of them.

Next day, April 3, we began the descent of these sinister rapids of the chasm. Colonel Rondon had gone to the summit of the mountain in order to find a better trail for the burden-bearers, but it was hopeless, and they had to go along the face of the cliffs . . .

Lyra, Kermit, and Cherrie, with four of the men, worked the canoes half-way down the canyon. Again and again it was touch and go whether they could get past a given point. At one spot the channel of the furious torrent was only fifteen yards across. One canoe was lost, so that of the seven with which we had started only two were left. Cherrie laboured with the other men at times, and also stood as guard over them, for, while actually working, of course no one could carry a rifle. Kermit's experience in bridge building was invaluable in enabling him to do the rope work by which alone it was possible to get the canoes down the canyon. He and Lyra had now been in the water for days. Their clothes were never dry. Their shoes were rotten. The bruises on their feet and legs had become sores. On their bodies some of the insect bites had become festering wounds, as indeed was the case with all of us. Poisonous ants, biting flies, ticks, wasps, bees, were a perpetual torment. However, no one had yet been bitten by a venomous serpent, a scorpion, or a centipede although we had killed all of the three within camp limits.

Under such conditions whatever is evil in men's natures comes to the front. On this day a strange and terrible tragedy occurred. One of the camaradas, a man of pure European blood, was the man named Julio of whom I have already spoken. He was a very powerful fellow and had been importunately eager to come on the expedition; and he had the reputation of being a good worker. But, like so many men of higher standing, he had had no idea of what such an expedition really meant, and under the strain of toil, hardship, and danger his nature showed its true depths of selfishness, cowardice, and ferocity. He shirked all work. He shammed sickness. Nothing could make him do his share; and yet unlike his self-respecting fellows he was always shamelessly begging for favours. Kermit was the only one of our party who smoked, and he was continually giving a little tobacco to some of the camaradas, who worked especially well under him. The good men did not ask for it; but Julio, who shirked every labour, was always, and always in vain, demanding it. Colonel Rondon, Lyra, and Kermit each tried to get work out of him, and in order to do anything with him had to threaten to leave him in the wilderness. He threw all his tasks on his comrades; and, moreover, he stole their food as well as ours. On such an expedition the theft of food comes next to murder as a crime, and should by rights be punished as such. We could not trust him to cut down palms or gather nuts, because he would stay out and eat what ought to have gone into the common store. Finally, the men on several occasions themselves detected him stealing their food. Alone of the whole party, and thanks to the stolen food, he had kept in full flesh and bodily vigour.

One of our best men was a huge negro named Paixão –
Paishon – a corporal and acting sergeant in the engineer
corps. He had, by the way, literally torn his trousers to
pieces, so that he wore only the tatters of a pair of old
drawers until I gave him my spare trousers when we
lightened loads. He was a stern disciplinarian. One evening he detected Julio stealing food and smashed him in
the mouth. Julio came crying to us, his face working with
fear and malignant hatred; but after investigation he was
told that he had got off uncommonly lightly. The men had
three or four carbines, which were sometimes carried by
those who were not their owners.

On this morning, at the outset of the portage, Pedrinho
discovered Julio stealing some of the men's dried meat.
Shortly afterward Paishon rebuked him for, as usual,
lagging behind. By this time we had reached the place
where the canoes were tied to the bank and then taken
down one at a time. We were sitting down waiting for the
last loads to be brought along the trail. Pedrinho was still
in the camp we had left. Paishon had just brought in a
load, left it on the ground with his carbine beside it, and
returned on the trail for another load. Julio came in, put
down his load, picked up the carbine, and walked back on
the trail, muttering to himself but showing no excitement.
We thought nothing of it, for he was always muttering;
and occasionally one of the men saw a monkey or big bird
and tried to shoot it, so it was never surprising to see a
man with a carbine.

In a minute we heard a shot; and in a short time three or
four of the men came up the trail to tell us that Paishon
was dead, having been shot by Julio, who had fled into the
woods. Colonel Rondon and Lyra were ahead; I sent a
messenger for them, directed Cherrie and Kermit to stay
where they were and guard the canoes and provisions, and
started down the trail with the doctor – an absolutely cool
and plucky man with a revolver but no rifle – and a couple
of the camaradas. We soon passed the dead body of poor

Paishon. He lay in a huddle, in a pool of his own blood, where he had fallen, shot through the heart. I feared that Julio had run amuck, and intended merely to take more lives before he died, and that he would begin with Pedrinho, who was alone and unarmed in the camp we had left. Accordingly I pushed on, followed by my companions, looking sharply right and left; but when we came to the camp the doctor quietly walked by me, remarking: "My eyes are better than yours, Colonel; if he is in sight I'll point him out to you, as you have the rifle." However, he was not there, and the others soon joined us with the welcome news that they had found the carbine.

The murderer had stood to one side of the path and killed his victim, when a dozen paces off, with deliberate and malignant purpose. Then evidently his murderous hatred had at once given way to his innate cowardice, and, perhaps hearing someone coming along the path, he fled in panic terror into the wilderness. A tree had knocked the carbine from his hand. His footsteps showed that after going some rods he had started to return, doubtless for the carbine, but had fled again, probably because the body had then been discovered. It was questionable whether or not he would live to reach the Indian villages, which were probably his goal. He was not a man to feel remorse – never a common feeling; but surely that murderer was in a living hell, as, with fever and famine leering at him from the shadows, he made his way through the empty desolation of the wilderness. Franca, the cook, quoted out of the melancholy proverbial philosophy of the people the proverb. "No man knows the heart of anyone," and then expressed with deep conviction a weird ghostly belief I had never encountered before: Paishon is following Julio now, and will follow him until he dies; "Paishon fell forward on his hands and knees, and when a murdered man falls like that his ghost will follow the slayer as long as the slayer lives . . ."

We buried him beside the place where he fell. With axes

and knives the camaradas dug a shallow grave, while we stood by with bared heads. Then reverently and carefully we lifted the poor body, which but half an hour before had been so full of vigorous life. Colonel Rondon and I bore the head and shoulders. We laid him in the grave, and heaped a mound over him, and put a rude cross at his head. We fired a volley for a brave and loyal soldier, who had died doing his duty. Then we left him for ever, under the great trees beside the lonely river.

That day we got only half-way down the rapids. There was no good place to camp. But at the foot of one steep cliff there was a narrow, boulder-covered slope, where it was possible to sling hammocks and cook; and a slanting spot was found for my cot, which had sagged until by this time it looked like a broken backed centiped. It rained a little during the night but not enough to wet us much. Next day Lyra, Kermit, and Cherrie finished their job, and brought the four remaining canoes to camp, one leaking badly from the battering on the rocks. We then went downstream a few hundred yards, and camped on the opposite side; it was not a good camping-place, but it was better than the one we left.

The men were growing constantly weaker under the endless strain of exhausting labour. Kermit was having an attack of fever, and Lyra and Cherrie had touches of dysentery, but all three continued to work. While in the water trying to help with an upset canoe I had, by my own clumsiness, bruised my leg against a boulder; and the resulting inflammation was somewhat bothersome. I now had a sharp attack of fever, but, thanks to the excellent care of the doctor, was over it in about forty-eight hours; but Kermit's fever grew worse, and he too was unable to work for a day or two. We could walk over the portages, however. A good doctor is an absolute necessity on an exploring expedition in such a country as that we were in, under penalty of a frightful mortality among the members; and the necessary risks and hazards are so great, the chances of disaster so large, that there is no warrant for increasing them by the failure to take all feasible precautions.

The next day we made another long portage round some rapids, and camped at night still in the hot, wet, sunless atmosphere of the gorge. The following day, April 6, we portaged past another set of rapids, which proved to be the last of the rapids of the chasm. For some kilometres we kept passing hills, and feared lest at any moment we might again find ourselves fronting another mountain gorge, with, in such case, further days of grinding and perilous labour ahead of us, while our men were disheartened, weak, and sick. Most of them had already begun to have fever. Their condition was inevitable after over a month's uninterrupted work of the hardest kind in getting through the long series of rapids we had just passed; and a long further delay, accompanied by wearing labour, would have almost certainly meant that the weakest among our party would have begun to die. There were already two of the camaradas who were too weak to help the others, their condition being such as to cause us serious concern.

However, the hills gradually sank into a level plain and the river carried us through it at a rate that enabled us during the remainder of the day to reel off thirty-six kilometres, a record that for the first time held out promise. Twice tapirs swam the river while we passed but not near my canoe. However, the previous evening Cherrie had killed two monkeys and Kermit one, and we all had a few mouthfuls of fresh meat; we had already had a good soup made out of a turtle Kermit had caught. We had to portage by one short set of rapids, the unloaded canoes being brought down without difficulty. At last, at four in the afternoon, we came to the mouth of a big river running in from the right. We thought it was probably the Ananás, but, of course, could not be certain. It was less in volume than the one we had descended, but nearly as broad; its breadth at this point being ninety-five yards as against one hundred and twenty for the larger river. There were rapids ahead, immediately after the junction, which took place in latitude 10° 58' south. We had come 216 kilometres all told, and were nearly north of where we had started. We camped on the point of land between the two rivers. It was extraordinary to realize that here about the eleventh degree we were on such a big river, utterly unknown to the cartographers and not indicated by even a hint on any map. We named this big tributary Rio Cardozo, after a gallant officer of the Commission who had died of beriberi just as our expedition began. We spent a day at this spot determining our exact position by the sun, and afterward by the stars, and sending on two men to explore the rapids in advance. They returned with the news that there were big cataracts in them, and that they would form an obstacle to our progress. They had also caught a huge siluroid fish, which furnished an excellent meal for everybody in camp. This evening at sunset the view across the broad river, from our camp where the two rivers joined, was very lovely; and for the first time we had an open space in front of and above us, so that after nightfall the stars and the great waxing moon were glorious overhead, and against the rocks in mid-stream the broken water gleamed like tossing silver . . .

Next day, April 8, we made five kilometres only, as there was a succession of rapids. We had to carry the loads past two of them, but ran the canoes without difficulty, for on the west side were long canals of swift water through the forest. The river had been higher, but was still very high, and the current raced round the many islands that, at this point, divided the channel. At four we made camp at the head of another stretch of rapids, over which the Canadian canoes would have danced without shipping a teaspoonful of water but which our dugouts could only run empty. Cherrie killed three monkeys and Lyra caught two big piranhas so that we were again all of us well provided with dinner and breakfast. When a number of men, doing hard work, are most of the time on half-rations, they grow to take a lively interest in any reasonably full meal that does arrive.

On the 10th we repeated the proceedings: a short quick run; a few hundred metres' portage, occupying, however, at least a couple of hours; again a few minutes run; again other rapids. We again made less than five kilometres; in the two days we had been descending nearly a metre for every kilometre we made in advance; and it hardly seemed as if this state of things could last, for the aneroid showed that we were getting very low down. How I longed for a big Maine birch-bark, such as that in which I once went down the Mattawamkeag at high water! It would have slipped down these rapids as a girl trips through a country-dance. But our loaded dugouts would have shoved their noses under every curl. The country was lovely. The wide river, now in one channel, now in several channels, wound among hills; the shower-freshened forest glistened in the sunlight; the many kinds of beautiful palm-fronds and the huge pacova-leaves stamped the peculiar look of the tropics on the whole landscape – it was like passing by water through a gigantic botanical garden. In the afternoon we got an elderly toucan, a piranha, and a reasonably edible side-necked river-turtle; so we had fresh meat again. We slept as usual in earshot of rapids. We had been out six weeks, and almost all the time we had been engaged in wearily working our way down and past rapid after rapid. Rapids are by far the most dangerous enemies of explorers and travellers who journey along these rivers.

Next day was a repetition of the same work. All the morning was spent in getting the loads to the foot of the rapids at the head of which we were encamped, down which the canoes were run empty. Then for thirty or forty minutes we ran down the swift, twisting river, the two lashed canoes almost coming to grief at one spot where a swirl of the current threw them against some trees on a small submerged island. Then we came to another set of rapids, carried the baggage down past them, and made camp long after dark in the rain – a good exercise in patience for those of us who were still suffering somewhat from fever. No one was in really buoyant health. For some weeks we had been sharing part of the contents of our boxes with the camaradas but our food was not very satisfying to them. They needed quantity, and the mainstay of each of their meals was a mass of palmitas; but on this day they had no time to cut down palms. We finally decided to run these rapids with the empty canoes, and they came down in safety. On such a trip it is highly undesirable to take any save necessary risks, for the consequences of disaster are too serious; and yet if no risks are taken the progress is so slow that disaster comes anyhow; and it is necessary perpetually to vary the terms of the perpetual working compromise between rashness and over caution. This night we had a very good fish to eat, a big silvery fellow called a pescada, of a kind we had not caught before.

One day Trigueiro failed to embark with the rest of us, and we had to camp where we were next day to find him. Easter Sunday we spent in the fashion with which we were altogether too familiar. We only ran in a clear course for ten minutes all told, and spent eight hours in portaging the loads past rapids down which the canoes were run; the balsa was almost swamped. This day we caught twenty-eight big fish, mostly piranhas, and everybody had all he could eat for dinner, and for breakfast the following morning.

The forenoon of the following day was a repetition of this wearisome work; but late in the afternoon the river began to run in long quiet reaches. We made fifteen kilometres, and for the first time in several weeks camped where we did not hear the rapids. The silence was soothing and restful. The following day, April 14, we made a good run of some thirty-two kilometres. We passed a little river which entered on our left. We ran two or three light rapids, and portaged the loads by another. The river ran in long and usually tranquil stretches. In the morning when we started the view was lovely. There was a mist, and for a couple of miles the great river, broad and quiet, ran between the high walls of tropical forest, the tops of the giant trees showing dim through the haze. Different members of the party caught many fish; and shot a monkey and a couple of jacú-tinga – birds akin to a turkey, but the size of a fowl – so we again had a camp of plenty. The dry season was approaching, but there were still heavy, drenching rains. On this day the men found some new nuts of which they liked the taste; but the nuts proved unwholesome and half of the men were very sick and unable to work the following day. In the balsa only two were left fit to do anything, and Kermit plied a paddle all day long.

Accordingly, it was a rather sorry crew that embarked the following morning, April 15. But it turned out a red-letter day. The day before, we had come across cuttings, a year old, which were probably but not certainly made by pioneer rubber-men. But on this day – during which we made twenty-five kilometres – after running two hours and a half we found on the left bank a board on a post, with the initials J. A., to show the farthest-up point which a rubber-man had reached and claimed as his own. An hour farther down we came on a newly-built house in a little planted clearing; and we cheered heartily. No one was at home, but the house, of palm-thatch, was clean and cool. A couple of dogs were on watch, and the belongings showed that a man, a woman, and a child lived there, and had only just left. Another hour brought us to a similar house where dwelt an old black man, who showed the innate courtesy of the Brazilian peasant. We came on these rubber-men and their houses in about latitude 10° 24′.

In mid-afternoon we stopped at another clean, cool,

picturesque house of palm-thatch. The inhabitants all fled at our approach, fearing an Indian raid; for they were absolutely unprepared to have any one come from the unknown regions upstream. They returned and were most hospitable and communicative; and we spent the night there. Said Antonio Correa to Kermit: "It seems like a dream to be in a house again, and hear the voices of men and women, instead of being among those mountains and rapids."

We had passed the period when there was a chance of peril, of disaster, to the whole expedition. There might be risk ahead to individuals, and some difficulties and annoyances for all of us; but there was no longer the least likelihood of any disaster to the expedition as a whole. We now no longer had to face continual anxiety, the need of constant economy with food, the duty of labour with no end in sight, and bitter uncertainty as to the future.

It was time to get out.

SLEDGE-TRACKS

Knud Rasmussen

Born in 1879, the Danish ethnologist Rasmussen led several expeditions to Greenland in support of his theory that the Eskimos were descended from migratory Asian tribes. His books include The People of the Polar North, *1908.*

We had reached our goal!

But one of our number was dangerously ill, and we were powerless to relieve him; the people we had hoped to meet with at Cape York settlement had left their houses, and our famished dogs were circling madly round us; we had hardly enough food left for one good meal, even for ourselves. To lighten our sledges we had stored our chests of supplies at Cape Murdoch, and a considerable proportion of the provisions that we had calculated would suffice for the journey thence to Cape York had been devoured by the dogs.

The forced pace of the last two days and nights had greatly exhausted us; for the moment, however, we were so much struck by all the new sights around us, by the strange, primitive human dwellings, that we forgot our fatigue in exploring the settlement. But it was not long before we flung ourselves down by our sledges and dropped asleep.

It is but a short rest, though, that a traveller can permit himself under critical circumstances. One of us soon woke again and roused the others. A more careful examination of the snow huts then revealed that it could not have been long since their owners had left them. In one of them there was a large seal, not cut up, which provided our dogs with a very welcome feast.

There were numerous sledge-tracks running northward, with only a light powdering of snow upon them; consequently men could not be far away.

I remembered a story told us by an old Greenlander whom we had visited in Danish West Greenland, on our way north.

He knew that they had kinsmen a long way north; but no one was certain exactly whereabouts. It was so far away. The following tradition he had heard as a child:

"Once upon a time there was a man who lived farther north than any of the settlements. He hunted bears every spring on a dogsledge.

"Once, during the chase, he came upon strange sledge-tracks, and made up his mind to seek out the people who had made them. So he set out on his bear-hunts the next year earlier than he was wont to do. The third day he came to houses different in appearance from those to which he was accustomed. But he met with no people; fresh tracks, though, showed that the settlement had been only recently left.

"When the bear-hunter drove off the following year he took wood with him, as a gift to the strangers; for he thought they must suffer greatly from the want of wood, as they used narwhal's tusks for the roof-beams of their houses.

"But he did not meet with the strangers on his second visit either. True, the tracks were newer than they had been the last time, but he did not dare to follow them up, and thus put a still greater distance between himself and his own village. He contented himself with burying the wood he had brought with him in the snow near the houses, and then, having presented his gifts, he went home.

"The third year he raised the best team of dogs that he had ever had, and earlier than was his custom he drove north after bears and the strange people. When at last he reached the village it was just as it had been the other years; the inhabitants had gone; but in the snow, where he had left his wood, they had hidden a large bundle of walrus tusks, and inside, in the entrance passage, lay a magnificent bitch and puppies. These were the return gifts of the strangers.

"He put them on his sledge and drove back home; but the people who lived north of all other men he never found."

And now, just as had been the case then, many sledge-tracks ran north, and again, as in the legend, it could not have been many days since they had been made.

It was an odd experience, creeping through the long, low tunnel entrances into the houses; with our furs on we could hardly pass. At the end, we came to a hole up through which we had to squeeze ourselves, and then we were in the house. There was a strong smell of raw meat and fox inside.

The first time one sees a house of this description one is struck by the little with which human beings can be content. It is all so primitive, and has such an odour of paganism and magic incantation. A cave like this, skilfully built in arch of gigantic blocks of stone, one involuntarily peoples mentally with half supernatural beings. You see them, in your fancy, pulling and tearing at raw flesh, you see the blood dripping from their fingers, and you are seized yourself with a strange excitement at the thought of the extraordinary life that awaits you in their company.

We walked round, examining all these things, which, in their silent way, spoke to us of the men and women who lived their lonely life up here. A little way from the houses, in a circle, were some large round stones, shining with stale grease. "Here they must have had their meals," suggested one of our Greenlanders. Already our imagination was at work.

Farther up, just under the overhanging cliff, lay a kayak with all its appurtenances, covered over with stones. Behind it was a sledge, with dead dogs harnessed to it, almost wholly hidden by the drifting snow. There, then, men lay buried with all their possessions, as Eskimo custom prescribes.

All that we saw was new to us and absorbingly interesting. At last we were on Polar Eskimo ground, and our delight at having reached our goal was unmeasured. If only we had been spared the calamity of our comrade's serious illness! He lay dazed and feverish, unable to stir, and had to be fed when he required to eat. At a council among ourselves, it was agreed that Mylius-Erichsen should remain with him, keeping the two seal-hunters, while Jörgen Brönlund and I drove on north as fast as our almost exhausted dogs could take us, to look for people. We calculated that at a distance of about sixty-four English miles from Cape York we ought to come across Eskimos at Saunders Island, and if not there, then at Natsilivik, some forty English miles farther north. All the provisions we could take were a few biscuits and a box of butter. Still we had our rifles to fall back upon.

The sealers had gone out to try their luck, and we waited for them to return – which they did empty-handed. Then we drank a little cocoa, and drove off along the glorious rocky coast, into the clear, light night.

In the neighbourhood of Cape Atholl we discovered fresh sledge-tracks, which we followed up. They led to a stone cairn, under a steep wall of rock, which cairn contained a large deposit of freshly-caught bearded seal. Ah! then we could not be far from human beings. The intense suspense of it! For it almost meant our comrade's life.

We had driven all night – some twelve hours, and a little way beyond Cape Atholl were obliged to pull up, to give the dogs a rest and breathing time. We had covered about fifty-six English miles at full gallop, and, should we be forced to drive all the way to Natsilivik, should have to make reasonable allowance for the empty stomachs of our poor animals. We flung ourselves down on the ice, discussed our prospects, ate a little butter – we simply dared not eat our biscuits – lay down on our sledges and went to sleep.

After three hours' rest we went on again.

We had only driven a little way when a black dot became visible in front. It developed and grew into a sledge.

"Jörgen! – Knud! – Jörgen! – Knud!"

We were half mad with relief and delight, and could only call out each other's names.

Speed signal! The dogs drop their tails and prick up their ears. We murmur the signal again between our teeth, and the snow swirls up beneath their hind legs. A biting wind cuts us in the face. At last! at last! people, other people, the new people – the Polar Eskimos!

A long narrow sledge is coming towards us at full speed, a whip whistles through the air, and unfamiliar dog-signals are borne on the wind to our ears. A little fur-clad man in a pair of glistening white bearskin trousers springs from the sledge and runs up to his team, urging the dogs on still faster with shouts and gesticulations. Behind him, sitting astride the sledge, sits another person, dressed in blue fox, with a large pointed hat on her head: that is his wife.

Our dogs begin to bark, and the sledges meet to the accompaniment of loud yelps. We spring off and run up to each other, stop and stare at one another, incapable of speech, both parties equally astonished.

I explain to him who we are, and where we come from.

"White men! White men!" he calls out to his wife. "White men have come on a visit!"

We have no difficulty in understanding or making ourselves understood.

I hasten to the woman, who has remained seated on the sledge. All sorts of strange emotions crowd in upon me, and I do not know what to say. Then, without thinking what I am doing, I hold out my hand. She looks at me, uncomprehending, and laughs. And then we all laugh together.

The man's name is Maisanguaq (the little white whale skin), his wife Meqo (the feather); they live at Igfigsoq, from twelve to sixteen English miles south of our meeting-place, and we learn that three or four other families live at the same place.

In our eagerness to arrive at Agpat (Saunders Island) we had cut across outside the bay on which Igfigsoq lies.

The snow on the ice at the entrance to the bay being hard, we had not been able to detect sledge-tracks which might have led us to enter it. But when we heard that there were far more people at Agpat, and that the hunting and sealing there were particularly good, I decided to drive straight on, and, by sledge post, advise my comrades to do the same.

Maisanguaq promptly seated himself across my sledge, his wife driving theirs, and we all set off together towards Agpat, carrying on the liveliest conversation meanwhile. The two ought really to have been at home by this time, but had turned back to show us the way.

Meqo was a capital dog-driver, and wielded her long whip as well as any man. In West Greenland you never see a woman drive, so I expressed my surprise; Maisanguaq laughed out with pride, and called out to her gaily to lash hard with her whip, it amused the white men, and Meqo swung her whip, and off we dashed, she leading.

"*Tugto! tugto!*" she cried, and the dogs bounded forward, and soon we began to near the high-lying little island on which Agpat lay.

Maisanguaq then told me that "many" people lived at

Agpat: there were three stone houses and five snow huts; and he burst into peals of laughter each time he thought of the surprise he was going to witness. "White men! White men!" he called out, whenever an instant's pause in the conversation occurred, and rubbed his hands with glee.

Suddenly he stopped short and listened, then jumped up in my sledge and looked behind. Another sledge had come in sight a long way to our rear.

"*Aulavte! aulavte!*" he called out. (That is the signal for a halt.) But my dogs did not understand him, and I had to come to the rescue by whistling to them.

Then he jumped out on the one side, and began to hop up in the air and slap himself on the legs. He continued to indulge in these extraordinary antics till he was quite red in the face from his exertions. This was an indication that something unusual was going on. The strange sledge came on at a gallop; as it approached, two young fellows sprang out and ran alongside, shouting. Maisanguaq began to yell too, and continued to flounder about like a madman.

At last the sledge came up to ours and stopped. The two young men were named Qulutana and Inukitsoq. First, of course, they wanted to know who we were, and Maisanguaq delivered himself of his lesson. Then the whole caravan drove on, laughing and shouting, towards Agpat.

Never in my life have I felt myself to be in such wild, unaccustomed surroundings, never so far, so very far away from home, as when I stood in the midst of the tribe of noisy Polar Eskimos on the beach at Agpat. We were not observed till we were close to the land, so the surprise and confusion created by our arrival were all the greater.

Maisanguaq recommenced his jumping antics by the side of the sledge as soon as we arrived within calling distance of the place, and then screamed out a deafening "White men! White men!"

The people, who had been moving briskly about among the houses, stood still, and the children left off their play.

"White men! White men!" repeated the young fellows who had joined us. Our dogs drooped their tails and pricked up their ears as a many-tongued roar from the land reached us. And then, like a mountain-slide, the whole swarm rushed down to the shore, where we had pulled up – a few old grey-haired men and stiff-jointed old crones, young men and women, children who could hardly toddle, all dressed alike in these fox and bear-skin furs, which create such an extraordinarily barbaric first impression. Some came with long knives in their hands, with bloodstained arms and upturned sleeves, having been in the midst of flaying operations when we arrived, and all this produced a very savage effect; at the moment it was difficult to believe that these "savages," "the neighbours of the North Pole," as Astrup called them, were ever likely to become one's good, warm friends.

Our dogs were unharnessed, and quantities of meat flung to them at once. Meat there was in abundance, and everywhere, in between the houses, you saw cooking-hearths. It was immediately apparent that these people were not suffering from privation.

On one's arrival at a settlement in Danish West Greenland, it is usual for the young women to help the new-comers off with their outdoor clothes. Now, for a moment, I forgot where I was, and as the Greenlandic custom is, stretched out my foot towards a young girl who was standing by my side, meaning her to pull off my outer boots. The girl grew embarrassed, and the men laughed. There was that winning bashfulness about her that throws attraction over all Nature's children; a pale blush shot across her cheek, like a ripple over a smooth mountain lake; she half turned away from me, and her black eyes looked uneasily out over the frozen sea.

"What is thy name?"

"Others will tell thee what my name is," she stammered.

"Aininâq is her name," put in the bystanders, laughing.

A jovial old paterfamilias then came up to her and said
with gravity:

"Do what the strange man asks thee!" And she stooped
down at once and drew off my boots.

"Move away; let me come!" called out an old woman
from the crowd, and she elbowed the people aside and
forced her way through to my sledge.

"It was my daughter thou wast talking to!" she burst
out eagerly. "Dost thou not think her beautiful?" and she
rolled her little selfconscious eyes around.

But Aininâq had slipped quietly away from the crowd
of curious beholders and hidden herself. It was only later
that I learnt my request to her had been construed into a
proposal of marriage.

Jörgen and I were now conducted up to the houses.
Sheltering walls of snow had been built up here and there
to form cooking-places, and round these the natives
clustered. A young fellow came up carrying a frozen
walrus liver, raw, which was our first meal; all the men
of the village ate of it with us, to show their hospitable
intent. Curious youngsters gaped at us greedily from
every side, and ran away when we looked at them.

When the pot had boiled, we were called in to the senior
of the tribe, the magician Sagdloq ("The Lie"); the boiled
meat was placed on the floor, and a knife put in our hands.

A lively conversation got under way. The people were
not difficult to understand, as their dialect differed but
little from the ordinary Greenlandic; they were surprised
themselves at the ease with which they understood us,
who yet came from such a distance.

After the meal, they immediately set about building us a
snow hut.

"There is a sick man with you, so you must be helped
quickly," they said.

They hewed large blocks out of the hard snow: those
were to be the walls of our new house. Then they set it up

in a hollow in the snow, and in the course of half an hour it stood complete.

A sledge was sent for our comrades, and by early morning we were all together.

The reception these pagan savages gave us was affectingly cordial; it seemed that they could not do enough for us. And just as they were on our arrival – helpful as they could possibly be, and most generous with their gifts – so they remained the whole time that we spent among them . . .

Our sick comrade, Count Harald Moltke, was by this time so far on the road to recovery that he could take a walk every day on the big flat outside our tent on Saunders Island. But in spite of the steady progress he was making, we dared not expose him to another winter in this harsh climate and under these primitive conditions, if we could possibly avoid it.

Two Scottish captains, whom we had met on June 27, would not undertake the responsibility of transporting him by vessel, but they had told us that not far behind them was another whaler, the *Vega*, which would be able to lend us a boat; they themselves could not spare one. If Moltke's health continued to improve, towards the autumn, when the channels were clear of ice, we might make an attempt to penetrate, along the Melville Glaciers, to Upernivik. We waited for the *Vega*, and went up the hills, on the look-out, whenever it was clear. But the waiting-time grew long. The *Vega* did not come. As is well known, she was packed in the ice in Melville Bay and lost.

By the middle of July we came to the conclusion that we must seek some other way out of our difficulties, if we wanted to reach Upernivik before the winter. And as an Eskimo, named Sâmik, in the Northern District, possessed a whaling sloop that he had received from Robert Peary, the American, we decided to place ourselves in communication with him and try to induce him to lend us

his boat, which could be returned to him later by a whaler
from Upernivik.

The time of year was not a favourable one for the
journey. Ice still lay over the fjord, and made kayak
travelling impossible. The attempt would have to be made
with dog-sledges. It was decided, therefore, that Mylius-
Erichsen and the Greenlander Gabriel should remain
behind with Harald Moltke, while I, with the Greenlandic Catechist Jörgen Brönlund, was to drive north and
open negotiations with Sâmik. In addition to Jörgen, I
chose, as escorts, two young Eskimos of about twenty
years of age, Sitdluk and Qisunguaq.

So two sledges left our encampment in Saunders Island
on July 17 at midnight and proceeded north. All the ice on
the south side of the island had disappeared, but on the
north coast there was still a narrow bridge of ice connecting it with the mainland: we should be able to cross by
that. But first we had to get our sledges over the high land,
2000 feet in height and bare of snow, and that was no easy
matter, as our way up and down led through ravines
where the streams had long since burst their ice covering
and rushed down with great force. Foreseeing what the
dificulties of our journey would be, we had limited our
baggage to our sleeping-bags and a little clothing, all the
provisions we had being a handful of biscuits and a little
tea and sugar; we should fall in with food enough on the
way.

"Men don't drag meat with them in the height of
summer!" as the Eskimos said. Nor did we take a tent
with us. We owned two, but one had to be left for Moltke;
the other had been torn by the dogs, and was consequently
unusable in wet weather. We should have to manage
Eskimo fashion; if it rained we must seek shelter among
the rocks.

Along wretched, half-melted ice, intersected by
streams, and after a twelve hours' journey, we reached
the mainland, where we had to camp, as the heat was too

much for the dogs. Towards midnight we went on, at first
on ice. We passed a few small islands, where we collected
eider-ducks', terns' and long-tailed ducks' eggs. The first
ice came to an end at the islands, and we went on for a
little way on floating ice-floes, but at last we were compelled to fall back on the land, though bare of snow. The
inland streams gave us a great deal of trouble. We were
obliged to pull the sledges ourselves, barelegged, when we
wanted to cross them, and, being glacier streams, they
were icily cold; our flaming scarlet legs tingled with the
freezing water.

We then came to the great bay, Iterdlagssuaq, across
the mouth of which it was easy going; but farther inland
the ice was cut up by the current and covered with water,
which often reached above the cross-bars of our sledges.
Towards midnight we succeeded in making the opposite
coast of the bay, without a dry thread upon us. There we
encamped, by a little stream-bed.

July 18. Towards evening we were awakened by pouring rain and obliged to seek shelter in a cave near by. Here
we were protected from the south-west gale and the
driving sleet. We remained thirty-six hours in the cave.

July 20. Towards morning it cleared up; we sprang
half-naked about the rocks, and dried our clothes and
sleeping-bags. We made a little tea, and boiled some seal's
skin – starvation fare. During the storm the dogs broke in
and ate our meat. We set out again towards evening.
Towards camping time, shot three seals; men and dogs
ate what they could. Sweet sleep followed.

July 21. Rain and storm again; we are sadly wet.

July 22. Good drying weather. We went on. The ice
unfortunately broken up; we had to drive on floes, the ice-
foot and on land. At the head of the fjord we made a halt to
reconnoitre; from there we had to travel along the glacier.
Jörgen, who had gone on in front, saw a reindeer, which
he shot. While we were engaged in skinning and cutting
up, the rain came on again. At the same time, a storm rose

amongst the rocks and glaciers, so violent that it swept
sand and stones down with it. We hastily erected a little
shelter, constructed of our sledges, covered with blubber,
and the freshly flayed seal-skins, and crawled inside.

For the third time we are weather-bound, even before
we have our clothes dried from the last wetting.

July 23. Rain and wind. We sit under an uninviting
dripping of blubber. When we are tired of telling tales –
and by degrees we have worked through the whole of our
childhood and our taste of manhood – we lie down to
sleep, or Jörgen begins to read aloud to us from his Bible.
I read the Revelation of St John, which impresses me
greatly in its imposing Greenlandic translation, Jörgen
clings to St Paul, and reads me the Epistle to the Romans.
Now and again an illusion of comfort visits us, and as we
grow absorbed in each other's narrations we manage to
forget that we are wet and hungry. It is only when silence
has fallen upon us all again that we notice how we are
slowly being pickled in the wet. The sleeping-bags are
drenched, the reindeer hair on them is beginning to fall
off in patches, and our clothes are smelling musty. Our
feet are white and swollen from the damp, and we are
cold.

Our spirits are on the verge of a breakdown, and we are
beginning to talk of our comrades at Agpat, who, on the
thorns of expectation, probably think that we have already
reached our goal.

When shall we be able to go on? Will it be possible to
get through at all? Or is this expedition, which was started
upon in such high hopes, to end merely in disappointment
– disappointment for us, and for those behind who are
waiting?

"Talk, Knud, talk! There will be no standing it, if we
are both silent. Tell us something, no matter what!" And
Jörgen rolls me over in my sleeping-bag. Sitdluk thrusts
his head out and shouts hopelessly into the roaring gale,
"*Qanigtailivdlugo! qanigtailivdlugo!*" which in translation

means, "Stop the rain! stop the rain!" For he believes that up among the rocks there live powerful spirits who can command the wind and stop the downpours of rain.

And Qisunguaq begins to reproach me with avarice. "You are so strange, you white men! You collect things you will never require, and you cannot leave even the graves alone. All this calamity is the revenge of the dead. Perhaps we shall die of hunger. Just because you took those stupid things!"

A few days before I had taken a scratching-pin, a needle-case, and a curved knife from an old grave. I console him by saying that the corpse would certainly have been satisfied with my exchange of gifts to the soul. It had had tea, matches, blubber and meat, just as they had stipulated. But Qisunguaq would not be appeased.

"The thoughts of the dead are not as our thoughts; the dead are incomprehensible in their doings!" he sighed.

"Stop, stop the rain!" calls Sitdluk despairingly up to the rocks.

"Tell us about Marianne, or Ellen, or Sara. Tell tales, and do not stop till we have forgotten where we are and think we are with them," demands Jörgen.

And memory hypnotises us back to experiences that lie behind; and fancy draws us ever in the same direction – back to vanished well-being, when we knew no privations; back to the delicacies of the Danish-Greenlandic kitchen, to the magnificent splendour of the shops. And thus, when one of us gets well under way with his narrative, we succeed in forgetting for a moment where we are, and friends, who perhaps think of us no more, Danes and Greenlanders, file past us, while the roaring stream outside thunders and swells with the rain.

The dogs, lying drenched in the wet, whine plaintively now and again; but the hills merely play with their yelping, and the echo of it rings across and across the fjord head.

July 24. Rained all night. Towards morning the storm

gave over. The clouds parted and the sun streamed down upon us. We attempted at three different places to cross the stream separating us from the drive up the glacier leading to Itivdleq on the other side of the mainland, but in vain.

By the time the water was up to our knees, the current was so strong that we almost lost our footing and were in danger of being carried off with it. Originally there were two streams only at the head of the bay, but in the last few days they have multiplied sadly. The terrific downpour has transformed the little valley into a whole network of streamlets. Altogether I counted eighteen, large and small.

An attempt at low water along the beach, leaping from one floe to another, was likewise unsuccessful. And the middle of the bay is now open water; the ice we were driving upon has been broken up by the storm. We are under siege. Seven glaciers shoot down to the head of the bay where we are; on the other side is the valley with the eighteen streams, and below it, the open bay itself.

July 25. Qisunguaq discovered a way up over a cliff about 2000 feet high, bare of snow. It was no easy matter to get the sledges up. Driving across the glacier was not without danger, either; there were many rushing streams, the passage of which gave plenty of trouble; I fell off twice and got wet through, but as there was a strong wind I soon got dry again. Some of the streams, with soft, deep snow on the sides, we had to cross by hurling ourselves over, to fall flat, rather than on our feet or legs, as otherwise we were in danger of disappearing altogether.

Late in the evening we have reached the place where begins the descent to Itivdleq, whence we were to cross to Qanâ. We are 2400 feet above the level of the sea and there is a superb view; but all our efforts have been wasted; Qanâ, where the boat is, is inaccessible. The ice is all broken up into floes.

It is night, and our journey has been a hard one; our

provisions are at an end; we can only fling ourselves down on our sledges and sleep our fatigue away. On the top of the hill, a terrific storm is howling.

July 26. We cannot get back to Agpat; and we must get into communication with men somewhere as soon as possible. Food we must have, and new footgear. We have tried to bind the soles of our kamiks (soft leather boots) together with thread; but they are so worn from the crumbling sandstone rocks and the sharp glacier ice that they are in holes that leave our feet bare. It is painful walking on the rocks, and it is abominably cold travelling on the ice.

We must attempt to reach Natsilivik; perhaps there are men there.

We break up towards midday and drive to the top of the glacier ridge, about 3400 feet up. We drive all day in a glorious sunshine through deep snow. Marvellously lovely glacier landscapes spread themselves out before us; there is a view over the whole of Whale Sound, with its islands, and the island of Agpat, and Wolstenholme with Jának. The sea is like a mirror, but up here, where we are driving, a fresh north wind is blowing, and it is cold – in spite of the sun.

The glacier drops gently down to Natsilivik, and we have an enjoyable drive downhill of two to three hours, with, when the snow is not too deep, good going.

We are above the clouds, for there hangs a thick fog down over Natsilivik while we are driving along in sunshine.

Down at the edge of the glacier, where we have to guide our team with great caution, as there is no snow, there are great glacier fountains, and several magnificent red water-springs, which give birth to red streamlets.

"It is the glacier bleeding!" says Qisunguaq of these great red springs, which gush up through narrow openings and rise in a thick stream, till they are scattered by the wind and fall away to the sides, like a waving crown of flowers.

At the edge of the glacier we leave our sledges and baggage behind and walk down to Natsilivik, where we arrive towards midnight.

No one there!

July 27. A dense fog further increases the difficulty of all search. Jörgen and Sitdluk have gone down to the houses at Natsilivik to see if there are meat deposits to be found.

Qisunguaq and I cross a ridge and make our way down to a creek, Narssaq, where there used to be tents.

We advance through the fog, seeing nothing and hoping for no more, our feet sore and our stomachs empty. After a few hours' toilsome march, we reach a rapid stream which we cannot cross; and we lie down under a great boulder, a discuss the position, and decide which of the dogs we shall be obliged to shoot, if we do not meet with people. We have eaten nothing for forty hours, and the last few days' traveling have been exhausting. Just as we are dropping asleep the fog lifts suddenly and we are inspired with fresh hope. We fling large stones into the stream, but the current carries them with it. At last one stone remains in place and we dare the crossing.

We are over; we run up the opposite bank, which is steep and high, and both utter wild cries of delight: at a distance of about 200 yards there are five tents . . . people! – and food . . . food!

THE REEF

Thor Heyerdahl

Heyerdahl was born in Norway and trained as an anthropologist. To test his theory that Polynesia was originally settled by Indians from South America, Heyerdahl and five colleagues sailed a balsa-wood raft from Peru to the South Pacific. The expedition might not have been good science, but it was high adventure. In the extract below, after 101 days at sea, Kon-Tiki *faced its supreme test – running aground on the Raroia coral atoll. The date was 7 August 1947.*

We saw that we had now only a few hours more on board the *Kon-Tiki*. They must be used in preparation for our inevitable wreck on the coral reef. Every man learned what he had to do when the moment came; each one of us knew where his own limited sphere of responsibility lay, so that we should not fly round treading on each other's toes when the time came and seconds counted. The *Kon-Tiki* pitched up and down, up and down, as the wind forced us in. There was no doubt that here was the turmoil of waves created, by the reef – some waves advancing while others were hurled back after beating vainly against the surrounding wall.

We were still under full sail in the hope of even now

being able to steer clear. As we gradually drifted nearer, half sideways, we saw from the mast how the whole string of palm-clad isles was connected with a coral reef, part above and part under water, which lay like a mole where the sea was white with foam and leapt high into the air. The Raroia atoll is oval in shape and has a diameter of twenty-five miles, not counting the adjoining reefs of Takume. The whole of its longer side faces the sea to eastward where we came pitching in. The reef itself, which runs in one line from horizon to horizon, is only a few hundred yards clear, and behind it idyllic islets lie in a string round the still lagoon inside.

On board the *Kon-Tiki* all preparations for the end of the voyage were being made. Everything of value was carried into the cabin and lashed fast. Documents and papers were packed into water-tight bags, along with films and other things which would not stand a dip in the sea. The whole bamboo cabin was covered with canvas, and specially strong ropes were lashed across it. When we saw that all hope was gone, we opened up the bamboo deck and cut off with machete knives all the ropes which held the centreboards down. It was a hard job to get the centreboards drawn up, because they were all thickly covered with stout barnacles. With the centreboards up the draught of our vessel was no deeper than to the bottom of the timber logs, and we would therefore be more easily washed in over the reef. With no centreboards and with the sail down the raft lay completely sideways on and was entirely at the mercy of wind and sea.

We tied the longest rope we had to the home-made anchor, and made it fast to the step of the port mast, so that the *Kon-Tiki* would go into the surf stern first when the anchor was thrown overboard. The anchor itself consisted of empty water cans filled with used wireless batteries and heavy scrap, and solid mangrove-wood sticks projected from it, set crosswise.

Order number one, which came first and last, was: Hold

on to the raft! Whatever happened we must hang on tight on board and let the nine great logs take the pressure from the reef. We ourselves had more than enough to do to withstand the weight of the water. If we jumped overboard we should become helpless victims of the suction which would fling us in and out over the sharp corals. The rubber raft would capsize in the steep seas or, heavily loaded with us in it, it would be torn to ribbons against the reef. But the wooden logs would sooner or later be cast ashore, and we with them, if only we managed to hold fast.

Next, all hands were told to put on their shoes for the first time in a hundred days, and to have their lifebelts ready. The last-named, however, were not of much value, for if a man fell overboard he would be battered to death, not drowned. We had time too to put our passports, and such few dollars as we had left, into our pockets. But it was not lack of time that was troubling us.

Those were anxious hours in which we lay drifting helplessly sideways, step after step, in towards the reef. It was noticeably quiet on board; we all crept in and out from cabin to bamboo deck, silent or laconic, and carried on with our jobs. Our serious faces showed that no one was in doubt as to what awaited us, and the absence of nervousness showed that we had all gradually acquired an unshakeable confidence in the raft. If it had got across the sea, it would also manage to bring us ashore alive.

Inside the cabin there was a complete chaos of provision cartons and cargo lashed fast. Torstein had barely found room for himself in the wireless corner, where he had got the short wave transmitter working. We were now over 4,000 sea miles from our old base at Callao, where the Peruvian Naval War School had maintained regular contact with us, and still farther from Hal and Frank and the other radio amateurs in the United States. But as chance willed, we had on the previous day got into touch with a capable wireless fan who had a set on Rarotonga in the Cook Islands, and the operators, quite contrary to all our usual practice, had arranged for an extra contact with him early in the morning. And all the time we were drifting closer and closer in to the reef, Torstein was sitting tapping his key and calling Rarotonga.

Entries in the *Kon-Tiki*'s log ran:

8.15: We are slowly approaching land. We can now make out with the naked eye the separate palm trees inside on the starboard side.

8.45: The wind has veered into a still more unfavourable quarter for us, so we have no hope of getting clear. No nervousness on board, but hectic preparations on deck. There is something lying on the reef ahead of us which looks like the wreck of a sailing vessel, but it may be only a heap of drift-wood.

9.45: The wind is taking us straight towards the last island but one we see behind the reef. We can now see the whole coral reef clearly; here it is built up like a white and red speckled wall which just sticks up out of the water in a belt in front of all the islands. All along the reef white foaming surf is flung up towards the sky. Bengt is just serving up a good hot meal, the last before going into action! It is a wreck lying in there on the reef. We are so close that we can see right across the shining lagoon behind the reef, and see the outlines of other islands on the other side of the lagoon.

As this was written the dull drone of the surf came near again; it came from the whole reef inside us and filled the air like thrilling rolls of drums, heralding the exciting last act of the *Kon-Tiki*.

9.50: Very close now. Drifting along the reef. Only a hundred yards or so away. Torstein is talking to the man on Rarotonga. All clear. Must pack up log now. All in good spirits; it looks bad, but *we shall make it*!

A few minutes later the anchor rushed overboard and caught hold of the bottom, so that the *Kon-Tiki* swung round and turned her stern inwards towards the breakers. It held us for a few valuable minutes, while Torstein sat hammering like mad on the key. He had got Rarotonga now. The breakers thundered in the air and the sea rose and fell furiously. All hands were at work on deck, and now Torstein got his message through. He said we were drifting towards the Raroia reef. He asked Rarotonga to listen in on the same wave-length every hour. If we were silent for more than thirty-six hours Rarotonga must let the Norwegian Embassy in Washington know. Torstein's last words were: "O.K. 50 yards left. Here we go. Goodbye." Then he closed down the station. Knut sealed up the papers, and both crawled out on deck as fast as they could to join the rest of us, for it was clear now that the anchor was giving way.

The swell grew heavier and heavier, with deep troughs between the waves, and we felt the raft being swung up and down, up and down, higher and higher.

Again the order was shouted: "Hold on, never mind about the cargo, hold on!"

We were now so near the waterfall inside that we no longer heard the steady continuous roar from all along the reef. We now heard only a separate boom each time the nearest breaker crashed down on the rocks.

All hands stood in readiness, each clinging fast to the rope he thought the most secure. Only Erik crept into the cabin at the last moment; there was one part of the programme he had not yet carried out – he had not found his shoes!

No one stood aft, for it was there the shock from the reef would come. Nor were the two firm stays which ran from the masthead down to the stern safe. For if the mast fell they would be left hanging overboard, over the reef. Herman, Bengt, and Torstein had climbed up on some boxes which were lashed fast forward of the cabin wall, and while Herman clung on to the guy-ropes from the ridge of the roof, the other two held on to the ropes from the masthead by which the sail at other times was hauled up. Knut and I chose the stay running from the bows up to the masthead, for if mast and cabin and everything else went overboard, we thought the rope from the bows would nevertheless remain lying inboard, as we were now head on to the seas.

When we realized that the seas had got hold of us, the anchor rope was cut, and we were off. A sea rose straight up under us, and we felt the *Kon-Tiki* being lifted up in the air. The great moment had come; we were riding on the wave-back at breathless speed, our ramshackle craft creaking and groaning as she quivered under us. The excitement made one's blood boil. I remember that, having no other inspiration, I waved my arm and bellowed "hurrah!" at the pitch of my lungs; it afforded a certain relief and could do no harm anyway. The others certainly thought I had gone mad, but they all beamed and grinned enthusiastically. On we ran with the seas rushing in behind us; this was the *Kon-Tiki*'s baptism of fire; all must and would go well.

But our elation was soon damped. A new sea rose high up astern of us like a glittering green glass wall; as we sank down it came rolling after us, and in the same second in which I saw it high above me I felt a violent blow and was submerged under floods of water. I felt the suction through my whole body, with such great strength that I had to strain every single muscle in my frame and think of one thing only – hold on, hold on! I think that in such a desperate situation the arms will be torn off before the brain consents to let go, evident as the outcome is. Then I felt that the mountain of water was passing on and relaxing its devilish grip of my body. When the whole mountain had rushed on, with an earsplitting roaring and crashing, I saw Knut again hanging on beside me, doubled up into a ball. Seen from behind the great sea was almost flat and grey; as it rushed on it swept just over the ridge of the cabin roof which projected from the water, and there hung the three others, pressed against the cabin roof as the water passed over them.

We were still afloat.

In an instant I renewed my hold, with arms and legs bent round the strong rope. Knut let himself down and with a tiger's leap joined the others on the boxes, where the cabin took the strain. I heard reassuring exclamations from them, but at the same time I saw a new green wall rise up and come towering towards us. I shouted a warning and made myself as small and hard as I could where I hung. And in an instant hell was over us again, and the *Kon-Tiki* disappeared completely under the masses of water. The sea tugged and pulled with all the force it could bring to bear at the poor little bundle of a human body. The second sea rushed over it, and a third like it.

Then I heard a triumphant shout from Knut, who was now hanging on to the rope-ladder:

"Look at the raft, she's holding!"

After three seas only the double mast and the cabin had been knocked a bit crooked. Again we had a feeling of triumph over the elements, and the elation of victory gave us new strength.

Then I saw the next sea come towering up, higher than all the rest, and again I bellowed a warning aft to the others as I climbed up the stay as high as I could get in a hurry and hung on fast. Then I myself disappeared sideways into the midst of the green wall which towered high over us; the others, who were farther aft and saw me disappear first, estimated the height of the wall of water at twenty-five feet, while the foaming crest passed by fifteen feet above the part of the glassy wall into which I had vanished. Then the great wave reached them, and we had all one single thought – hold on, hold on, hold, hold, hold!

We must have hit the reef that time. I myself felt only

the strain on the stay, which seemed to bend and slacken jerkily. But whether the bumps came from above or below I could not tell, hanging there. The whole submersion lasted only seconds, but it demanded more strength than we usually have in our bodies. There is greater strength in the human mechanism than that of the muscles alone. I determined that if I was to die, I would die in this position, like a knot on the stay. The sea thundered on, over and past, and as it roared by it revealed a hideous sight. The *Kon-Tiki* was wholly changed, as by the stroke of a magic wand. The vessel we knew from weeks and months at sea was no more; in a few seconds our pleasant world had become a shattered wreck.

I saw only one man on board besides myself. He lay pressed flat across the ridge of the cabin roof, face downwards, with his arms stretched out on both sides, while the cabin itself was crushed in like a house of cards, towards the stern and towards the starboard side. The motionless figure was Herman. There was no other sign of life, while the hill of water thundered by, in across the reef. The hardwood mast on the starboard side was broken like a match, and the upper stump, in its fall, had smashed right through the cabin roof, so that the mast and all its gear slanted at a low angle over the reef on the starboard side. Astern, the steering block was twisted round lengthways and the crossbeam broken, while the steering oar was smashed to splinters. The splashboards at the bows were broken like cigar boxes, and the whole deck was torn up and pasted like wet paper against the forward wall of the cabin, along with boxes, cans, canvas, and other cargo. Bamboo sticks and rope-ends stuck up everywhere, and the general impression was of complete chaos.

I felt cold fear run through my whole body. What was the good of my holding on? If I lost one single man here, in the run in, the whole thing would be ruined, and for the moment there was only one human figure to be seen after

the last buffet. In that second Torstein's hunched-up
figure appeared outside the raft. He was hanging like a
monkey in the ropes from the masthead, and managed to
get on to the logs again, where he crawled up on to the
debris forward of the cabin. Herman too now turned his
head and gave me a forced grin of encouragement, but did
not move. I bellowed in the faint hope of locating the
others, and heard Bengt's calm voice call out that all
hands were aboard. They were lying holding on to the
ropes behind the tangled barricade which the tough
plaiting from the bamboo deck had built up.

All this happened in the course of a few seconds, while
the *Kon-Tiki* was being drawn out of the witches' kitchen
by the backwash, and a fresh sea came rolling over her.
For the last time I bellowed "hang on!" at the pitch of my
lungs amid the uproar, and that was all I myself did; I
hung on and disappeared in the masses of water which
rushed over and past in those endless two or three seconds. That was enough for me. I saw the ends of the logs
knocking and bumping against a sharp step in the coral
reef without getting over it. Then we were sucked out
again. I also saw the two men who lay stretched out across
the ridge of the cabin roof, but none of us smiled any
longer. Behind the chaos of bamboo I heard a calm voice
call out:

"This won't do."

And I myself felt equally discouraged. As the masthead
sank farther and farther out over the starboard side I
found myself hanging on to a slack line outside the raft.
The next sea came. When it had gone by I was dead tired,
and my only thought was to get up on to the logs and lie
behind the barricade. When the backwash retreated, I saw
for the first time the rugged red reef naked beneath us,
and perceived Torstein standing bent double on gleaming
red corals, holding on to a bunch of ropes' ends from the
mast. Knut, standing aft, was about to jump. I shouted
that we must all keep on the logs, and Torstein, who had

been washed overboard by the pressure of water, sprang up again like a cat.

Two or three more seas rolled over us with diminishing force, and what happened then I do not remember, except that water foamed in and out, and I myself sank lower and lower towards the red reef over which we were being lifted in. Then only crests of foam full of salt spray came whirling in, and I was able to work my way in on the raft, where we all made for the after end of the logs, which was highest up on the reef.

At the same moment Knut crouched down and sprang up on to the reef with the line which lay clear astern. While the backwash was running out, he waded at the double some thirty yards in and stood safely at the end of the line when the next sea foamed in towards him, died down, and ran back from the flat reef like a broad stream.

Then Erik came crawling out of the collapsed cabin, with his shoes on. If we had all done as he did, we should have got off cheaply. As the cabin had not been washed overboard, but had been pressed down pretty flat under the canvas, Erik lay quietly stretched out among the cargo and heard the peals of thunder crashing above him while the collapsed bamboo walls curved downwards. Bengt had had a slight concussion when the mast fell, but had managed to crawl under the wrecked cabin alongside Erik. We should all of us have been lying there if we had realized in advance how indissolubly the countless lashings and plaited bamboo sheets would hang on to the main logs under the pressure of the water.

Erik was now standing ready on the logs aft; and when the sea retired he too jumped up on to the reef. It was Herman's turn next, and then Bengt's. Each time the raft was pushed a bit farther in, and when Torstein's turn and my own came, the raft already lay so far in on the reef that there was no longer any ground for abandoning her. All hands began the work of salvage.

We were now twenty yards away from that devilish step

up on the reef, and it was there and beyond it that the breakers came rolling after one another in long lines. The coral polyps had taken care to build the atoll so high that only the very top of the breakers was able to send a fresh stream of sea water past us and into the lagoon, which abounded in fish. Here inside was the coral's own world, and they disported themselves in the strangest shapes and colours.

A long way in on the reef the others found the rubber raft, lying drifting and quite waterlogged. They emptied it and dragged it back to the wreck, and we loaded it to the full with the most important equipment, like the radio set, provisions, and water-bottles. We dragged all this across the reef and piled it up on the top of a huge block of coral which lay alone on the inside of the reef like a large meteorite. Then we went back to the wreck for fresh loads. We could never know what the sea would be up to when the tidal currents got to work around us.

In the shallow water inside the reef we saw something bright shining in the sun. When we waded over to pick it up, to our astonishment we saw two empty tins. This was not exactly what we had expected to find there, and we were still more surprised when we saw that the little boxes were quite bright and newly-opened and stamped "pine-apple", with the same inscription as that on the new field rations we ourselves were testing for the quartermaster. They were indeed two of our own pineapple tins which we had thrown overboard after our last meal on board the *Kon-Tiki*. We had followed close behind them up on to the reef.

We were standing on sharp, rugged coral blocks, and on the uneven bottom we waded now ankle-deep, now chest-deep, according to the channels and stream-beds in the reef. Anemones and corals gave the whole reef the ap-pearance of a rock garden covered with mosses and cactus and fossilized plants, red and green and yellow and white. There was no colour that was not represented, either in

corals or in algae, or in shells and sea slugs and fantastic
fish which were wriggling about everywhere. In the
deeper channels small sharks about four feet long came
sneaking up to us in the crystal-clear water. But we had
only to smack the water with the palms of our hands for
them to turn about and keep at a distance.

Where we had stranded we had only pools of water and
wet patches of coral about us, and farther in lay the calm
blue lagoon. The tide was going out, and we continually
saw more corals sticking up out of the water round us,
while the surf which thundered without interruption
along the reef sank down, as it were, a floor lower. What
would happen there on the narrow reef when the tide
began to flow again was uncertain. We must get away.

The reef stretched like a half-submerged fortress wall
up to the north and down to the south. In the extreme
south was a long island densely covered with palm forest.
And just above us to the north, only 600 or 700 yards
away, lay another but considerably smaller palm island. It
lay inside the reef, with palm-tops rising into the sky and
snow-white sandy beaches running out into the still
lagoon. The whole island looked like a bulging green
basket of flowers, or a little bit of concentrated paradise.

This island we chose.

Herman stood beside me beaming all over his bearded
face. He did not say a word, only stretched out his hand
and laughed quietly. The *Kon-Tiki* still lay far out on the
reef with the spray flying over her. She was a wreck, but
an honourable wreck. Everything above deck was
smashed up, but the nine balsa logs from the Quivedo
forest in Ecuador were as intact as ever. They had saved
our lives. The sea had claimed but little of the cargo, and
none of what we had stowed inside the cabin. We ourselves had stripped the raft of everything of real value,
which now lay in safety on the top of the great sun-smitten
rock inside the reef.

Since I had jumped off the raft, I had genuinely missed

the sight of all the pilot fish wriggling in front of our bows. Now the great balsa logs lay right up on the reef in six inches of water, and brown sea slugs lay writhing under the bows. The pilot fish were gone. The dolphins were gone. Only unknown flat fish with peacock patterns and blunt tails wriggled inquisitively in and out between the logs. We had arrived in a new world. Johannes had left his hole. He had doubtless found another lurking-place here.

I took a last look round on board the wreck, and caught sight of a little baby palm in a flattened basket. It projected from an eye in a coconut to a length of eighteen inches, and two roots stuck out below. I waded in towards the island with the nut in my hand. A little way ahead I saw Knut wading happily landwards with a model of the raft, which he had made with much labour on the voyage, under his arm. We soon passed Bengt. He was a splendid steward. With a lump on his forehead and sea water dripping from his beard, he was walking bent double pushing a box, which danced along before him every time the breakers outside sent a stream over into the lagoon. He lifted the lid proudly. It was the kitchen box, and in it were the Primus and cooking utensils in good order.

I shall never forget that wade across the reef towards the heavenly palm island that grew larger as it came to meet us. When I reached the sunny sand beach, I slipped off my shoes and thrust my bare toes down into the warm, bone-dry sand. It was as though I enjoyed the sight of every footprint which dug itself into the virgin sand beach that led up to the palm trunks. Soon the palm-tops closed over my head, and I went on, right in towards the centre of the tiny island. Green coconuts hung under the palm-tufts, and some luxuriant bushes were thickly covered with snow-white blossoms, which smelt so sweet and seductive that I felt quite faint. In the interior of the island two quite tame terns flew about my shoulders. They were as white and light as wisps of cloud. Small

lizards shot away from my feet, and the most important
inhabitants of the island were large blood-red hermit
crabs, which lumbered along in every direction with
stolen snail-shells as large as eggs adhering to their soft
hinder-parts.

I was completely overwhelmed. I sank down on my
knees and thrust my fingers deep down into the dry warm
sand.

The voyage was over. We were all alive. We had run
ashore on a small uninhabited South Sea island. And what
an island! Torstein came in, flung away a sack, threw
himself flat on his back and looked up at the palm-tops
and the white birds, light as down, which circled noise-
lessly just above us. Soon we were all six lying there.
Herman, always energetic, climbed up a small palm and
pulled down a cluster of large green coconuts. We cut off
their soft tops, as if they were eggs, with our machete
knives, and poured down our throats the most delicious
refreshing drink in the world – sweet, cold milk from
young and seedless palm fruit. On the reef outside re-
sounded the monotonous drumbeats from the guard at the
gates of paradise.

"Purgatory was a bit damp," said Bengt, "but heaven
was more or less as I'd imagined it."

We stretched ourselves luxuriously on the ground and
smiled up at the white trade wind clouds drifting by
westward up above the palm-tops. Now we were no
longer following them helplessly; now we lay on a fixed,
motionless island, really in Polynesia.

And as we lay and stretched ourselves, the breakers
outside us rumbled like a train, to and fro, to and fro all
along the horizon.

Bengt was right; this was heaven.

FLIGHT TO APIA

Ernest K. Gann

Ernest Gann was born in 1910 and combined a career as a pilot with that of a writer, principally of adventure novels, most famously The High and the Mighty. *His non-fiction includes the autobiographical* The Flying Circus. *Gann died in 1991.*

My heart had long been scorched with envy, for other men were lofting to regions I could never achieve. It was the year of the Geminis, of plans for the moon, of supersonic transport design, of fighters slashing thrice the speed of sound. Like most people I had no choice but to remain an observer, a grubby role for one who has flown with eagles. Perhaps that is why I instantly agreed when Freddie called and asked, "How would you like to fly a DC-3 from San Francisco to Apia?"

If there is anyone who does not know where Apia is, then it is in Western Samoa, which is very far over the South Pacific horizon.

It had been nineteen years since I had flown a DC-3. Where now was my hard-won wisdom? There was the belief I had always held that a wise man never tries to go back.

And yet . . . Apia, a siren whispered the name. An author named Robert Louis Stevenson is buried in Apia and if he could make it in a sailing craft, certainly I should be grateful for a DC-3. The analogy would be abused, I knew, by well-meaning, jet-minded friends.

"A *DC-3?* It's four thousand over-water miles to Samoa!" A preliminary measuring reminded me it was *four thousand, three hundred and fifty miles.*

"You'll go crazy! It will take you thirteen hours just to Honolulu . . ." *My specially designed pessimistic computer insisted it would take longer.*

"A jet takes only four hours plus. Stay home and write books. No one ever drowned writing and making a fortune."

But how much had they lived?

"What happens if one engine quits?"

According to my recollection most DC-3s eventually arrived at their destination if they carried enough fuel. In my private manual I firmly believed the only time there was too much fuel aboard any aircraft was if it was on fire. As for single-engine emergencies, I had enough familiarity with the proper mixture of fright, sweat, and faith to remain convinced "it can't happen to me."

"All DC-3s are ancient. What about metal fatigue? If you take a tin can and bend it a million times . . . well?"

Well? Never having flown with the handicap of an engineering degree, I had never worried about such things. But I would bend as gently as possible.

Freddie, while masquerading as just another Pan American pilot, was, as everyone knew, the uninaugurated president of the Pacific Ocean. On the telephone he had advised, "The father of our country will be your navigator."

I was pleased because *this* George Washington was a stocky, alert, New Zealander, at the moment Operations' Manager-Chief Pilot-all around-high chieftain of Polynesian Airlines. And he smiled easily. This infant airline had been flying a route pioneered by Captain Cook, rechecked by William Bligh, and publicized by Somerset Maugham and James Michener. With a single borrowed DC-3, Polynesian Airlines had been serving Apia in Western Samoa, Pango Pango in American Samoa, flying thence to Atitaki and Rarotonga, or westbound to Tongatapu and Fiji. Now, after two years of operation Polynesian had taken an important step. Business was so good they had resolved to buy an airplane they could call their own. Following sound advice they had bought a DC-3.

Freddie said, "John Best will be Flight Engineer. He can also do some of the flying when you want a stretch."

Best was also a New Zealander. Though still in his early twenties he approached genius as an aircraft mechanic. It was he who had nursed Polynesia's single rented DC-3 so tenderly, soothing its brow against all weariness. Many people believed the line operated four airplanes.

"And who," I asked Freddie, "will be the co-pilot?"

"Co-pilots for ferry flights are hard to come by . . . you can sort of switch around."

Freddie is easily given to sweeping statements when bothersome details threaten his multitudinous affairs. He is a man who likes to launch projects. If allowed he will plan your coming week, month, year, or life.

"Freddie," I said patiently, "George Washington is going to be very busy navigating and when he is not actually holding an octant in his hand he should be catching a few minutes sleep. John Best should be checking fuel consumption and a lot of other things. Without even knowing what the winds will be, it will certainly take us fourteen hours or so just to make Honolulu. That is a long time for these bifocaled eyes to be staring at instruments. There should be a co-pilot, someone—"

"What about Dodie? She could double as stewardess."

I swallowed thoughtfully. Dodie was my girl Friday secretary. It was true that she was taking flying lessons and was almost ready for her private license, but when she

signed on for her job, the fringe benefits did not include a
possible voyage in a life raft. Personally, I would feel much
safer a thousand miles from the nearest land in a DC-3 than
on any freeway, but Dodie's decision to go might hinge on
loyalty. I remembered only too well that ferry flights were
never the same as routine passenger flights. There would be
the usual makeshift arrangement of extra fuel tanks installed for one flight only, and of course a subsequent weight
overload. Yet the ferry flights I knew about had arrived at
their destinations in good grace . . . almost always.

"I'll ask her."

Thus it was that the fourth member of our crew was a
girl named Dodie. Do not offer adventure to a certain kind
of female unless you want them to accept.

The San Francisco night is unusually soft, and a near full
moon is rising across the Bay. It is Friday the thirteenth,
which may have accounted for three lucky takeoffs and
landings I had executed during my afternoon reunion
with a DC-3. After nineteen years . . . there she stands
quite as resolute as ever, a bit paunchy-looking perhaps
with the new type landing gear doors, but otherwise the
blood sister of those I had flown regularly from New York
to Cleveland and Chicago in 1939, to California in 1940,
and across the Atlantic to Greenland and Iceland when
there were no radios to guide us because the towers for
constructing same were our cargos.

Below the cockpit window I notice her christened name
– *Savaii*, the name of the second island of the two which
constitute the new nation of Western Samoa. John Best
has painted the red and blue national flag on her tail.

Beyond *Savaii* is the enormous San Francisco airport.
Jets keen their elephantine way along the runways, others
sigh down one after another for their landings, still others
blast their hot breaths against the night with power we
had never dreamed of only a few years ago. I watch them
soar towards the moon.

The contrast seems almost too much for the *Savaii*. The brilliant hangar light is cruel to her, the new paint becomes the pitiful striving of an old harridan trying to look her best at a relative's wake. There is something sheepish about her. And why not? In a few moments I will guide this anachronism along taxi-ways five times wider than she requires. The takeoff runway is so long that even with an overload *Savaii* should be able to make an ascension from one end, fly momentarily, and land at the other end with room to spare.

John Best comes to my side. "We are ready."

"All tanks topped off and checked?"

"Personally . . ."

After a few minutes we are taxiing slowly towards a moon path on San Francisco Bay.

George Washington calls the control tower and I try to persuade myself his New Zealand accent is to blame for the patronizing tone in the controller's voice. The tone changes to consolation when he recites our airways clearance to Honolulu. Beneath the obligatory technical mishmash he seems to be saying, ". . . now, not to worry. But are your life jackets handy?" The coward within me is momentarily resurrected, then dies one of his ten thousand deaths.

When we run up the two engines and check the magnetos we sound like vacationists playing with their outboards on a quiet lake. Just behind us, crouched like a prehistoric monster, is an American Airlines jet. I must know the pilots, or at least the captain. Long ago, beyond the swiftly closing mists of aviation time, we must have flown over the same routes as comrades, in DC-3s which really *were* brand new and glistening, and of which we were extremely proud. And it is very possible the rest of the captain's crew have never flown an airplane with a propeller on it.

I am reasonably sure what they are saying on the flight deck of the American 707 while they contain their impatience with this obstructive gnat, "Some people have it tough . . . flying a beat-up old DC-3 to Honolulu."

Lo, how the mighty have fallen.

Moments later *Savaii* demonstrates that however humble, she is far from beat-up and is not about to join the fallen. In spite of the overload she soars from the runway like a frightened sea gull. As altitude and airspeed mount I yell triumphantly, "We are in orbit!" the night allows me the deception of playing astronaut. And those who have been there have told me there is no more "G" sensation transmitted to their backsides by a Saturn 5 at blastoff than a pair of Pratt and Whitneys. And during the launch at least, I have a better view of the stars from a DC-3.

Four minutes later the shadowed land slips from beneath us and we are over the darker ocean. It is, as the gooney bird flies, 2,091 miles to Honolulu. The tower bade us farewell with a hint of good riddance, and George Washington has switched to the en route radio frequency.

As I ease *Savaii* upward, four thousand memories assail me, for I have as many hours in DC-3s. In cramped cocoons nearly identical to this one, I had frozen in the Arctic and melted in the Tropics. I had been sublimely content in autumn evenings above the shores of Lake Erie and awed by the aeronautical cruelties lurking in Catskill thunderstorms. Living so many hours in these noisy little cavities, I had belly-laughed over inconsequentials, dreamed ambitions never to be satisfied, scribbled naive notes for books I would never write, made lifelong friends, and wept for some who were slain. In these drafty little cubicles of aluminum lined with green leather I had known shame, lust, triumph, and near despair. And I had learned humility.

It is little wonder that after an absence of nineteen years I have absolutely no difficulty reaching for every control, absorbing the information offered by every instrument, or responding to the tolerant flight demands of a DC-3.

These things, all of them, are engraved in my mind
forever. Like the prisoner of Zenda, I know my cell.

We are supposed to report our arrival over "Briney", a
radial intersection twenty-two miles offshore. We have
not troubled to inform Air Traffic Control that we lack
the electronic gear for such an exact fix. They would not
understand our reasoning or our temporary reliance on
dead reckoning. Yet air traffic controllers, like all the rest
of us, are comfortable with the familiar. For years they
have been clearing jets to "Briney" and no matter what
their computers tell them they obviously cannot believe
the near static target on their radar screens. Are we a
balloon? How can we be so lackadaisical in reaching
"Briney"?

They call three times to ask when we estimate arrival.
When George Washington gives them an educated guess
they wait only a few minutes before calling again.
Wouldn't any self-respecting flying machine long ago
have passed "Briney"? In contrast to the old blips swimming quickly about their screens we are apparently stuck
in the celestial mud.

"They won't believe me!" George Washington's eyes
are hurt. I wonder what would happen if I should pick up
my own microphone and scold them for insulting his
name.

To the controller's relief we eventually decide we are
arrived at "Briney". He is rid of us. We have also
struggled to 6,000 feet. The moon peers benignly over
my left shoulder as I level *Savaii* and ease the engines into
long-range cruising power. Far above us moves the modern world of flight. Here, with our two engines snoring
like contended pigs we slide along smoothly enough.
Anachronism be damned! The top-gallants and royals
are set. The breeze is drawing fine. Sail on!

Soon we are free of our radar fetters, and George
Washington retires to his small navigating table situated
just behind my seat. A curtain between us shields his light

from the cockpit, but where it should button against the curving side of the fuselage there is a separation. The buttons are missing and so a narrow band of reflected light is created on my side window. As if observing him on a miniature television screen I can watch George Washington settle down to work at his flight log and chart. He opens a book of tables and scribbles with his pencil. He wets his lips several times and frowns. He is making computations concerning the stars and planets which will be our beacons during the balance of the night. Suddenly, I am sorry for those who no longer use the heavens to guide their way.

You there, aloft in your jets so high above us! Are you content with the magic of your Inertial Navigation System? Do those impersonal, ultra-efficient, cold green numbers flicking across the panels of your obsequious machine now seem to match the beauty of the stars we use in our subterranean world? If so, I fear you are lost men bound to genuflect before an electronic marvel and I do not envy you.

Now for us, there is only the firmament, the vast ocean, and ourselves.

I am reluctant to turn on the automatic pilot, wishing to prolong this very special, rather sensuous experience, the return to an old and willing love. *Savaii* responds to my slightest touch . . . a change of altitude twenty feet . . . a few degrees off course . . . ah. Beyond the windshield is *Savaii*'s broad snout. The moon outlines it clearly now and it droops down to a line of fluff balls, innocent little clouds marching along the black line of the sea.

For a time I seem to be alone with *Savaii*, staring at the fluorescent instruments exactly as I had done through so many long nights, almost hypnotized by their somnolent gentle motions, slipping pleasantly into that unique trance peculiar to night flying, that strange mixture of alertness and lethargy which somehow magically adds up to inner peace.

How many nights had I sat in just this way? During the Korean War it seemed we carved a track through these same skies; so many times did we pass back and forth with our cargos of fresh men out, and torn men home. And before that there was a steamship company which employed me to fly their first attempts to leave the surface for the air. But those flights were made in much bigger four-engined airplanes, so heavily manned and relatively sumptuous there were two bunks for resting when we pleased.

Dodie is standing in the moonlight beside me. I pretend to be working instead of luxuriating. She blinks at the rows of instruments.

"Coffee . . . tea . . . or milk?" Her nasal tone is part of our agreement. I had said that she could come if she rehearsed the stewardesses' chant to perfection.

"No thanks. Sit down and fly."

She needs a hundred-mile cross country for her private license. Though flying *Savaii* will not satisfy the FAA it will at least make a startling entry in her logbook. I take my hands and feet away from the controls. *Savaii* wavers momentarily, then settles obediently back to business. In the moonlight I watch Dodie's knuckles turning white. It will pass. *Savaii* is far larger and heavier than the little planes she knows. She will soon relax.

John Best has come forward. He scratches at the curly locks of his hair and I wonder if all New Zealanders are curly-headed since George Washington's hair is much the same.

"Are you ready to go on the fuselage tanks?"

"Wait. Let's burn off the auxiliaries another fifteen minutes."

"Right."

"Did you like the United States?"

"Yes . . ."

I wonder at a strange lack of enthusiasm in his voice.

"You wouldn't care to migrate . . . become a citizen?"

"No, thank you, skipper." Cold and flat. Too bad. John Best is the kind of young man we need.

Midnight. The cockpit has been like a miniature stage upon which our limited dramatis personae appear, speak their few lines in the subdued light, then exit into the darkness from whence they came.

Dodie has gone back to the cabin to tinker with the buffet. The heater is not working properly. John Best has turned four fuel valves so that now *Savaii*'s engines are sucking life from the long metal tanks which are lashed in the area normally occupied by passenger seats. Each tank holds four hundred gallons and passage between them is barely possible.

Two hours ago George Washington came forward to announce that his first star fix placed us in central China. Then he chuckled and pounded on the side of his head.

"I not only mixed up my Greenwich time, but was looking in the south latitude tables instead of north."

Later he returned with a second fix which was as near perfect as man could ask.

George Washington is a good navigator. Now, reflected in my side window, I can see him winding his octant. There had been so many nights over the North Atlantic when I had performed the same manipulations although our octants were not nearly so fancy. In these same type airplanes, we had done our own navigating. While the co-pilot flew the airplane I would go back to the cabin, climbing over bodies and cargo with octant in hand. If lucky I could catch a significant star through one of the cabin windows or the narrow skylight above the toilet. Sometimes it was necessary to signal the co-pilot for a turn to the right or left and thus reveal a certain star. It was a clumsy arrangement and our "fixes", if they could be dignified with the title, were heavily dependent on imagination. And hope. But we made it to Labrador and Greenland and Iceland as we would make it this night to the island of Oahu. In the intervening years the only apparent change is the addition of an astrodome through which George Washington observes the identical stars.

Dawn. It comes slowly for we are bound away from it and even our leisurely pace delays our pursuit by the sun. We are weaving between towering cumulus which would be dwarfed to toadstools by high-flying jets but appear as formidable bastions to us. We pass in dreamlike sequence from one to another and around the next. We are a butterfly seeking its way through a forest.

George Washington is patiently trying to transmit a position report on the radio. He holds his flight log in one hand and the microphone in the other while he reads off the long list of numbers which describe our whereabouts, our future whereabouts, comment on the weather, and our fuel endurance. It is a frustrating business which must be attempted every hour. Listening to my own headset as we strive for the most elementary communication with our fellow men, I am disillusioned. As it was long ago. In an emergency we would be more dependent on God and Pratt and Whitney than electronics for our survival. In the midst of fantastic progress, aviation has neglected its Achilles heel. I cannot detect how en route long-range radio communications have made the slightest improvement in the past fifteen years.

Now the moon rides ahead of us. Against the pale sky of a new day it looks a fake, like something the property man forgot to take down. The stars have taken their leave so George Washington has retreated to the cabin for a well-earned rest. He will resume his duties when the sun is high enough to offer a good shot. I have also rested, slumbering like a child while John Best twisted the knobs on the automatic pilot. And now it is his turn to close his eyes.

Dodie brings me tea, apologizing for its cool temperature.

"The buffet is *cassé*."

I tell her it is too early in the morning for such corny

rhymes. She has also brought a sandwich of salami and
cheese and while I munch at it and watch the glorious
dawn, Dodie flies *Savaii.*

I glance down at the ocean and appreciate how the
depths of the clouds are still wrapped in gloom. Yet a
moment later, still munching, I see the left wing tip
twinkle with the first touch of sun. Here is great contentment. All is as it should be in my aerial world.

Thirteen hours and fifty-three minutes after taking off
from San Francisco, *Savaii*'s tires kiss the runway at
Honolulu. And again we have offended the normal order
of things. The control tower, speaking its annoyed mind,
confesses it knows not what to do with us. We wait,
orphaned in the middle of the vast airport while great
jets scream past. Who are we who dare bring ancient
history into the hectic morning business of a great airport?
Go away, flying Dutchman! There is no longer any
appropriate nest for an aged DC-3.

Finally we are directed to a lonely tin hangar, itself an
anachronism. A man from the State of Hawaii arrives in a
yellow truck to collect $29 for the landing fee.

Twelve hours later we are airborne again, bound for
Apia. And on this second night, climbing in the humid
Hawaiian sky, I am suddenly possessed with the fancy
that this whole flight is a dream. I will awaken any instant
and this candy-floss airplane will vanish. My hands now
caressing the controls will grasp only air. Or perhaps, as
the lights of Honolulu sink into the depths, *Savaii* will
become a submarine with this unbelieving Captain Nemo
trying to fit his anachronistic craft into reasonable harmony with the instructions rattling in my earphones.

Earphones? Anachronism upon anachronism. These
heavy pre-World War II types always made me feel like
a yoked ox.

Honolulu Departure Control has us on their radar
screen. The controller himself is loquacious with local
gossip. ". . . you have traffic at two o'clock."

We peer at the night and see a great nothing. Even the stars are obscured by a cloud level we have yet to reach.

"Traffic, slow moving . . . at ten o'clock . . . two miles."

There. The blinking lights of an aircraft off to our left. He slips swiftly overhead and is gone. In earlier days we might have been innocent of his presence.

The controller asks if we have "VOR" equipment.

"Negative."

I hope he will reply, "How quaint . . ." but there is only silence.

The omission of VOR in *Savaii* is deliberate. Of what use would such sophistication be when the simple islands of the South Seas have no stations to transmit the necessary signals? Our next radio navigational aid will be a plain old-fashioned, nondirectional beacon located on Canton Island, over 1,600 miles of ocean and sky to the southeast. There is nothing in between. Now the situation is the same as our departure from San Francisco. Lacking the sophisticated electronic aid of VOR equipment we cannot depart the busy Honolulu area with sufficient exactitude to please Air Traffic Control. We are quite capable of wandering off on our own, but such carefree license was for leather-jacketed country bumpkins – not for the now in aviation.

"I will vector you on course", the controller announces. "Turn right to one eight five degrees."

I oblige. Big Brother is watching us. He can see aircraft we cannot see so it is wiser to let him escort us toward the great outdoors. Where we are bound the entire sky will more certainly be ours.

"Turn left to one seven zero degrees. You are now forty miles southeast of Koko Head . . . good night."

Thank you and good night, dear Big Brother. You cannot imagine how silly it feels flopping around in your radar-controlled world on the beak of this ancient pelican. We are not pressurized so we can open the side windows when we please and toss our gum out or the wrapping of a sandwich or anything else which is messy and displeases us. We can open the window and stick out our noses and sniff at the moist lukewarm air, or peer down at the black sea, or enjoy an unadulterated view of the heavens. This, Big Brother, is something you cannot do in a jet.

Midnight again. At this time last night we were far to the east of Honolulu in regions heavily traveled by sea and air; here with our chances of seeing another aircraft or any ship on the sea infinitesimal, I rediscover a wonderful loneliness. Once, the New Bedford whalers sailed this area, and long before the incredible migration of Poly- nesian peoples followed this same general line in reverse until they came upon the Hawaiian Islands. And during World War II the skies were busy. But now . . . nothing. Our first flights across the North Atlantic had been much the same. We were entirely self-reliant, a condition which sweetens all loneliness. We worried about many things, but not about collision.

We are cruising at 6,000 feet again. The stage moon has been hung for another performance, this time shoved around until it is perched on *Savaii*'s nose. The cumulus buildups which normally surround the Hawaiian land masses have been left behind. Below there is only the sea shimmering in the moonlight with here and there lost dumplings of vapor looking for a parent.

It is dark in the passageway which leads aft from the cockpit. George Washington is standing on a ten-gallon oil drum taking his first fix of the night. The octant hangs from the center of the star-studded astrodome and seems to be a projection of George Washington's body.

John Best has switched to the cabin-ferry tanks and is standing beside me. His youthful face is intent on the fuel pressure gauges. He wants to be certain there is no air lock in the ferry system. In this vigilance he has my hearty endorsement.

"She seems to be feeding fine, skipper."

"Yes . . ."

John Best reaches for the booster pump switches and flips them off one at a time. The pressure needles sag and then revive. He turns back into the blackness and soon Dodie arrives to sing the coffee-tea-or-milk song. There is a look in her eyes which has nothing to do with refreshment.

"You really came up here to fly, didn't you?"

"I confess . . ."

"Take over, Mrs. Mitty. The sky is all yours."

For a time I sit half-dreaming in the square of moonlight framed by the windshield. And as inspired by so many similar nights I find myself marveling at fortune's inexplicable arrangements. During those easily memorable times when I flew open cockpit Wacos, Birds, Ryans, Stearmans, and anything else I could beg or borrow, how could I have envisioned these circumstances? Below is an ocean with the nearest land already hundreds of miles away. On my right is a young lady flying a heavy twin-engined aircraft better than I had hitherto thought she might do. Yes, perhaps I should stow my male chauvinist helmet and goggles away forever and admit there are no longer any great physical demands upon a pilot. At least it was some consolation to realize "they" have not so far automated the weather.

Or man's resistance to fright – as I would later be reminded.

Hours later it is my turn to rest in the cabin. I lie down on our makeshift bunk and discover the belt of Orion framed in the nearest window. There is Rigel on the right; Betelgeuse on the left, and farther out in left field is Procyon twinkling as brightly as I have ever seen it. Here, near the tail, the engines' muffled drone is soothing and mixed with the hissings of countless drafts spewing from as many small openings in the fuselage. It is true non-supercharged fresh air and I breathe deeply of it. Who could not sleep here with the tail swinging so gently back and forth as if some long gone aviator would rock me in the cradle of his heights?

Just before dawn I make my way forward between the fuel tanks and pause by George Washington's tiny cubicle. He has crossed the last of three small lines and holds the tip of his pencil upon it.

"I doubt if I'll have another fix until mid-morning. We are coming up on the intertropical front now and I should suppose we'll do a bit of bouncing about."

We have passed the equator and are in a region once known to sailing ship men as the Doldrums.

"Why don't you get some sleep?"

"I rather think I shall. I'm tired of bucking the bloody radio. Nandi is guarding us now."

Nandi is in Fiji, a long way over the horizon – like 2,000 miles.

I move forward to the darkened cockpit and tap John Best on the shoulder. He surrenders his seat with a smile.

"Just in time. There's some fire up ahead."

During my absence the moon has rolled from the left side of *Savaii*'s nose to the right. Presently it occupies a lozenge-shaped clear space in the sky and illuminates a long wall of cumulus which extends much higher than *Savaii* could ever climb. Occasionally the fat and bulbous tumors, charged with their interior lightning, flicker brilliantly. Then they become quiescent for a while and soon, as if commanded by an energy-hungry Wotan, commence flashing again.

I watch the show from my front-row balcony seat. It appears to be no more of a threat than any other intertropical front I have ever seen, which if reviews were given for spectacle would place it considerably below a line of Appalachian thunderstorms and far down the honors list from the permanent thunderstorm front which lies off the west coast of Africa. There I had played audience to extravaganzas so visually terrifying I had wanted to crawl under my seat and hide, yet once a part

of the performance I discovered they invariably had more
bravado than bite. But this?

I remember a night when I had been overly casual about
entering a line of thunderheads assembled over the Irish
Sea and in two minutes found myself praying audibly for
immediate salvation. Obviously my airplane would not
survive. I resolved then and there that I would never trust
a line of cumulus no matter how flabby their appearance.

Dodie, now awakened, joins me in the cockpit while I
guide *Savaii* along winding cloud streets pressed on both
sides by gigantic ramparts. Occasionally we reach a dead
end and plunge into cloud. Then rain hisses at the wind-
shields, *Savaii* is rudely jostled, and I ask Dodie to pull on
a bit of carburetor heat. But these sessions are brief, not at
all ugly, and soon we are gliding along another street.
There are times when it is necessary to change course as
much as twenty degrees to avoid the larger anvil-headed
cumulus which really might be grisly. I always compensate a like number of degrees in the opposite direction lest
George Washington have complaint that his carefully
plotted course has been fouled. Our extra wanderings
will not consume more than ten minutes. Why trade this
much peace for that much war?

After an hour or so, when the dawn light has over-
powered the moon's, we pass beyond the front. Now there
are strange rills of curiosity passing through each of us,
for soon there must be something to see. There? No . . . it
is too early. Another ten minutes . . . maybe fifteen.

There!

Canton Island is an ill-defined bronze blob on the sea
horizon which appears to have been dropped from the
cloud stretching above it. All of *Savaii*'s crew are gathered in the cockpit for their first sight of land since the
night before. The intervening time has been like a passage
from another life.

Very abruptly we are brought back to our immediate
existence.

For suddenly there is a violent spasm of shudderings and regurgitations from both engines.

Our human responses are immediate. Dodie's hands try to squeeze juice out of the plastic control wheel. George Washington, ever the cool one, purses his lips and frowns. John Best disappears into the cabin.

With the speed of a d'Artagnan I turn on both main fuel tanks and hit the booster switches. When the engines settle back into their usual sonorous melody and my heart slides back down and off my tongue, I find it difficult to believe a former helmet and goggle man could have moved so fast.

John Best returns to the cockpit wearing the frown of a man betrayed.

"I don't understand it. The cabin tanks were still reading thirty gallons on my measuring stick."

"Do you abide by Murphy's law in New Zealand?"

"Ah? . . . Yes."

"When the plumbing system was installed someone bent a pipe up when it should have been bent down, or vice versa."

"It must be."

Fright, being merely a spark of fear, is much more quickly extinguished. Having swallowed my heart I affect a nonchalance suitable to the occasion. For lack of other gestures to fix the image I calmly call Canton and give our identification and destination.

At once I regret having opened the liaison. For the man who resides somewhere on that lonely atoll asks, "Are you landing Canton?" There is an unmistakable plaintiveness in his voice – a yearning.

"Negative."

From the atoll there is only the silence of disappointment. Then hopefully, should we change our minds, the voice recites the surface wind and altimeter.

"Thank you . . . so long." Even a little DC-3 has managed to pass over Canton Island.

Once we leave Canton it seems we have already arrived, although Samoa lies almost seven hundred nautical miles beyond. Yet it is close enough to rouse the homing instinct in half our crew. George Washington goes about his navigating with increasing zest instead of succumbing to the natural wilting which marks the very last part of most long flights. He keeps trying to tell Nandi our estimated arrival time in Apia, though he might as well holler down a barrel which is exactly what both he and the Nandi station operator sound like.

I turn to chide him. "You've been homesick."

"Of course."

John Best is also becoming increasingly restless. There is no room to pace, but he makes innumerable trips from the cabin to the cockpit. He will stand beside me for minutes, looking over the nose, scanning the horizon although he knows very well it will be hours before any land will appear. He borrows my pocket computer so he can calculate our true airspeed.

"One hundred and sixty knots true . . ." Not quite true because his heart has added a knot for hope and perhaps two more knots for anticipation and his heart has hinted to his eyes that if he leans far enough to one side when he reads the airspeed indicator it will appear to read faster than if he looks directly at it.

Now suddenly, in a frenzy of activity, everyone is taking pictures of each other and of the sky which is now dulled by a high overcast and certainly the least photogenic sky since we left San Francisco. I put it down to a mutual urge to disperse minutes, something to do while the faithful engines drone on, something to keep hands occupied while time segments drag between arithmetical fact and desire.

In contrast I become morose and find myself behaving like a sentimental fool. In spite of a certain weariness I do not really want this anachronistic flight to end. I touch the elevator trim tab in a way that should be reserved for a woman, then catch myself pretending to wipe at a spot of grease. I know it will be a very long time before I will fly a DC-3 again.

Faleolo is the airport for Western Samoa, located a long twenty-two miles from Apia. It is one of the world's fast vanishing grass airports, which makes it a sensuous pleasure to land any airplane.

It is a strip of green confined by the sea on one side and ranks of coconut palms on the other. George Washington had given our arrival time hours before. He had predicted 1:35. It is 1:35.

I point to the brooding island, most of which is shrouded in gray, soggy-looking clouds.

"You lied, George Washington. We will not be on the ground until thirty-eight."

Three minutes. Three minutes deviation in a flight that had commenced over 4,000 miles away.

I call for the landing gear to be lowered. George Washington recites the litany of the cockpit check list, and after fifteen hours in the sky we slide down through the warmth to the grass.

There are many people waiting to greet us. They place welcoming leis around our necks and admire *Savaii* as if she were the sleekest supersonic transport.

Walking away from *Savaii* I paused to look back at her. And I saw beyond the people clustered all around her, volubly expressing their wonder. Suddenly I knew my long nourished envy of astronauts had been eased. For had our aerial voyage been beyond the moon, I thought, our sense of detachment would have been much the same. Now I knew there had been no true measurement of the distance from our fellow earthlings. *Savaii*, a phantom from the past, had been our space ship carrying us above reality and in her we had made a reluctant reentry. Thus may the useful life of a thing be prolonged and that of some men temporarily exalted.

IN PATAGONIA

Patrick Symmes

In 1952, the young and pre-revolutionary Ernesto "Che" Guevara and his friend Alberto Granado set off from Argentina on an eight-month motorbike trip around South America, which Guevara recorded in The Motorcycle Diaries. *Half a century later, Guevara and Granado's trip was retraced by Patrick Symmes on a BMW R80 GS motorbike called 'Kooky' and recorded in his book* Chasing Che. *Symmes, a journalist and travel writer, lives in New York City.*

There are moments on a motorcycle when all the glory of motion is distilled into one purposeful package. Chasing curves over a swelling landscape, a motorcycle enters the pure expression of physics and is bound to the road in a way no car will ever know. The rider and machine are literally balanced on the infinitely thin line where centripetal force meets gravity. Despite this state of suspended disaster, the sensation of risk is largely a sensation; the motorcycle is in harmony with the road, and risk comes overwhelmingly from other drivers. Any moment of travel on a motorcycle is a light and essential moment, an agile rebuke to a life conducted in one place.

The raw force of the engine is not hidden beneath a hood, but alternately purrs and growls a few inches from the knees, demanding the consciousness of power. Sealed behind glass, insulated by climate control systems and music, the driver of a car knows nothing about the directions of the wind, the lay of sunlight, the small changes in temperature between a peak and a valley, the textured noise of differing asphalts, or the sweet and sour aromas of manured fields or passing pine forests. Engaged in all the senses and elements, balanced in the present tense, a rider on two wheels can taste moments of oneness with the road.

Alas, this wasn't one of those moments. After three hard days and two bad nights I came finally to a sliding, squirming halt in a thick pebbly gravel at the end of Valdés Peninsula. The truck driver had been right. I was on my own.

National Route 3, as the road south was called, had been pockmarked, scarred, and prone to sudden fits of gravel, all in all a merciless experiment in moving fast down a dangerous yet utterly boring route that lasted hour after hour, morning and afternoon, day after day, interrupted only by brief interludes in hideous gas stations manned by surly men dishing overpriced fuel. This shakedown cruise was pure pain: the new Plexiglas windscreen on the bike proved too short by a few inches, so that a sixty-five-mile-an-hour wind slipped over the top and tugged at my helmet all day, pressing the chin strap into my neck; the tip of my nose burned red and then peeled; my shoulders and behind complained incessantly; I became very dirty. Later I would miss the Ruta Nacional 3, of course, but I didn't know that at the time.

Patagonia is immense and more impressive than lovely in its austere vastness. With every mile south the land turned a lighter brown. Green grasses faded to tan clumps on a canvas of powdery soil. Where the road cut near the sea I saw a churlish and black Atlantic dressed with

constant whitecaps. It was an ever-diminishing landscape: flatter, emptier, windier, a desert without sand,
hot by day and cold by night. The last hundred miles of
the peninsula were on a loose gravel track that caught the
wheels and threw me down twice. I'd topped up my tank
in the pathetic town where the gravel began, and each
time the bike fell over gasoline trickled out of the carburetors, wetting the stones. The dark stains evaporated
quickly in a wind that ripped off the Atlantic at twenty-
five miles an hour, an offshore blast that smelled only of
fathomless distance, of the great expanse of ocean east
toward Africa and south toward the ice.

Valdés Peninsula is a geologic oddity, thrust far into the
cold currents of the South Atlantic yet home to the lowest
point in South America, a broad, white salt pan some
thirty-five meters below sea level that I had passed
quickly on my way in. This featureless plain was the
dullest tourist site I'd ever seen, but every day a bus
pulled to a halt beside it, disgorging groups of visitors
who were expecting the Patagonia of wall calendars. The
buses progressed around the peninsula, pausing at ocean
vistas and heading always to the north point, where, if you
arrived at high tide, you might see one of the local orcas
charge the beach, scattering – and only occasionally
catching – the seal pups that played tauntingly in the
surf. The rest of the peninsula was satisfyingly empty, a
landscape without utility poles or houses or pavement.

I'd finally come to a halt at Caleta Gonzalo, a zipper of a
bay at the ocean end of the hundred-mile peninsula.
Twice a day, Caleta Gonzalo opened along its length
and closed again, breathing water in and out in an enormous tidal swing that exposed almost ten miles of mud,
then reflooded it. Steep cliffs dropped down to a beach
where a dozen obese sea elephants brayed and dozed.
Despite the briny stink of the tidal flats, the beach looked
attractive. I'd driven back and forth for miles, scaring up a
rare Patagonian fox and several loping guanacoes but

failing to spot even a single dip or hollow to shield my tent
from the wind, nor any man-made structure to provide lee
shelter. From on high you could spy the magellanic
penguins as they waded into the water and fell over with
a cute belly flop. In an instant these waddling land
creatures were reborn as subsurface birds, their useless
wings now fins that helped them school in speedy flocks
through the undersea.

Everywhere, the elements sounded their warnings. A
blood-orange light fled the setting of the sun behind me,
and the wind already carried a premonition of how cold it
would be in half an hour. I needed shelter quickly. Night
was minutes away, and in this unpopulated zone I was
ready to ignore the No Camping signs sprinkled thoughtfully along the cliff, but I knew why they were really
there. At high tide the beach would disappear, and the
water came in like a flash flood. If you were asleep on the
beach you would never make it. A month before my
arrival a careless camper had been killed that way.

I drove south on the bay road, rounding bluff after bluff
in search of any sheltered spot, but the ground was flat
everywhere and scoured by the violence of the air. If I'd had
a car I could have slept in it, but instead I needed protection
from elements that cared nothing for "oneness."

Hurrying along, I almost passed the little farm nestled
in a dell where the cliffs briefly faded away and a cluster of
buildings touched the high-water line. There were four
sheep ranches on the Valdés Peninsula, and these buildings were an outstation on the biggest, which ran more
than 40,000 head.

This is where my filth came in handy. If there was one
thing I was learning to admire about the young Ernesto
Guevara, it was his unmitigated gall. As story after story
in his diary showed, the man was absolutely shameless, a
master at the traveler's art of scamming, borrowing,
begging, or otherwise landing accommodation, favors,
food, clothes, money, introductions, jobs, dance partners,

and liquor. When it came to freeloading, Guevara was a prince. "We aren't that broke," he once wrote to his mother after cadging a bed in a hospital, "but explorers of our stature would rather die than pay for the bourgeois comfort of a hostel."

Menaced on both sides by barking black dogs, I rode down the driveway of the ranch, dismounted, and clapped twice. Then I waited the customary two minutes, the black dogs barking all the while, circling slowly as I stood stock still. I spent the time preparing a little speech. I had to sound needy, yet not desperate. I had to plead for a roof, neither so demanding that I would offend nor so tentative that I would be rejected. I had to balance a humble tone with the subtle implication that I was a person of enormous importance, deserving of aid. For proof of the latter, I carried in my breast pocket a letter of introduction from a New York magazine, ready to spring forth like a passport from the Other World.

When he came out – a fat, greasy fellow in a sun-bleached PARIS ELLE T-shirt, his hair wild in the wind – he didn't wait for my speech. He looked at the setting sun, the distant horizon, and above all the dirt on my clothes.

"Come in, come in," he said, "you had better spend the night." His name was Florio, and he had the buttery handshake of a man who handled sheep. He waved at the dogs, who fell silent, and led me inside.

My bed was the floor of the cookhouse. After three twelve-hour days of riding my ugly cockroach of a motorcycle, I slept soundly and long. The broken cement felt like a down mattress.

The hens woke me when they strutted into the shed and bobbed nervously, emitting feed-me clucks. The tin roof played a twangy tune, like an instrument in the wind that had risen during the night. Outside it was blowing hard enough to send an unhappy hen rolling beak-over-talon past the shed from time to time.

Florio listened to the radio, measured the wind, and
sent his son David out to tell me that I was grounded. It
was gusting to forty-five miles an hour now, and I could
not drive. The boy told me this and kept talking. The dam
of solitude first leaked and then gushed. Nine years old,
living in isolation with his father and 40,000 sheep, the
boy needed nothing so much as to speak. As I stood
silently with him in the sunshine, both of us leaning
against the wind, he unleashed everything at once, a gale
of words about the neighbors, who lived an hour away,
and the level of water in the well, which was low, and the
whales and sharks that came into the bay. He named the
starving cats that wandered the yard eyeing the chickens,
and explained the work histories of both black dogs, along
with the good qualities of various birds, the murderous
nature of foxes, and which of every animal that walked or
swam was good or bad, which cherished or hated. He
talked of the orcas that came into the bay to hunt seals and
tasty sea lion pups, and of the tourists who came on great
lumbering buses to watch the orcas hunt, and of the water
truck, which was three days late, and of the strange
English boy he met once at a boarding school, a boy
who spoke very oddly, almost as though he had different
words for things.

"*Myaw myaw myaw*; we couldn't understand anything
he said," David explained. The fever or speech ran on,
burning at the boy so badly that he twitched and jumped
and jumbled words, hunching down to tell me about the
coloration of chicken eggs, then jumping up to describe
the stars we would see at night, and the paths of airplanes,
and the cost of soccer balls, and his fervent desire to drink
Coca-Cola. "I go through mountains of shoes my father
says I'm crazy he can't believe it but I don't do anything
except when it's raining and the mud gets everywhere and
the rain kills the chickens that one lays white eggs it's the
only one the *patrón* comes to visit sometimes and I
showed him but if it's an east wind it's cold and wet

and that kills the chickens or the fox comes and gets them which is why they sit in their bush all night where the dogs don't chase them I like the cats better my kitten is better will you take a picture of him?"

By my watch he talked for twenty-five minutes without interruption. What finally stopped him was that I belched, and at this he fell over in the dirt and chicken shit and began laughing his head off, the fever of an entire solitary winter broken by a fit of endless giggles. He'd never heard a foreigner belch before. Before he could start talking again, I asked him if he'd ever heard of Che Guevara.

David looked broken by the question. My tone told him it was an adult matter, something serious and from the outside world, but I was mouthing words as meaningless as those of the strange little English boy at boarding school. This was something from beyond the realm of foxes and sea elephant pups and good and bad winds. "Does he play football?" he asked tentatively.

Later I risked the short trip to the north shore, but the orcas never came and the seals sunned themselves unmolested. When I got back Florio was still sitting inside at the same table, his ear tuned to the transistor voice of the world. There was no news from the atmosphere.

In the morning I lay on the floor listening to the roof, which struck a lower tone than the day before. The shed was decorated with old shears and handmade knives hanging from the wall, their rusty points dangling down in the general direction of my sleeping bag. The tools were waiting for October, for the 40,000 sheep to finish converting grass into wool and then to line up in the chutes and paddocks and march in steady panic under these sharpened edges.

Little David came to the door carrying the same message from his father that I had heard in the tin roof: the wind was down in the twenties. David stood just inside the doorway of the cook shed, silent but clearly crestfallen by my decision to abandon him to the sheep and cats and chickens and orcas. He watched with wide eyes as I handled each of my possessions in turn, brushing stray down from my sleeping bag and stuffing it away, nestling my tiny cook stove in a saddlebag, dropping my flashlight into the zippered tank bag that would fit on the bike between my knees, one piece of kit after another. You could carry a lot if you packed carefully.

"This is the airplane that brought you here," he said. I turned and saw he was pointing at one of the last things I packed, the book of outdated hotel listings and dubious restaurant recommendations that was supposed to be guiding me across South America. It lay open to the very first page, an advertisement for SAETA, the Ecuadorean airline. Like all airline ads it showed a clean jet rising up in a blue sky. I told David that I had come on a different airplane.

"From where?" he said. I turned to the map of Argentina in the guidebook and showed him the Valdes Peninsula and how it lay far to the south of Buenos Aires.

"Is Buenos Aires in your country?"

This was serious. I unpacked my big map of South America and explained that Buenos Aires was in his country, while mine lay still farther to the north. He pointed to the north of Argentina: "Here?" Farther north, I replied. He looked slightly defeated by the news that there was more than one airplane, but I gave him a set of batteries for his transistor radio, which had died months ago. Now, like his father, he could have a one-way conversation with the world. I said good-bye to Florio, who looked relieved to see me go and asked that I send David a book, which I did.

Driving out the peninsula, the wind knocked me over twice more, sending me into knee-scraping mounds of pebbles. When the bike blew over the second time the windshield cracked. Gasoline leaked from the carburetors again; I watched the liquid evaporate from the stones in horror, quickly righting the bike each time but losing several pints that I could not afford to lose. Yesterday's trip to the north shore suddenly seemed a foolish waste of fuel. I hit the reserve tank with an hour still to go. Somehow I made it to the steep ridge of hills at the neck of the peninsula, but the motor began to cough and hesitate on the way up the last hill. I threw the petcock from *Res*. back to *Auf* and got one last burst of power that pushed me up to the crest at a wobbly five miles an hour. It was two paved miles from there to the gas station, but all downhill, and I eventually coasted into the little settlement of Puerto Piramides like some pathetic bicyclist. I mailed a postcard to my girlfriend and bought a vanilla milk shake and a full tank of gas, and then sat on a chair on the beach drinking the milk shake, watching the tide surge right past the No Parking signs, up and over the legs of the chair, and while I sipped my milk shake the water ran forth and back beneath me, chilling the aluminum.

ROMANCING THE STONE

Quentin Chester

Quentin Chester's books include The Wild Calling, *a collection of his columns for* Wild *magazine. An "accidental adventurer", Chester lives in Adelaide, Australia.*

Thunder boomed off the walls of the gorge and lightning flooded the tent with flashes of spectral blue. Then the rain came: an overture of slow, heavy drops building to a crescendo of pelting water. Our nylon canopy suddenly felt very thin. Sleep was out of the question, so while the elements raged we lay huddled together, teetering between moments of child-like fear and wonder. At the same time there was reason to rejoice, for the storm gave our bushwalk the only thing it really lacked – water. The sounds outside were heavy metal but it was still music to our ears.

Earlier that day we had set out from Grindels Hut on a five-day sojourn in the Gammon Ranges. It was a broiling October afternoon. Late spring can be a risky time to wander into the arid north of the Flinders Ranges. What little rain that does fall in these parts usually arrives in summer downpours. But during the preceding summer the storms had bypassed the ranges and we arrived after a

long winter of cloudless skies. There was a strong likelihood that most, if not all, waterholes would be dry.

Nevertheless, we made a pact to give it a go on the
grounds that this was no ordinary walk but a kind of
pilgrimage. We had journeyed halfway across the continent from our exile in Sydney to walk in these gorges. It
was also a time for making pacts. Twenty-four hours
earlier Dale and I had exchanged wedding vows at the
altar of the same Adelaide Hills church where I was
baptised. It may have been a coincidence but throughout
the ceremony the iron roof over our heads echoed to the
sound of hailstones clattering out of the heavens. Everywhere we went, it seemed, the elements were in uproar.

The decision to celebrate the first days of marriage in the
Gammons seemed preordained. Over the years our lives
had followed paths which at different times had intersected, diverged and run parallel. The constant that
finally brought us together was a passion for the Flinders.
Our common ground was an amalgam of landscapes and
memories. All those frosty nights around smoky, resinous
campfires, the mornings spent wandering boulder-strewn
creek beds with corellas screeching from the treetops, and
countless days on the sheer ramparts of Wilpena, climbing orange walls under panes of blue sky, hanging on for
dear life.

The Gammons had become part of these heartlands.
The terrain I had encountered on previous walks grabbed
my imagination. Fortified by outlying peaks and perimeter ranges the core of this wilderness is a baffling,
defiant expanse of plateaus, craggy summits and deep
chasms. The acute inaccessibility of this place and the
extravagance of its landforms lend the Gammons a mys-
tique unlike anything else I had experienced in the Flinders. I wanted to see more and it seemed fitting to share it
with my now even more significant other.

By daybreak the ranges were still once more. We woke

feeling dazed and drowsy, though not for the usual honeymoon reasons. Opening the tent flap revealed a gorge transformed. The dusty walls now glistened with water tumbling down from the high ridges. We sat by a stream burbling over the rocks of Italowie Creek, the same rocks that the day before had been flint-dry underfoot. While the billy boiled on the stove, breezes shook the branches of the pines and rivergums that arched over our camp. Water droplets sprayed brightly down through the morning light, landing with a hiss on the billy lid. We then raised our mugs of tea and toasted the weather gods for their wedding gift.

Upstream towards Junction Waterhole the creek narrowed. Stormwater continued to pour off the slopes all around us, falling in iridescent sheets across exposed slabs and cascading down steep gullies. Gurgling sounds filled the gorge. The normally bleached vegetation was now vivid with saturated colour. Upright trunks of callitris pines stood jet black with robes of glossy green needles. Eucalypt bark shone in hues of olive and amber. Even the yaccas and spinifex bushes looked damp and lush.

We soaked up the sights. By midday we reached the junction, a convergence of creeks marked by flat benches of stone. The main waterhole was overflowing as the waters continued to surge down from the plateau high above us. A brisk southerly had stripped the sky of any lingering cloud and the cliffs and jagged spires around the junction shone in the clear air. Without the burden of our rucksacks we investigated nearby ridges and ravines, scrambling over the warm rocks feeling a lightness of heart and head. At dusk we pitched our tent at the foot of a mountain. It seemed too good to be true, but according to the map the name of this summit was Mr Changeweather.

That night sleep came swiftly. But then in the early hours of the morning we both woke suddenly to what sounded like an avalanche or distant explosion. There was a rumbling echo, then silence. "What was that!?" asked

Dale. I looked out the tent but the sky was clear and the gorge stood still in the light of a full moon. "I don't know, there aren't any thunderclouds, perhaps it was a falling branch or a rock slide," I said. I crawled back into my sleeping bag. As I dozed off a whimsical voice whispered in my ear, "Did the earth move for you too dear?"

The Gammon Ranges are infamous for strange, unnerving sounds. According to the Adnyamathanha people, the traditional custodians of this area, the ranges are the home of the serpent Akurra. Legend has it that Akurra descended from Yackie Waterhole to drink from the salt lakes west of the ranges. Having drained the lakes the bloated serpent crawled slowly back into the high country and in doing so created the gorge along Arkaroola Creek. At resting places along the way he formed springs and waterholes before finally returning to Yackie. The great Akurra still sleeps at the waterhole and his noisy stomach continues to sends strange tremors throughout the Gammons.

There are other, more prosaic, explanations for the rumblings in the ranges, including the possibility of seismic activity and the theory that chunks of rock must eventually part company with the gorge walls. Indeed on our walk we came across evidence of freshly fallen blocks. But, notwithstanding the science of the matter, our route the next day took us close to Akurra territory. Just to be on the safe side I suggested to Dale that we tread softly. "No point in waking the big snake," I explained.

The jumbled boulders of Streak Gorge led us to a saddle on the rim of the main plateau. At these elevations there is an abrupt change in vegetation. Crowded stands of acacias and mallee eucalypts pose a challenge to even the most enterprising bushwalkers. We made a short diversion through the scrub to the rounded summit of Four Winds Hill. From this vantage point the spectacle of the surrounding terrain was laid bare. An expanse of

undulating plateau extended to the south-west. To the
north lay Mainwater Pound and the distant tops of the
Blue Range. But dominating the view were the prodigious
ravines that dissect the eastern flank of the ranges.

In other parts of the Flinders Ranges the sandstone
strata are usually tilted at rakish angles, which give the
ridges their striking ripsaw appearance. But in the heart of
the Gammons the Pound quartzite has remained horizontal to form a lofty plateau. Sitting atop this formation
we gazed down into the shadowy depths of the gorges.
There the sediments of ancient seabeds were revealed in
an immensity of stone. Never had geology seemed quite so
romantic. Throwing caution to the four winds I kissed the
woman next to me.

It was C. Warren Bonython, one of the most ardent
explorers of the region, who named this summit during
his pioneering crossings of the plateau in the late 1940s.
For him it is a pivotal point in the Gammons because it
marks the place where three major drainage basins meet.
Being a dedicated man of science, Warren's accounts of
the area bristle with learned observations but they also
reflect a personal mythology of place not unlike that of the
Adnyamathanha people: "The rounded summits swell
upward, the spurs sprawl outward like the limbs of some
great monster, and the sides break away in raw red rock
which, with its sparse growth of shaggy scrub, contributes
a menacing air to the scene."

Descending back to the saddle it seemed hard to believe
that it took until 1982 for this remarkable landscape –
which forms the great bulk of the Gammons – to be
included in the national park. For nearly 20 years Warren
Bonython had lobbied to make this a reality. The eventual
purchase of Balcanoona Station by the government in
1979 was a start but subsequent delays in dedicating this
acquisition led to disquiet about the future of the area.
Matters came to a head in 1981, culminating in a lively

meeting of conservationists and bushwalkers at which the minister responsible finally gave a commitment that the dedication would proceed.

The campaign to conserve the Gammons may have lacked the histrionics of the Franklin Dam fight but the views expressed were no less deeply held. People who had spent years quietly delving into the intrigues of the ranges voiced their concerns. The vigour of this public sentiment was a sign that the Gammons, for all its undoubted academic interest and rare scenic value, is ultimately a place of the heart, a place that stirs the passions – and not just of honeymooners.

After a night camped on the edge of the plateau we descended into The Terraces. This succession of rock pools and waterfalls was awash. Water cascaded over the stone tiers like champagne spilling down a pyramid of glasses. We abandoned any attempt to stay dry and went with the flow, climbing down the rock steps. Wind funnelling up the gorge flicked spray from the falls up into our faces as we clung precariously to small ledges, our fingers and toes parting the effervescing curtains of water.

In these secluded realms there are no tracks or landmarks, only the serpentine watercourse. And yet the confines of the gorge walls are strangely liberating. Our sense of time passing was suspended and we lost ourselves in the intimate obscurity of the natural world, marvelling at the weather-hewn stone shapes and the enterprise of trees and shrubs clinging to the steep walls.

On a sunny ledge below Fern Chasm we found an echidna curled in a ball, mimicking a clump of triodia. Further along a startled pair of yellow-footed rock wallabies leapt across our path and bounded effortlessly into a cave on a buttress high above. The gorges may be the ideal habitat for a variety of creatures but suitable accommodation for newlyweds was hard to find. Eventually we settled on a small rock platform, an island in the stream.

By first light the water level had subsided almost

completely. Only a thin ribbon of water trickled past our tent. The pre-dawn air was cold and even the slightest breeze had a numbing effect. Dale sensibly remained ensconced in her sleeping bag while I sat hunkered over the stove, watching the high rim of the gorge and willing the sun to hurry into our camp.

When I saw silhouettes moving on the skyline, I thought my shivering must have been affecting my eyesight. But the shapes kept moving and eerie, almost childlike, complaints echoed across the gorge. "Have we got company?" asked a sleepy voice from the tent. "Yes, a wanton herd of horned and bearded ruminants," I replied sonorously. "Ah," said Dale emerging, "the things you see when you haven't got your gun."

Goats are the scourge of the Flinders Ranges and despite ongoing efforts to control their numbers they continue to ravage the landscape. It was a melancholy realisation that the recent rains would be a boon to their population. Sadly, even a wilderness as sublime and seemingly unassailable as the Gammons requires more than national park status. Its survival depends on sympathetic intervention.

We continued our descent from the ranges with freshening breezes whistling up the gorge. Dale went ahead while I paused to take photos. It was a relief to be moving in the warmth of the sun at last, rock-hopping down the cobbled creek boulders. The creek bed was now dry but the waterholes were still brimful.

I arrived at a deep pool to find a pile of cast-off clothing and my bride disporting herself in the cool, dark water. Nothing from Dale's broad vocabulary of encouragement or humiliation could induce me to join her. "Think of the windchill factor," I said, edging past the pool. "I'll just scout on ahead a bit." I stole away, thinking I'd gotten off lightly. Then from the chill waters came a shout "Bearded ruminant!"

*   *   *

Later that day I managed to salvage some self-esteem by navigating a course over the ridge to Wildflower Creek. Dale's estimation of our whereabouts had proved to be somewhat awry. But keeping score seemed pointless given the views of Cleft Peak that confronted us, looming fearsome and craggy over the creek. And so the afternoon passed, at times following in one another's footsteps, at other times striking out alone.

On our final night we camped near Grindels Hut with a view back to the ramparts of Mt John Roberts and the shadowy profile of the plateau beyond. I retrieved a bottle of champagne we had cached in a water tank near the hut. Under the light of early evening the surrounding hills were dark ochre, tinged with green swathes of new grass. It looked like the promised land. Sipping champagne from enamel mugs we celebrated our return to the Flinders and being reunited with our younger selves. We celebrated breaking new ground, together. When the moon finally rose it was round and full and the colour of honey.

AMERICAN HORSEMAN

A.F. Tschiffeley

Tschiffeley was a Swiss adventurer who rode from Argentina to Washington in the 1930s. His journey took two and half years, and he finished on the same two ponies he started with – Mancha and Gato, Argentine Criollos which had formely belonged to a Patagonian Indian chief, "I-have-feathers".

In one of the small coastal towns a Spaniard introduced himself to me. He looked a pleasant sort of fellow, and told me he had lived quite a number of years in the Argentine. In the evening we chatted for some time, and during the course of conversation he said that no man's education was complete unless he had seen one of the low "dance-halls" that exist in some of the small towns along the Peruvian coast, and when I expressed my willingness to see and learn he offered to act as guide. Soon we were on our way towards the place that was situated about a mile out of the little town. The dance-hall was merely a large adobe hut, and the interior was lit by two oil lamps. Along the walls were rough benches on which some dirty, ragged and bare-footed men sat, whilst others were standing in front of a counter made of old packing-cases where alcohol was being despatched. The boss of the place was a fat and greasy mestizo woman with strands of black hair hanging over her face, hair that was coarse and wiry like a horse's mane. Several equally repulsive females were acting as "dancing-partners" to any man who wished to pay ten cents for the pleasure of having one of them. I have seen some villainous faces in some of the "western hair-raisers", but since I have been in that dance-hall it is obvious to me that the producers of these films have not been "educated", as my Spanish guide would say. The type of villian we usually see in the "movies" are mere cherubims compared to the men I saw that night. The majority were mestizos, or what I would like to call "criss-cross breeds" between Indian, Spanish, Chinese and negro blood. One specimen was black, pock-marked, had Chinese slit eyes, and curly hair with a red tint!

Somehow our presence did not seem to please, and particularly one fellow kept casting nasty glances towards us, glances that said more than words could have done. When my companion became aware of it he took offence, and soon the inevitable happened; both jumping at each other like tigers. Some intervened and the two were separated, and then somebody suggested going outside to fight it out. The Spaniard took off his coat and handed it to me, and when we were outside the two started at each other. Owing to the darkness it was impossible to see what was happening, but after some quick shuffling, wrestling, fierce growling and many terrible oaths there was a piercing shriek, and then all was silence, a silence that was only broken by the heavy breathing of the two exhausted fighters. Presently I heard moans, and then somebody struck a match. The Spaniard was standing over his opponent who was on the ground, and upon striking another match we noticed that the man who lay writhing on the ground had been stabbed in two places.

Only now did I begin to realize the seriousness of my situation, for here was I all alone with the Spaniard, who after all was only a chance acquaintance, and the others were many, and for all I knew they might try to avenge their badly-wounded friend, who was now moaning and rolling over on the ground. Whenever I was in a town or in a more or less decent village I never carried my fire-arms, for they were heavy, and the sight of them might offend people. On this occasion I had come out unarmed, and fearing the worst I thought I would try to get out of this ticklish situation by bluffing. I jumped on a low adobe wall that fenced off a field and shouted that if anybody moved I would shoot. Obviously somebody had long ago advised the police that there was trouble, for soon several terribly excited "vigilantes" arrived on the scene, waving their arms, rifles and swords like actors in a stage version of the storming of the Bastille. One who had come with a lantern led the procession back towards the town, a few helping to carry the wounded man, who was evidently in a serious condition. Once at the police station the "jefe" (chief) and a doctor were called, and everybody, except the Spaniard and myself were thrown into the filthy "calabozo". The jefe's language was most apolo-getic for what had happened to me, and the Spaniard, being a good friend of his, was told to embark on a sailing vessel that was to leave the little port next morning, for in case the wounded man should die it would be just as well if the guilty party could officially be announced as having escaped. When I saw the last of that little town, I pro-mised myself never again to visit a "dance-hall" in Peru, and I did not find it difficult to keep that promise!

Still following the hot, sandy coast, we came to a large sugar plantation, not far from which stands a fortress that was built by the ancient Chimu Indians. It is a colossal piece of work, entirely made of adobe and built in high terraces that appear like a square hill from the distance. Near the main fortress are high walls, and the way every-thing was built leaves no doubt that these ancients had a certain scientific knowledge of warfare. Some of the paint with which the walls were coloured still remains, neither weather nor centuries having been able to make it fade or to destroy it. The colours that exist are red, black and yellow, the same as are found on pottery that dates back to the Chimu period.

The fortress of Paramonga consists of two main strongholds. One of these is situated on a hill, the waves of the Pacific Ocean beating against its inaccessible cliffs which face west. The eastern side of that hill has a steep and sandy slope where numerous mummies, wrapped in coloured cloths, were buried and have now become uncovered by the shifting and sliding sands. The main fortress is roughly half a mile east from there, and the two were probably separated by a swamp in former times, but today the low flat stretch of land between the two is dry, and sugar-cane is successfully cultivated by a Japanese settler who entertained me splendidly when I happened to call at his place during my rambles among the ruins. Although subterranean passages and burial places exist here, the natives are afraid to explore them, for many strange tales and superstitions have been handed down from one generation to another. As I had not time enough, I could not do more than have a general look over these interesting relics of the past.

From Paramonga north there is a vast desert, close on a hundred miles from one river to the next, and as there is no water to be found there I was obliged to make the crossing in one journey. For this reason I had to wait for the full moon before I could, with a certain degree of safety, attempt this long ride.

There was an outbreak of bubonic plague whilst I was there, and quite a number of plantation workers died, whilst many more were ill. The authorities raided their filthy quarters, and it was a pathetic sight to see their owners howling and wailing as they walked behind their filthy belongings which were being carted out to be burnt, together with some ancient mummies that had been discovered near there in an old burial ground. I took every precaution against the horrible disease and was particularly careful never to lie down to rest unless I had previously sprinkled my bed with insect powder, for fleas and similar pests transmit the germs of bubonic plague. It was uncomfortable to have to remain in this place with the danger of catching the plague, but I was between the devil and the deep blue sea; for before attempting to cross the desert ahead of us I had to be careful to make my plans, and as I intended to start in the evening it was necessary to wait until the moon was at its brightest. I had heard many terrible stories about this sandy wilderness, its very name, "Matacaballo" (Horse-killer), gave me food for reflection.

After four days' waiting I was ready to start, and as I did not intend to carry water for the horses, I was careful not to give them anything to drink the day before we left, for I wanted them to be thirsty and therefore not likely to refuse a good drink immediately before starting out. For myself I packed two bottles of lemon juice in the saddlebags, and the only food I took with me were a few pieces of chocolate that had been in my pack for some days. Towards evening we were ready, and when the sun was setting we crossed the river, on the other side of which the rolling desert starts. I waited until the horses had finished their drink, and after they had pawed and played with the cool water I mounted, and soon we were on the soft and still hot sands that made a peculiar hissing sound under the hoofs of the animals. The indescribable colours of a tropical sunset were reflected on the glittering waves of the ocean, and the old Indian fortress assumed a tint of gold. Even the inhospitable sandy wastes had changed their dread and desolate appearance, for now the sand dunes and undulations were one mass of colour, from golden brown to dark purple, according to light and shadows. A few belated sea-birds were hurriedly flying towards their distant roosting-places on some rocky island; everything seemed to be different now, except the regular, eternal rolling of the breakers on the shore. No sooner had the last clouds ceased to glow like fading beacon fires than darkness set in, and after a while the moon rose over the mountain ranges in the far east, slowly, majestically; and more than welcome to me.

The sensation of riding on soft sand is a peculiar one at first, until the body becomes used to the peculiar springless motion of the horse. Knowing that such conditions mean a great strain on the animal I could not help moving in the saddle, uselessly endeavouring to assist my mount. We were twisting and winding our way through among high sand dunes and, whenever it was possible, I guided the animals down to the wet sand on the beach where I would urge them into a slow gallop. Often we came to rocky places or to land-points which stretched far out, and thus I was forced to make a detour inland again, frequently for considerable distances. For the first few hours I observed everything around me and admired the brilliance of the moon that made the ocean glitter like silver, and gave the often strange sand formations a ghostly appearance. Soon even all this became monotonous to me, and every time I stopped to rest the horses for a while or to adjust the saddles, I lit a cigarette to help pass the time away. Shortly before dawn I had to halt for quite a long time, for the moon had gone down behind some clouds and we were left in darkness; it would not have been wise to continue lest I should take the wrong direction or lead the horses into places where the sand is so soft that they would sink in up to their bellies.

My instinct for finding the direction had developed to a notable degree by this time, probably because I had not very much to think about besides keeping the horses' noses facing the right way, but even when I knew exactly which way to go, fogs or darkness on several occasions made me think it wiser to wait until I could see.

The first rays of the morning sun were hot, and I rightly anticipated that the day was going to be a "scorcher". The horses plodded along as if they realized that they were in the midst of a serious test, and when it was about one hour after noon I noticed that they lifted their heads and sniffed the air. Immediately after they hurried their steps, and I believe they would have broken into a gallop if I had permitted them to do so. I was wondering why the horses were so keen to hurry along, and within an hour I knew the reason, for we arrived at the river, and I am certain that the animals had scented water long before I could see it; obviously Mancha and Gato still possessed the instincts of the wild horse.

Great were my feelings of relief when we left the Matacaballo desert behind us and, in spite of my already high opinion of the horses' resistance, I admired the splendid behaviour they had shown during so long and trying a journey – a journey that would have killed most horses unaccustomed to such conditions. After I had unsaddled them they had a good drink, and then I gave them a much-needed bath. When this had been done I turned them loose in a small field with good grass, and after both had rolled, stretched and shaken themselves, they started to eat, and anybody might have believed they had only just returned from a short canter. I only realized how tired and played out I was when I sat down on my saddles whilst a woman in a hut prepared some food for me, and I thought I had only dozed off to sleep for a few moments when I awoke in the evening. The good woman, knowing that I needed sleep more than food, had kept my meal warm for me, and once I had the first taste of it I did not stop until the last grain of rice and the last bean had disappeared. It had taken us exactly twenty hours to cross the desert, and I have no desire ever to make another such ride.

All the coastal villages are much alike, equally depressing, hot and miserable. A few houses and huts, a couple of uneven and sandy roads, sometimes a tumbledown adobe church, hens and pigs roaming about in search of refuse that is simply thrown out of the houses into the street, and on the roofs a few mournful-looking "gallinazos" (buzzards) waiting to pick up bits of filth at which other animals refuse even to look. At the doors of some houses, and particularly in front of the "palacio municipal", a primitive construction that is no better than the rest of the dilapidated houses, men can be seen loitering all day and, although they never seem to work, they always appear to have money enough to buy alcohol, and once they are stimulated by its temporarily elevating effects they talk in such sums of money that even the most powerful Wall Street magnates would prick up their ears. Rich mines, large estates, social reform, are discussed and debated, and once the bottle is empty and the men full, they again fall into silence or shuffle home, happy and satisfied after a good day's work.

Malaria is very common in some of the regions along the rivers, and Indians who come from the mountains to work in the cotton and sugar plantations invariably fall victims to this tropical fever. Once the effects of malaria have rendered them unfit for work, the landowners simply dismiss them, the existing law that is supposed to protect the unfortunate semi-slaves against this crime hardly ever being observed.

Whilst I was riding along in company of a native who was on his way to another village, we had a most unpleasant experience with a snake. On a sandy plain we had dismounted to have a short rest, when suddenly the man shouted to me in a very excited manner. A small snake had crawled under his mule, probably in order to take advantage of the only shady spot within miles. The frightened man said that this was a particularly venomous reptile, and that its bite would without doubt kill his mule. We tried to tease the snake away by throwing pebbles at it, and fortunately the mule was very tame and did not move. However, instead of coming away from under the beast, the snake tried to climb up one of its legs, and I held my breath, expecting the mule to move or stamp, but somehow it did not seem to feel anything. We were lucky to be able to attract the snake away at last, and I immediately killed it with a leather strap I had ready for that purpose.

I had sometimes hired guides to take me through bad and tricky parts, but most of these men were so useless, lazy and impertinent that I much preferred to travel alone, and leave the rest to chance.

We had crossed another long and weary stretch of sandy desolation in which walls and other remains of the old Indians could be seen, and when we arrived at the river it was already dark. I knew that a village was not far from the opposite banks of the river, and as I had eaten nothing all day. I was keen on crossing in spite of the prevailing darkness. I rode along the bank until I thought I had found a suitable place to cross, and there I made the horses wade out. I had not expected to find such a strong current and began to wonder if it would not be wiser to turn back, and just then the horse I was riding was swept off its feet. Very foolishly I still had the pack-animals tied to the wide girth of my mount, the usual manner in which lead-horses are taken along the pampas. Before I had time to think, the three of us were swept down-stream, and it was due more to luck than to ability that we landed safely back on the shore from which we had started. Besides having had a longer drink than I had bargained for, I rightly suspected in what a mess I would find the contents of my saddlebags next day. I had no desire to make a second attempt to cross the river that night, so I resigned myself to fate and prepared to wait for daylight. I let the horses look after themselves among the coarse grass near the river, whilst I went to spread my soaked blankets at the foot of a sandy hill close by, for there it would not be damp, and the sand was still comfortably warm after the day's terrific heat. In spite of my raving appetite and my wringing wet clothes I was soon fast asleep, but during the night I was several times awakened by a strange noise that sounded like the beating of drums, or as if a motor launch were travelling on the river. As I could see nothing I continued to sleep, and only awoke when the sunrays were beginning to be hot. When I looked about, I found that I had slept near a "gentilar" as the ancient Indian burial-grounds are called. There are many of these along the Peruvian coast and, after seeing a few, one takes hardly any more notice of all the skulls and bones that lie about on the sand, which has shifted with the passing centuries. The horses must have had a good feed, for they were waiting for me, and when all was ready we crossed the river without much diffculty, and when we arrived in the village I fully made up for arrears in the food line.

While conversing with some people I told them about my nasty experience in the river the night before, and when they heard where I had slept all wanted to know if I had heard the "manchang". This word sounding rather like Chinese to me I asked them what it meant, whereupon they all started to explain in chorus that the sandhill where I had slept was haunted, and that the dead Indians of the "gentilar" danced every night to the beating of drums. So many terrible superstitious stories did they tell me about the "manchang" that I began to think I was lucky to be still alive. Later I had occasion to speak to an educated gentleman who had come to visit me, and he said that both Baron von Humboldt and Raimondi had once upon a time investigated the strange phenomenon of that hill, and that they had expressed the opinion that the peculiar sounds that are frequently heard during the night were due to underground waters which moved as the temperature changed. Another theory that has been brought forward is that when the sea breezes blow from a certain direction and the air hits the sandy ripples on the slopes of the hill, it will produce this strange sound. Somehow both explanations appealed to me as being sensible, but I feel inclined to think that the former is more likely to be correct.

After all these trying journeys I rested for two days, for there was plenty of grass for the horses, and I, for a change was able to even enjoy a few decent meals again.

One evening I thought I would pass a couple of hours away by going to see some moving pictures which were announced for that night. The "teatro" was merely a large shed with a tin roof, and the films shown were old and worn out, but yet the audience seemed delighted with the show. All of a sudden everybody made a rush for the door; there were a few shrieks from women, and the whole place shook. Before I had even time to think what was happening the place was empty, only myself and two women who had fainted remaining there. Even then I could not make out what had happened, but when I went outside I was told that there had been an earthquake. I had been under the impression that the trampling and rushing crowd had shaken up the place. Luckily nobody was hurt in that stampede for the open, but a few had sustained minor bruises and knocks and the rest had come out of it with only a good fright. No one seeming keen on going back, the management announced the show as having terminated; much to my surprise nobody protested or asked for "money back".

Earthquakes are very common occurrences along the Peruvian coast, but as the houses and huts are so lightly built, and the roofs being merely light covers to protect against the fierce sun, it is rarely that much harm is done. As I have mentioned before, rains are practically unknown in these regions, and so the houses are simply covered with bamboo canes, mud and straw.

Fording some of the wide and usually slow-flowing rivers was not without its dangers, treacherous quicksands lurking where one least expects to find them. If anybody happened to live near a river I had to ford, I always offered a good reward if he were willing to show me the best place where to cross, but often I had to try my luck alone.

One evening, after a long day's riding, I came to a solitary hut near the mouth of a river where a fisherman and his family lived. I was very hungry and thirsty, and looked forward to a change of diet, for I had lived on sardines and biscuits for some days. Two children were playing in the sand outside the hut, and as it was always my policy to make friends with the youngsters in order more easily to approach the parents, I thought I would do the same here, and so gave them my last biscuits and the remaining tin of sardines. I thought this was a good investment and a safe gamble to get something more agreeable to my taste from the grateful parents later on, but to my bitter disappointment I was told that they had run out of supplies and that there would be nothing to eat until next morning when the man was going out fishing. I was given some hot water with which I brewed myself some tea, and even this I had to drink without sugar, my supply having come to grief whilst crossing a river. The next journey being a long one I had to start early, and so I had to do another day's hard riding on an empty stomach, and it can easily be imagined how I blessed those children and how pleased I was with myself for having given them that tin of sardines and the biscuits.

After a few hours we came to a river that had a very bad reputation for quicksands, and so I rode up-stream until I came to a hut where another fisherman lived. He was willing to help me across. He had a pony which, he told me, served to drag his net through the shallow water along the beach. Mounted on this animal he came to show me the way, but he only did this after having received five *soles* (Peruvian standard currency) in advance for his services. We had nearly reached the other side of the shallow but wide river when suddenly his pony's hindlegs sank into the sand. Knowing what this meant, I hurried my horses along, made a semi-circle around my guide, and was fortunate enough to reach the dry shore. Without losing a moment I untied the lasso I always had handy, and then cautiously waded back to where the man was still sitting on his animal, which was sinking deeper and deeper. As soon as I had thrown him the lasso he put it around the pony's neck; then he jumped off and came towards me, all the time holding on to the lasso in case he also should sink in. Whenever a horse sinks into a quicksand hindlegs first, it is of no use to try to pull him out from in front, but to save him one has to pull in such a manner as to make him fall on his side. This frees his hindlegs and gives him buoyancy, and then one can usually rescue him. Should the animal be left alone he will gradually sink in and finally drown, and the more he struggles and fights the quicker will he sink. Working like Trojans we finally rescued the guide's pony, and in case the same thing should happen to him again I waited until he had safely reached the home shore.

IN CHIEF YALI'S SHOES

Tim Cahill

Tim Cahill is an editor-at-large for Outside, *and the author of seven books including the collections of travel-writing* Jaguars Ripped My Flesh, A Wolverine is Eating My Leg, Pecked to Death by Ducks *and* Pass the Butterworms.

"Wabintok Mabel," Chief Yali Mabel whispered, by way of reverent introduction.

He held a lit candle under Wabintok's black and desiccated face. Flickering yellow light illuminated the mouth, which was open wide in a soundless, twisted scream. It was, I understood, a privilege to view Wabintok here, in the sanctity of the men's hut.

"*Wah,*" I said. The Dani expression is, in my opinion, the finest word for "thank you" in the human vocabulary.

"*Wah,*" Chief Yali replied politely.

"*Wah,*" a number of the other men said.

The small circular wooden hut smelled of straw, of countless fires, of singed pig fat. Wabintok himself smelled of smoke, and, yes, singed fat. He was, by some village estimates, four hundred years old. I'd never slept in the same hut with a smoked mummy before.

Chief Yali spoke with some awe about Wabintok, who was his ancestor and a great hero of the Mabel family. "*Bintok*," Yali explained, is the Dani word for bamboo knife. Wabintok means "Thank you, Bamboo Knife." Chief Yali's ancestor had been a great warrior, a master of the bamboo knife, in the time of ritual war, before the first outsiders came to the valley of the Dani four generations ago.

The valley, the Grand Baliem Valley, is located in the highlands of New Guinea, specifically in the Indonesian western half of the island, called Irian Jaya. The valley is a mile high, almost fifty miles long, and is home to an estimated one hundred thousand Dani people, short sturdy Papuans who, according to one guidebook "are just now emerging from the Stone Age."

I suppose that's so. Dani women wear grass skirts. The men often wear nasal ornaments made of bone. They sometimes wear feathered headdresses and paint their bodies with special-colored clay. The Dani men are phallocrypts, which means that aside from feathers and bones, they wear penis sheaths. And nothing else.

In the men's hut, where Chief Yali invited me to spend the night, the Mabel family men all said that the time of ritual war was past. It was forbidden by the government, illegal. And yet, Yali, a handsome, powerful man who looked to be in his late thirties, sported at least five small circular scars.

If there was no war, I asked in a roundabout manner, who had fired all those arrows into Yali's chest and back? Well, it seemed that while there was no war, there were battles now and again.

And so I spent the night around a smoky fire, gnawing the charred remnants of what had been a piglet a few hours before. We laughed and sang and pounded on logs and talked of glorious battles. We pledged a kind of brotherhood and spoke of the spirit each man feels in his belly and in his heart.

It seemed to me that Yali could make a hell of a living in America leading "wild man" weekends. He made me promise that I'd come back and visit him, with at least one of my wives.

Just last month, I mailed Yali a present he had desperately wanted and I had solemnly promised to send him. Certain culturally aware friends thought the gift insensitive. Such goods would "spoil" the naked Dani. Well, a promise is a promise, a brother is a brother, and screw the culturally aware. I like to think of the chief in his feathered headdress, his body paint, and his penis gourd: Yali Mabel, standing proud, wearing his new leather Redwing boots. I know what Yali said when he got the package. He said, *"Wah!"*

KAMPALA HALT

Christopher Portway

Christopher Portway was born in England in 1923, is a member of the British Guild of Travel Writers and a Fellow of the Royal Geographical Society. His many books include The World Commuter: Great Journeys by Train.

I had some hours to kill at Nakuru, so spent them exploring this quite large and prosperous town. Its railway station was the smartest in East Africa, I was told, and certainly its locomotive sheds held offerings that deflected my morbid thoughts from the gathering crisis up the line. I had arrived at this paragon of stations at 3.30 a.m., having spent a night on the tiles. However, my Uganda Mail, when it drew in soon after 3.00 p.m., was resplendent with sleepers, one of which was mine. The very fact that the train had not been cancelled or seemingly curtailed and showed every sign of an intention of going through to Kampala cheered me up no end.

Nakuru vanished and, out of the window, I caught more glimpses of the Rift Valley, only now it was becoming more fertile as the red soil deepened and lush foliage folded round the line.

Eldoret, they will tell you, is where the bank was built

around its safe. Again, it was the railway that made the town, though it was through an accident that the big safe fell from a wagon; found to be too heavy to move, a building was constructed over it and things grew from there. Unfazed by its unscheduled beginnings, Eldoret flourishes as a busy market town, the last sizeable community before Uganda.

I had several companions in the compartment who drew me into animated conversation and pressed me to edible delicacies from an assortment of newspaper packages. One of the men was a Ugandan law student from Nairobi University who was returning to Kampala to see his parents. He thought he could stay a couple of days and make it back to Kenya before the border finally closed. This, likewise, cheered me up some more since my plans were to remain in the Ugandan capital just for one day. The train schedules offered a nine-hour stay, which I felt was adequate for a brief glimpse of the city. The coach in which we were travelling was composed of compartments making up into four beds at night.

It was nothing less than pure bloody-mindedness that kept the train standing at the border station of Malaba for all of five hours that night. Neither the law student nor myself were able to sleep with the rumours and counter-rumours that were circulating as money-changers and Kenyan border police stamped up and down the corridor. Cold daybreak saw us stomping impatiently alongside the stranded train, so that when the Ugandan authorities finally gave us the green light to let the train go we almost missed it, and in retrospect I rather wished we had. Rolling across a wide brook I glimpsed a notice reading "You are entering the Republic of Uganda" which evoked in me a similar sense of foreboding to that of crossing the one-time East-West German border into the totalitarian Communist East.

Ten minutes later we drew into Tororo, on the Ugandan side of the border, and the train filled up again. An immigration official examined my passport, acidly pointing out that I had no need of the visa I had prudently obtained from the Ugandan High Commission in London.

"This is a free and democratic country," he added. "We welcome British visitors wholeheartedly." He stamped the passport and afforded me two days on Ugandan soil, though I only wanted one.

The train did its best to make up for lost time but, with numerous scheduled halts en route, it was a forlorn hope that I would get more than a fraction of my nine hours in Kampala. Every station was a hive of activity, the colourful crowds having little to do with the train's arrival, but grouping there simply because the station represented the local community centre; the place where the action was, and where they would be most likely to sell their goods. Even though I possessed no Ugandan currency, I nevertheless became the recipient of a bunch of thirty bananas on account of the fact, it was explained, that I looked hungry.

As we crossed the Nile over the great bridge at Jinja – Uganda's Sheffield – I sensed an air of crisis at its station. The crowds were less exuberant here and uniformed police more in evidence; indeed even while the train stood at the platform I watched two of them arresting a man.

This region of Uganda is a green and pleasant land, well watered and fertile. Exotic blossoms and bloated leaves pressed against the track and my student friend treated me to a running commentary on their botanical details.

It was raining when we reached Kampala and the grey clouds did nothing to enhance a city of nearly empty dual carriageways, tall buildings in need of renovation and beautiful colonial homes run to seed. I estimated that my planned nine-hour sojourn had been cut to four, which worried me not at all. My friend escorted me up the stairs to the station concourse.

An officious-looking man in civilian clothes stood behind a desk close to the ticket barrier surveying the happy jostling crowd with distaste. His gaze fell on me.

"You. Here!" he bawled.

"You talking to me?" I asked with equal hostility.

The man demanded my passport and that of the student. To me he barked, "Why have you and your friend come here?" as he thumbed through the pages. I sensed the start of something more ominous than mere immigration control, and noticed too the unease of my companion.

"I've come to spend a few hours in Kampala," I explained, adding hurriedly that I had met the student on the train and that we were not together. The student gabbled his own reasons for his visit.

"Wait here." The man moved away, taking our passports. We watched him arrogantly pushing through the crowd, knocking a woman almost to the ground as he went.

He returned a while later to take us to a bare office where a colleague sat, smiling sardonically, at a table. We were not invited to sit down. The second man started to question me.

"Why have you come to Uganda? What is the purpose of your visit?"

I answered his questions as best I could, expressing my interest in the East African Railway network though aware that my reason sounded inadequate, even provocative to an African unappreciative of his railway. The student was steadfastly ignored though, out of the corner of my eye, I caught his unease growing into stark terror. He was sweating profusely, plainly aware of what these evil men had in mind.

"What is your connection with this man?" came the question I was half expecting.

I repeated the fact that we were no more than travelling companions and that once out of the station we would be going our different ways. Neither of our questioners seemed to believe this, and a few moments later the two of us were taken outside and pushed into the back of an antiquated black saloon car. As we were driven through the town the rain fell in buckets and I almost managed to convince myself that, in the circumstances, this was the best way of seeing Kampala.

Seldom have I witnessed a more depressing city. The shops were no more than eye-sockets in a face of empty streets where policemen hung around the intersections. Halfway up a hill the car engine began to cough and the driver to moan loudly about the shortage of fuel coupons even for official vehicles. I now understood the reason for a deficiency of traffic. When the engine finally expired we all had to abandon its dry interior and push the thing all the way to the Kampala Police Headquarters. In minutes we were wet through.

Inside the blank-faced building a stench of stale sweat, rancid tobacco and an unidentifiable sweet odour permeated the bare-walled corridors. Handcuffed prisoners, wild-eyed and perspiring, passed by in the charge of young policemen. The student's face had gone deathly pale and I guessed he knew more about Ugandan security police methods than I did.

In an office almost as bare as the corridors we found ourselves before another inquisitor, this one likewise in plain clothes. The furnishings were a cheap desk, a couple of hard-backed chairs, a filing cabinet, a telephone and, on the wall, a lop-sided photograph (unframed) of Idi Amin. Previous interrogation scenarios of which I had been witness went through my mind. Such sparse furnishings fitted the Gestapo, the Czech STB and the Soviet KGB, though nobody in Nazi and post-war Communist days would dream of displaying a lop-sided Fuhrer or an unframed Stalin.

Ugandan interrogation style differed too. Not particularly unpleasantly did the new man sitting opposite me repeat the same questions, though adding a new emphasis. It wasn't so much why had I come to his country, but why for so brief a period? To this I gave him the double reason; this being that my passport had been endorsed by the Ugandan authorities at the border for only two days, though one would suffice since my chief interest lay with the railway. He also wanted to know why I was in a carriage with a Ugandan exile returning to his country (when everyone else was leaving), and why we had exchanged addresses (the "incriminating" scraps of paper had been found when my wallet and pockets had been searched). This had been the student's request and a very harmless one but, abruptly, I was aware how small incidences could be blown up into a balloon of guilt and suspicion. Then came the next hurdle.

"How is it your passport indicates you are a company director and this card pronounces you a journalist?" (At that time British passports had to show the bearer's profession).

To explain that I was once a company director and had retained the title in my passport in preference to the sometimes provocative "journalist" would only complicate matters, even though here was an example of just such provocation. So I offered the white lie that I was still a company director and that I was a journalist, though only a travel journalist, in my spare time.

To two fresh interrogators in another room I repeated these explanations, which sounded even less plausible each time I uttered them, but I stuck to it. And you know, there comes a moment when you actually begin to believe that you *are* a spy or whatever it is they are trying to suggest you might be. It creeps up on you when they catch you out on some harmless answer to a question. I felt the symptoms and resolved to keep my answers *simple* and to stick to them the second and third time round.

For instance: What school did I attend? I was asked. I gave the one I attended the longest. There was no need to bring up the other two.

My regimental association membership card came up for scrutiny. What rank did I hold? they wanted to know.

"Corporal," I replied, giving the lowest rank I had held, though I had actually risen to that of captain. Pride alone stopped me from saying "private".

"Which army?" came the next enquiry. I had to admit it was British.

My camera produced much attention. I was asked what photographs I had taken on Ugandan soil and truthfully reported that I had taken none. They made sure I was telling the truth by exposing the film.

Every now and again I would point out the fact that if they were going to charge me with anything, I had the right to see a representative of my government, though this seemed to be of no consequence to my interrogators. And there comes, too, a point in all interrogations when there is a lull in proceedings during which one can mount a counter-attack of the "Why the hell am I here? What crime am I supposed to have committed?" sort of thing which, if nothing else, raises morale if not the roof.

No longer was my student friend with me and I was never to set eyes on him again as I was taken from room to room to be harangued by a sequence of questioners all demanding to know what I was up to. Occasionally I was asked if I was hungry, to which I replied, truthfully, that I was.

"What would you like?" they enquired.

Optimistic to the bitter end I suggested steak and chips.

"Do you want some tea?"

"That too, please."

Neither the steak nor the tea put in an appearance, of course, but I felt grateful for the enquiry. It added a slice of normality to the proceedings.

Sometimes the questioning was undertaken in an abusive manner with accusations flung at me in angry outbursts. I was a spy sent by Kenya to make contact with somebody. I was intent upon prying into the workings of the railway. I was sent to undermine the Ugandan regime, the student being my contact. Mostly, however, the questioning was mildly administered of the "Come on, you can tell us everything and we'll let you go" sort of manner, which was the more ominous.

Everything I said had to be typed in triplicate by a

series of clerks who were no more than one-finger typists. Everybody with whom I came into contact wore the depressing air of a black Gestapo, this emphasised by the fact that I had finally recognised the source of the sweet smell my nose had picked up as we had entered the building. It was of rotting flesh: a recollection dredged up from my wartime experience.

The questioning, together with repeated searching of my duffel bag, continued for two whole days and nights with little respite. Occasionally I was left alone, presumably so that I could ponder upon my alleged sins, and I took the opportunity for a catnap. But just as I nodded off, in someone would come with the same line of questioning and it would all start again. A single glass of water was all I could manage to extract to keep body and soul intact.

And then, suddenly, I was told I could go. A moment of disbelief kept me rooted to the spot and then I was off, bundling my belongings, strewn over the table, into my bag. My sense of urgency to get to the railway station must have communicated itself to my guards because they broke into a run to get to the car. Abruptly they were no longer my guards but the means of catching a train, if there was one, to Kenya, or as near as I could get to Kenya.

At the station I found I had to wait for several hours for a train to Tororo, some five miles from the border, and my return ticket was still valid for it. Not that this mattered, for when the train did arrive it was overrun by a huge crowd that overflowed on to the outside of the coaches. I joined a trio of anxious youths on the steps of a second-class coach. Rain still splashed down but I was too relieved to care.

For 15 minutes nothing happened and then, without any warning, the overloaded train slunk away through the suburbs of Kampala. I never felt so pleased to see the back of a city as I did this one.

But my good fortune was short-lived, for as we approached the gradient to Seta, the English Electric diesel ground to a halt. A wave of panic washed through the coaches. Up front a crowd gathered round the green locomotive with its distinctive yellow stripe. Everybody yelled advice and instructions to the driver and, such was the desperation to proceed, some passengers began trying to *push* it. The atmosphere was tense, with more and more men joining the pushing contingent while their women-folk stood in silence by the track, under the downpour, with their babies and small children. At the third attempt the wheels gripped the track and we were away again, everybody hurling themselves back into the coaches. In the mêlée I won a seat in a coach.

Back at Tororo they grabbed me again. I couldn't believe it. As everybody left the train with, presumably, the intention of joining an expected connection that would take them into Kenya, a posse of uniformed police intercepted me, gave a cursory glance at my passport, and bundled me into an office in the station. And there I was grilled again, this time by uniformed interrogators. I complained loudly that I had been officially released by their compatriots in Kampala, but this seemed to cut no ice with them. Instead I was curtly told not to answer back. Then came the bombshell. *I would be returned to Kampala on the next eastbound train.* My sense of relief plummeted to that of grave concern.

However, there was no train to Kampala scheduled until the following morning. In the meantime I was consigned to a draughty waiting-room, the door securely locked and a sentry placed outside it. At least my new oppressors fed me as I was becoming weak with hunger. I had also fathomed a superficial reason for my re-appre-hension since my permitted stay in Uganda had expired which, technically, made me an illegal alien. But I felt this to be no more than a ploy in the general scheme of things. It was all becoming a bad dream.

The room into which I had been put was, to all intents and purposes, a prison cell. It held no more than a wooden bench on which previous inmates had carved their names, and one window, high in the wall, which was too small to use as an escape exit. As darkness fell the elderly guard with an old Lee Enfield rifle joined me in the room. Beyond an occasional grunt he never spoke a word. We sat in stoic silence through the first half of the night, with me trying to get some sleep on the narrow bench. The darkness of the room was confounded by a low-wattage bulb suspended from the high ceiling.

Escape was now firmly in my mind; the idea of a return to that hellhole of Kampala Police Headquarters was unbearable. The border was not more than five or six miles distant and, though the Ugandan Army was supposedly massed along it, I presumed it would be facing the other way. And, after all, nobody was stopping the massed migration out of the country. Furthermore I was unable to believe that the Amin regime had caught up with the finesse practised by the European Communist regimes so far as their methods of discouraging illegal emigration across the former Iron Curtain was concerned.

I pondered upon these matters as the night wore on, even managing a brief doze too, until my guard, snoring stentoriously, had fallen into a deeper sleep. And, glory be, he had left the key in the inside lock of the door. All I had to do was to pick up my duffel bag and let myself out, which I promptly did. It was all too easy; I even felt a pang of conscience about allowing the man to take the rap for losing a prisoner.

Nobody was about the station platform as the first streaks of dawn showed in the sky. And the rain had ceased. I made straight for the almost complete darkness of the trees and, keeping the railway to my right and in sight so as not to lose direction, strode out for the border. I fastened my eyes on a distant hill, now visible against the lightening sky, which I judged to be in Kenya. Foliage dripped incessantly as if it were raining again.

I bumped into the Army a moment before I became

aware that I had company: a bunch of soldiers trying to get their radio to work. Too late to take avoiding action, I exhibited interest in what they were doing and, telling them that I was once a soldier myself, offered my help since I knew the type of Second World War apparatus they were using.

The group seemed more concerned with the state of their equipment than with my presence amongst them, but I still felt obliged to explain that I had missed the last train to Nairobi and was therefore walking to the border. After all, an Englishman walking into someone else's war zone at dawn I felt needed some explanation.

Though the soldiers had no need of my assistance, which was just as well, they could not have been friendlier, one of them presenting me with a bottle of lager. Rashly I enquired whether one of their vehicles and a driver could be presumed upon to give me a lift to the border. The corporal said he'd have to ask his officer, and I wondered whether I was pushing my luck too far.

But not so. A lieutenant came over, showing not the slightest surprise at my being where I was. He apologised for not being able to take me to the physical border, though a driver would drop me close by. This suited me fine.

And so it came about that, in the warm, petrol-reeking cab of a 15-hundredweight Bedford truck I made the border area without even having to walk there. The driver pointed me in the direction of the border post and, with a wave, returned the way he had come.

With the vehicle out of sight I left the road and struck out across pleasant rolling country in front of the conical hill for which Tororo is known, and also the landmark I had wrongly gauged to be in Kenya. And there was the railway again. Parallel with it I turned eastwards and came to the brook that forms the physical demarcation line between the two countries. I got my feet wet by failing to jump the obstacle.

IN A LOST VALLEY

Ralph Izzard

Ralph Izzard was born in Essex, England, in 1910. For many years he was a foreign correspondent for the Daily Mail, *and was a member of that newspaper's Abominable Snowman Expedition of 1954. Among his books of travel writing are* The Abominable Snowman Adventure *and* Smelling the Breezes. *Izzard was the founder of Television Exploration Ltd., a television company which specialized in travel documentaries.*

It was round about the end of the war [the Second World War] that rumours began to circulate of an "extinct" monster moving along the Himalayan border. The stories were embroidered and went to rather absurd lengths. This can happen to a grain of perplexing evidence when it is carried verbally from mouth to mouth, the latter often being organs of a primitive order. And then the grapevine breaks into news-print.

Dimensions of the mystery beast were so exaggerated that at first there was the usual dismissal of the report as being just a good tall story dreamed up to relieve the tedium and tragedies of the receding war years. Nevertheless, there was in fact good reason to believe that a hitherto unknown creature of swamps and rivers existed in the region at one time, and just possibly still did in the unexplored terrain of Northern Assam.

Some of the rumours came from highly creditable sources. The correct sequence of events is this: Dr. C. Freür von Haimendorf, the noted anthropologist, now Professor of Oriental Studies at London University, first reached the valley of the Apa Tani tribe in 1944. He brought back an account of stories he had heard of there being at one time "monsters" in the central swamp of that area. In 1945 Charles Stonor and James Philip Mills, of the Indian Civil Service, went to the valley. They visited it again in 1946. James Mills' daughter went with them, and during a dangerous pilot expedition, undertaken mostly on research in the tribal field, James Mills' daughter died of the same lethal malaria that had attacked H. W. Tilman and his Sherpas during his 1939 visit. Up till that time they were merely investigating vivid tribal memories of a Plesiosaurus-type creature which everyone believed was certainly extinct. They were on serious research, and highly qualified for it by their long experience and travels in those remote areas in the course of their administration – in Charles Stonor's case too – among the primitive and little known tribes of North Assam.

In 1947 Stonor was again in the area about fifty miles distant from the Apa Tani Valley. He ran into a Dafla tribesman who assured him that in the Rilo Valley, the Dafla territory we eventually visited, the *Buru*, as the monster was called, still existed.

The whole matter suddenly became alive and urgent. That was when I was called in. We mounted our expedition to Rilo in 1948 – the only *Buru* search in which I took part, and my worst expedition.

Our investigating party eventually set out after many preparations, backed by official approval and scientific encouragement, to discover how much truth lay behind the so far unsubstantiated story of monsters in swamps. It had been given some substance when I was in New Delhi by A. P. F. Hamilton, then Director of the Indian Forestry Service. It was he who first told me about Charles Stonor, the eminent zoologist. Stonor, then Tribal Agricultural Officer of the North-east Frontier Area of Assam, and based on Shillong, had also reported on the *Buru*. He had reported that during his travels he had heard of a "Lost Valley" where, according to tribal account, there might still be a saurian species which buried itself in the mud in the winter and emerged in the summer.

From anyone other than Stonor this would have sounded too much like Conan Doyle's *Lost World*, but his reputation as a brilliant and sound zoologist of absolute integrity lent importance to his claim. That was how we met, and after the usual preliminaries and organising, that was how we joined forces in an expedition consisting of Stonor, Frank Hodgkinson and myself.

The hazardous journey could never have taken place but for Stonor's knowledge and encouragement. He was by the nature of his appointment as well as his several years' of studies in tribal ethnology well qualified to guide us in the then practically unknown areas where such tribes led their primitive and often dangerous lives.

There is still a small but dogged body of scientific and hunting opinion who are prepared to give dinosaurs a chance of survival, not the vast bulky creatures which once roamed the earth, but primitive saurians living beneath the waters, never coming to land, or very seldom. The data, or myth, if it be myth, of the Loch Ness and its elusive amphibian is a case in point.

Too many down-to-earth and informed persons with no axe to grind quote evidence of "Something unusual" in certain deep waters or swamps to dismiss reports entirely, while one discounts the exaggerations and jokes. In recent years "things" of a like nature were reported from Malaysia and elsewhere, not by superstitious tribes only but by some Europeans.

As modern research has proved that huge creatures of undetermined shape and size live in the very lowest depths of sea, the same could be true of profound fresh-water depths.

It is important to differentiate between the two tribes associated with the *Buru* stories – the Apa Tani and the Daflas. The Apa Tanis are remarkable in that they occupy only a single self-contained pocket in the area and have a much higher civilisation than the surrounding Daflas. The Apa Tanis are sedentary cultivators, while the Daflas are the more primitive shifting cultivators, burning a patch of forest, sowing a single crop, and then moving on to burn another patch of forest when secondary under-growth takes over the first burnt patch. Apart from forest collecting, this is the most primitive form of agriculture of all.

The central area of the Apa Tani Valley consists partly of widely separated cultivated rice-fields. It is irregular in shape, with innumerable large and small inlets of flat and running in between low projecting bracken-covered spurs on which about seven large villages of the tribe are situated. The valley is elevated plateau surrounded by a rim of mountains. It lies between two river valleys, that of the Kamla to the north, and the Panior (or Panir) running south. It is the only valley of that character in the Himalaya of this region, and is reminiscent on a much smaller scale of the great valley of Nepal. At that time neither the Apa Tani Plateau nor the surrounding country had ever been surveyed. The swamp, already referred to, which was the bed of the valley, appeared to consist of a thick layer of silt superimposed on gravel. The climate provides winter frosts and regular falls of snow. This despite the tropical conditions under which we ourselves later worked on our survey.

The outer region of this territory is populated by that other tribe, the Daflas. These are semi-nomadic, and are probably later immigrants than the Apa Tanis.

In investigation of traditional stories about local monsters one has to bear in mind the culture and social level of the Apa Tani tribe. They were at the time of our visit, and no doubt still are, a primitive people. Their organisation can be compared with that of the Naga tribe of the Assam-Burman border, with the Abor, and with more obscure tribes scattered over this immense and varied Himalayan region. They have no knowledge of writing, no art whatever, and their religion is a simple, form of Animism without the slightest admixture of Buddhism or Hinduism. Their political organisation is of the same corporate type as that of the Naga tribes. In contrast to their primitive background and fluid mode of governing influenced by conditions of climate, hunting, and crops, they are highly efficient agriculturists.

Their isolation is quite remarkable. A great many never leave the confines of their small valley, and the tribe seems to have founded no off-shoots in the surrounding region.

Against such a background survived the tradition of "monsters" making sporadic appearances in the swamps.

Leading men of different villages were approached. They were questioned separately through reliable interpreters, and research proceeded with the greatest care so that those interviewed had no inkling of the scientific nature of the enquiry, and so could not embroider their reports to suit preconceived notions.

The Apa Tanis discovered the beast they called Buru when they first came to the valley. It was about three and a half to four metres long. The head was about fifty centimetres long, and lengthened to a great snout at the tip while the eyes lay behind the snout. The teeth, said tribesmen, were flat like a man's except for a pair in the upper and lower jaws. Those were large and pointed like those of a tiger or bear. The neck was well under a metre in length, and here they specified that it could be stretched out or drawn in. This was described in expressive pantomime. The body was roundish, with a girth "just what a man could put his arms around". The tribesmen were demonstrative in their mime, and went on to speak of the creature's tail which they said was long and fringed, and there seemed to be a spine effect. To explain their meaning they made a small crude model by placing leaves along the sides of a stick.

The creature's legs were fifty centimetres with claws on the feet which looked like the fore-feet of a "burrowing mole". The skin suggested a scale-less fish. No hairs were apparent, but three lines of short blunt spines ran down the back and along each side. The colour was dark blue blotched with white, and a broad band of white ran down the belly.

The Buru, they state, lived entirely in the water and never came to land. They were not often seen as their habitat was water deeper than the height of a man. They would put their necks up out of the water, and make a hoarse bellowing noise. This too was imitated by informants. Sometimes they were seen nosing in the muddy banks of a lake, and when doing so they wagged their head and neck from side to side. They did not kill or eat men. It was not thought that they ate fish, but "lived on the mud". As for the young, and their breeding habits little seemed to be known.

A story was told of a man of the Tagomi clan who went with his wife and family to live away from his village and built a house on the extreme edge of a lake at a spot later known as Duta Lapang. During heavy rains his construction gave way, and the house and five occupants collapsed into the water, and they were all drowned. There was a buru nosing about at the time, and the house fell on top of it. The accident was seen by a boy of the household who happened to have gone out to answer the calls of nature just before the house disintegrated. That buru was never seen again, and it was not known if it had been killed.

The Apa Tanis who were questioned told how their ancestors began to drain their lake by opening an outlet whereby a stream called the Kal left the valley. As the ground was drained it was turned into rice-fields. Time went on, and there was less and less water deep enough for the burus. It became possible to trap them in deep pools and kill them. This was done by piling earth, stones, and logs into a pool where there was a buru and thereby burying it. The creatures used to wave their heads and long necks from side to side above the mud in their struggles. This was imitated by a man waving his arms from side to side.

Incidentally, though this may seem irrelevant and possibly frivolous, when recently I was engaged in describing these strange mystery beasts to an interested listener, it evoked in that person's mind an odd memory of the first scene in that occasionally macabre and highly coloured *Fantasia* film of Walt Disney! Just a passing reference, but it is a thought that no science or serious problem of anthropology or zoology is entirely safe from the makers of entertainment. However, it does little harm, and is generally treated at its own level.

Chief informants on the killings and haunts of the burus were priests and headmen. One was a priest of Duta village named Chigo Nime. A story about one particular buru came from Ṭakhe Bdha, a man from the village of Hang. Here was his version: There was once a buru in a pool near Hang. All the people gathered together, and omens were taken to see if it should be destroyed. Now in Hang village four magic plates of red metal were kept. These were called *Mamla* and had sharp razor-like edges. The buru bellowed, and suddenly the *Mamla* plates left the village of their own volition and went and cut the buru to pieces under water. Its blood surged up from below suffusing the surface of the water with crimson. Then the people threw in earth, stones, and logs, and made a mound over the place.

Three of the original *Mamla* plates had been destroyed or lost, but a small piece of metal from one is preserved in Hang village. No stranger is ever allowed to see it.

According to this man's stories, no one knew how many generations ago the burus were killed, but it happened after the foundation of the villages mentioned. Four were known to have been killed. The historical order of their destruction was remembered. The sites were known to everyone.

During searching parties' second visit to the valley, an old priest was interrogated. He was much respected among the Apa Tanis, and was known as Tamar of the village of Hang. He was well over seventy years of age, somewhat crippled with rheumatism, and never left his village. He had little contact with men from outside villages, and had not been present at previous enquiries, nor had former tribesmen who had been questioned gone first to him for information on the new visitors' behalf.

Tamar described the buru as like a very big snake. It had three hard plates on top of its flat head, was long with an elongated tail peculiar for flanges down the side. When asked if the buru ever caught men, Tamar replied that a Dafla of the Tago clan was once pulled into the water by a buru which grabbed his legs with its tail. It had no legs, explained Tamar, but wriggled like a worm. This description was probably given because witnesses of the past who had handed down this data had only caught a glimpse of the creature. Probably they had not realised that it had legs of a kind which were comparatively short. The priest's description of the skin colour tallied with other reports given as dark blue and blotched. When asked if the buru made any noise Tamar produced a high-pitched bellow in imitation.

The buru ate mud, he went on. When asked why then had it killed the Dafla of the Tago clan, he explained that the man had been out hunting and finding a young buru asleep on a mud bank had speared it. So the mother buru had killed the man and then pulled him into the water. This was alleged to have happened on the banks of the River Kal. But how had the adult buru known the man

who had killed her young, Tamar was next asked. She just
knew, he insisted. When questioned on the buru's breeding habits, he said the young were born alive. There were
no eggs. Were there many burus? someone enquired.
There were many, he said, but when there was snow they
stayed deep under water, and only came out in warm
weather to curl in the sun and bask on the mud banks.

Then for a test came the repeated enquiry as to how the
animals used to be killed. Tamar's description of the
killing of some burus by *Mamla* plates, and by piling
earth, stones, and logs on top of their watery haunts,
tallied with former stories of their destruction. But Tamar
did not know how long ago all this had happened, he
added. It was very long ago, and the present Tago clan of
these days were different from the Tago people of past
times.

"Do you know of any other animal like the buru?"
someone now asked Tamar, and went on to enquire if he
knew of the crocodiles of the Brahmaputra. The ques-
tioner turned to another man present who came forward,
and after speaking to Tamar, said that he himself had seen
crocodile. After more consultation with the priest, both
men stated that the buru was not the same reptile.

The theme now turned upon legend and beliefs. Tamar
was asked if the buru had magical powers. This was
denied with emphasis. He qualified this when asked
why had people killed them, by stating that the burus
were killed simply because they were troublesome. Did
the burus kill many people, someone else insisted, asking
an associated question in a different form. The burus had
only killed one man, was the down-to-earth reply. As for
remains of bones, teeth, the burus had possessed those,
but all this was long ago, and there were no relics of bones
or teeth lying around to be found now. They had all gone.

In existence were several sites known as places where
burus were killed. They were: The Hari site in the main
valley between the eastern edge of the swamp and the

central stream. The actual site was marked by a small
pool. It was the only place in the valley where it had been
impossible to drain for rice cultivation. The Bela site, the
one at Hang, and another at a place called Haja comprised
this collection of strange spots. The site at Hang was
distinguished by a circular raised patch of long grass in
the middle of a rice plot. When asked why that central
patch was not cultivated, and whether it was supposed to
be unlucky, the tribesmen replied non-commitally that it
was not especially unlucky.

Those sites were never excavated. The burials had
taken place seven generations back, they thought. They
added that a man named Takhe Sahe of Hang village had
once found a skull purporting to be a buru's in a corner of
a spot called Chogo. The skull was like a pig's, with a long
flat snout, forked at the tip. Takhe Sahe had taken it back
to his house, but died soon after. That the skull was a
buru's was only his own and contemporary inference.
However after the man's death it was suspected of being
unlucky and thrown away.

As regards accuracy of the above descriptions, one
thing must be said: all who have made contact with
primitive people ignorant of the written word, have been
struck by the extraordinary accuracy and tribal memory,
and the vividness of tradition.

Before our own departure, and at times during the first
stages of our march to find the buru, or its remains, we
considered the dragon myth from which it might have
stemmed, as the uninitiated might think. The dragon is a
symbol, and not a legendary monster. It was produced by
merging and readapting of ideas among many peoples
already of comparatively high civilisation. The dragon
can be symbolic of either good or evil. It would cease
being the symbol it has always been if it took the form of a
once-reality, even with civilised peoples. For such primitive mentalities as those of the Apa Tanis and the
Daflas to create a traditional myth from an animal they

always tried to destroy because it was "troublesome" would be most unlikely. In their simple estimation there was nothing magic or awe-inspiring about the buru. Its image remained in their minds because of its former nuisance value.

Through many years of poking about in odd corners of the earth I have preserved an open mind on the subject of fabulous and dangerous beasts, never seen face to face, but generally reported as having been sighted by the dead-and-gone cousin of a second cousin of some local character. But I can say this; during our buru expedition, it was the momentary conviction that I was going to be eaten alive by a dinosaur which gave me the biggest fright of my life.

That moment came when I found myself up to my neck in the middle of a mile-wide swamp in the centre of an even more distant "lost valley" in the heart of those Himalayan foothills of Northern Assam. We had reached our goal in our quest for the buru after what seemed endless hacking our way through one of the cruellest jungles in the world.

The valley is called Rilo, also in the "white" area of the map marked "Tribal Territory". That means the area is still virtually unexplored, and it warns the inexperienced and the uninitiated to keep out. Anything may happen in such places, and anything often does. It did then.

The tribesmen were the Dafla tribe, the same name as part of the Assam territory now marked on the map. These people are of Tibeto-Burman stock, and they are utterly unlike the Indians who would try to administer them by remote control. A wise principle at times. There is a contemporary connotation there with the sporadic Naga difficulties Indian administration often encountered, and still faces (at times).

The Daflas we met wore head-dresses of black and white barred Great Hornbill feathers, and they hunted

with split bamboo bows and poisoned arrows. The poison
is derived from pulped aconite paste kneaded round the
shaft just behind the arrowhead. The stuff is alleged to be
strong enough to kill a bear within twenty minutes.

The swamp at Rilo was really a very deep lake covered
by a quaking carpet of tangled vegetation. In the middle
was an open patch of water about the size of an average
swimming pool. It was in probing gingerly towards this
pool that disaster overtook me. I fell in.

My problem was how to get out, for every time I pressed
down the weeds sank beneath me and I with them. For
some moments I rested my head on my one good arm which
I lay across the weeds. Three weeks before this I had broken
a collarbone, and my left arm was still strapped tightly up
under my right ear. Trying not to panic, I lay quiet,
thinking the situation out carefully. Then a horrible thing
happened. There was a sudden upsurge of water in the
centre of the "swim-pool" beside me. Watchers on the edge
of the swamp – they could not reach me – told me afterwards
that what they thought happened was that there had been a
big eruption of marsh gas, probably released by my own
movements. It had caused a wave of water to expand
outwards in ever increasing circles. Things looked rather
different from my chin-high view of the swamp. I saw the
eruption all right, and then, following it, what I took to be a
wave heading straight in my direction. The appalling
thought struck me that at that very moment a "prehistoric
monster", probably a primitive crocodilian, was cruising
towards me in the free water below, prepared to drag me
down by the heels.

Then the miracle happened. How, I can't remember
now, but think it must have been the result of one of those
superhuman efforts that provide the individual with
unusual physical prowess in a terrifying emergency. Before you could say "Pleisosaurus" I was out on top of the
weeds, and at first crawling, and then floundering, I
finally reached the edge of the lake.

It was the first violent effort I had made since my accident in which I felt not a twinge of pain in my injured shoulder.

On our march through the jungle, up gorges, and across streams, we received the same description as had been given to Charles Stonor by Apa Tanis on the occasions of his first enquiries with J. P. Mills. The length, size, shape of the buru, and peculiarities of limbs, especially the tail, mostly tallied with other reports. That tail length was alleged to be nine feet long, and its "flanges" were powerful and used for burrowing in the mud. All this was physically demonstrated to us more than once, without any prompting or leading questions that might have influenced those being questioned. Stonor, who had recognised this was no common crocodile, mentioned that he had considered excavating the Apa Tani burial sites, but they were too formidable to tackle single-handed. At the time he had determined to return so as to mount a small expedition to examine them more closely. That was in 1947 while making a third journey to the vicinity of the Apa Tani Valley. That was when in an area about fifty miles away, Charles Stonor had the chance encounter with the Dafla tribesman who told him of the hitherto unsuspected existence of the Rilo Valley where at last we found ourselves.

In Rilo, in much more remote Dafla country, the swamp had not been drained, and at the height of the monsoon season the water rose so that it became a vast lake.

"At that time," said the Dafla, "as many as eight or ten burus may be seen breaking the surface of the lake together. They rise with great disturbance and splashing, come straight out of the water, stay for a few moments, and then disappear down again."

"How big are they?" Stonor asked.

"About the same size as the mithan."

The tame bison, or "mithan", to give it its local name,

is the centre of Dafla economic life, and any animal approaching its size would automatically be compared with it.

"If you come in the rainy season you are certain to see them," was the next assurance.

The chance of the buru, even if not in such numbers, being still alive in this until then unexplored area, was the incentive that had brought Charles Stonor, Frank Hodgkinson, and myself to this well-named "Lost Valley". Charles was convinced that if one did not attempt discovery of the truth now, the opportunity might not occur again.

So here we were with our equipment: porters, rations, presents for headmen, collapsible boats, and powerful photographic apparatus. Fool-proof photographic evidence is vital for success on such an expedition.

"It will be no picnic party," had been Charles' laconic warning. He knew his territory well. It certainly was not.

We had set out for Rilo at the beginning of the monsoon. Our jumping-off point had been Charduar in a more civilised part of the country where we had obtained much advance information, and had helpful meetings with Frank Noble, formerly a colonel in the Indian Army who knew the land, and tribal (and hunting) conditions from years of experience. Our conversations were useful. Charduar had too been H. W. Tilman's jumping-off point on his ill-fated 1939 expedition.

Our plan was the ambitious aim of lassoing a buru, dragging it to the bank, examining it closely, and then letting it go. We had a rifle with us for good reason. But this was qualified with stringent warnings from Stonor, who, from his experience, stressed that in penetrating virtually unexplored areas one may be regarded as a dangerous intruder, and must on no account suggest the idea of being armed for purposes of intimidation. Though we did possess this weapon, we had no intention of shooting the buru, whatever it might turn out to be. So rare a creature, if still in existence, must be left unharmed.

We reached Rilo as the first white men ever to do so, after an appallingly difficult march through dense sub-tropical rain forests. No man in his senses goes into the Northern Assam jungle during the monsoon. At night one is tormented by mosquitoes which carry particularly virulent malaria. By day one is tortured by Dim-Dam flies which raise maddeningly irritating blood blisters. Snakes abound, and the floor of the forest quivers with leeches impossible to keep from one's skin. I have counted as many as forty leeches on each leg at the end of a day's march, and have plodded on for miles with blood squelching in my boots.

The march had begun with three days through the almost impenetrable forest of the northern Brahmaputra plain. This area teems with wild elephant, tiger, and panther, including an unusually high percentage of the much-prized black panther. Occasionally Great Hornbills clattered about in the branches above our heads. Though those attractive clowns of the forest were officially "protected" this made little impact in tribal territories where both bills and feathers were highly valued as head decorations.

Game thinned rapidly as soon as we mounted into the foothills of the Dafla country. Daflas, whose only occupations then were hunting, trading, and raiding, were poor porters. Pay disputes were incessant, and as we drew farther away from civilisation, minor pilfering developed to a considerable scale when whole loads began disappearing with their carriers into the jungle, and those goods were hardly ever recovered.

In calculation of our supplies we had made some allowances for the unpredictable local co-operation, but never had we expected quite such wholesale depletion of equipment and sustenance. Even kerosene drums were punctured in the vain hope that they might contain drinkable spirits, to the disappointment of the investigators, no doubt, but no return of the kerosene.

Fortunately we had with us a stiffening of Gurkha porters for part of the way, loaned to us by Sir Akbar Hydari, at that time Governor of Assam. But of these Gurkhas three soon went down with malaria, and two more had to be left behind to look after them.

Our personal servants were two Mission-domesticated Naga head-hunters named Orenimo and Pio Pio who enlivened the march with Salvation Army tunes sung to their own highly improper texts. Also with us was a Kasi cook with the improbable name of Washington. He too was another Mission product. He had originated from the Kasi tribe in which men perform the household duties while the women are off doing the hunting, trading, and in former times even raiding.

"If only Washington could knit," said Frank Hodgkinson, "he'd make an ideal husband for a Kasi wife."

Orenimo had a half secret which no one ever mentioned after a while, as he would get so embarrassed. That so-called secret was actually a family burden, or distinction. It depended on the way you viewed it. He had an aunt who was a witch and famous for having effected some remarkable cures of tribal maladies. "How's your old witch of an aunt?" was a question that could send Orenimo into contortions of dismay and mental discomfort. For his peace of mind, the crucial query was rarely put to him, for he was a good bearer, wore sensible shorts and bush shirt, even while treasuring a photograph of himself in full tribal regalia.

The witch aunt was reputed to have a familiar that was a snake. In view of that asset we would sometimes feel that the old lady, whom we never met, by the way, might have been persuaded to do something to ease our apprehension of stepping upon one of those jungle risks. She must have had some control over their movements! But we never suggested to Orenimo that she might use her influence. It was best to leave well alone. His assistant, Pio Pio, was his junior and a distant Naga relative. Orenimo would have felt his prestige damaged had he failed to produce some aunt-like tribal "magic".

In all, our party had mustered 120 men, an indication of the difficulty of the going, for we formed no more than a light reconnaissance team charged by various interests with getting undeniable proof of the buru's existence. If all went well, we planned to return with a full-scale expedition the following year.

As we stood on the rim of Rilo Valley, we recognised that it was quite as plausible a sanctuary for animals believed to be extinct as had been Sir Arthur Conan Doyle's *Lost World*. It was about four miles long and three across, and the sides, hundreds of feet high, were almost sheer, and quite unscaleable for any monster of the type we were seeking.

A chickenpox epidemic had broken out at Rilo and in surrounding villages, and as this was its first appearance it had proved particularly virulent and had killed off about thirty people. Consequently, we would have to be careful to do nothing that might offend the spirits. Should any unorthodox behaviour of ours coincide with further deaths, conditions might become awkward for us. Nonetheless, one had to remember that a favourite trick of frontier tribes who did not like the intrusion of visitors was to spread rumours of an epidemic ahead of a European party, and so hope to divert them from their villages. Europeans were not always popular. They had a way of asking too many embarrassing questions.

The Daflas we met and our own troop of bearers, guides – so-called – and our camp domestics, were then diverted by us into talking about our objective, the buru. Stories of strange animals, or reports of "sports" from known species which may have existed in the vast remoteness of Assam, were, and probably still are, numerous enough. They make common talk when strangers to an area have to be impressed. We took all those tales with reserve. Yet, to side-track a little, there is a belief, for instance, founded on quite sound reasoning, that somewhere, at some time or other, a black tiger will again be shot by some hunter. Black panther are not unusual in certain parts of Assam. Excessive skin pigmentation accounts for that. A black panther is the extreme opposite of an albino panther. Albino tiger are fairly common, but certainly not black tiger although in 1772 in South-West India, the water-colourist James Forbes made a fine painting of a black tiger. As Forbes was a man of all-round ability and a Fellow of the Royal Society, his record can be taken as certain. Since that time there have been three more sightings by Europeans in 1842 and 1914 in Assam, and in 1904 in South-East Burma, while Charles Stonor himself had interrogated a headman in the Mishmi Hills to the east of the Dafla country who swore there were black tiger in the vicinity. Five records only in nearly 200 years of what must be a truly awe-inspiring beast.

Previously, before setting out, Colonel Frank Noble of the Assam Rifles had told us of a story that existed among his men who were for the most part recruited from Gurkha settlers. They stated that not so long ago a gigantic animal had been seen to cross the Brahmaputra and take refuge in the mountains to the north where it was supposed to have survived.

However, interesting as such records were, we resolutely refused to classify the buru with such freaks, or such fantasies. We ran through a list of all the known animals which could possibly fit the buru descriptions given by Apa Tanis and by Daflas, and we drew a blank. Our verdict at the time was: "Probably a hitherto unknown animal: just possibly a prehistoric one."

That something unidentified and mysterious existed, we had no doubt.

To the few people outside our own immediate small circle both here and elsewhere who had been told confidentially of the object of our mission, we had pointed out that they must reckon with more than fifty per cent chance of total failure, and we advised against pre-publicity. The absurdity of those previous reports was remembered, and made us extra cautious. To the uninformed who enquired en route as to the aim of our expedition, Charles Stonor had produced fluent and convincing phrases about surveying new areas for drainage and cultivation. This information was conducted with such expert authority that no one suspected our true cause.

A stiff descent down through thickets of cane, bamboo, and giant tree ferns brought us to the floor of the valley. Here we at last set camp near a settlement of Daflas who later proved surly, dirty, and rather dishonest neighbours. In many respects the valley was a beautiful place. Sprays of scented orchids hung from trees. Brilliant butterflies as big as bats hovered in the air, and great masses of brambles held raspberries as large as full-grown strawberries.

Among ourselves that night we became optimistic, and rated our chances of success at about seventy per cent. We talked far into the night, Charles, the eager, earnest zoologist with a monopoly of knowledge of local conditions, Frank Hodgkinson, jungle trained and our able and very experienced photographer, and myself. Here we were, a jungle pilot search party, each with his own qualifications, even though mine were no more than my wartime sailor's knowledge of practical seamanship, small-boat management, and the like. What I knew might come in useful, again it might not.

Our arrival had ended that nightmare journey across mountains, through jungles, and lesser swamps which were formidable enough to tackle. The leeches continued to hang tenaciously to our legs despite boot protections, and we spent camp evenings, after day-long investigating, in disposing of them, and treating ourselves for various

stings, and coping with thorn extractions. This ritual
would take place as a relief from daytime torture before
Washington unsmiling, but with punctilious ceremony,
would set out tea and other so-called refreshment and
nourishment before us while Dafla porters unpacked gear,
or set up or reorganised tents. Often these functions took
place in pelting rain and thunderstorms with lightning
turning the whole landscape into a sort of other-planet
territory while the fury lasted.

In between such ordeals at the end of our forced
marches, visits and ceremonial welcomes and presenta-
tion of gifts to various village headmen came as light
relief. But sometimes these too became tedious, anxious
though we were to create the right impression and so gain
co-operation when needed.

All the time we were straining to get on with the job at
the final swamp of Rilo as we watched and waited for the
right weather. The amount of rice spirit drinking at those
convivial get-together affairs did not agree with all of us
either. Yet we had to keep up a good face and take part in
greeting exchanges and compliments if we wanted to
obtain chickens and eggs and other edible provisions as
we went from one community to the other. And some of
the social atmosphere had to be kept up for policy even
now that we had reached our action-stations.

A short walk from our camp brought us to a mount
whence we could overlook the swamp. Our first sight of it
was disconcerting. For as I have already described when
detailing my accident in the middle of it, apart from that
central patch of water, it was covered with matted weeds,
a tangled and deceptive carpet as I discovered to my cost
when I ventured upon it. However, even if our joint
inspections from above were disappointing, it was still
early in the monsoon season, and we comforted ourselves
with the surmise that there was plenty of time left for the
lake to fill, and so set the scene for what we required – a
buru – just one would do – to heave itself out of the rising

waters, and give us a chance of capture, even if only by photographic lens.

Interrogation of the local Daflas had not been neglected. We had already ascertained that no buru had been seen during the present season. Yet all claimed to have seen it a number of times in the past, and none of them could be shaken from their descriptions of its appearance and habits which Charles had noted down during his original questionings. All this data was added to the various other stories we had collected on the way. Now the general opinion among the local tribe and our boys was that the buru was due to appear any day since the *real* rains were nearly due and the swamps would flood.

Unable to contain our impatience, Charles and I would leave Frank Hodgkinson busy with film and photo equipment, and make our way swamp-wards.

We made our way to our observation mount with the village headman, Pinjin, and with Paning and Padma, our two new interpreters. We dropped downwards from our shelf through a narrow belt of jungle and two enclosures that had been stockaded against raids by mithan, the local cattle that seemed to be the backbone of Dafla husbandry. Mithan were currency, barter, dowry, and exchange commodity rolled into that one type of black and white and piebald beast. Mithan are as different from European domestic cattle as a water buffalo is from a Devon Red.

On our observation this time, we saw that the great swamp which from Dafla accounts would already be a huge lake caused by the approaching rains, contained no open water at all except two small pools each about twenty yards long and ten across. They lay about thirty yards apart. Charles was as taken aback as I was by the comparative absence of water where at last buru might emerge, but grimly he took out his huge telescope, and began focusing it on the pools. To negotiate the unreliable trembling quagmire and reach the pools would be impossible on foot as my own venture later proved, even if

we could contrive ladders to pay across the bright green
treacherous sedge and vegetation. Our rubber boats
seemed the answer for when the great floods came.
Yet, especially after my later escape from a sticky end
in the swamp, we did not relish the risk of snagging
hidden logs or weeds when afloat, and finding ourselves
sinking in a deflated boat in the depths of alleged buru
haunts.

The idea of the boat was abandoned.

It was not until the full force of the monsoon had broken
over us after weeks of gruelling search, accidents, and
surveys while conditions deteriorated both in food supplies and in social contacts with our neighbours and
porters that we realised gradually the impossibility of
our quest, and how fantastic were the hopes we had
cherished. During those weeks we had nothing dry to
wear or sleep in, and what is more, we saw as the waters
rose that our "Sargasso Sea" of weeds was rising too with
the flood.

But even then, the urge to reach that central patch of
water became an obsession with us. It was our last chance
of catching a glimpse of the animal for which we had come
all the way to, until then, unexplored territory, and
endured the trials of the last few weeks. We kept the
patch of open water constantly under observation through
Charles' telescope. Occasionally we were raised to a high
pitch of excitement and expectancy when we spotted
ripples and dark shadows cross the surface. Then our
hopes wavered. Those ripples and mysterious heavings
could have been caused merely by wind or cloud effects. It
was imperative though to know for certain.

The problem was – how? A stream did meander
through the swamp, and that was what had tempted us
to consider the boats, two Air Force dinghies we had
brought along with us. But the stream was fouled with
jagged tree trunks. Just as we had dismissed the idea of

using the boats on the swamp to get to the open water, so now we did not relish risk of damaging the dinghies and being precipitated into the stream. Also, a few days before, a fifteen-foot King Cobra had passed right through the camp and headed downstream into the swamp. The King Cobra is the deadliest of snakes, and as it is often truculent is best left undisturbed. An alternative plan to the boats had been to construct three bamboo ladders and leapfrog them over surface weeds. But this had proved such back-breaking work, it soon exhausted us and had to be abandoned. It was on that occasion in complete desperation, we had set out on foot across the weeds, and I fell in. My companions at the time were in too unstrategic positions paces away from me to be able to do anything to help. Their approach even if they could have floundered to where I struggled would only have hindered my efforts.

Now reviewing the whole survey we decided that we had shot our bolt, for there is a limit to physical endurance in such expeditions beyond which one cannot venture if one hopes to escape alive. Behind us, rivers were rapidly swelling with rain and threatened to become unfordable, which would cut off our retreat to the plains. Food was low, and we had already been reduced to livening up our rice menus by grubs hacked out from rotting tree stumps.

Another factor which compelled us to admit defeat was our rapidly worsening relations with the Daflas. None of us were inclined to run the risk of a poisoned arrow in the back. If capable of killing a bear within twenty minutes, those aconite-smeared weapons could dispose of the human frame with equal speed, especially if that lethal paste had been freshly pulped – a condition which apparently adds considerably to the stuff's potency. And the long marches and terrible camping conditions had already caused enough misery arising from such side-issues as insect attack and frequent hairbreadth avoidance of snakes.

As time went on, eggs, chickens, meat and indeed any fresh food became impossible to obtain by barter or by any other inducements. The reason for our increasing unpopularity we had suspected, and soon confirmed. The Daflas considered themselves surrounded by a vast horde of spirits, the majority of which were evil. Dafla life was in fact one long struggle to neutralise hostile spirit influences. The so-called "wise" men who at first had been voluble in their buru tales, the creatures' haunts, habits, and size, now spread the word that our presence in the valley could bode no good for anyone. Our intrusion into the swamp, the home of particularly malevolent spirits, could easily result in dire calamity for the community.

It would prove no easy task to find a less sophisticated tribe than those Daflas. Although the country we had penetrated was geographically contained within the frontiers of India, the vast majority of tribesmen had never seen an Indian from the plains, or from the more western Himalayan regions, let alone any white men. Few, if any, had ever heard of the almost legendary figure of Gandhi, or of Nehru, or of any other Indian leader. They knew no other laws but those of their own communities, and recognised no authority other than that of their village headmen.

While we were at Rilo and around, Charles Stonor had collected more data on the Daflas than even his own great experience in the tribal field of knowledge had already given him. In this he had recruited the help of one Taning, a trustworthy member of our team of porters, guides, interpreters, and handymen. At the time he allowed me to see his notes, and to quote from them.

He confirmed that the Daflas were divided more or less into the eastern and the western stocks. The eastern branch were those Daflas among whom we were. They were probably in the majority. Their way of life was extremely primitive, and they were far behind the Naga tribes in any degree of civilisation. They did not weave, had not evolved any form of art, and had no blacksmiths or metal workers of any kind. The nearest one could get to data on their crafts was in sparse replies that their only handiwork was pot-making. This was of very rough and unfinished type. Their cultivation too was rough and haphazard. Eastern Daflas lived in long communal houses that had no partitions and had several hearths running along down the centre. A so-called rich man might have a longhouse of over two-hundred feet in length, and he would possess twelve or more hearths. Each hearth was the home of a family, either of the owner's relations, or of his dependants. Some of the bigger houses were said to harbour up to two hundred and fifty people. They built their villages over widely dispersed ridges. A village of fifteen longhouses might cover a square mile.

The western Daflas built in more compact form to create a pattern effect. Houses were separated inside in sections and were more solid. These people had more initiative than their eastern neighbours. They could weave, using nettle fibre. Here the men did a fair amount of metal work. Their crops were tended by the women while the men concerned themselves with the more spectacular duties of cutting the ever encroaching jungle each winter, and burning down great patches to provide the women with a brief season's cultivation before the forest took charge again.

All those performances were carried out only if there was no sign of annoyance or warning from those ever-hovering spirits they were always propitiating. This was often done by carving wooden symbols representing birds, beasts, and other objects of worship. All this equipment for the assistance of the living and the dead would be cheek-by-jowl at times with a dead ancestor's everyday utensils such as a drinking bowl or implement of cultivation to help the traveller until the soul reached its journey's end.

The sacrifice of mithan to placate the spirits was also

commemorated. This was shown by large panels sur-
mounted by crude carvings on long poles. Sometimes
they were carved to represent horns; on other monuments
were crude symbols of birds on the wing. Such signs of
beliefs occurred frequently among many tribes of the
Assam frontiers, and even in parts of Burma.

The local priests break the yolks of eggs to divine
portents. This tells them which spirit has been offended,
and whether the sacrifice in apology must be mithan, goat,
pig, or fowl. Keeping the wicked of the disembodied
world at bay, and keeping the fairly harmless ones sweet,
was quite an expensive business for the ordinary tribesman, but he never considered refusing to bring forth a
sacrifice if omens demanded one. Still, this did create
some sort of control, though of loose administration. For
the Daflas, it was an improvement on former times when
tribes raided one another's communities, the causes being
debts, jealousies, or the dreaded "sickness carrying". A
village epidemic could bring forth fierce retribution upon
the next community.

Meanwhile, as we prepared for our still debated departure, under impetus of driving rain heralding the real
monsoon, the jungle vegetation thrived in gigantic strides,
and five pools now appeared on the Rilo swamp as we
watched from our lookout posts. The mountains around
the valley appeared smoke-veiled with low-hanging cot-
ton-wool clouds. Everything one touched was damp and
sticky with monsoon moisture. Blankets "sweated" and
the tents teemed with Dim-Dam, sand flies, and thumb-
nail-sized jungle ticks. Lizards scampered everywhere,
and frogs would leap from nowhere, often landing on our
shoulders. Those Daflas who still served us would return
from hunting with their legs streaming with blood from
leech bites.

We went about the camp with damp boots and damp
and dirty clothing as it was useless to wash anything.
Damp got into the cameras, and much film was lost. Then

we hit on the method of putting them over the kitchen stove. The only bright spot in camp was a flower. It was known as the Pakke Orchid and to our delight, it suddenly burst into bloom, displaying a glorious, fragile fleece of thirty-three blossoms.

Our observation of the swamp became spasmodic. There was no point in sitting in pouring downfalls when the swamp was covered with obliterating veils of water. When clouds showed signs of lifting we watched. If the buru was to appear in traditional manner, it must be now on the eve of our departure, or never, as far as we were concerned.

On one occasion when the rain had lifted, I was on the lookout alone except for an Apa Tani called Tameng. He was a reliable chap, as tribesmen go, and now he happened to be snoring gently on the platform behind me. I was reflecting on the strange lives these people led as I sat staring across over the empty swamp, when I heard a low drumming sound in the air. The noise grew louder, and I noticed it was emitted by the most enormous hornet I had ever seen even in this land of outsize insects. Its body was about three inches long and striped with black and amber bands, a giant, jet-propelled piece of flying mechanism. Suddenly alarmed, I saw it change course and wheel towards me. I sat rigid, rooted to the spot, for I could feel its wing beats ruffling the hair at the back of my neck. Then it swerved away with one of those quick spasmodic turns that one notices at times in the small and relatively harmless wasp-flies or hover-flies in a peaceful summer garden in Britain. It was fascinating to note the similar movements in that ogre of an insect.

Tameng must have heard it in his sleep. In one move-ment he had bounded up like a released spring, drawn his *dao*, and smashed the raider out of the air with the edge of the blade. Here was immediate reflex action arising out of deep sleep. Poor Tameng, still bleary-eyed from dis-turbed rest, glared at me at first as if I had supplied this interruption. Then he grinned, and settled down to snore again, the giant hornet shattered on the ground, soon to be devoured by the red ants.

Shortly after this incident Charles appeared. He looked very serious. He told me we were in for the final dis-illusionment. I think he felt the responsibility too strongly. Probably because his experience and previous knowledge of the buru reports had been the factors that led us into this wild comfortless country. That morning, he related, he had gone to the village and had met a hunting party who with cheerful temporary reversal from non-co-operation to eagerness to inform, told him they had seen the buru in the swamp the previous afternoon. Charles remembered how at about the same time as that of their alleged sighting, during his stint at our observation post, he had seen with the naked eye some puzzling shadows and movements on the surface of the pool. However, with the aid of the telescope they next appeared to him to be nothing more again than the wind ruffling the surface. In an unguarded moment he had replied to the hunters too hurriedly: "You really mean that you saw shadows on the surface of the pool?"

At that, the Daflas had nodded their heads up and down in the characteristic manner primitives assume when white men are delaying their own pursuits with discussion and argument that now bores them.

They grunted assent to his supposition. It was as good as saying: "Well, if you think that is all the buru is, you may well be right."

This was such an astonishing change of opinion after all we had assembled of evidence in the past gruelling weeks, not to mention the advance data we already possessed, that Charles after that last encounter had now come to me and to Frank Hodgkinson to call a new council of war. That we were soon leaving Rilo was certain, but still, what to do next before we departed? Should we still linger, extending our sojourn just a little more, just in case of the miracle of the swamp happening?

Supplies and friendships were running dangerously low.

First we needed some solace for this final shattering denial of the buru's existence by its protagonists. We looked for the last remaining bottle of rum. It had been looted too.

Charles was inclined to write the buru off by accepting this new Dafla opinion. Our third companion was inclined to argument, and so was I. After all, we were not romantics, we said, but a scientist, a professional photographer and a journalist.

All of us were hard-bitten and highly sceptical when "told the tale". The most sceptical of all had always been Charles, the scientist, searching for argument to disprove his own evidence, so that if that evidence were true analysis would strengthen it. That, of course, is the right approach to those zoological imponderables we hear about from time to time. It makes for real evidence when the time is ripe – if it ever is in the inaccessible and dangerous parts of the world that still remain in spite of the wider implications of present-day space exploration.

We finally decided that even if our expedition had ended in no tangible evidence, the detailed and tallying descriptions of the buru taken from many different tribesmen could not be dismissed as so much racial legend and superstition. There was nothing supernatural in the buru reports, except in the Apa Tani tale of the lethal Mamla plates and the spirit control they seemed to believe was attached to them. It occurred to us as unbelievable that successive generations of men depending on hunting for their livelihood could ever have been deceived into making an animal out of shadows on the surface of pools. Their very calling demanded keen observation of wild animals. Also, the whole countryside had been positive that now burus only appeared at Rilo.

What was the link between the alleged Rilo burus and those of the Apa Tani Valley which was fifty miles distant over a succession of mountains where lived another tribe speaking another language? No tracks led east to the Apa Tanis. Burus of the Apa Tani were known to have been extinct for centuries. Why should the same species of animal suddenly re-appear at Rilo which had only been inhabited a mere ten years actually at the time of our expedition? Nobody had anything to gain by making out such reports.

The only reason for the Daflas' change of front now, we all agreed after discussion, was that the tribesmen had grown tired of us. There was no more that could be extracted from our camp, so the best way to get rid of us was to deny the monster's existence. Probably the hunting party's statement to Charles of having seen the buru had been made by someone not yet briefed by the headman on their growing antagonism to our presence at Rilo. Hence the surprising *volte-face* when they agreed that what they had seen was just the effect of shadows and wind.

The Apa Tanis' first stories of the buru were almost certainly the genuine ones, and tallying reports from the Daflas previous to their campaign against us were also a logical follow-up.

The monsoon was now well upon us, and apart from the worst hardships of all – "ordeal by insects" – there were too many risks to face if we did not hurry away. Soon the rivers would be in flood and we would be marooned in the swamp until June. Soon, no porter would be able to help us up and down the treacherous, slippery tracks to get back to near-civilisation. We could have faced staying on if the buru had shown itself; now we packed and departed, knowing that lingering would have been senseless waste of time and money, as well as rather suicidal in view of the climate and tribal hostility.

"The wind of change" written about many years ago by

that inimitable author of India, E. M. Forster, and quoted during an African visit in more recent years by an eminent British statesman, was blowing vigorously across the whole of the sub-continent when we came back.

We were more dead than alive, our clothes rotting off our backs, and we found that British rule had passed to Indian hands.

The Northern Assam tribes, who had no alternative but to accept Indian rule, soon became disturbed. To the east, where we had nearly left our skins, trouble soon spread, and the Indian Army engaged in "Police action" against the Naga headhunters along the Burman front.

Charles, Frank Hodgkinson and I left India that summer.

OPEN BOAT

F.A. Worsley

Frank Worsley was the captain of HMS Endurance, *the ship used by Sir Ernest Shackleton in his 1914–16 expedition to Antarctica. When the* Endurance *became trapped and crushed by ice, the ship's party of twenty-eight men drifted on an ice floe for five months before, as Worsley recounts here, taking to three small boats on 16 April 1916. Their destination was Elephant Island in the South Shetlands.*

Just in time – two hours after noon – we reached a narrow arm of open water. As the pack edged away from us the floeberg rolled and almost dipped one side into the sea. With a rush we slid the boats down the six-foot cliff into the water.

The *James Caird* caught on a ledge of ice, but her crew smartly pushed her off and saved her from capsizing. We hurled the stores in without stowing and, leaping on them, pushed and poled the boats out into safety. It was a narrow enough escape.

Dodging in and out through loose patches of pack, we sailed two miles west into more open sea. Then the *Stancomb Wills* fell astern and got into trouble. It was blowing half a gale from northeast, and it looked as though the *Wills* would be jammed on a lee shore – the front of the main pack.

My boat being the fastest, Shackleton sent me back to tow the *Wills* clear. It was sunset by the time we overhauled and rejoined Shackleton.

We continued to sail west until we saw a floe large enough to promise some shelter for the night. At dusk we made fast in its lee.

As we tended the boats and ate cold rations, Green and How landed the galley and boiled the milk. While this operation was proceeding some of our irrepressibles were making impatient calf noises to amuse Green, until we were all handed mugs of glorious hot milk. The galley was then embarked.

Suddenly masses of ice eddied round the floe, threatening to hole the boats. We cast off hurriedly. During the night we dodged from one patch of ice to another, but could get no shelter.

"A cold, wet, rotten night – all hands wet and shivering – with rain at first and snow showers. One oilskin only in the *Docker*. No sleep. After midnight the temperature fell to 25° of frost, and we could not get enough rowing to keep us warm. I wanted to pull slowly to the west all night for the sake of progress and to keep the men warm, but Sir Ernest would not agree. He feared the danger of holing the boats against the ice and the difficulty of keeping them together in the dark. At dawn we set sail and steered west-southwest on the starboard tack. This twenty-four hours we have seen numerous fulmars, snow petrels, silver petrels, giant petrels (almost as big as albatrosses), stormy petrels, and Antarctic petrels. Hundreds of crabeaters in all directions on the pack and many whales.

"April 12. 62°15′S, 53°07′W. Strong northwest breeze. Cloudy and misty, with sleet showers. The temperature during the last three days has been going up and down – mostly down – but we had no thermometer in the *Docker*."

When our crop of minor frostbites increased, we hailed Hussey in the *Caird*. "What's the temperature, meteorologist?" Our youthful humorist invariably gave the information wrapped up in comic abuse. This was received politely if the temperature was reasonably cold, but if it was below zero he got a hot reply. The northwest wind brought the temperature nearly up to freezing point, but no pleasure to us. It turned the snow to sleet and rain, which froze on men and stores, making us wet, cold, and miserable. Fortunately our previous experiences had so toughened us that we managed to weather it out.

After breakfast, as soon as the horizon cleared, I took observations for longitude with the sextant. At noon I observed the latitude.

When I worked out the position, it was a terrible disappointment. I had previously told Shackleton that I thought we had made thirty miles towards Elephant Island. The sights proved we were thirty miles farther away and had been driven nineteen miles farther south. Shackleton ran the *James Caird* down to us and asked, "What have we made, Skipper?" "Thirty miles astern, sir," I muttered. It was so bad that he did not tell the men. He merely said, "We haven't done as well as we expected." Even so I got a black look or two.

In retrospect, the childlike mentality of many of the party, in respect to our progress, had its humorous side. On the pack ice, which was outside any human control, they seemed to hold me responsible for the drift. At noon, when I worked out where the ice had carried our camp, I was asked, "What have we done?" If I replied "Four miles north," it was "Well done, Skipper, have a cigarette." If I said "Fourteen miles north," I became the hero of the day. Cigarettes, bits of bannocks and lumps of chocolate were offered to me. On the other hand, if we drifted eight miles south, I received black looks and was avoided like a pestilence. Like the Ancient Mariner, "Instead of the cross the albatross about my neck they hung." Few besides Shackleton sympathized with me.

This last setback came when it was imperative to make speed to the land. A strong head current had poured out from the Bransfield Strait, which lay ninety miles west of us.

The current had been speeded up by the heavy northwest gale which we knew, by the swell, had been blowing off Cape Horn. Our advance had been completely reversed and we had been carried south into the pack again.

Though the responsibility must rest on the leader of an expedition, I can never forget my acute anxiety for the next two days. If there was a mistake in my sights, which were taken under very difficult conditions, twenty-eight men would have sailed out to death. Fortunately the sights proved correct. We made the island ahead fifty hours later.

Shortly after noon we suddenly ran out of the main pack into open sea, with bergs and small islands of pack scattered about. There was a long swell from the open sea, and we flattered ourselves we were going to make a good passage either to the island or else to Graham Land, the northern extreme of the Antarctic Continent.

We sailed past a strange berg that resembled a pig-faced prehistoric monster. It rolled slowly to the swell. For five minutes at a time the grotesque face rolled down 100 feet into the sea. A long pause and it slowly rolled up again, the water pouring in torrents down the monster's face. It seemed to us to be weeping tears of rage at our escape from the pack.

"In the evening we saw enormous 'woolpacks' of cumulus to northwest – the aftermath of the gale which had raised the great swell. They were breaking up. These great cumulus are seldom or never seen over pack ice. The sea appeared open to southwest, and the heaviest pack lay behind us to the east.

"From here onward, to the departure of the *James*

Caird from Elephant Island, was written from memory
nine months later, as I was too busy to do so in the boat,
what with steering, navigating with frostbitten fingers,
etc. etc."

The sea was clear to southwest, and the wind having
increased and hauled northwest was ahead for the island.
Sir Ernest discussed with Wild and me the advantages of
making for Hope Bay in the north of Graham Land, and
decided that was the best course under the circumstances.

We sailed west-southwest into the dusk, but later met
long streams of ice that we could not weather. To avoid
being caught between the streams in the dark, we made
fast to the largest floe we could find. Unfortunately it was
not large enough to give us much shelter from the rising
gale. The sea was too rough for the cook to land his galley,
so we boiled milk over a "Primus" in each boat.

We made a practice of eating our food and swallowing
our milk at far greater heat than normal men could have
borne. So we gave our chilled bodies warmth enough to
keep us alive against cold, fatigue, and lack of sleep.

The painters of the *Caird* and the *Docker* were made
fast on the floe, and the *Wills* moored between us. The
three boats lay side by side during supper. Later the seas
running round the floe bumped and chafed the boats, so
that we had to slack the other two astern of us.

As the last of our supper was vanishing at its usual
amazing rate, the wind suddenly shifted to southeast. The
boats drove broadside on to the jagged edge of the floe. To
save them being stove in, we hurriedly cut our painter,
losing valuable rope, and pushed off.

All that night in the open sea we "bothered" about – as
our seamen did *not* say. The *James Caird* made fast astern
of us and the *Stancomb Wills* astern of her. Most of the
time we pulled ahead, towing the two boats to prevent
them bumping. We had the best of it – the exercise kept us
from freezing, and also kept us awake. I am keen on

rowing and enjoyed my spells at the oars. Some were not usually keen on rowing, but all preferred it, that night, to the shivering spells between.

The temperature suddenly fell to 36° of frost. It was so cold that our Burberry overalls crackled and ice and frost fell off us as we rowed. When the moon came out, we saw that beards were white with frost, moustaches knobbed with ice, and each man's breath formed clouds of vapour, showing white against his grubby face.

Snow showers swept up from southeast and the surface of the sea froze in spite of wind and swell. This made patches of sludgy ice into which we towed the boats for smoother water. Another compensation – the sudden change of wind that almost spoiled our supper – had given us a fair wind for Elephant Island.

So far this boat escape had been a "rake's progress". We had rowed. We had sailed. Shackleton and I had taken turns at towing the smallest boat. We had been hindered by pack ice, head winds, currents, and heavy swells. We had hauled up on the ice and escaped again. Now, after three days of toil and exposure, without sleep, we were forty miles farther from Elephant Island.

In spite of all, the men, inspired by Shackleton, were magnificent. Their courage and humour came to the front when most needed. It was well that they had been toughened and tempered to hardness for this ordeal, by the progressively severer conditions which we had undergone since leaving civilization.

Shackleton and several of us had been trained in square-rigged ships. After the cold of South Georgia our party worked the *Endurance* through 3,000 miles of pack ice – a fine, hard, open-air life. Then came 1,000 miles drift, with temperature down to 100° of frost, but in the comfort of the ship. Then 600 miles drift in gale-worn tents lying by night on snow that, melted by the heat of our bodies, ran into our sleeping bags until we lay in pools of ice-cold water. Now that conditions were worse the men, like true British seamen, ceased complaining and said, "Grin and bear it. Growl and go."

At dawn on the thirteenth, it blew strong from south-east, with clear weather. Cumulus – typical of open sea – scudded across the blue sky.

The men were bleary-eyed from exposure and want of sleep. Shackleton hailed me. I took the *Dudley Docker* alongside. After a short talk we decided to take advantage of the fair wind and steer, again, for Elephant Island. The food stores were distributed amongst the boats, so that, if they separated, no one would go short.

Sail was set, and we steered northwest. As the boats gathered way before the fair breeze our spirits rose. We forgot our disappointments. We were making headway to the land – solid land! How fine it would be to feel good earth beneath our feet, after sixteen months spent on the accursed heaving, restless ice. We felt the exhilaration that yachtsmen feel. We were yachting though in a rather overperilous manner.

As we rolled along we chipped and scraped off the ice that had formed during the night on the bows and sterns of our three craft. We could not cook while we were sailing, so Shackleton gave permission for every man to eat as much biscuit, cold ration, nut food, and West Indies loaf sugar as he liked. This was a fairly safe order as we had found by experience that, "short commons" had so contracted our stomachs that we were unable to eat too much at one time.

It was more than sixteen months since the party had been in a rough sea. Several were "off colour" for two days, but four were seasick and unable to eat. I was sorry for them. It was bad enough for frostbitten men to be huddled in deep-laden boats while seas broke over them, without having seasickness added. However, our amusement was aroused by the dismay of one who was fond of saving his food and, later, eating it in front of others who had not been so frugal. This procedure had an infuriating effect on most of the hungry onlookers. Now this man, suffering from seasickness, gazed impotently at us – ravening sea wolves – making the rations disappear. He got scant sympathy.

Sailing on at a fair rate we came into areas of loose pack ice, interspersed with many lumps. Taking turns, we leaned over the bows, poling the lumps away with indifferent success. Many were too heavy to be moved quickly enough. The *Caird* struck one that holed her above the water line. Soon after we saw a piece of sealskin protruding through the hole to keep the water out. After that we reefed sails to avoid more damage to the boats.

At noon we again came into an area of comparatively open water. Shackleton led in the *Caird*, followed by the *Docker* and the *Wills* in that order. Occasionally he sent me ahead to prospect, but generally his orders were for the boats to keep within thirty yards of each other.

Our sails showed dark in contrast to the patches of white pack. We looked like a fleet of exploring or marauding Vikings. Sailing on we came to large areas of freezing sea with slush and "pancakes", through which we forced the boats at much reduced speed.

Lying about in the slush and on the "pancakes" were countless thousands of dead fish, some of which were eight inches long. They had been caught and frozen by the sudden freezing of the sea. They looked like splashes and bars of silver glistening in the sun. The petrels and Cape pigeons were enjoying an unusual feast. Like the birds, we would have relished a splendid meal of fish, but we dared not waste time gathering them.

In the afternoon the temperature rose slightly, the sea thawed and became more open. We made good headway, but had to take a second reef in the sails as the boats were shipping much water and steering badly in the rising wind and sea.

At sunset I thought the wind would soon moderate, and advised Shackleton to stand on all night, but he consid-

ered it safer to heave to. This we did by means of three
oars bent on to the *Docker*'s painter for a sea anchor. The
other boats were made fast astern of us.

We had sailed clear of the pack ice so quickly that there
had been no time to lay in a stock of ice for drinking water.
All hands were suffering painfully from thirst. However,
by superior cunning, we in the *Docker* had secured four
precious blocks of ice. These we "whacked out", with
comparative honesty, amongst the other crews. By very
strict rationing we managed to make the ice last all night.
It seems strange that men in such cold weather, frequently soaked by seas breaking over them, should have
suffered more from thirst than hunger, but so it was.
Throughout the night Shackleton was concerned with the
welfare of the men. He always took great care of them, but
now, owing to the incessant hardships, he was obviously
anxious. At intervals he hailed us and the *Wills* to find
how we were faring. The answers were always cheerful,
but Marston raised a laugh by humorously shouting, "All
right, but I'd like some dry mitts." There was nothing dry
in the boats except our parched mouths. Shackleton
replied, "I left a pair at home. You can have them if
you'll drop in and tell 'em I'm coming." The humour may
have been slightly heavy, but we were eager to seize on
any excuse for a laugh.

The sea, breaking over the boats, froze in great masses
on bows and sterns. The temperature was below zero, but
we could not waste precious matches looking at the
thermometer. There was no real sleep that night, though
some dozed in each other's arms for warmth.

After dark the wind moderated, as I had foretold,
which, however, did not prove that Shackleton's decision
was wrong. But I had a twofold anxiety. One was that
delay might give time for a heavy gale to rise. The other
was about the men. Some were becoming exhausted with
fatigue, intense cold, and lack of sleep for three days and
nights. We knew there was more to follow. Next night the

delay ran us into a gale so furious that it was providential neither of the smaller boats foundered.

At daybreak on the fourteenth there was a gentle south-west breeze and clear weather. A magnificent and gorgeously beautiful sunrise raised our spirits, but not our hopes. It was a high dawn presaging a gale.

It had been impossible to sleep in the two open boats. In the *Docker* we laid our flimsy tent on the ice-clad boxes of stores. Pulling its folds over us, we compressed ourselves into a shivering mass of humanity. We were like those monkeys which, during a cold night in the forest, lock themselves into a ball for mutual warmth. If one gets left out and, pushing in, disturbs the others, a furious row ensues. So it was with us. When some shivering unfortunate on the outside tried to push in, there instantly arose a frightful burst of profanity and dire threats of vengeance from the disturbed men.

Greenstreet and I bore this till some time after midnight. We then crawled out, swung our arms, stamped our feet, punched each other, and occasionally solaced ourselves by smoking. We used four valuable matches.

When daylight came we stood looking for some minutes at the writhing mass of suffering men clearly outlined under the tent. It shook and heaved up and down. It trembled and wriggled. Ever and again, at some fresh convulsion, it emitted terrible oaths profaning the morning air. Suddenly we could stand it no longer. We burst into such yells of laughter that we roused the crews of the other boats as well as our own. We were possibly a bit overwrought, but even now, years after, I laugh whenever I recall that scene.

In the growing light we cleared the boats of the heavy accumulations of ice that were weighing them down. Before we could ship the rudder we had to chip and scrape all ice off the stern and clear the gudgeon holes before we could get the pintles in.

After this we ranged alongside the *Caird* and tacked a square of sealskin over the hole in her bows. A good temporary patch that would keep the water out in a high sea. The next job was to haul in the painter and recover the oars which we had been using as an improvised sea anchor. When we reached the oars we found each encased in ice to the thickness of a man's thigh. We had to chip them clear before we could lift them aboard. Setting sail, we stood north, and again all hands were cheered by our progress.

For breakfast we had cold rations. There were a few very small lumps of ice remaining. These we sucked slowly. When they were finished we became so terribly thirsty that we were unable to eat. We then resorted to chewing pieces of raw bloody seal meat.

This stayed our thirst as well as our ravenous hunger for a while, but later we were more parched than before. Probably this was due to salts in the seal's blood.

In the *Wills* Blackborrow's feet were badly frostbitten. Nothing could be done then except that Dr. McIlroy occasionally massaged the sufferer's feet. Blackborrow, the youngest of the party, was twenty years old. That may have accounted for the fact that he was the only one to suffer permanently from frostbite. Shackleton and the other six Antarctic veterans had come through well, but equally so had Greenstreet, the two doctors, Clark, Wordie, and I. Most of us had suffered no more than frostbitten fingers which all were liable to. The only notice we took of a frostbitten finger was to remove our sodden mitts and massage the finger until it recovered.

Shackleton said to me, later, "All the time I was attending to the boats and watching the condition of the men, Wild sat calmly steering the *Caird*. He never batted an eyelid. Always the same confident, blue-eyed little man, unmoved by cold or fatigue. He was a tower of strength, as I knew he would be."

This was only what we all expected of that grand veteran of the Antarctic, but it was typical of Shackleton to praise his friend so generously.

As the daylight strengthened, we saw to northeast the lofty snow-clad peak of Clarence Island tipped with pink against the sunrise. A little later the peaks and ice uplands of Elephant Island showed cold and gloomy, thirty-five miles to the north-northwest. They were both exactly on the bearings I had laid off. Shackleton, always generous with praise, congratulated me on the accuracy of my navigation under difficult conditions, after two days of dead reckoning working in and out amongst floes with no accurate means of checking compass courses and two nights drifting at the mercy of winds and currents.

I took my honours unblushingly, but to tell the truth there had been a large element of luck in making this good landfall. I had been very anxious, for our lives depended on reaching land speedily. My worries departed; the men forgot thirst, hunger, and fatigue. All cheered up visibly in spite of the forbidding look of our goal.

Since Elephant Island was uninhabited, Worsley, Shackleton and four others then sailed 800 miles in the James Caird *to the whaling stations of South Georgia.*

ACROSS SOUTH GEORGIA

Ernest Shackleton

The legendary Sir Ernest Shackleton led the ill-fated Endurance *expedition to Antarctica (see pp. 302–313), which
he later chronicled in* South. *He died in 1922, aged forty-
eight, on his fourth Antarctic expedition, and is buried in the
whalers' cemetery in South Georgia.*

From South:

A fresh west-southwesterly breeze was blowing on the
following morning (Wednesday, May 17), with misty
squalls, sleet, and rain. I took Worsley with me on a
pioneer journey to the west with the object of examining
the country to be traversed at the beginning of the overland journey. We went round the seaward end of the
snouted glacier, and after tramping about a mile over
stony ground and snow-coated debris, we crossed some
big ridges of scree and moraines. We found that there was
good going for a sledge as far as the northeast corner of the
bay, but did not get much information regarding the
conditions farther on owing to the view becoming obscured by a snow squall. We waited a quarter of an hour
for the weather to clear but were forced to turn back
without having seen more of the country. I had satisfied

myself, however, that we could reach a good snow slope leading apparently to the inland ice. Worsley reckoned from the chart that the distance from our camp to Husvik, on an east magnetic course, was seventeen geographical miles, but we could not expect to follow a direct line. The carpenter started making a sledge for use on the overland journey. The materials at his disposal were limited in quantity and scarcely suitable in quality.

We overhauled our gear on Thursday, May 18, and hauled our sledge to the lower edge of the snouted glacier. The vehicle proved heavy and cumbrous. We had to lift it empty over bare patches of rock along the shore, and I realized that it would be too heavy for three men to manage amid the snow plains, glaciers, and peaks of the interior. Worsley and Crean were coming with me, and after consultation we decided to leave the sleeping bags behind us and make the journey in very light marching order. We would take three days' provisions for each man in the form of sledging ration and biscuit. The food was to be packed in three sacks, so that each member of the party could carry his own supply. Then we were to take the Primus lamp filled with oil, the small cooker, the carpenter's adze (for use as an ice axe), and the alpine rope, which made a total length of fifty feet when knotted. We might have to lower ourselves down steep slopes or cross crevassed glaciers. The filled lamp would provide six hot meals, which would consist of sledging ration boiled up with biscuit. There were two boxes of matches left, one full and the other partially used. We left the full box with the men at the camp and took the second box, which contained forty-eight matches. I was unfortunate as regarded footgear, since I had given away my heavy Burberry boots on the floe, and had now a comparatively light pair in poor condition. The carpenter assisted me by putting several screws in the sole of each boot with the object of providing a grip on the ice. The screws came out of the *James Caird*.

We turned in early that night, but sleep did not come to

me. My mind was busy with the task of the following day.
The weather was clear and the outlook for an early start in
the morning was good. We were going to leave a weak
party behind us in the camp. Vincent was still in the same
condition, and he could not march. McNeish was pretty
well broken up. The two men were not capable of managing for themselves and McCarthy must stay to look after
them. He might have a difficult task if we failed to reach
the whaling station. The distance to Husvik, according to
the chart, was no more than seventeen geographical miles
in a direct line, but we had very scanty knowledge of the
conditions of the interior. No man had ever penetrated a
mile from the coast of South Georgia at any point, and the
whalers I knew regarded the country as inaccessible.
During that day, while we were walking to the snouted
glacier, we had seen three wild duck flying towards the
head of the bay from the eastward. I hoped that the
presence of these birds indicated tussock land and not
snow fields and glaciers in the interior, but the hope was
not a very bright one.

We turned out at 2 a.m. on the Friday morning and had
our hoosh ready an hour later. The full moon was shining
in a practically cloudless sky, its rays reflected gloriously
from the pinnacles and crevassed ice of the adjacent
glaciers. The huge peaks of the mountains stood in bold
relief against the sky and threw dark shadows on the
waters of the sound. There was no need for delay, and
we made a start as soon as we had eaten our meal.
McNeish walked about 200 yds. with us; he could do
no more. Then we said good-bye and he turned back to
the camp. The first task was to get round the edge of the
snouted glacier, which had points like fingers projecting
towards the sea. The waves were reaching the points of
these fingers, and we had to rush from one across to
another when the waters receded. We soon reached the
east side of the glacier and noticed its great activity at this
point. Changes had occurred within the preceding

twenty-four hours. Some huge pieces had broken off, and the masses of mud and stone that were being driven before the advancing ice showed movement. The glacier was like a gigantic plough driving irresistibly towards the sea.

Lying on the beach beyond the glacier was wreckage that told of many ill-fated ships. We noticed stanchions of teakwood, liberally carved, that must have come from ships of the older type; ironbound timbers with the iron almost rusted through; battered barrels and all the usual debris of the ocean. We had difficulties and anxieties of our own, but as we passed that graveyard of the sea we thought of the many tragedies written in the wave-worn fragments of lost vessels. We did not pause, and soon we were ascending a snow slope, heading due east on the last lap of our long trail.

The snow surface was disappointing. Two days before we had been able to move rapidly on hard, packed snow; now we sank over our ankles at each step and progress was slow. After two hours' steady climbing we were 2500 ft. above sea level. The weather continued fine and calm, and as the ridges drew nearer and the western coast of the island spread out below, the bright moonlight showed us that the interior was broken tremendously. High peaks, impassable cliffs, steep snow slopes, and sharply descending glaciers were prominent features in all directions, with stretches of snow plain overlaying the ice sheet of the interior. The slope we were ascending mounted to a ridge and our course lay direct to the top. The moon, which proved a good friend during this journey, threw a long shadow at one point and told us that the surface was broken in our path. Warned in time, we avoided a huge hole capable of swallowing an army. The bay was now about three miles away, and the continued roaring of a big glacier at the head of the bay came to our ears. This glacier, which we had noticed during the stay at Peggotty Camp, seemed to be calving almost continuously.

I had hoped to get a view of the country ahead of us from

the top of the slope, but as the surface became more level beneath our feet, a thick fog drifted down. The moon became obscured and produced a diffused light that was more trying than darkness, since it illuminated the fog without guiding our steps. We roped ourselves together as a precaution against holes, crevasses, and precipices, and I broke trail through the soft snow. With almost the full length of the rope between myself and the last man we were able to steer an approximately straight course, since, if I veered to the right or the left when marching into the blank wall of the fog, the last man on the rope could shout a direction. So, like a ship with its "port," "starboard," "steady," we tramped through the fog for the next two hours.

Then, as daylight came, the fog thinned and lifted, and from an elevation of about 3000 ft. we looked down on what seemed to be a huge frozen lake with its farther shores still obscured by the fog. We halted there to eat a bit of biscuit while we discussed whether we would go down and cross the flat surface of the lake, or keep on the ridge we had already reached. I decided to go down, since the lake lay on our course. After an hour of comparatively easy travel through the snow we noticed the thin beginnings of crevasses. Soon they were increasing in size and showing fractures, indicating that we were traveling on a glacier. As the daylight brightened the fog dissipated; the lake could be seen more clearly, but still we could not discover its east shore. A little later the fog lifted completely, and then we saw that our lake stretched to the horizon, and realized suddenly that we were looking down upon the open sea on the east coast of the island. The slight pulsation at the shore showed that the sea was not even frozen; it was the bad light that had deceived us. Evidently we were at the top of Possession Bay, and the island at that point could not be more than five miles across from the head of King Haakon Bay. Our rough chart was inaccurate. There was nothing for it but to start up the glacier again. That was about seven o'clock in the morning, and by nine o'clock we had more than recovered our lost ground. We regained the ridge and then struck southeast, for the chart showed that two more bays indented the coast before Stromness. It was comforting to realize that we would have the eastern water in sight during our journey, although we could see there was no way around the shoreline owing to steep cliffs and glaciers. Men lived in houses lit by electric light on the east coast. News of the outside world waited us there, and, above all, the east coast meant for us the means of rescuing the twenty-two men we had left on Elephant Island.

The sun rose in the sky with every appearance of a fine day, and we grew warmer as we toiled through the soft snow. Ahead of us lay the ridges and spurs of a range of mountains, the transverse range that we had noticed from the bay. We were traveling over a gently rising plateau, and at the end of an hour we found ourselves growing uncomfortably hot. Years before, on an earlier expedition, I had declared that I would never again growl at the heat of the sun, and my resolution had been strengthened during the boat journey. I called it to mind as the sun beat fiercely on the blinding white snow slope. After passing an area of crevasses we paused for our first meal. We dug a hole in the snow about three feet deep with the adze and put the Primus into it. There was no wind at the moment, but a gust might come suddenly. A hot hoosh was soon eaten and we plodded on towards a sharp ridge between two of the peaks already mentioned. By 11 a.m. we were almost at the crest. The slope had become precipitous and it was necessary to cut steps as we advanced. The adze proved an excellent instrument for this purpose, a blow sufficing to provide a foothold. Anxiously but hopefully I cut the last few steps and stood upon the razorback, while the other men held the rope and waited for my news. The outlook was disappointing. I looked down a sheer precipice to a chaos of crumpled ice 1500 ft. below. There was no way down for us. The country to the east was a great snow upland, sloping upwards for a distance of seven or eight miles to a height of over 4000 ft. To the north it fell away steeply in glaciers into the bays, and to the south it was broken by huge outfalls from the inland ice sheet. Our path lay between the glaciers and the outfalls, but first we had to descend from the ridge on which we stood.

Cutting steps with the adze, we moved in a lateral direction round the base of a dolomite, which blocked our view to the north. The same precipice confronted us. Away to the northeast there appeared to be a snow slope that might give a path to the lower country, and so we retraced our steps down the long slope that had taken us three hours to climb. We were at the bottom in an hour. We were now feeling the strain of the unaccustomed marching. We had done little walking since January and our muscles were out of tune. Skirting the base of the mountain above us, we came to a gigantic bergs-chrund, a mile and a half long and 1000 ft. deep. This tremendous gully, cut in the snow and ice by the fierce winds blowing round the mountain, was semicircular in form, and it ended in a gentle incline. We passed through it, under the towering precipice of ice, and at the far end we had another meal and a short rest. This was at 12:30 p.m. Half a pot of steaming Bovril ration warmed us up, and when we marched again ice inclines at angles of 45 degrees did not look quite as formidable as before.

Once more we started for the crest. After another weary climb we reached the top. The snow lay thinly on blue ice at the ridge, and we had to cut steps over the last fifty yards. The same precipice lay below, and my eyes searched vainly for a way down. The hot sun had loosened the snow, which was now in a treacherous condition, and we had to pick our way carefully. Looking back, we could see that a fog was rolling up behind us and meeting in the valleys a fog that was coming up from the east. The creeping grey clouds were a plain warning that we must get down to lower levels before becoming enveloped.

The ridge was studded with peaks, which prevented us getting a clear view either to the right or to the left. The situation in this respect seemed no better at other points within our reach, and I had to decide that our course lay back the way we had come. The afternoon was wearing on and the fog was rolling up ominously from the west. It was of the utmost importance for us to get down into the next valley before dark. We were now up 4500 ft. and the night temperature at that elevation would be very low. We had no tent and no sleeping bags, and our clothes had endured much rough usage and had weathered many storms during the last ten months. In the distance, down the valley below us, we could see tussock grass close to the shore, and if we could get down it might be possible to dig out a hole in one of the lower snowbanks, line it with dry grass, and make ourselves fairly comfortable for the night. Back we went, and after a detour we reached the top of another ridge in the fading light. After a glance over the top I turned to the anxious faces of the two men behind me and said, "Come on, boys." Within a minute they stood beside me on the ice ridge. The surface fell away at a sharp incline in front of us, but it merged into a snow slope. We could not see the bottom clearly owing to mist and bad light, and the possibility of the slope ending in a sheer fall occurred to us; but the fog that was creeping up behind allowed no time for hesitation. We descended slowly at first, cutting steps in the hard snow; then the surface became softer, indicating that the gradient was less severe. There could be no turning back now, so we unroped and slid in the fashion of youthful days. When we stopped on a snow bank at the foot of the slope we found that we had descended at least 900 ft. in two or three minutes. We looked back and saw the grey fingers of the fog appearing on the ridge, as though reaching after the intruders into untrodden wilds. But we had escaped.

The country to the east was an ascending snow upland dividing the glaciers of the north coast from the outfalls of the south. We had seen from the top that our course lay between two huge masses of crevasses, and we thought that the road ahead lay clear. This belief and the increasing cold made us abandon the idea of camping. We had another meal at 6 p.m. A little breeze made cooking difficult in spite of the shelter provided for the cooker by a hole. Crean was the cook, and Worsley and I lay on the snow to windward of the lamp so as to break the wind with our bodies. The meal over, we started up the long, gentle ascent. Night was upon us, and for an hour we plodded along in almost complete darkness, watching warily for signs of crevasses. Then about 8 P.M. a glow which we had seen behind the jagged peaks resolved itself into the full moon, which rose ahead of us and made a silver pathway for our feet. Along that pathway in the wake of the moon we advanced in safety, with the shadows cast by the edges of crevasses showing black on either side of us. Onwards and upwards through soft snow we marched, resting now and then on hard patches which had revealed themselves by glittering ahead of us in the white light. By midnight we were again at an elevation of about 4000 ft. Still we were following the light, for as the moon swung round towards the northeast our path curved in that direction. The friendly moon seemed to pilot our weary feet. We could have had no better guide. If in bright daylight we had made that march we would have followed the course that was traced for us that night.

Midnight found us approaching the edge of a great snow field, pierced by isolated nunataks which cast long shadows like black rivers across the white expanse. A gentle slope to the northeast lured our all-too-willing feet in that direction. We thought that at the base of the slope lay Stromness Bay. After we had descended about 300 ft. a thin wind began to attack us. We had now been on the march for over twenty hours, only halting for our occasional meals. Wisps of cloud drove over the high peaks to the southward, warning us that wind and snow were likely to come. After 1 a.m. we cut a pit in the snow, piled up loose snow around it, and started the Primus again. The hot food gave us another renewal of energy. Worsley and Crean sang their old songs when the Primus was going merrily. Laughter was in our hearts, though not on our parched and cracked lips.

We were up and away again within half an hour, still downward to the coast. We felt almost sure now that we were above Stromness Bay. A dark object down at the foot of the slope looked like Mutton Island, which lies off Husvik. I suppose our desires were giving wings to our fancies, for we pointed out joyfully various landmarks revealed by the now vagrant light of the moon, whose friendly face was cloud-swept. Our high hopes were soon shattered. Crevasses warned us that we were on another glacier, and soon we looked down almost to the seaward edge of the great riven ice mass. I knew there was no glacier in Stromness and realized that this must be Fortuna Glacier. The disappointment was severe. Back we turned and tramped up the glacier again, not directly tracing our steps but working at a tangent to the southeast. We were very tired.

At 5 a.m. we were at the foot of the rocky spurs of the range. We were tired, and the wind that blew down from the heights was chilling us. We decided to get down under the lee of a rock for a rest. We put our sticks and the adze on the snow, sat down on them as close to one another as possible, and put our arms round each other. The wind was bringing a little drift with it and the white dust lay on our clothes. I thought that we might be able to keep warm and have half an hour's rest this way. Within a minute my two companions were fast asleep. I realized that it would be disastrous if we all slumbered together, for sleep under such conditions merges into death. After five minutes I shook them into consciousness again, told them that they had slept for half an hour, and gave the word for a fresh start. We were so stiff that for the first two or three hundred yards we marched with our knees bent. A jagged line of peaks with a gap like a broken tooth confronted us. This was the ridge that runs in a southerly direction from Fortuna Bay, and our course eastward to Stromness lay across it. A very steep slope led up to the ridge and an icy wind burst through the gap.

We went through the gap at 6 a.m. with anxious hearts as well as weary bodies. If the farther slope had proved impassable our situation would have been almost desperate; but the worst was turning to the best for us. The twisted, wave-like rock formations of Husvik Harbor appeared right ahead in the opening of dawn. Without a word we shook hands with one another. To our minds the journey was over, though as a matter of fact twelve miles of difficult country had still to be traversed. A gentle snow slope descended at our feet towards a valley that separated our ridge from the hills immediately behind Husvik, and as we stood gazing Worsley said solemnly, "Boss, it looks too good to be true!" Down we went, to be checked presently by the sight of water 2500 ft. below. We could see the little wave ripples on the black beach, penguins strutting to and fro, and dark objects that looked like seals lolling lazily on the sand. This was an eastern arm of Fortuna Bay, separated by the ridge from the arm we had seen below us during the night. The slope we were traversing appeared to end in a precipice above this beach. But our revived spirits were not to be damped by difficulties on the last stage of the journey, and we camped cheerfully for breakfast. While Worsley and Crean were digging a hole for the lamp and starting the cooker I climbed a ridge above us, cutting steps with the adze, in order to secure an extended view of the country below. At 6:30 a.m. I thought I heard the sound of a steam whistle. I dared not be certain, but I knew that the men at the whaling station would be called from their beds about that time. Descending to the camp I told the others, and in intense excitement we watched the chronometer for seven o'clock, when the whalers would be summoned to work. Right to the minute the steam whistle came to us, borne clearly on the wind across the intervening miles of rock and snow. Never had any one of us heard sweeter music. It was the first sound created by outside human agency that had come to our ears since we left Stromness Bay in December 1914. That whistle told us that men were living near, that ships were ready, and that within a few hours we should be on our way back to Elephant Island to the rescue of the men waiting there under the watch and ward of Wild. It was a moment hard to describe. Pain and ache, boat journeys, marches, hunger and fatigue seemed to belong to the limbo of forgotten things, and there remained only the perfect contentment that comes of work accomplished.

My examination of the country from a higher point had not provided definite information, and after descending I put the situation before Worsley and Crean. Our obvious course lay down a snow slope in the direction of Husvik. "Boys," I said, "this snow slope seems to end in a precipice, but perhaps there is no precipice. If we don't go down we shall have to make a detour of at least five miles before we reach level going. What shall it be?" They both replied at once. "Try the slope." So we started away again downwards. We abandoned the Primus lamp, now empty, at the breakfast camp and carried with us one ration and a biscuit each. The deepest snow we had yet encountered clogged our feet, but we plodded downward, and after descending about 500 ft., reducing our altitude to 2000 ft. above sea level, we thought we saw the way clear ahead. A steep gradient of blue ice was the next obstacle. Worsley and Crean got a firm footing in a hole excavated with the adze and then lowered me as I cut steps until the full 50 ft. of our alpine rope was out. Then I made a hole big enough for the three of us, and the other two men came down the steps. My end of the rope was anchored to the adze and I had settled myself in the hole braced for a strain in case they slipped. When we all stood in the second hole I went down again to make more steps, and in this laborious fashion we spent two hours descending about 500 ft. Halfway down we had to strike away diagonally to the left, for we noticed that the fragments of ice loosened by the adze were taking a leap into space at the bottom of the slope. Eventually we got off the steep ice, very gratefully, at a point where some rocks protruded, and we could see then that there was a perilous precipice directly below the point where we had started to cut steps. A slide down a slippery slope, with the adze and our cooker going ahead, completed this descent, and incidentally did considerable damage to our much-tried trousers.

When we picked ourselves up at the bottom we were not more than 1500 ft. above the sea. The slope was comparatively easy. Water was running beneath the snow, making "pockets" between the rocks that protruded above the white surface. The shells of snow over these pockets were traps for our feet; but we scrambled down, and presently came to patches of tussock. A few minutes later we reached the sandy beach. The tracks of some animals were to be seen, and we were puzzled until I remembered that reindeer, brought from Norway, had been placed on the island and now ranged along the lower land of the eastern coast. We did not pause to investigate. Our minds were set upon reaching the haunts of man, and at our best speed we went along the beach to another rising ridge of tussock. Here we saw the first evidence of the proximity of man, whose work, as is so often the case, was one of destruction. A recently killed seal was lying there, and presently we saw several other bodies bearing the marks of bullet wounds. I learned that men from the whaling station at Stromness sometimes go round to Fortuna Bay by boat to shoot seals.

Noon found us well up the slope on the other side of the

bay working east-southeast, and half an hour later we were on a flat plateau, with one more ridge to cross before we descended into Husvik. I was leading the way over this plateau when I suddenly found myself up to my knees in water and quickly sinking deeper through the snow crust. I flung myself down and called to the others to do the same, so as to distribute our weight on the treacherous surface. We were on top of a small lake, snow-covered. After lying still for a few moments, we got to our feet and walked delicately, like Agag, for 200 yds., until a rise in the surface showed us that we were clear of the lake.

At 1:30 p.m. we climbed round a final ridge and saw a little steamer, a whaling boat, entering the bay 2500 ft. below. A few moments later, as we hurried forward, the masts of a sailing ship lying at a wharf came in sight. Minute figures moving to and fro about the boats caught our gaze, and then we saw the sheds and factory of Stromness whaling station. We paused and shook hands, a form of mutual congratulation that had seemed necessary on four other occasions in the course of the expedition. The first time was when we landed on Elephant Island, the second when we reached South Georgia, and the third when we reached the ridge and saw the snow slope stretching below on the first day of the overland journey, then when we saw Husvik rocks.

Cautiously we started down the slope that led to warmth and comfort. The last lap of the journey proved extraordinarily difficult. Vainly we searched for a safe, or a reasonably safe, way down from the steep ice-clad mountainside. The sole possible pathway seemed to be a channel cut by water running from the upland. Down through icy water we followed the course of this stream. We were wet to the waist, shivering, cold, and tired. Presently our ears detected an unwelcome sound that might have been musical under other conditions. It was the splashing of a waterfall, and we were at the wrong end. When we reached the top of this fall we peered over cautiously and discovered that there was a drop of 25 or 30 ft., with impassable ice cliffs on both sides. To go up again was scarcely thinkable in our utterly wearied condition. The way down was through the waterfall itself. We made fast one end of our rope to a boulder with some difficulty, due to the fact that the rocks had been worn smooth by the running water. Then Worsley and I lowered Crean, who was the heaviest man. He disappeared altogether in the falling water and came out gasping at the bottom. I went next, sliding down the rope, and Worsley, who was the lightest and most nimble member of the party, came last. At the bottom of the fall we were able to stand again on dry land. The rope could not be recovered. We had flung down the adze from the top of the fall and also the logbook and the cooker wrapped in one of our blouses. That was all, except our wet clothes, that we brought out of the Antarctic, which we had entered a year and a half before with well-found ship, full equipment, and high hopes. That was all of tangible things; but in memories we were rich. We had pierced the veneer of outside things. We had "suffered, starved, and triumphed, groveled down yet grasped at glory, grown bigger in the bigness of the whole." We had seen God in his splendors, heard the text that Nature renders. We had reached the naked soul of men.

Shivering with cold, yet with hearts light and happy, we set off towards the whaling station, now not more than a mile and a half distant. The difficulties of the journey lay behind us. We tried to straighten ourselves up a bit for the thought that there might be women at the station made us painfully conscious of our uncivilized appearance. Our beards were long and our hair was matted. We were unwashed and the garments that we had worn for nearly a year without a change were tattered and stained. Three more unpleasant-looking ruffians could hardly have been imagined. Worsley produced several safety pins from some corner of his garments and effected some temporary repairs that really emphasized his general disrepair. Down we hurried, and when quite close to the station we met two small boys ten or twelve years of age. I asked these lads where the manager's house was situated. They did not answer. They gave us one look – a comprehensive look that did not need to be repeated. Then they ran from us as fast as their legs would carry them. We reached the outskirts of the station and passed through the "digesting-house," which was dark inside. Emerging at the other end, we met an old man, who started as if he had seen the Devil himself and gave us no time to ask any question. He hurried away. This greeting was not friendly. Then we came to the wharf, where the man in charge stuck to his station. I asked him if Mr. Sorlle (the manager) was in the house.

"Yes," he said as he stared at us.

"We would like to see him," said I.

"Who are you?" he asked.

"We have lost our ship and come over the island," I replied.

"You have come over the island?" he said in a tone of entire disbelief.

The man went towards the manager's house and we followed him. I learned afterwards that he said to Mr. Sorlle: "There are three funny-looking men outside, who say they have come over the island and they know you. I have left them outside." A very necessary precaution from his point of view.

Mr. Sorlle came out to the door and said, "Well?"

"Don't you know me?" I said.

"I know your voice," he replied doubtfully. "You're the mate of the *Daisy*."

"My name is Shackleton," I said.

Immediately, he put out his hand and said, "Come in. Come in."

"Tell me, when was the war over?" I asked.

"The war is not over," he answered. "Millions are being killed. Europe is mad. The world is mad."

Mr. Sorlle's hospitality had no bounds. He would

scarcely let us wait to remove our freezing boots before he took us into his house and gave us seats in a warm and comfortable room. We were in no condition to sit in anybody's house until we had washed and got into clean clothes, but the kindness of the station manager was proof even against the unpleasantness of being in a room with us. He gave us coffee and cakes in the Norwegian fashion, and then showed us upstairs to the bathroom, where we shed our rags and scrubbed ourselves luxuriously.

Mr. Sorlle's kindness did not end with his personal care for the three wayfarers who had come to his door. While we were washing he gave orders for one of the whaling vessels to be prepared at once in order that it might leave that night for the other side of the island and pick up the three men there. The whalers knew King Haakon Bay, though they never worked on that side of the island. Soon we were clean again. Then we put on delightful new clothes supplied from the station stores and got rid of our superfluous hair. Within an hour or two we had ceased to be savages and had become civilized men again. Then came a splendid meal, while Mr. Sorlle told us of the arrangements he had made and we discussed plans for the rescue of the main party on Elephant Island.

I arranged that Worsley should go with the relief ship to show the exact spot where the carpenter and his two companions were camped, while I started to prepare for the relief of the party on Elephant Island. The whaling vessel that was going round to King Haakon Bay was expected back on the Monday morning, and was to call at Grytviken Harbor, the port from which we had sailed in December 1914, in order that the magistrate resident there might be informed of the fate of the *Endurance*. It was possible that letters were awaiting us there. Worsley went aboard the whaler at ten o'clock that night and turned in. The next day the relief ship entered King Haakon Bay and he reached Peggotty Camp in a boat. The three men were delighted beyond measure to know that we had made the crossing in safety and that their wait under the upturned *James Caird* was ended. Curiously enough, they did not recognize Worsley, who had left them a hairy, dirty ruffian and had returned his spruce and shaven self. They thought he was one of the whalers. When one of them asked why no member of the party had come round with the relief, Worsley said, "What do you mean?" "We thought the Boss or one of the others would come round," they explained. "What's the matter with you?" said Worsley. Then it suddenly dawned upon them that they were talking to the man who had been their close companion for a year and a half. Within a few minutes the whalers had moved our bits of gear into their boat. They towed off the *James Caird* and hoisted her to the deck of their ship. Then they started on the return voyage. Just at dusk on Monday afternoon they entered Stromness Bay, where the men of the whaling station mustered on the beach to receive the rescued party and to examine with professional interest the boat we had navigated across 800 miles of the stormy ocean they knew so well.

When I look back at those days I have no doubt that Providence guided us, not only across those snow fields, but across the storm-white sea that separated Elephant Island from our landing place on South Georgia. I know that during that long and racking march of thirty-six hours over the unnamed mountains and glaciers of South Georgia it seemed to me often that we were four, not three. I said nothing to my companions on the point, but afterwards Worsley said to me, "Boss, I had a curious feeling on the march that there was another person with us." Crean confessed to the same idea. One feels "the dearth of human words, the roughness of mortal speech" in trying to describe things intangible, but a record of our journeys would be incomplete without a reference to a subject very near to our hearts.

TRAVELS WITH PEGASUS

Christina Dodwell

Christina Dodwell was born in 1951. Her travel books include Travels with Fortune, In Papua New Guinea, *and* Travels with Pegasus, *her account of flying a microlight across West Africa with David Young.*

We flew south towards the Niger River, which lies six miles from the town. "Isn't that one of Tom and Michele's irrigation schemes?" David said as we overflew some neatly laid out rice fields with straw windbreaks. Beyond them was the river, then only the desert, rows of parallel dunes remarkable for their red tops and white valleys. The colours blended on the slopes into shades of pink.

Our engine temperatures were not reading evenly; one cylinder was much too hot. We hoped the instrument was misreading. By pressing the glass David could make the needle drop to normal. I suggested we flew along with him making the gauge read a safe heat.

We thought we were on a straight line course, heading ultimately for Douentza again, but as usual it was impossible to tell how the wind at this height was affecting our line. There were few landmarks to judge by. After one and a half hours we expected to pass the west tip of Lake

Garou and go over Lake Niangay. At one and three-quarter hours we still hadn't seen any lakes, only scrubby bush desert. Niangay should have been twenty-three miles wide, how could we miss it?

David thought he could pick out the shape of a dry lake-bed which he said must be Lake Niangay. People in Tombouctou had assured us the lakes still existed, and I felt certain that, even if they were seasonal, not permanent as the map showed, they could not have leafy bushes growing in them.

Then we spotted a derelict-looking village which tied in on the map with David's theory of dry lakes. Refusing to agree, I studied the map and suggested the village could be one of several we might see if we had drifted east with less of a crosswind than anticipated. It still frustrated me not being able to know either our ground speed or the sideways drift. Below us was another vastness of parallel dunes in pink and white. Twenty minutes later we saw a lake. It shouldn't have been there. Its shape bore no relation to anything on the map.

David did some rapid calculations and said that if by chance this was Niangay, we were flying into headwinds and we'd never make it to Douentza. We climbed to 4,500 feet to give us a better view, then we cruised around in loops, casting for signs. In one bushy basin I thought I saw an elephant, but this was too far north for elephants, I told myself, it was more likely to be an anthill. I switched my attention back to looking for shapes which might be marked on a map. As before, none of the ground features fitted any part of our map. It was time to admit we were lost.

Our fuel gauge showed ten litres left; we needed to stop and refuel from the jerrycans, and our muscles were stiff from two and a half hours' flying. We landed on a spacious purple gravel sweep, with a few anthills and many dead trees, skeletal white in the glaring sun. While we sat in the shade of the wing and pored over the maps, some Peul tribesmen appeared in billowing robes and with swords slung from their shoulders. I asked if they knew where we were.

Unfortunately none of them could speak French, only Fulde. Twelve years ago I had learnt some words of Fulde, useful phrases like "Where is . . .?" and now I racked my brains to remember. *Ipi* sprang to mind but I suspected that was "where is" in Zulu. Slowly some words came: *ndiam*, meaning lake or water; *dar larde*, in the bush; and *me ander*, I don't know. With these and by watching the Peuls' reactions to area names and finding out which ones were local, then pointing in the direction of each name, we attempted to centre our position. The men were puzzled but helpful, though their idea of direction could be totally misleading, as we had found before.

The man beside me had pulled out a dainty silver tobacco pipe of tiny trumpet shape whose wider end was beautifully engraved with patterns, and, after filling it with dusty Tuareg tobacco he lit it by striking a knife against a stone flint over a scrap of fluffy tinder.

Despite our pact that we would never fly in the midday thermals, we decided it would be better than sitting in the heat of the desert. So we took off, and David lopped one of the wingtips into a dust-devil to help us gain lift.

Pegasus purred along comfortably; there were stretches of calm air and stretches where we bubbled along on soft thermals. Below us the pale sand had dark smooth outcrops of rock like stone dunes. Sometimes the whole view looked like a burned pie crust.

Moving south we came to some belts of scrub, which we guessed might be Benzema pan since our map marked water-holes there. Benzema was where there were still some herds of elephants, said to be the remnants of the herds that supplied Hannibal with his elephants for crossing the Alps.

An hour later we spotted a 3,000-foot mountain barrier

dead ahead. This was reassuring, our map showed we should follow them west and they'd lead us to Douentza. These were the mountains we had already flown along the southern side of when we had camped the night in a wind trap.

The north side was no better. Turbulence broke out around us and with one fearful jolt we rocketed up faster than the gauge could show. We were still a few miles from the north-facing cliffs of the mountains but obviously we were encountering seething wind currents spinning back from the wall. A lurch sideways made me grab for handholds, a wump down, and another, I tightened my seatbelt.

It was like hitting holes in the air; we seemed suddenly to stop flying and drop straight down. David stayed silent and concentrated on flying us through it. Twice we "went negative" as gravity forces shot fast towards the border of human limits, and I wondered how much more stress the microlight could take before breaking up.

We tried to climb out of the turbulence, and at 6,000 feet we reached the top of the inversion layer. The air was very cold but less rough. It was rather stunning to fly along level with the flat plateau on the mountain massif, seeing down the sheer drops of its cliffs, and being able to pick out impressive isolated cylindrical peaks towering 1,000 feet higher.

The visibility was deteriorating rapidly with thick dust in the air. And we were tiring fast, we had been flying for four and a half hours. I didn't know whether to feel thirsty and hungry, or sick from the continual pockets of turbulence. We gritted our teeth and went on.

It was with great relief that we finally landed at Douentza. In the evening I met someone who said there had not been water in Lakes Niangay and Do since 1973, and when I asked about the lake we'd seen to the south he said, "Oh yes, that's Benzema, it's a very flooded waterhole."

We had both been right: Lake Niangay was where David had seen its shape, but it hadn't been a lake for so long that bushes had grown. Even the elephant had been in the right place. The incident boosted my faith in David's navigation. He had never actually been lost today, and as a pilot he had certainly come through an evil rough flight with flying colours.

At sundown I sat for coolness on the roof of Fiona's house and was busy writing when I heard music. It was the thumpings of many women pounding millet with wooden pestles, each thud echoing off several mud walls, combined with the handclaps by some women on an upstroke, and others snapping two fingers together or calling a thrilling ululation to encourage their companions, all blending into a rhythmic harmony.

Dawn on the rooftop was punctuated with calls to prayer: "*Allah-ah-hab! Allahaaah-washbar!*" The last two syllables came out with terrific gusto and abrupt staccato endings.

I piloted the morning's flight, to make myself get over the horrors of the last one. At take-off Pegasus didn't do her usual hurtle forward and pop away from the ground; this time she seemed reluctant to let go. David explained he'd moved the trike's hang-pin into its front hole which changed its pitch and made the wing take longer to reach flying speed, less economical on fuel but it would give us greater speed in flight, and meant the aircraft would be more quickly responsive to my hands on the bar.

We were heading in a good tailwind south-west back to Sévaré and the delta. Visibility was great, showing all the cracks in the mountain range beside us; deep sheer ravines made black knife-sharp shadows. From the ravine's narrow mouths came tongues of white sand, dry stream-beds seasonally running a short way into the desert.

A bit of light turbulence sent me scurrying up to 3,000 feet where the air was smooth. It was lovely flying.

Northwards I could see for about forty miles, infinite dune crescents which made flecked scrolling patterns. After an hour, despite our altitude, thermals started bursting off the ground and catching us quite forcefully.

It was hard work keeping the microlight on course. The air was jerking around and we were forced along with it. "Don't fight it," said David, so I relaxed and discovered that by using the bar lightly but firmly, I could feel how to fly.

We saw the River Niger and the glint of lakes in the delta after one and a half hours' flight; my muscles were aching from having to recorrect our course, and the turbulence was increasing as the sun's heat hit the land.

The wind-sock at Sévaré airport was horizontal, indicating a fifteen-knot crosswind, as we descended and made a pass over the runway because our radio wasn't working. The controller couldn't hear us, but we could hear him telling us, "You are inedible. Say again. You are inedible."

Then he saw us, recognised us and cleared us to land.

VICTIM OF RAMADAN

Shiva Naipaul

The travel writer Shiva Naipaul died in 1985, aged forty. His books include Fireflies, The Chip-Chip Gatherers *and* Beyond the Dragon's Mouth. *An annual prize in his memory is awarded by the* Spectator.

The idea was simple enough and, on the face of it, harmless: to spend a few days in Fez and write a short piece about it. Idly, I set off for Morocco. But I would not have gone if, beforehand, I had received this letter which I found awaiting me on my return to London. ". . . I want [the New York editor wrote to me] . . . that sense of place which the great travel writers of the past so wonderfully evoked and which I hope to restore, albeit in a more modern idiom . . . photographically, I see this as a dramatic, riveting story which should provide wonderful contrast to a piece such as the English Lake Country or trekking through New Zealand. In words and pictures, the redolence of spices, the ceaseless counterpoint of languages in the market; the silence of the Arab mosque, the clamorous and enveloping crowds of the street – all that should be conveyed by both words and pictures . . ." Really, there is no need for me or anyone else to have actually been sent to Fez. The dramatic and riveting story could and should have been composed in Manhattan. It would have been far more convincing, far more convenient and much cheaper.

Nor, perhaps, would I have gone if I had known it was the holy month of Ramadan and been forewarned of the privations and dangers to which I would be exposing myself during this season of austerity and exacerbated religious sensibility. In Morocco, as I was soon to discover, the dietary strictures of Ramadan are enforced on the Faithful by state power: Muslims caught eating, drinking or smoking between the hours of sunrise and sunset can be jailed for six months. But, as Royal Air Maroc bore me swiftly over the brown coast of Christian Spain, traversed the wrinkled neck of the Mediterranean and swooped low over the beaches of Islamic North Africa, I had no conception of what lay ahead. Tribulation began almost immediately: while waiting for my luggage to be disgorged from the aircraft a policeman bore down on me, grasped my arm and ordered me to extinguish the cigarette I was smoking. Other, more obvious foreigners were smoking too but they were not troubled by his zeal. It was my misfortune to look as if I ought to have been a Muslim and, therefore, to be treated like one. Argument was useless – and, possibly, full of potential peril. Most Moroccans had never heard of Hindus; and the few who had seemed to think that my ancient religion was merely an eccentric form of Islam.

At my hotel I was told that the restaurant would not be open until 8.30 in deference to the nutritional needs of the staff who would be eating for the first time that day. I went into the bar. The barman looked askance at me. Out on the terrace I could see French and German tourists drinking tall, icy glasses of beer. I ordered a Scotch. He frowned at me. I showed him my room key, showed him my passport. The waiters watched and whispered. Reluctantly, I was served.

As I crossed the market square of the Grand Socco, my shoulder bag lightly brushed the arm of a young man. It was nearing noon and extremely hot. He stopped, turning back towards me, his face sullen with rage as he pointed at his arm. I apologised. He did not, however, seem to want a peaceful solution, but continued to advance on me. I apologised a second time – a little more profusely. This appeared to mollify him slightly. Muttering curses, he went on his way. "It is Ramadan," I was assured again and again whenever I sought from my Moroccan acquaintances an explanation for some display of enigmatic brutishness. Under a blazing sun, men deprived of food and drink operate on short fuses. The Faithful become unpredictable, liable to explode at any moment, to reach for their knives. Ramadan may bring men closer to Allah and Paradise but not, it would seem, to tolerance and compassion. It is a scarifying – not a softening – experience; it must entrench the association of religious purity with suffering and violence.

Ramadan alters the rhythms of life. By day, lethargy reigns, all effort directed towards the conservation of energy. Inert bodies lie sprawled in parks and pools of shade. In field and factory men slow down waiting for the sun to disappear. After dusk and the break of the fast they return to life. At night, the streets of downtown Tangier swarmed with sated and voluble promenaders. Hordes of men crowded bright cafés and restaurants, drinking sweet coffee and mineral water. The atmosphere would become almost festive. Until the small hours of the morning there poured through the open windows of my un-airconditioned room the babble and roar of human activity – for there was a second meal to be eaten at two or three o'clock in the morning. In Fez, almost the whole town, it seemed, would migrate by car and bus to the resort oasis of Sidi

Harazem. There, under a nearly full moon floating above the encircling hills, the smoke of kebab fires hazed the air, plump Berber tribeswomen sang and danced in concrete pavilions, pious beggars recited sutras from the Koran. In the swimming baths which have been built there, bikini clad women splashed unaffectedly in close proximity to strange men – a reminder of the comparative mildness of Morocco's Islamic regime; a mildness which, I sensed, may be under threat. Over all of them, on chanting beggars as well as bikini-clad girls, there arched the enforced rhythms of Ramadan, regulating metabolism and mood. Islam, especially during this holy month, is an inescapable reality clamped down on everyone and everything. The unstable cycle of torpor and release, of denial and satiety, induces a kind of claustrophobia. I recall seeing from a train a peasant clad in coarse robes making his obeisance towards Mecca in a bleak, sunburnt field. When the world becomes a mosque, there is nowhere to seek refuge.

The package tourists who sweep in and out of towns like Fez are a fortunate breed. Sealed off by their air-conditioned coaches from the dusty anarchy through which they move, protected from its assaults and treacheries by their well-trained handlers, they are immune from reality. They come, they take their photographs, they go away. It is a splendid way to travel. I returned from Fez to Tangier, exhausted, after four days. During that time, I had been harried by cheating merchants, felled by a bad stomach and threatened with grievous bodily harm by my guide because I refused to allow his rapacity. The congested alleys and lanes of the medina had quickly lost their charm. I recoiled from the ceaseless counterpoint of language in the marketplace and the clamorous, enveloping crowds. I brought back with me on the long train ride not the redolence of spices but the stench of animal droppings, of heaps of rotting vegetables, of dripping, uncured hides destined for the tanneries. The cloying sourness of the medina seemed to cling to my clothes, to exude from the pores of my skin. Mostly, though, as the train crawled through sunlit, semi-arid dereliction, there hovered before me the feral cunning that had darkened the face of my guide as he sought to terrorise me. It had been a pitiless performance. I thought I would rest for a day or two in Tangier before setting out in search of further adventure.

The hotel I chose was pleasant and sedate – washed in white and green-shuttered. From its terraced garden, planted with bougainvillea and oleander, pines and palms, there was a view of the town and, beyond, the Mediterranean. When there was no mist I could see the mountains of Christian Spain. They were a comforting sight.

Even my guide book, which usually made mountains out of molehills, admitted that there was nothing much to see in Tangier. I had seen what there was to see – the Kasbah, the medina, a palace, a few heavy old guns. Freed from guilt, I felt I could stick to the hotel. Within its high walls my alien status was accepted and I could do much as I pleased. Grateful for the opportunity to recuperate from Fez, I sat by the swimming pool and watched the sun-bathers. My attention came to rest on two men with dark glasses and a little girl. This was not only because the child was making a nuisance of herself. I was intrigued by the language they were speaking, not French or Spanish or German or Dutch. From what exotic corner of Europe did that guttural sing-song emanate? With a slow start of surprise, I found myself able to pick up the occasional English word. Gradually, it dawned on me that they were, in fact, speaking English; that they were from Liverpool. When the older of the two men, both of whom seemed mildly drunk, knocked over his glass of beer into an ashtray filled with stubs, the girl shrieked with joy. She held the ashtray close to his lips. "Drink it! Drink it!" The man demurred, but without force. She insisted, joy turning to rage. "I want you to drink it! I want you to drink it!" The high-pitched voice cut like a knife through the peace of the afternoon. I could only wonder at the childish desire to inflict public humiliation.

Later, I went down to the palm-lined sea front. The sun was low, colouring the tops of the apartment blocks whose roofs bristled with television antennae. In Tangier they consider themselves triply blessed: they can receive, in addition to the local service, Spanish and Gibraltar television. I rested on a decaying concrete bench facing the sea, my skin irritated by the prickly heat of late afternoon. Armed policemen paraded in pairs, on the lookout for any signs of impiety. The day's fast was drawing to an end and the vendors of kebabs were stoking their fires. Young French and German vagrants, bohemianly rough, struggled by under the weight of backpacks. There wandered by a barefooted girl of European provenance. She was wrapped, sarong-style, in a strip of green cloth, exposing shoulders flayed by over-exposure to the sun. Meandering at a snail's pace along the corridor of palms, she murmured to herself frequently stopping to stare vacantly about her, plucking distractedly at the pages of what looked like a passport. Hers was a stylish delinquency, a studied throwback to vanquished hippiedom. A ragged youth circled about me. He offered hashish, he offered boys, he offered girls. Night was falling. I walked uphill through nearly empty streets: at this hour of impending release Tangier retired indoors. As I neared the hotel, a gun boomed through the dusk, muezzins wailed. Another day of abstinence was over. Fearlessly, I lit a cigarette.

The Liverpudlians dominated breakfast, the shrieks of the little girl now joined to the penetrating voice of her American mother – who was dilating on her feminist views. At the table next to mine a demure English couple exchanged scandalised whispers.

"They drink like fish," the lady said. "They make a real spectacle of themselves. When they get drunk, they even begin to sing . . ."

After breakfast I went out on the terrace overlooking the garden. The morning was clouded and humid; the town was quiescent. A sea mist obscured the mountains of Spain. Tranquillity was shattered by the arrival of the Liverpudlians. They were quarreling about money.

"I try to ask a straight question," the American was saying, "and I get bullshit."

"Calm yourself," urged the man who had almost been compelled to drink out of the ashtray.

The American would not calm herself. "I don't like this fucking space at all, let me tell you. This trip is my bag. I want to know what's going for what . . . I'm not that spaced out. But this whole scene's too far out . . . too fucking far out. I can't relate to it. It bugs my head, man . . ."

The little girl shrieked. He of the ashtray started to sob, laying his head on the shoulder of his friend.

On the street below, a group of veiled women walked slowly downhill, carrying clanking milk churns.

"I don't want to be bugged," the American shouted. "I wanna keep my head straight, relate to my own space. I don't want no fucking MCP to lay some heavy sexist trip on me . . ."

The veiled women disappeared around a corner. But I could still hear the clanking of their milk churns.

"You know," the writer said, "I believe in the Islamic *identité*."

He was Moroccan, he lived in Paris, but returned home four or five times a year so that he could keep in touch with his "roots". We were sitting in an open-air restaurant in the small, white-washed town of Asilah on the Atlantic coast of Morocco, about an hour's drive from Tangier. The restaurant lay in the shadow of a fifteenth-century Portuguese fort. Atlantic waves exploded against the remnants of a sea-wall. Asilah had had a turbulent past. Octavius had deported its people to Spain because they had supported Mark Antony. In 1578 King Sebastian of Portugal had landed here in a disastrous attempt to conquer Morocco. It had formed part of the Spanish zone during Morocco's colonial period and was restored to it only in 1956 when the country regained its independence. (The Spanish still hold the enclave of Ceuta.) It seemed a peculiar place to be talking about *identité*.

"The strict enforcement of Ramadan might seem harsh to you," he said, "but it helps to remind the people of who and what they are. Ramadan brings us back to ourselves. It renews our sense of being Muslim."

I suggested that *identité*, in the sense in which he understood it, strangled rather than liberated men; that it took no account of the historical process and was a sad and overheated reaction to Western dominance.

He laughed. "We are dealing with eternal truth," he said. France was a decaying country, a cemetery. Would I deny that the West was riddled with moral and spiritual disorder?

Disagreement was silenced by the memory of the American woman. Between him and her, I felt lost.

The mountains of Spain beckoned: it would be pleasant, I thought, to traverse the Mediterranean, to escape Ramadan for a few hours. I decided to make a day trip to Algeciras. There was confusion on the dock. My first attempt to board the ferry was repulsed: my exit card had not been properly stamped. I returned to the long, slow-moving queue.

A German voice spoke close to my ear. "Is it possible to ask where to get one of those?" He pointed at my exit card. I told him; he ran off.

Some minutes later, the voice spoke again. This time it was tinged with panic. "Why do they all have blue cards?

I do not have a blue card. What does the blue card mean? Is it possible for you to explain?"

It was not possible for me to explain because I myself was not in possession of a blue card. Looking around, I saw what he meant. Blue cards everywhere. We both ran off. It seemed likely that I might miss the ferry.

"Writer?" the immigration officer asked. "What do you write?"

"Books . . ." I hazarded.

"Books? You are a writer of books? What kind of books? Please tell."

I could not grasp what this might have to do with a day trip to Algeciras. Nor did it seem the appropriate place or time to embark on a literary discussion.

"I write stories," I said.

"You are a journalist, perhaps?" He scrutinised my face, comparing it with the photograph in the passport. With deliberation, he studied the official record of my travels.

"You are a great voyager," he said. It was not intended as a compliment. "What have you been doing in Morocco?"

"Nothing," I replied truthfully. "Tourist," I added, also with considerable truth.

He scowled, grudgingly applied his stamp and flung the passport unceremoniously in my direction. I headed for the good ship *Ibn Batouta*.

"Passport . . ."

By the gaping jaws of the ferry I submitted to another cross-examination. The officer fingered my shoulder bag. "Open . . . open . . ."

I opened it up. He examined my guide book, thumbed the novel (*A Passage to India*) I was reading, sniffed my cigarettes, explored every pocket and niche of the bag. At last, I was allowed on board. But already I was exhausted. My day trip between Islam and Christianity, between Africa and Europe, had gone sour on me.

The white huddle of Tangier receded. A sign above the bar declared that it was forbidden to serve alcohol to Muslims. Not wishing to provoke a jihad, I contented myself with coffee. Going up on deck, I stared at the corrugated Spanish coast. In the distance loomed the rectangular, misty mass of Gibraltar. Dolphins frolicked close to the bows of the ship. To cross from the Spanish enclave of Ceuta into Morocco was, by all accounts, a murderous business; to cross from the British enclave of Gibraltar into Spain could, by all accounts, be a murderous business; and, as I was now discovering, to cross from Tangier to Algeciras was no joy ride – not, at least, for those who called themselves writers. How much nicer to be a dolphin.

"That is the Rock." I turned to find a wizened American dowager, incandescently clad in an emerald green trouser suit, standing beside me. "That is what the Brits call Gibraltar," she added.

I thanked her for the information.

"Where are you going to in Spain?" she asked.

"Only as far as Algeciras." I pronounced it with a "g".

"Alheciras," she corrected. "It's a Spanish name, you know."

I thanked her for the information and sidled away. How much nicer to be a dolphin.

The Spanish let me in. There was little to do in Algeciras. I drank some wine in a café not far from the ferry terminal, deafened by a churning cement mixer. At five, I returned to the ferry terminal. The Spanish let me out. Morocco, however, had other ideas. The boatride was a nightmare. Orders to submit to immigration control were ceaselessly relayed on the Public Address system. Islamic righteousness had turned it into a prison ship.

"You're a writer . . . what do you write? . . . are you a journalist? . . . what have you been doing in Morocco . . . you need a visa to enter our country . . ."

"But I have a visa."

"It is expired. It is suitable for only one entry. You cannot enter Morocco. You will return to Spain."

"But I have all my luggage in a Tangier hotel . . . I have a plane ticket, a passage booked . . ."

Silence.

"Let me at least make a phone call."

"Stand back!" Oriental despotism had spoken and I was shoved away.

"It is Ramadan," said a Belgian lady who lived in Tangier – and who had befriended me. It was from her, with the mountains of North Africa hard and high in the afternoon light, that I learned of the death of the Shah of Iran.

"Such a shame," she said, "that only Sadat should have had the courage to attend his funeral."

I had been in Iran; I had written about the Shah; I had judged harshly. But now I could sympathise. He must have known about that *identité* which, one day, would eat Iranians alive. Against that hard and high North African skyline, he became a little easier to understand. That *identité* had proved itself locust-like in its voracity: it was even trying to eat me up. I was sad that only Sadat had had the courage to attend his funeral.

We docked; the passengers disembarked. "Hope to see you again," intoned the PA. On came the cleaners. The Belgian lady promised to get in touch with my Moroccan acquaintances, but she was nervous and would commit neither names nor addresses to writing. Two hours later, I began my third crossing of the Mediterranean. If the Spanish were surprised to see me back so soon, they did not show it. At two o'clock in the morning I set out to look for a hotel. Ragged and luggageless, I did not rate my chances very high. But the four star Reina Christina took me in without a murmur. How dreadful it was to wake up the next morning. Unshaven, my head swimming with fatigue, my clothes crumpled, I considered my position.

I decided I would call on the British Consulate. They were courteous but completely unhelpful.

"It is your problem," I was told. The man smiled charmingly and shrugged. It was Ramadan. The Moroccans were always difficult during Ramadan. They could exercise no influence over them.

I wandered around the streets of Algeciras, unable to face the Moroccan consulate, feeling and looking like a tramp, reflecting wistfully on the failure of the Christian Reconquest of Spain to extend itself to the shores of North Africa. I drank glasses of Fundador and cups of black coffee. Resolution returned and I went in search of the Moroccans. I submitted to the same old questions, filled out forms in triplicate, tried to remember the names of my grandfathers and grandmothers, had to decide who in London I could use as "references". When I lit a cigarette, officials screamed at me and pointed at a portrait of King Hassan. In the end, I was given a visa valid for five days. It occurred to me that I should avoid the ferry and take the hydrofoil which goes from Tarifa. Late that afternoon, I crossed the Mediterranean for the fourth time.

Policemen in brown robes and yellow slippers shepherded us off the hydrofoil, barking orders. I had begun to detest these under-developed Moroccan faces, trapped, it seemed to me, in a perpetual adolescence; a perpetual puberty.

My passport was seized and put away. "Stand aside!"

I was too stunned to protest. I was made to wait until all the other passengers were processed. Files were searched. Eventually, it was agreed that I could re-enter Morocco. I found a taxi.

At the gate of the dock a policeman halted us.

"Where's passport . . . where's luggage . . . where you stay in Tangier – where's airplane ticket . . . what you do here? Eh? Eh?" In due course, I was allowed to proceed.

"I seen you in Tangier," the taxi-driver said. "I seen you walking around. Tourist?"

I did not answer. The world was becoming too small, too dangerous. Early the next morning, I went to the airport.

More shouting. More barked orders. My luggage was searched once, twice, a third time. I appeared to be running a gauntlet. The immigration officer demanded that I write down the titles of my books.

"What magazine you write for? You journalist? Give name of magazine . . . give name . . ."

But I did not give any names. To lie seemed the safest course. I continued down the gauntlet. Just when I thought I had made it to the relative safety of the departure lounge, a policeman waved me aside. I was taken away into a room full of other policemen. My mouth went dry. I realised that anything could happen among the lesser breeds without the Law. My shoulder bag was opened up; my books were leafed through; hands crept up my trouser legs, were inserted into my shirt.

"You like hashish . . ." said one of the grinning policemen.

"Where you keep the hashish?" asked another with an adolescent leer. "Where? Suppose we find a little hashish on you . . . what then? Moroccan jail not good, no?"

Miraculously, I got out of there. Half an hour later, high over Spain, my mouth was still dry.

THE HAUNT OF THE ANACONDA

Percy Fawcett

Lieutenant-Colonel Percy Fawcett DSO was born in England in 1867 and led several expeditions to the Amazon and Mato Grosso. In 1925 he disappeared without trace in the Brazilian jungle whilst searching for a lost city. With Fawcett perished his son Jack, and their friend Raleigh Rimmell. Below, Fawcett recounts a journey along the Abuna River in 1906–7.

"You'd better look out for yourselves on the Abuna!" was the warning everybody seemed to enjoy giving us. "The fever there will kill you – and if you escape that, there are the Pacaguaras Indians. They come out on the banks and make a boat run the gauntlet of poisoned arrows!"

"A German engineer was attacked there the other day, and three of his men killed," said someone. Another nodded confirmation ponderously and shook a finger at us.

"Not so long ago forty-eight men went up the Rio Negro – that's an affluent of the Abuna – in search of rubber. Only eighteen came out, and one of them was stark, staring mad from the experience!"

Had we listened to all the grim warnings we should

have got nowhere. By this time I was beginning to form my own opinions, and was not prepared to believe all the tales I heard about savages.

It was one of the gloomiest journeys I had made, for the river was threatening in its quiet, and the easy current and deep water seemed to promise evils ahead. The demons of the Amazonian rivers were abroad, manifesting their presence in lowering skies, downpours of torrential rain and sombre forest walls.

Before reaching the confluence of the Rapirran we stopped at the *barraca* of a Tumupasa Indian called Medina, who had made a fortune in rubber. In this filthy place Medina had a daughter who was one of the prettiest blonde Indians I have seen – tall, with delicate features, small hands, and a mass of silky golden hair. Beautiful enough to grace a royal court, an asset to any European ballroom, this superb girl was destined to join the harem of the manager at Santa Rosa and languish as the fifth member of that enterprising Frenchman's seraglio. I took several photographs of her, but together with all those of the Abuna, except a few developed at Santa Rosa, they were destroyed by the constant damp . . .

We were drifting easily along on the sluggish current not far below the confluence of the Rio Negro when almost under the bow of the *igarité* there appeared a triangular head and several feet of undulating body. It was a giant anaconda. I sprang for my rifle as the creature began to make its way up the bank, and hardly waiting to aim smashed a .44 soft-nosed bullet into its spine, ten feet below the wicked head. At once there was a flurry of foam, and several heavy thumps against the boat's keel, shaking us as though we had run on a snag.

With great difficulty I persuaded the Indian crew to turn in shorewards. They were so frightened that the whites showed all round their popping eyes, and in the moment of firing I had heard their terrified voices begging me not to shoot lest the monster destroy the boat and kill everyone on board, for not only do these creatures attack boats when injured, but also there is great danger from their mates.

We stepped ashore and approached the reptile with caution. It was out of action, but shivers ran up and down the body like puffs of wind on a mountain tarn. As far as it was possible to measure, a length of forty-five feet lay out of the water, and seventeen feet in it, making a total length of sixty-two feet. Its body was not thick for such a colossal length – not more than twelve inches in diameter – but it had probably been long without food. I tried to cut a piece of the skin, but the beast was by no means dead and the sudden upheavals rather scared us. A penetrating, foetid odour emanated from the snake, probably its breath, which is believed to have a stupefying effect, first attracting and later paralysing its prey. Everything about this snake is repulsive.

Such large specimens as this may not be common, but the trails in the swamps reach a width of six feet and support the statements of Indians and rubber pickers that the anaconda sometimes reaches an incredible size, altogether dwarfing that shot by me. The Brazilian Boundary Commission told me of one they killed in the Rio Paraguay exceeding *eighty* feet in length! In the Araguaya and Tocantins basins there is a black variety known as the *Dormidera*, or "Sleeper", from the loud snoring noise it makes. It is reputed to reach a huge size, but I never saw one. These reptiles live principally in the swamps, for unlike the rivers, which often become mere ditches of mud in the dry season, the swamps always remain. To venture into the haunts of the anaconda is to flirt with death.

"Savages!"

The cry came from Willis, who was on deck watching the approach to Tambaqui Rapid. Dan and I tumbled out of the shelter and looked in the direction the negro was

pointing. Several Indians were standing on the bank, their
bodies painted all over with the red juice of the *urucu*, a
bean common in the forest. Their ears had pendulous
lobes, and quills were thrust from side to side through
their nostrils, but they wore no feather head-dresses. It
was my first sight of these people, whom I took to be
Karapunas.

"We'll stop and make friends with them," I said; but
before the order to put into the bank could be given our
Indian crew had spotted them. There were cries of alarm
and the paddles moved at a frenzied rate.

Shouts came from the savages, and loosing their great
bows they shot some arrows in our direction. We couldn't
see them coming, but one ripped through the side of the
boat with a vicious smack – through wood an inch and a
half in thickness, and right through the other side as well!
The force behind that arrow amazed me, and without
seeing for myself I would never have credited such
penetrating power. Why, a rifle could scarcely do more!

It was the custom of these savages to come out two or
three hundred strong on the banks, and give any passing
boat a hot reception. The middle of the river was within
range from either side, so there was no escaping them. I
knew an instance on another river of a steamer being
attacked in the same way. An arrow transfixed an Englishman through both arms and chest, and pinned him to the
deck with such force that it took some time to release him.

The *igarité* slid through the water at so lively a clip that
we soon came up to the Tambaqui Rapid and rushed it
without mishap, the crew still paddling furiously in their
fear of more arrows. It was not a very formidable rapid –
by no means as bad as the next one, Fortaleza, which had a
ten-foot fall, and of which the noise alone was frightening.
The water rushed with a flurry of foam over an outcrop of
the same granite that is to be found in the Madeira and all
rivers to the east of it between eight and ten degrees South
Latitude – the significance of which I came to recognize

later, when studying the geology of the ancient continent. The boat had to be portaged past this fall, hauled overland on rollers made from tree trunks – a labour that left us well-nigh exhausted, so short-handed were we.

On the bank lay the half-dried body of a dead anaconda, its hide nearly an inch thick. Possibly when quite dry it may have shrunk to less than that, but even so the fine tough leather would equal in quality that of the tapir.

Four hours below Fortaleza we reached the confluence with the Madeira River, so wide that it seemed like an ocean after the narrow Abuna . . .

At the mouth of the Abuna *charque* and rice were the only foodstuffs. No one bothered to fish or hunt, or even to dress, and sweating in their filthy rags they sang their drunken catches or groaned in the throes of sickness, as the case might be. No medicines were available, and even if any had been, there was no mind clear enough to administer them. The only healthy person was a young German who came in on his way up river, a cheerful and wholesome youth who made no bones about Anglo-German relations. The burning desire of Germany, he said, was for war, in order to damage the commercial prosperity of her rivals and secure colonies.

After eight days in this vile place we managed to obtain passage aboard *batelónes* with freight for Villa Bella, a port at the mouth of the Mamoré and half-way back to Riberalta. As we pushed out into the river there came to us like a dirge of farewell the tinkle of the guitars and drone of voices . . .

In the smooth stretches the crew of twenty Indians paddled; but where the water was swift and broken the boat had to be swung round rocks at the end of a long rope. Great skill was needed to avoid the ever-present dangers, and by nightfall the crew were utterly exhausted. The moment they threw themselves down on the hot rocks beside the river they were fast asleep, and in consequence pneumonia was rife amongst them – so much so that sometimes a whole crew would be carried off by it, and the boat forced to await the arrival of a fresh crew before it could go on.

Four of the men in our boat died during the first half of the voyage. Any man who fell ill became the butt of the rest, and when he died there was tremendous hilarity. The staring corpse was tied to a pole, and sparsely covered in a shallow trench scraped out with paddles on the river bank, his monument a couple of crossed twigs tied with grass. For funeral there was a drop of *kachasa* all round, and ho for the next victim!

The river here was over half a mile wide, but full of rocks, and the swift current made navigation difficult. The dangerous little rapids of Araras and Periquitos were passed without difficulty, but the more formidable one of Chocolatal took three days to negotiate. Life here was far from dull. The pilot went out to inspect the road where the *batelónes* would be portaged to by-pass the rapid, and was shot by Indians not half a mile from the boat. We found him with forty-two arrows in his body.

INTO THE BELLY OF BOLIVIA

Kent Black

Kent Black is a travel writer and contributor to Outside
magazine.

Mario knelt by the left front tire, sprinkled it with alcohol
from a small bottle, and said a prayer to Pachamama, the
earth mother. Those of us who had stepped out of the
truck to watch were in favor of any edge we could get.
This road in the Bolivian Andes looked as if it'd been
nailed by concentrated strafing, and the cliff to our left
gave way to nothing we could see but darkness. As the
truck descended jerkily, we focused on Mario's uncanny
ability to slide around corners without pitching us into the
void.

Matt, a 26-year-old from Colorado, nudged me. "You
know the left rear tire is just hanging off in space, right?" I
unscrewed the cap of one of our bottles of *singani*, a potent
Bolivian brandy, took a good swig, and passed it along.
Only Tim, our trip's naturalist, was brave enough to
glance out his window. He turned suddenly, seized the
singani bottle, and drank a steady five-second pull. It was
then that we all said a little prayer to Pachamama.

It's never a bad idea to invoke some extra deities when

you're traveling in the Third World – especially if you're planning to venture deep into the Amazon where there are no human settlements, no radio contact, and no possibility of rescue. Eleven of us had signed up to do just that . . . for fun. It was a trip that would take us across the 14,000-foot altiplano, along the eastern shores of Lake Titicaca, over a 15,000-foot pass in the Andean Apolobamba Range, and then down to its eastern flanks to the Rio Tuichi, which we'd follow via raft and kayak through the heart of Madidi National Park. None of us expected our shirttails to touch our butts for the next 11 days.

Our group had hooked up in La Paz, Bolivia's 12,000-foot-high capital, which, surrounded by the higher altiplano, resembles nothing so much as a big city swallowed by the world's largest sinkhole. Still, it's good for acclimatizing. It's also good physical conditioning to weave in and out of the potential rallies that are a daily feature of the city's life. And it's a great place to leave. We did the next morning, figuring we'd sail across the altiplano, skirt Titicaca, hump it over the Andes, and arrive at the hot springs that was our intended first night's camp a bit after teatime. After all, our trip's leader and organizer, Sergio Ballivian of Explore Bolivia, had said, sphinx-like, "It's not really that far."

We soon figured out that Sergio is a master of understatement. The first night's campsite wasn't far if you're packing a compact transporter from the Starship Enterprise. Otherwise, it's a long, long way (the 150-mile route took 14 hours). Sergio had once told us to expect a little mud; we spent half the day digging out the truck and slogging through the stuff. Sergio told us that "the next day is going to be a little tougher"; this was when it became necessary to inebriate the tires and call for Pachamama's diving intervention.

When we awoke and crawled from our tents on the third morning, addled from Mario's version of Mr Toad's Wild Ride and fuzzy from the *singani*, we found ourselves

in a grassy field in Santa Cruz del Valle Ameno. Our trip's
co-leader, Greg Findley, owner of Mukuni Wilderness
Whitewater Expeditions and a veteran Zambezi guide,
was whipping up some scrambled eggs and sausage with
fellow Montanan, Chuck Champe, who'd come along to
cook and captain the paddle boat. Surrounding us were
the administration of buildings from the Madidi National
Park, and standing in front of them were what seemed like
half the town. These people had evidently come out to
have a look at the scraggly, bleary-eyed foreigners emerging from their multicolored cocoons.

As we amused our audience by trying to organize gear,
our Tuichi expert, Pancho Novak, a former army ranger
and mahogany logger, arrived with the porters and a
string of small horses that would portage our boats and
gear the 15 miles to the river. According to Sergio, Pancho
knew the Tuichi like no other man in Madidi, having
ridden logs down the river to the market in Rurrenaba-
que. Renegade mahogany cutting was discontinued with
the park's creation in 1995, and Novak, like most of the
curious onlookers in Santa Cruz, was hoping tourists like
us were going to create a new job market by making the
Madidi one of the most visited parks in South America.

It certainly has the credentials. Its 4.7 million acres
(Yellowstone, by contrast, has 2.2 million acres) include
Andean ranges, montane cloudforests, savanna, dry tropical forests, and lowland rainforests. The park is also one
of the most biodiverse regions on earth, providing habitat
to more than 1,000 species of birds, 44 percent of all New
World mammals, and 38 percent of all neotropical am-
phibians. We figured if we got a glimpse of just 10 percent
of what was out there, it'd, be more than most of us had
seen in years of trekking around North America.

We were an odd-looking safari: trekkers with oversize
daypacks, kayak- and raft-laden horses, and porters lug-
ging or balancing everything from paddles to pots and
pans. By mid-morning, we were stretched into a line all

the way across the 200-yard field. Entering the forest was
a bit like a jungle version of *Through the Looking Glass*;
one minute we were walking in sunlight and order, the
next minute we'd entered a green tunnel full of unidentifiable sounds and shadows.

As the thick mud of the trail threatened to suck our
sports sandals off with every step, Tim explained that we
were in the Yungas, the region of humid montane slopes
(aka cloudforests) of the eastern side of the Andes between
2,000 and 10,000 feet. We pulled wild coffee beans off
bushes and crushed them in our hands for their fragrance,
orchids that would have cost $20 from a Park Avenue
florist littered the trail, and all around us giant stands of
bamboo and ferns reached up to where bromeliads hung
from tree branches, their broad pink leaves like obscene,
drooping tongues. Escaping the dense cover along the
ridgetops, we spotted Andean condors floating above the
valley. The intense heat and humidity made the going
slow for both pack-laden humans and horses. But at least
we were spared the constant drizzle that is usually a
feature of cloudforests.

"Last year on my second Tuichi expedition, the rain
was so intense the porters almost mutinied," Sergio
recounted when we collapsed to have lunch in a small
meadow. "It was right here, in fact. The porters were
going to drop all the equipment and head back to Santa
Cruz. Then Pancho got up and gave them a speech like he
was a Bolivian General Patton. They all stayed."

That night we camped on an exposed ridge above the
forest canopy, where we spent hours hitting off a rum
bottle and counting falling stars. Our resulting slothful-
ness the next morning would have its consequences: while
we slept soundly, the porters filled the water jugs from the
stream below camp but neglected to inform anyone of this
"favor." Before the mix-up was, discovered, five people
had filled their canteens and drunk the unfiltered water.
The unlucky parties were identifiable during that day's

long, hot march through Madidi's inter-Andean dry forest by their sudden dashes off the trail.

It was on a small ridge in this habitat of grasslands, scattered trees, and cacti that Tim spotted a pair of rare harpy eagles, the true kings of Amazonia. Standing nearly three and a half feet tall with claws like a grizzly's, they snatch monkeys right out of trees.

We hit the Tuichi late that afternoon like pilgrims to the River Jordan and set about rigging up the two 14-foot rafts, the cataraft, the paddle boat, and three kayaks. By the next morning, we were ready to boat. Well, almost. First, rituals had to be observed. In El Alto, the ramshackle antiplano city above La Paz, a few of us had invested in several large bags of coca leaves. Long a staple of Andean *campesino*, coca alleviates hunger, fatigue, altitude sickness, and susceptibility to cold and heat – in short, it's the perfect chew for adventure travel.

In Pancho, we had found a coca mentor. Every morning before his first mouthful, he'd offer up three leaves to Pachamama, asking her to keep us safe during our travels. After dropping the leaves one by one onto a blanket, he'd read them for a favorable sign and, satisfied, would give us the thumbs up and we'd all mumble a "Thank you, Pachamama" before stuffing in our morning cud.

The next couple of days of river travel were mostly easy going, the Class II and III rapids providing good paddling practice, getting us soaked and proving that you can indeed freeze your ass off even in the Amazon basin. Keeping up a killer pace of 30 to 40 miles a day, we finally got the knack of interpreting Sergio's assessment of our trip. "Just around the next bend" usually meant a couple of miles. "Just a couple hours more to camp" meant we were probably going to be setting up our tents in the dark. Though Pancho may have known the Tuichi better than any man in the forest, the unfortunate truth is that the river changes dramatically every rainy season. We found that a lot of "perfect" camp spots were either underwater or washed away.

The river's edge is like the forest's shopping mall; every creature eventually comes to its banks. Multicolored macaws and lime-green parrots flew across the river from treetop to treetop as we floated underneath, kingfishers skipped alongside us and herons, startled by our approach, took off in slow-motion climbs. Huge colonies of yellow and white butterflies raised themselves off the sandy banks en masse as if unseen hands were lifting up a rug. And everywhere we sighted capybaras, the world's largest rodents, which look like labrador retriever-sized hamsters with enormously fat asses. One day when we pulled up to a sandbar for a break, clearly imprinted from the water's edge back to the tree line were the prints of a tapir, the largest mammal of this lowland forest. Directly alongside the tapir prints were those of a large jaguar with a cub. Pancho studied them carefully. "Mue, my fresca," he pronounced.

A whole new crew seemed to get to work in the forest during the night shift. After we'd eaten, downed a little rum around the campfire, and retired to our tents, the voices of the forest jacked up a few dozen decibels into a cacophony of hoots, whistles, and strange groans and screams. Together with the sound of the Tuichi pouring solidly over rocks, it produced an almost narcotic effect: The more I tried to differentiate sounds, the quicker it put me to sleep.

Day seven of our Tuichi expedition started ominously. We'd entered San Pedro Canyon the night before and there was a certain nervous tension as we prepared to spend the day running what Sergio promised was a series of Class-IV-plus rapids. It didn't help that there was a cold rain or that half of the crew were weak from intestinal bugs or that all of us were desperately trying not to create any open wounds by scratching our numerous sand-fly bites. I stood with Pancho near the river's edge as he offered his daily prayers to Pachamama. After dropping the leaves onto the ground, he arched an eyebrow, then got to his feet and stalked off. There was no thumbs-up this day.

The Tuichi had changed. There was a rumble, a growl, a force to it that we hadn't felt upstream. The river had risen significantly during the last 16 hours of rain and it was possible that rapids that had been Class IVs yesterday would be Class Vs today. Sergio had told me the night before that he'd first been struck by the idea of running the river after reading *Back from Tuichi*, a book by Israeli Yossi Ghinsberg, which relates the story of his ill-fated 1981 expedition. His log raft had broken apart in the rapids, and for two weeks he'd wandered the forest until being rescued. Pancho, it turned out, had lost one of his logging partners when their raft broke apart and pinned the man underwater. Sergio had made the first complete descent of the Tuichi in 1996, and ours was the fourth "official" one. "This is not a river to take lightly," Sergio told us. "Something bad happens out here, and we're on our own." If this was understatement, we were in for a hell of a ride.

Immediately after leaving camp we hit a boiling Class IV and then a series of Class III rollers. The crew in my paddle boat barely had time to catch a breath when we came upon the next rapid, a Class IV that had a hard left turn where the river slammed into a rock face and then dumped over a mid-river rock into a raft-gobbling hole. Digging in, we made the turn with enough momentum to launch over the hole. It was only 9 a.m. and we were whipped.

The canyon narrowed in places to less than a hundred feet, and the force of the water sometimes made it difficult to hear Chuck's commands. The kayakers, Beverly, Pete, and Kevin, were having a high old time, though it was a little more serious work for Sergio, Greg, Smiling Dave (a river guide in Alaska), and Matt on the oars of the heavy, gear-burdened rafts. Just after clearing an unexpectedly powerful Class IV called Bandera, Roja, Matt got too close to the raft in front of him and had to backpaddle.

"It killed my momentum," he said afterward, "and the next thing I knew we'd dropped into a hole and couldn't clear it."

It might've been almost funny watching the raft slowly flip and catapult its passengers into the water if there'd been any decent eddies. As the upside-down raft shot by, one of the paddlers in my boat leaped onto it from our bow and managed to keep it close to shore until enough people gathered to flip it back over.

The next section of rapids involved some Class IIIs and easy Class IVs that provided some respite before the monster Sergio was anticipating at Puerto del Diablo. But as we got close, one of the kayakers dropped into a hole and found herself pushed under a ledge. After trying three times to roll, she decided to bail out of her kayak and swim to the surface. But by now she was exhausted and numb from the cold water. Slightly downstream from her, Sergio could see that she was no longer swimming and might be in trouble.

"I threw the safety line and then she went under again," he recalled later. "When she came up she had it wrapped around her neck. Obviously, I didn't want to pull on it, but we were drifting downstream right into Puerto del Diablo. I knew if I didn't get her in the boat before we hit it, she'd be a goner." Screaming at her to swim and pulling at the rope, Sergio managed to get her to the boat in time to swing it into the last big eddy.

It took us two and a half hours to scout and run Puerto del Diablo. The rain had transformed what was normally scary enough Class V whitewater into 200 yards of solid, terrifying froth. A series of huge waves and holes made it necessary to cut far right, ferry left, and then get into position to miss a giant slab of rock in the center of the river. Bad positioning for this final maneuver meant getting pinned against the rock by an unrelenting force

of water. Not a pleasant thought. While scouting Diablo I
slipped on a mossy rock, fell a few feet, and cut my leg, but
too much was happening to pay any attention to it.

The run itself went by in an adrenaline blur. Though I
was digging hard, looking ahead, and trying to hear
Chuck's commands, I remember at one point the raft
dropped suddenly off a big wave into a hole – I looked up
into a sky of white foam and screamed, "Pachamama!"

About four the next morning I woke up convinced
some small animal was gnawing on my shin. I turned on
my headlamp. In the 12 hours since I'd scraped my leg
on the rocks above Puerto del Diablo, the opportunistic
organisms of the Amazon had invaded the one-and-a-
half-inch cut and turned it into a pulsing, red, walnut-
size infection. There was nothing I could do but squeeze
a little antibiotic ointment onto it, cover it with a waterlogged bandage, and go back to sleep, hoping for the
best.

Late the next day, we finally reached Chalalán, the
preserve and eco-lodge built by the Quechua-Tacana
from the nearby village of San José de Uchupiamonas.
Our crew was silent from a combination of fatigue after a
long day of paddling slow water, madly itching bug bites
and assorted other ailments, and the satisfaction of having
escaped the river relatively unscathed. Pachamama had, at
least, been democratic.

The appearance of Chalalán at the end of the half-mile
trail from the river transformed our whinging and whining into a kind of enthusiasm that hadn't been much in
evidence since we'd left La Paz. Laughter erupted and
dancing might've followed given half the chance. Trays of
cold fruit juice appeared, and, not long after, liter bottles
of Pacena beer. Even in the dark, the simple, rustic beauty
of the main dining room and three traditional cabins
constructed from chonta palm and jatata leaves made
us feel we'd stumbled on an Amazonian Shangri-la. We'd
only been away from civilization for a week, but all of us

felt we had experienced something rare, something that will probably vanish from the earth before we do.

Later that evening, after everyone had either gone to bed directly after consuming the excellent dinner and Chilean wines, or gone out on the lake in canoes looking for gators, I rocked in a chair in front of the dining room, nursing a whiskey and soda. The young employee who'd brought me the drink stopped to chat awhile, and asked what had happened to my leg. After I peeled off the bandage and explained, he told me he'd be back in a few minutes. Returning with a small clay pot of mud, some leaves, and a spool of gauze, he examined the cut and slapped a bit of the mud on it. He then laid on the leaves, wrapped it in gauze, and told me to leave it there for a couple of days. I thanked him and, when he'd left, downed my whiskey in a single gulp.

Two days later in La Paz, I removed the poultice and washed the cut. The swelling was down and the infection nearly gone. Later I learned that some of the mud in the forest contains a fungus that acts as a natural antibiotic. Throughout our journey down the Tuichi, all the moments of exhilaration and wonder had been tempered by my vision of the forest, with its inch-long stinging abuná ants and poisonous eyelash vipers, as a malevolent force. Now I wasn't so sure. I told Pancho about it that afternoon.

"Pachamama," he said, nodding. "For every bad thing in the forest, she makes something good."

IN DISGUISE TO EVEREST

J.B.L. Noel

*The British adventurer J.B.L. Noel was the first white man
to come within forty miles of Everest. His 1913 journey was
undertaken in disguise, since the approaches to "The Mother
Goddess of the World" were officially barred to westerners.
Not until 1921 was the restriction lifted.*

Having already accomplished a good deal of mountain
travel on the borders of India and Tibet, I decided in 1913
to seek out the passes that led to Everest and if possible to
come to close quarters with the mountain. Everest!
hitherto unapproached by men of my race; guarded, so
fantastic rumour said, by the holiest lamas dwelling in
mystic contemplation of the soul of the giant peak, com-
muning with its demons and guardian gods! It was an
alluring goal.

I thought that if I went with only a few hillmen from
the borders of Tibet and India, I should avoid the attention a group of white men would attract. This proved to
be the case. I was within 40 miles of Everest before a force
of soldiers turned me back.

To defeat observation I intended to avoid the villages
and settled parts generally, to carry our food, and to keep

to those more desolate stretches where only an occasional shepherd was to be seen. My men were not startlingly different from the Tibetans, and if I darkened my skin and my hair I could pass, not as a native – the colour and shape of my eyes would prevent that – but as a Moham- medan from India. A Moslem would be a stranger and suspect in Tibet, but not as glaringly so as a white man.

I dared not hope to escape observation entirely, but thought I could minimize it and perhaps reach my goal before an intercepting party would catch me up. I planned the route from the writings of Sarat Chandra Das.

I intended to cross the mountains by a high pass which was not used by the Tibetans nor watched by them. It cut off the populated districts of Southern Tibet round Khamba Dzong and Tinki, and it would open, I hoped, a high level road behind Kangchenjunga to the gorge of the Arun, and then to Everest's eastern glaciers.

All this was an ambition of years, and the result of careful study and preparation. It would have been im- possible of accomplishment but for the help of the men who had travelled with me before. I could impart my plans to them. They were simple wild men of the moun- tains. I talked their tongue and they trusted me as I did them. If you travel with a man, you must either fall out with him or make him your good friend.

Adhu was a Bhutia with all the vigour of his race and the youth of the twenties. His broad Bhutia face smiled all day long whatever happened – that is chiefly why I took him.

Tebdoo was a Sherpa Nepalese, a rough but golden- hearted fellow who knew everything that there is to be known about mountains and wild sheep. After this jour- ney he said he would come to work for me in India; and refused to believe that there were no wild sheep to hunt there. But at the end of the journey I had to part with him and send him back to wild Nepal. I honestly regretted doing so.

Badri, a little man from the mountains of Garhwal, had always been a favourite companion of mine on journeys in the Himalaya. I kept him beside me to carry the rifle and camera. He had a keen appreciation of mountain scenery; perhaps not for the beauty an artist would find in it but, born and bred among mountains, he felt their peculiar charm, that something which draws, gladdens and masters the soul of a hillsman. How impatient and miserable he was on the plains of India before we were able to start for the Himalaya! The keen, hardy, vigorous little figure felt lonely among the Hindoo people in that flat land. But as the days went on and the time for the start came nearer he responded to the delight of making "bandobast". Then all day he was light-hearted and happy.

I intended to be free to wander where I wished, unencumbered, so took no more baggage than would go into two small tin trunks from the native bazaar, a supply of blankets and two native tents. I concealed in the trunks two cameras and instruments for drawing and mapping; a boiling-point thermometer for altitudes; a good take-down model American rifle, that could be tucked away in any blanket, with plenty of ammunition; also my revolver, and automatic pistols for the men.

Enthusiasm filled me for this adventure. Darjeeling was to be made the base for meeting Adhu and Tebdoo and buying ponies. Then we would plunge into the heart of the great forests that clothe the foot-hills of the Himalaya. We would pass through the tangled thickets of the tropical forest, climb into the regions of pine, larch, juniper and rhododendron, then beyond the tree line through snow-bound passes into unmapped Tibet.

"Why, look, Sahib! There are the mountains!"

I was awakened by little Badri, who had climbed into my carriage on the Bengal Express that runs from Calcutta overnight to Jalpaiguri and Siliguri. At Jalpaiguri at daybreak the traveller gets his first sight of the forests of the Terai with their stagnant morasses, clearings of rice-fields and tea gardens. A dull green forest-clad wall of hills rises abruptly out of the hazy stretch of plain. Here and there on the distant slopes the white tin roofs of the teaplanters' bungalows flash in the sunlight. Some of them occupy solitary clearings in the green mantle of forest which covers every inch of the hills.

If the morning is clear, far to the north, overtopping the tangle of green hazy foot-hills and rising to an incredible height, may be seen a serrated line of dazzling white peaks extending the whole length of the horizon from east to west, the great range of the Himalaya.

A little toy-like train starts from Siliguri. It is called the crookedest, and it is the tiniest mountain railway in all the world. Yet it does a giant's work. It climbs 8,000 feet in 40 miles to Darjeeling on the hilltop. It journeys from the plains through the heat of the tropical forests, through the Terai where tigers lurk and tea-planters cultivate clearings. Up and up it goes, turning and twisting and shunting backwards and forwards. A dozen times it makes figures of eight and zigzags and loops, where the engine passes the tail of the train, and the driver leans out and talks to the passengers in the end coach.

The track is laid along the cart road; and the engineer whistles to wake up the bullock carts and frighten away chickens and children in the village streets. At night time a man sits in front of the engine, holding a great tar torch to light the track and see that no stray tigers or elephants cause a bump!

At Ghoom comes the first view of the snows. That view rewards hours of waiting, when finally it reveals itself as the train, rocking from side to side, flies round a corner. So unexpected is the height of Kangchenjunga, the third highest mountain in the world, 28,000 feet, that people often mistake its silver spearhead for a cloud formation.

I remember the remarks of the people in the compartment, mostly residents, some invalids, and businessmen who would not leave their newspapers to look at any mountains. They agreed that Kangchenjunga, a spire of ice that pierces the heavens, is a mighty sight, but their attention was given to collecting their parcels and guessing if "So-and-so" would perhaps be at the station to meet them. We were running into Darjeeling.

Darjeeling, like all Indian hill stations, is built on the very top of the hill. It has its fine club houses – its Gymkhana Club where a London quartette plays for dances, apparently all day and all night. There is a Scotch Mission, a Barracks, a Hospital, and an Observation Point to which tourists ride in a rickshaw, to lean over an iron railing and look down 6,000 feet into the steaming valleys below. From there the eye can sweep in a panorama embracing tropical forests and eternal snow.

At two o'clock in the morning, the hotel porter rings a 12-inch brass bell outside your door, and comes again every ten minutes to make certain that you do not forget that ponies and rickshaws are waiting to take you to Tiger Hill where people go to see the sun rise on Kangchenjunga and Mount Everest. It is an unforgettable spectacle. Kangchenjunga commands the attention because it is so prominent, so near, and so huge. Far away to the west is a mass of huge peaks. Among them the guide points out a pyramid peeping behind the others and seeming to be smaller; that mountain is Everest.

Just as interesting as the first sight of the mountains is a first acquaintance with the hill people. In the market place on Sunday morning may be seen a throng entirely different from the people of the plains of India. They are jovial, happy folk, and you see no veiled women's faces. There are jolly Bhutia girls – very pretty some of them, but they win you most by their high spirits and their laughter. Everyone of them is naughty. They smoke cigarettes all day long. They do most of the hard work, while the Bhutia men collect in circles to gamble for hours with dice at the street corners, or else lounge against walls, grin broadly, and doff their hats to anyone from whom

they think they can get baksheesh. They are good-hu-
moured; handsome; with gaily coloured clothes, raucous
joking voices, and tangled, loose, flowing hair. They earn
enough to get drunk on by pulling rickshaws or by
carrying luggage to the Everest Hotel. Both men and
women are immensely powerful. There is a true story
told of how a Bhutia woman porter once carried a grand
piano unaided 500 feet from the station to this same hotel.

It is these people with whom one lives when wandering
in the forests and mountains beyond Darjeeling. They
make jovial travelling companions; but the traveller must
understand them and know how to manage them. They
have a habit of calling at their pet drinking houses in
outlying villages and getting hopelessly drunk, leaving
him without bed and supplies the first night out.

I selected my ponies with great care. A man can entrust
his life to a good pony and not even bother about holding
the reins along the narrow paths through gorges and
across precipices, they are so sure-footed.

Adhu and Tebdoo having been met according to plan,
all was ready for the start. The cool of Darjeeling and the
breeze that refreshed the hill-tops changed rapidly as we
dropped down and down into the Tista Valley nearly
7,000 feet below. We found ourselves entering the humid
forest, whose vegetation grew thicker and thicker until the
trees and the twisted creepers that climb over them,
interlaced above, formed a tunnel of greenery hiding
the sky.

We were dropping down mile after mile. The road was
the hottest I had ever felt. The blazing sun boiled the
thick, damp, rotting jungle into a thousand oppressive
smelling vapours. Swarms of insects filled the air with
incessant hum and buzz. There came land leeches to
attack our legs from the ground and fix themselves to
our boots; others on the trees above, warned by some
instinct – wonderful but horrible, since they are blind –
swung their bodies in the air on our approach and

dropped down on us as we passed below. There is no escape from the leech. You must make up your mind that you are going to lose a lot of blood. To compensate slightly there were remarkable butterflies on this road. They were gigantic, measuring up to four inches across the wings and unequalled for colour and diversity.

During the next few days' march, each bend of the road – and the track was twisting and turning continuously through the forests following the bank of the river – opened a new peep of the Tista, here a broad flood broken into foam by large boulders in mid-stream, and flanked by steep mountain walls, from which the superabundant vegetation hung down and trailed into the water. We crossed a chasm by a wire suspension bridge, a frail structure swinging and lurching under every step, where the torrent below had carved itself a gorge, only some 30 feet wide, but almost 300 feet deep.

As we continued day by day the path climbed higher and higher, and the scenery changed as if by magic. The tangled jungle dropped away and we entered a smiling valley. There were meadows dotted with pine, larch, and rhododendron, with Alpine flowers and primulas beside clear streams that meandered through the pasturages.

Lachen occupies a shelf high above the torrent which tears and foams through a 500-foot cleft below. The village stands on a shelf thrown out from the flanks of snow-capped Lamadong, in a recess snug and protected from the cold. It was here I planned to leave the ponies and get six of the hardy hillmen of this village to come on with me to Tibet. They had been hunting with me on a former occasion.

Here, while making these arrangements, my men first seemed to realize the nature of our journey. They became filled with doubts and fears. "We have no man who knows those parts," they said. "How will we find the way to this mountain in Nepal that the Sahib wishes to see?" They had little faith in my map; and, truth to tell, I had little too. They feared maltreatment should we enter Nepal; and they told stories of the fierceness and exclusiveness of the Nepalese.

We went on to a high grazing ground called Tangu, 13,000 feet, where I could acclimatize and prepare for the rough work. One day, in order to spy out the geography and to exercise my men, I decided to make the ascent of one of the surrounding peaks, which promised from its position to reveal the panorama ahead. We started before dawn to climb the snow-covered slopes. The ground was smooth and of even inclination, and there was no difficulty in making good pace all the way. Finally we gained the summit of the ridge, and found that we could not have taken a more lucky direction. We were looking at the giants of the Himalaya from their very midst.

It was shortly after dawn. The slanting rays of the sun caught the fantastic crest of the immense mountain Tsenguikang in a bright flaming glow. Mists scattered, and flying erratically in whirls and eddies, chased each other over the shining ridges, now hiding the peak entirely, now evaporating and revealing fresh vistas of ice and rock and precipice.

Looking west in the direction of Kangchenjunga we saw the first pass over the ridge towards the tangle of snow mountains into the heart of which we were to go. Deep below us was the cleft of the valley through which we had come from India. It continued to the north towards the Koru Pass that leads to Tibet, but is watched by Tibetans and guarded by the fortress of Khamba Dzong on the other side of the divide. There was no way for us into Tibet there. To the north we saw the landscape broadening, and in the far distance we got a glimpse of the plateau land of Tibet that stretches on for hundreds of miles, bleak deserted plains that roll away to Central Asia.

I could not have struck a better place for observation. The boiling-point thermometer measured the altitude as

16,700 feet. There was not a cloud to spoil the splendid view; and I lingered, contemplating the solitudes and admiring and storing in memory the beauties of the crystal air and turquoise sky. The men grew cold in the biting wind that blew in fitful gusts over the ridge. Although fine as a view-point, an exposed ridge at this height is no place for a doze.

From here I was to strike to the west and take a high level track that would take us out of the Indian Empire behind Kangchenjunga into Southern Tibet.

We carried fourteen days' food with us. The first pass of 16,000 feet was no great obstacle. In two days we were across, spending one night at a Tibetan camping ground called Chabru, where there is a cave making a fine shelter. From there we looked down to the high verdant pasture lands of Lhonak where the Tibetan shepherds come in the height of summer by the Naku Pass from Khamba Dzong. The valley is a lofty secluded basin at an elevation of 16,000 feet, surrounded by walls of snow. In a hidden nook deep in the heart of undiscovered lands we stood alone among the solemn majesty of the sentinel mountains.

We sampled the variable Tibetan climate, where the sun shines in the rarefied air with dazzling brightness and burning heat. The rays parch the lips and tan the skin, even blistering it. Suddenly the sun may veil over and the wind spring up. Then – pile on your thickest clothes if you would not feel perished with cold.

I challenged Tebdoo to a race down the hill. In the mountains it is often easier to run down slopes than to walk; and, indeed, when one is tired, it is often a relief to break into a run. But you must have strong knees and a good stick to lean back upon. Tebdoo, who was at heart only a boy, delighted in amusements of this kind, and won the race, at the cost of his skin boots. However, he could mend them quickly by sewing on a new piece of the untanned sheepskin which all hillmen carry in their bokkus.

We pressed forward through this country and got behind Kangchenjunga, where our course turned again to the north to cross the high Chorten Nyim Pass. The pass is a cleft in the mountains, blocked by snow and the debris of rock avalanches. I had learned that the Tibetans had abandoned the pass, and by crossing it I hoped to get into Tibet unobserved.

The day before crossing we made camp on a shelf looking right across to Kangchenjunga's precipices to the south. That evening I spent watching. It is in the evening that these mountains wear their most fairy-like aspect. Vapours and mists, evaporating, form themselves again, and coil worshipfully round the cliffs and ridges. Kangchenjunga's precipices rise 12,000 feet sheer from the glacier below. As I watched, the slanting shafts of light crept up the fluted precipices and caused their draperies of ice to scintillate as with fire. On the eastern side the shadows gathered. Twilight conquered, the depths became a dark chaos – in such shadows might have been enacted the primal mysteries before Time began – but the summits of Kangchenjunga remained aflame, like beacons high above the night-enveloped world below, and seemed to shine with a luminosity all their own.

With the darkness came biting frost; and I turned quickly to creep into the tent and wrap a blanket round me.

I brought three of the men into my tent, as there was plenty of room, while their tent was overcrowded. They curled themselves up side by side, wrapped tightly in blankets, and so kept each other warm. I woke in the cold and darkness of the night to stir the smouldering juniper logs of the fire. Outside all was silent, and nothing could be seen except the still shining ghost-like mountain spires of Kangchenjunga.

Unable to sleep because of the cold, I remembered eerily how once, in a previous Himalayan adventure, I had seen at the monastery of Gantok, the capital of Sikkim, the annual festival of the worship of the god of Kangden-Dzod-Nga, Kangchenjunga – this mountain. The pageant took place in the presence of the Maharaja and Maharani before the Chief Magician's temple in the garden of their palace, with a retinue of brightly clad Lepcha guards.

The god is called Dzod-Nga, meaning "Five Treasures". He is the war god, and every year the ceremony must be held to placate him, and to foster the martial spirit of the nation, while the lamas invite Dzod-Nga to guard the faith of the State and to bring peace and security to the people.

Flashing sword dances are accompanied by the blare of lamas' trumpets, processions of temple gods, and other religious ceremonies.

In the dance of the Dorge-Gro-Dosjidros – the mystic step – the triumph of Truth over Evil is believed to be accomplished. This dance is held with loud cries, led by the Maharaja at his throne, and echoed in a chorus of thousands from his assembled subjects – "Ki-Kihubu! Ki-Kihubu!" It is the voice, as is also the thunder in the heaven, of the war god who consumes mountains of dead as his food and drinks oceans of blood as draughts and relishes the organs of the senses for dessert. "Ki-Kihubu – I am the blood-drinking and destroying god! Glory to Maha-Kala! Should any love his life, keep out of my way. Any wishing to die, come into my presence. I will cut the red stream of life – glory to Maha-Kala-Ki-Kihubu."

The dancers work themselves into a frenzy, wounding each other with their swinging swords, and imitate a fight between the followers of the war god and his enemy. Heralds of the Sword chant loudly:

"This blood-dripping sword is the despatcher of lives. It is made of the substance of the thunderbolt, welded by a thousand wizard smiths. In the summer it has been tempered in the white mountain tops, in the winter it has been tempered in the ocean beds. It has imbibed the heat of fire and the venom of the ocean. It has been dipped in

poisons. Its edge has been ground on the man-slaughter-
ing boulder. When waved over the head it emits sparks of
fire. When lowered point downwards it drips blood and
fat. It is my dearest and most cherished friend – My name
is the Lightning-like Life Taker! Ki-Kihubu!"

All very ludicrous and, to the Western mind, when the
first impressions begin to pall, even rather tiresome. But
alone in these remote mountains, in the icy depths of their
night, those raucous cries came echoing through my
memory. This was the very home of that mountain
god. Giant shapes flung themselves to the skies all round
me. Who was I to violate with impudent temerity these
forbidden solitudes? The wind howled, now miserably,
now angrily round our tiny tent. I shivered, and although
I told myself that it was the bitter cold, I began to wonder,
if – after all . . . !

Next morning we shook ourselves up at an early hour; our
blankets stiff with frozen dew. We had a hard march
before us.

The pass looks like the work of a giant axe that has split
a narrow cleft in the mountains, and left the bottom raw
and splintered. Huge fingers of rock point vertically
between cliffs on either side. When we reached the foot
we found the debris of avalanches precipitated from above
– the danger that had caused this pass to be abandoned by
the Tibetans. Rocks fell as we climbed, and we met an
exhausting obstacle in the loose shingle that slipped
beneath our feet. Even the highest and loneliest Himalayan passes are crossed occasionally, as this one used to
be, by shepherds, and in their migration in search of grass
they perform amazing feats getting their yaks and sheep
and goats, their families and foodstuffs across. The animals, each carrying a light load of tsampa and tea sewn
into little wooden bags, balanced and strapped to each
side, find their own way. The yaks are so surefooted, on
ice and rock, that they can go almost anywhere a man or

goat can go. The shepherds sing and whistle shrilly and hurl stones from their slings to urge and guide them.

But we were not yaks, and the men felt the burden of their loads, heavily laden as they were with our reserve food. One man complained of noises in the head; Adhu's nose started to bleed. The air was dead – mountain climbers know this condition as "stagnant air" – but the men called it "La-druk", the Poison of the Pass. They say it is the evil breath of the Zhidag – the Spirit of the Mountains.

But on the top we found good air and the men became happy and began to sing mountain songs. They built cairns, tied strips of coloured rags to them, lifted their caps and cried, "*Om mani padme hum.*" These cairns were to counter the evil spirits.

But their flags did not drive away the low spirits which began to assail me. When I looked down to the desolation below, I felt discouraged. Ahead was the unknown – a foodless, inhospitable, forbidding waste. Moreover the obstacle of the pass we had just crossed would lie like a barrier across our homeward tracks. We did not dare to look back to the lovely grassy meadows of Lhonak, lest they should lure us from our goal. We had to nerve ourselves to go forward to the north – to Tibet. We would have to find some shelter by the glacier to spend the night. Next day, we would look for the pilgrim's shrine of Chorten-Nyim, reported by the early native explorers as lying where the mountains drop to the plains.

The men became anxious for our safe descent to Tibet, for the prospect was indeed threatening. A staircase of rocky ledges conducted to the terraces of ice which formed the head of the glacier below. Where glaciers at their source break away from the rock walls of the mountains, they leave gaping cracks, sometimes invisible under snow crusts, and a great danger when descending passes. We had to make our way, cautiously avoiding immense

cracks down which we could look, sometimes 50 feet, into
dark recesses.

That night we sheltered in a nook by a glacial lake. In
the mountains I think one can scarcely find a prettier sight
than these glacial lakes. They are like pale blue translu-
cent cups filled with emerald water.

A night spent on a glacier holds many sensations. The
stars at night in the rare air seem to be larger and brighter
than you have ever known before. The slowly moving ice
gives out weird noises as it rends itself, opening out new
fissures with reports like pistol shots. Surface stones slip
and gurgle down into the thinly frozen water of the lakes.
Now and then louder noises, sometimes reaching a deafening crash, tell of rocks falling from above. The melted
snow water, lodging in cracks during the day, freezes at
night, and expands and loosens the rock. You will hear
also what the natives name "the music of the wind". Ice
pinnacles whistle shrilly as their sharp edges cut the wind
and the ice caverns moan deeply as it eddies in their
hollows. Wrapped in your blanket, your breath freezing
on its edge, uncomfortable on rough stones, your native
companions – for you feel no colour bar when sleeping out
in such conditions – huddle close. You are glad to have
them near, as you wait for the dawn to come.

Morning showed no signs of life or vegetation. We
found the way, avoiding boulders and crevasses, left the
broken ice and walked to the side of the valley. After some
miles we came unexpectedly to a little stone hut on a
promontory where the valley closes to a neck. The hut was
deserted. I expect it was the identical one mentioned by
Sarat Chandra Das as the first Tibetan guard post; but it
was no longer inhabited by any Tibetan guard.

Adhu discovered the shrine by following the line of
chortens which are put up to guide pilgrims from the
north and are built on the hillocks. The shrine, a place of
special sanctity, lies hidden in a secluded nook. Numbers
of tame birds and blue pigeons inhabit the cliffs and are

fed by the nuns who live at the shrine. The spot has a special beauty in its solitude and in its gaunt surroundings. The valleys converge with white tongues of glaciers protruding from the cavernous mouths of the mountains that stand behind dark and solid.

The shrine is circled by a well-worn pilgrim's path, marked with mendongs, and poles with flying prayer flags. As we approached we behaved as pilgrims, lifted our hats, cried, "*Om mani padme hum*," and contributed stones to the foot of the chortens.

We entered and I took a dark corner to hide in while Adhu conversed with the nuns. We found that the chief nun and two others were quite blind, which relieved me of some anxiety. There were altogether seven nuns living at the shrine.

"Are you pilgrims?" they asked.

"No, we are travellers from India."

"Make offering to our shrine that no misfortune may overtake your journey. And take these potions to bring strength and love to your lives, for you Outer Men" (meaning men of earthly affairs) "prize these things for the body more than those things for the soul. Live more for the inner life," they said.

We made suitable offerings to the shrine, placed grains of rice in the bowls by the butter lamps beneath the god images; accepted the pills and love potions the nuns gave us. Then the nuns brought out goat-bladders of yaks' milk and *chung* from their bokkus and gave us to drink. Adhu talked with them and obtained information for our journey. The nuns said we were brave to come by the snowy road; they even said we might sleep here, but we feared other people might arrive. We thanked the nuns for the wise things they had told us, to which they answered, "We know your darkness" (ignorance) "and we will pray for you." Then we took our departure.

Here at Chorten Nyim we were at the exit from the high mountains. To the north we contemplated the plateau of

Tibet, the highest desert of the world. It has much of the character and appearance of an Arabian or an Arizona desert, with the same breadth and space of sandy, rocky soil, intersected with ranges of undulating hills, bare of trees; but it has this difference, that the far horizons show snowy peaks.

In depressions between the hills, more like shallow basins than defined valleys, is seen the green of the marsh-lands along the banks of lakes and winding rivers. Beyond the grass-lands sandy wastes continue ruffled and blown into dunes by the wind. As in all deserts, there is shimmering sunshine and clear sky, yet the sky of Tibet seems to have a special blue all its own. As in other deserts, the day is hot and the night is cold. Here is experienced a difference of 50° between day and night. All is peace and breadth and solitude; guarded by snowy mountain barriers that wall away the outer world and lend an impression of majestic loftiness to this peaceful plateau. We felt ourselves to be above the other world – veritably on the roof of the world.

We continued due west, following a high level line over the spurs of the mountains, switchbacking over ridges and across deep glacier valleys. We could make little headway, and finally we were stopped altogether by deep canyons. We descended to the bottom of one by a funnel, but could not find any way out beyond. We were obliged to turn back and take a lower level route by the plain, hiding ourselves and passing villages at night, making detours to avoid the dogs that, hearing every movement of men and animals within the distance of a mile, barked and howled. These Tibetan mastiffs, found in all the Dok-pa shepherds' encampments, are magnificent yet savage animals. Attacking, they show fangs like wolves, and their ferocious appearance is heightened by the immense scarlet ruffs of yak hair which the Tibetans place round their necks like Elizabethan collars. These dogs are prized for their ferocity, and the mark of their breeding is the depth of their bark. The Tibetans say their bark must ring like a well-made gong. Once I had to shoot one of these mastiffs that rushed out and bit one of my men badly.

We had now fairly well escaped the fortresses of Khamba Dzong and Tinki Dzong; and I wanted to bear into the valleys in the direction of Nepal, which promised more friendly concealment than the plains. But I was vague as to the way to the Langbu Pass, so we decided boldly to turn into a certain village that we saw in the opening of a valley leading south-west.

Our approach caused the keenest excitement, the barking of dogs and the barring of doors. Along the sky line of the roofs were the flying prayer flags and bunches of dried grass, and we noted peeping heads observing us from the apparently deserted houses. Keeping on our way, and meeting people, we boldly insisted on being given a house to live in.

The people are forbidden by the lamas and Dzongpens to furnish information to strangers; but they do not do more than offer a passive resistance and answer "No" or "I do not know" to everything. They would, however, always give information in return for presents secretly conveyed, and at night time they would give us food in return for money. The Tibetan peasant himself is friendly, generous and hospitable, although with the same freedom that he gives his own things to you he will also make you a present of other people's things and take what he fancies of yours. In the spacious folds of his bokkus he stows away anything up to the size of a cooking pot.

A man and woman befriended us at this village, which we found was called Eunah, and gave us to eat and drink at their house. We climbed a wooden staircase to the living-room above the stable which always occupies the lower floor of a Tibetan house. There were no windows, but a circular hole in the ceiling let in light and let out the smoke of the yak-dung fire burning in the chula, or earthenware pot. There was also the dim light of the butter lamps burning before the family shrine. We sat round the fire on sheepskins and Tibetan woollen rugs and brought out our wooden tea bowls from our bokkus to drink buttered tea and eat tsampa.

I behaved just as one of my own men, except that I conversed in the Indian language, using a few Tibetan words that I knew.

Our visit, although no doubt causing our presence in the country to be reported to the governors of the fortresses, served its purpose, in that we found out from the people the way to the Langbu Pass. We got the information out of two boys who said, "Go to Changmu tomorrow – bridge to cross – go little along the river to two chortens. Then go up between high stones and you will find yak paths."

This we did, passing the curious rock-hewn settlement of Changmu, consisting of about a hundred caves like huge pigeon-holes high up on the sheer face of a sandstone cliff. They were cave dwellings and we kept some distance away, not knowing what the hidden inhabitants would do. In Tibet there are many such caves, and they are said to be connected with passages leading out to the tops of the cliffs. They make splendid dwellings, protected from cold and heat and enemies alike.

We found the chortens the boys spoke of, and the yak paths that led into the mountains to the west. We breasted the bridge which separated us from the valley of the Langbu Pass. Below our feet was the winding valley of the Gye River. A track could be seen along the open red sandy hillsides. On we went, doing about 18 miles that day by my pacometer, and camped by the stream, where we found fuel and could light a fire.

By climbing 1,500 feet up the hillsides I observed that evening the position of the Langbu Pass, also that of another pass to the south, leading back over the main chain to Nepal and giving access probably to the Kambachen Valley somewhere near the foot of the Kangchen

Glacier. This would make a back door from Lhonak to Southern Tibet through a corner of Nepal. There is still another pass that way, the Chabuk-la; but it is said to be very difficult.

Next day we struck out towards the Langbu Pass, crowned by the fine mountain called the Langbu Singha. The all-important question was: could Everest be seen from the top of the pass?

When I reached the top, I was staggered by a magnificent view of towering snow mountains. The centre peak of the range rose as a glittering spire of rock clothed with clinging ice and snow. Beyond rose a higher peak twisted like a hooked tooth, a precipice on the north side and a névé on the south. To the left of this again was a long, flat-ridged peak, fantastically corniced with overhanging ridges of ice.

What fine mountains! But they were none of them Everest: they were too near. Everest was still about 60 miles away. These mountains were about 23,000 feet in height. I named them – Taringban (meaning "Long knife" in the Lepcha language) and Guma Raichu (meaning "Guma's tooth" in Tibetan).

Presently, while watching the panorama, the shifting of the clouds revealed other high mountain masses in the distance; and directly over the crest of Taringban appeared a sharp spire peak. This, through its magnetic bearing by my compass, proved itself to be none other than Mount Everest. A thousand feet of the summit was visible.

Although this fine panorama and the discovery of mountains hitherto unknown was in itself a reward, still it was also a disappointment, because it indicated an utter barrier. The only existing map showed the Kama Valley joining the Arun at the same place as the Tashirak River. I had planned to follow down the Tashirak Valley to reach the Kama Valley and then to go up this valley to Mount Everest. The maps were entirely wrong. This mountain range stood between me and Mount Everest; and the Tashirak River flowed south instead of west. I was opposed by an enormous mountain obstacle; and I felt it was impossible to overcome it. After remaining an hour on the top of the pass, during which time the men said copious prayers and built a chorten, to which they attached the usual strips of cloth, we went steeply down to the open meadows which surround the village of Guma; and there we found a shelter for the night among some dirty sheep pens and huts plastered with mud and dung. The people were not unfriendly.

We proceeded towards Tashirak in some trepidation as to whether we would be stopped by the Dalai Lama's Rice Officer, who holds the toll bridge with a guard of soldiers. There was nothing for it but to go straight on and talk to him. He requested us not to cross, so we went away and made a camp on our side of the river some distance off. We struck camp, however, at about two o'clock in the morning, forded the river in the dark under terrible difficulties, and so lost two loads of our food. But I breathed again.

I hoped the valley would bend west towards the Arun. But it went on persistently south and we eventually found ourselves descending to forest lands with the valley becoming more and more narrow.

We met an encampment of Nepalese traders with their yaks carrying borax, salt, wool, skins and yak tails. They are enterprising, honest, engaging and handsome men and women, these Nepalese who spend their lives crossing the mountains, trading between Tibet and Nepal. They talked openly and pleasantly and told no lies in answer to my questions.

"This road does not go to Kharta," they said. "Down the river you will come to Hatia, which is in Nepal, and the Maharaja's guards live there to see that no strange people enter. Go up that valley," they said, pointing to a lateral valley to the west, "and you will find a Gompa [monastery] high up, from which you can see all mountains."

They spoke of a great mountain Kangchen Lemboo Geudyong. Could this be Mount Everest? They knew Kangchenjunga, which they called Kangchenzeunga. They spoke of another great mountain which had a lake in its centre, which might well be a reference to Makalu, the "Arm-chair Peak", which has been observed from India to have a curious cup-like formation near its summit. Geographers think this is filled with a glacier.

These Nepalese invited me and my men to stay in their camp, which we did for a little while, and they replenished our supplies of mutton, butter, ghee, salt and tea.

We regretfully parted from them; and struck off to the westerly valley to reach the Monastery they had spoken of, and to look across, as I hoped, to Mount Everest.

We found a strongly fortified wall built across the valley – a wall that had been made during the wars between Nepal and Tibet. I little thought how useful that wall would soon be in other ways. Now we used it as a shelter against the wind where we made our camp; pretty soon it was to protect us against Tibetan bullets.

Next morning Adhu came to the tent to say that a Tibetan captain and guard sent to prevent us following the upper road to Pherugh were watching some little distance away. I went down with my men and, forcing the captain to dismount, asked him what he meant by posting soldiers on us as if we were common thieves. I found that he was the Captain of the Tashirak guard, and in the background was no less a personage than the Tinki Dzongpen himself and his followers.

They rode shaggy Tibetan ponies bridled in brass and silver and saddled in coloured numdahs. Each pony carried bulky slung leather saddle-bags and blankets; and from the general appearance of the party it was obvious they had travelled far. We learned later that the Dzongpen, hearing of our presence, had ridden

150 miles to meet us, covering the distance in three days.

An interview was arranged which lasted two hours, and was carried on for some time in rather a heated manner. The Dzongpen showed his surprise that we had been able to find our way into Tibet over the high pass, and was suspicious because we had chosen to come by such an unusual way.

"For what reason have you come to Tibet? At the time of the War" (the 1904 Mission to Lhasa) "many white men and men of India came, but since that time no one has entered the country."

They repeated again and again the same sentences: "No foreigners may come to Tibet. We do not know what you want, or for what reason you come."

I complained that I had received only discourtesy and opposition in Tibet, whereas all Tibetans coming to India were free to travel where they wished, and were received as welcome visitors. This was, I protested, indeed a disgrace to Tibetan civilization and Tibetan culture.

The whole party became very excited at this juncture and all started to shout and talk together. The soldiers crowded round and unstrapped their matchlocks in a threatening manner. It was impossible to understand what they were shouting about or what plan they might be proposing. All I could make out was the Dzongpen saying: "Go back the way you came."

I argued, but he was insistent. Then I tried the Tibetan game. I temporized, told him I would think it over and give him a reply the following day. The discussion then took another turn. He dropped his blustering authoritative tone, and became delightfully courteous. He told me he would have to get permission from Lhasa for us to pass through his province, and he begged me by no means to travel on or it would cost him his head. So I consented to wait for instructions from his superior. But such a permission, in the unlikely event of his even seeking it, and in the unlikelier event of its being accorded, would take weeks to arrive. I knew they were only procrastinating. In a very few days the Dzongpen would inform me that Lhasa had refused, and that I was to quit Tibet immediately. I was tempted to steal away and push on with my hillmen. I was nettled, meeting this opposition when so near to my goal, and at the prospect of failure after so much effort.

I knew that his force of soldiers could not deter me. They were armed with an ancient variety of matchlocks, and at 30 yards range the charge of slugs they would fire would be harmless; but the Dzongpen had, in the latter part of the interview at least, been so polite that I naturally hated to do anything that would cause him to be beheaded!

Happily, this idea of fighting the Dzongpen forces was quickly dismissed. Certainly it would be impolite, and moreover there seemed to be no need of it. He returned to the charge and again urged me to quit Tibet immediately.

But it was my turn to procrastinate. Delay might produce an opportunity to steal away unobserved. When he saw that I would give him no decided answer, he said he would not remain in that inhospitable gorge until I had made up my mind, but would go home. He ordered me to remain where I was. He would return on the following day for my decision.

He galloped down the ravine, his party stringing along behind him. I watched them, none too pleased with the turn of events, and well "on the boil". Life at high altitudes does not conduce to placidity and evenness of temper, and the arrogance of the soldiers, and their unconcealed smug satisfaction at having discovered and made us halt, had distinctly got on my nerves. One of the men remained behind longer than the rest. Finally he too started, but in passing he jostled his horse against me rudely. I jumped ahead and seized his bridle. I meant to hold him and complain to the Dzongpen, but he struck me across the face with his whip and tore the bridle from my grasp. Highly enraged, I ran after him. He galloped for several hundred yards with me in pursuit. Then he dismounted and swung his clumsy matchlock into action.

I was fired on by that grotesque instrument! It made enough noise for a cannon. Where the slugs went I could never tell – all over the place, I think. I slipped behind the ruins of the Tibetan wall. I placed a shot from my American rifle over his head, and he went off so fast, and made me laugh so much, that I did not think it worth while to follow it with another one.

Things seemed to be none the worse for this incident, save that my face smarted a bit from the blow of the whip; but my men thought otherwise. They were tremendously excited and highly perturbed. With the exchange of fire they thought the whole of Tibet would descend on us. They absolutely refused to go on.

There was nothing to be done but to turn our backs on the approaches of Everest, the mysterious Lamasery and the valley of the mountain.

Within forty miles, and nearer at that time than any white man had been! I leave you to imagine my chagrin and disappointment.

It took us six long weeks to get back to India.

FARTHEST NORTH

Robert E. Peary

The American naval officer and explorer Robert Edwin Peary (1856–1920) is generally acknowledged to be the first man to have reached the North Pole overland, doing so on 6 April 1909.

Perhaps a man always thinks of the very beginning of his work when he feels it is nearing its end. The appearance of the ice-fields to the north this day, large and level, the brilliant blue of the sky, the biting character of the wind – everything excepting the surface of the ice, which on the great cap is absolutely dead level with a straight line for a horizon – reminded me of those marches of the long ago . . .

Near the end of the march I came upon a lead which was just opening. It was ten yards wide directly in front of me; but a few hundred yards to the east was an apparently practicable crossing where the single crack was divided into several. I signalled to the sledges to hurry; then, running to the place, I had time to pick a road across the moving ice cakes and return to help the teams across before the lead widened so as to be impassable. This passage was effected by my jumping from one cake to

another, picking the way, and making sure that the cake
would not tilt under the weight of the dogs and the sledge,
returning to the former cake where the dogs were, encouraging the dogs ahead while the driver steered the
sledge across from cake to cake, and threw his weight from
one side to the other so that it could not overturn. We got
the sledges across several cracks so wide that while the
dogs had no trouble in jumping, the men had to be pretty
active in order to follow the long sledges. Fortunately the
sledges were of the new Peary type, twelve feet long. Had
they been of the old Eskimo type, seven feet long, we
might have had to use ropes and pull them across hand
over hand on an ice cake.

It is always hard to make the dogs leap a widening
crack, though some of the best dog drivers can do it
instantly, using the whip and the voice. A poor dog driver
would be likely to get everything into the water in the
attempt. It is sometimes necessary to go ahead of the dogs,
holding the hand low and shaking it as though it contained
some dainty morsel of food, thus inspiring them with
courage for the leap.

Perhaps a mile beyond this, the breaking of the ice at
the edge of a narrow lead as I landed from a jump sent me
into the water nearly to my hips; but as the water did not
come above the waistband of my trousers, which were
water-tight, it was soon scraped and beaten off before it
had time to freeze.

This lead was not wide enough to bother the sledges.

As we stopped to make our camp near a huge pressure
ridge, the sun, which was gradually getting higher,
seemed almost to have some warmth. While we were
building our igloos, we could see, the water clouds lying
to the east and south-east of us some miles distant, that a
wide lead was opening in that direction. The approaching
full moon was evidently getting in its work.

As we had travelled on, the moon had circled round and
round the heavens opposite the sun, a disk of silver opposite

a disk of gold. Looking at its pallid and spectral face, from which the brighter light of the sun had stolen the colour, it seemed hard to realize that its presence there had power to stir the great ice-fields around us with restlessness – power even now, when we were so near our goal, to interrupt our pathway with an impassable lead.

The moon had been our friend during the long winter, giving us light to hunt by for a week or two each month. Now it seemed no longer a friend, but a dangerous presence to be regarded with fear. Its power, which had before been beneficent, was now malevolent and incalculably potent for evil.

When we awoke early in the morning of April 3, after a few hours' sleep, we found the weather still clear and calm. There were some broad heavy pressure ridges in the beginning of this march, and we had to use pickaxes quite freely. This delayed us a little, but as soon as we struck the level old floes we tried to make up for lost time. As the daylight was now continuous we could travel as long as we pleased, and sleep as little as we must. We hustled along for ten hours again, as we had before, making only twenty miles because of the early delay with the pickaxes and another brief delay at a narrow lead. We were now half-way to the 89th parallel, and I had been obliged to take up another hole in my belt.

Some gigantic rafters were seen during this march, but they were not in our path. All day long we had heard the ice grinding and groaning on all sides of us, but no motion was visible to our eyes. Either the ice was slacking back into equilibrium, sagging northward after its release from the wind pressure, or else it was feeling the influence of the spring tides of the full moon. On, on we pushed, and I am not ashamed to confess that my pulse beat high, for the breath of success seemed already in my nostrils . . .

The last march northward ended at ten o'clock of the forenoon of April 6. I had now made the five marches planned from the point at which Bartlett turned back, and my reckoning showed that we were in the immediate neighbourhood of the goal of all our striving. After the usual arrangements for going into camp, at approximately local noon, on the Columbia meridian, I made the first observation at our polar camp. It indicated our position as 89° 57'.

We were now at the end of the last long march of the upward journey. Yet with the Pole actually in sight I was too weary to take the last few steps. The accumulated weariness of all those days and nights of forced marches and insufficient sleep, constant peril and anxiety, seemed to roll across me all at once. I was actually too exhausted to realize at the moment that my life's purpose had been achieved. As soon as our igloos had been completed, and we had eaten our dinner and double-rationed the dogs, I turned in for a few hours of absolutely necessary sleep, Henson and the Eskimos having unloaded the sledges and got them in readiness for such repairs as were necessary. But, weary though I was, I could not sleep long. It was, therefore, only a few hours later when I woke. The first thing I did after awaking was to write these words in my diary: "The Pole at last. The prize of three centuries. My dream and goal for twenty years. Mine at last! I cannot bring myself to realize it. It seems all so simple and commonplace."

Everything was in readiness for an observation at 6 p.m., Columbia meridian time, in case the sky should be clear, but at that hour it was, unfortunately, still overcast. But as there were indications that it would clear before long, two of the Eskimos and myself made ready a light sledge carrying only the instruments, a tin of pemmican, and one or two skins; and drawn by a double team of dogs, we pushed on an estimated distance of ten miles. While we travelled, the sky cleared, and at the end of the journey, I was able to get a satisfactory series of observations at Columbia meridian midnight. These observations indicated that our position was then beyond the Pole.

Nearly everything in the circumstances which then surrounded us seemed too strange to be thoroughly realized, but one of the strangest of those circumstances seemed to me to be the fact that, in a march of only a few hours, I had passed from the western to the eastern hemisphere and had verified my position at the summit of the world. It was hard to realize that, on the first miles of this brief march, we had been travelling due north, while, on the last few miles of the same march, we had been travelling south, although we had all the time been travelling precisely in the same direction. It would be difficult to imagine a better illustration of the fact that most things are relative. Again, please consider the uncommon circumstance that, in order to return to our camp, it now became necessary to turn and go north again for a few miles and then to go directly south, all the time travelling in the same direction.

As we passed back along that trail which none had ever seen before or would ever see again, certain reflections intruded themselves which, I think, may fairly be called unique. East, west, and north had disappeared for us. Only one direction remained and that was south. Every breeze which could possibly blow upon us, no matter from what point of the horizon, must be a south wind. Where we were, one day and one night constituted a year, a hundred such days and nights constituted a century. Had we stood in that spot during the six months of the Arctic winter night, we should have seen every star of the northern hemisphere circling the sky at the same distance from the horizon, with Polaris (the North Star) practically in the zenith.

WINGS OVER THE POLE

Richard Evelyn Byrd

*The American explorer Richard Evelyn Byrd and his pilot
Floyd Bennett were the first to reach the North Pole by air.
Their historic journey started at 12.30 a.m. on 9 May 1926.*

With a total load of nearly 10,000 pounds we raced down
the runway. The rough snow ahead loomed dangerously
near but we never reached it. We were off for our great
adventure!

Beneath us were our shipmates – every one anxious to
go along, but unselfishly wild with delight that we were at
last off – running in our wake, waving their arms, and
throwing their hats in the air. As long as I live I can never
forget that sight, or those splendid fellows. They had
given us our great chance.

For months previous to this hour, utmost attention had
been paid to every detail that would assure our margin of
safety in case of accident, and to the perfection of our
scientific results in the case of success.

We had a short-wave radio set operated by a hand
dynamo, should we be forced down on the ice. A
hand-made sledge presented to us by Amundsen was
stowed in the fuselage, on which to carry our food and

clothing should we be compelled to walk to Greenland. We had food for ten weeks. Our main staple, pemmican, consisting of chopped-up dried meat, fat, sugar and raisins, was supplemented by chocolate, pilot-bread, tea, malted milk, powdered chocolate, butter, sugar and cream cheese, all of which form a highly concentrated diet.

Other articles of equipment were a rubber boat for crossing open leads if forced down, reindeer-skin, polar-bear and seal fur clothes, boots and gloves, primus stove, rifle, pistol, shotgun and ammunition; tent, knives, axe, medical kit and smoke bombs – all as compact as humanly possible.

If we should come down on the ice the reason it would take us so long to get back, if we got back at all, was that we could not return Spitzbergen way on account of the strong tides. We would have to march Etah way and would have to kill enough seal, polar-bear and musk-ox to last through the Arctic nights.

The first stage of our navigation was the simple one of dead reckoning, or following the well-known landmarks in the vicinity of Kings Bay, which we had just left. We climbed to 2,000 feet to get a good view of the coast and the magnificent snow-covered mountains inland. Within an hour of taking [to] the air we passed the rugged and glacier-laden land and crossed the edge of the polar ice pack. It was much nearer to the land than we had expected. Over to the east was a point where the ice field was very near the land.

We looked ahead at the sea ice gleaming in the rays of the midnight sun – a fascinating scene whose lure had drawn famous men into its clutches, never to return. It was with a feeling of exhilaration that we felt that for the first time in history two mites of men could gaze upon its charms, and discover its secrets, out of reach of those sharp claws.

Perhaps! There was still that "perhaps", for if we should have a forced landing disaster might easily follow.

It was only natural for Bennett and me to wonder whether or not we would ever get back to this small island we were leaving, for all the airmen explorers who had preceded us in attempts to reach the Pole by aviation had met with disaster or near disaster . . .

As we sped along over the white field below I spent the busiest and most concentrated moments of my life. Though we had confidence in our instruments and methods, we were trying them for the first time over the Polar Sea. First, we obtained north and south bearings on a mountain range on Spitzbergen which we could see for a long distance out over the ice. These checked fairly well with the sun-compass. But I had absolute confidence in the sun-compass.

We could see mountains astern gleaming in the sun at least a hundred miles behind us. That was our last link with civilization. The unknown lay ahead.

Bennett and I took turns piloting. At first Bennett was steering, and for some unaccountable reason the plane veered from the course time and time again, to the right. He could glance back where I was working, through a door leading to the two pilots' seats. Every minute or two he would look at me, to be checked if necessary, on the course by the sun-compass. If he happened to be off the course I would wave him to the right or left until he got on it again. Once every three minutes while I was navigating I checked the wind drift and ground speed, so that in case of a change in wind I could detect it immediately and allow for it.

We had three sets of gloves which I constantly changed to fit the job in hand, and sometimes removed entirely for short periods to write or figure on the chart. I froze my face and one of my hands in taking sights with the instruments from the trapdoors. But I noticed these frostbites at once and was more careful thereafter. Ordinarily a frostbite need not be dangerous if detected in time and if the blood is rubbed back immediately into the affected parts. We also carried leather helmets that would cover the whole face when necessary to use them.

We carried two sun-compasses. One was fixed to a trapdoor in the top of the navigator's cabin; the other was movable, so that when the great wing obscured the sun from the compass on the trapdoor, the second could be used inside the cabin, through the open windows.

Every now and then I took sextant sights of the sun to see where the lines of position would cross our line of flight. I was very thankful at those moments that the Navy requires such thorough navigation training, and that I had made air navigation my hobby.

Finally, when I felt certain we were on our course, I turned my attention to the great ice pack, which I had wondered about ever since I was a youngster at school. We were flying at about 2,000 feet, and I could see at least 50 miles in every direction. There was no sign of land. If there had been any within 100 miles' radius we would have seen its mountain peaks, so good was the visibility.

The ice pack beneath was criss-crossed with pressure ridges, but here and there were stretches that appeared long and smooth enough to land on. However, from 2,000 feet pack ice is extraordinarily deceptive.

The pressure ridges that looked so insignificant from the plane varied from a few feet to 50 or 60 feet in height, while the average thickness of the ice was about 40 feet. A flash of sympathy came over me for the brave men who had in years past struggled northward over that cruel mass.

We passed leads of water recently opened by the movement of the ice, and so dangerous to the foot traveler, who never knows when the ice will open up beneath and swallow him into the black depths of the Polar Sea.

I now turned my mind to wind conditions, for I knew they were a matter of interest to all those contemplating the feasibility of a polar airway. We found them good.

There were no bumps in the air. This was as we had anticipated, for the flatness of the ice and the Arctic temperature was not conducive to air currents, such as are sometimes found over land. Had we struck an Arctic gale, I cannot say what the result would have been as far as air roughness is concerned. Of course we still had the advantage of spring and 24-hour daylight.

It was time now to relieve Bennett again at the wheel, not only that he might stretch his legs, but so that he could pour gasoline into the tanks from the five-gallon tins stowed all over the cabin. Empty cans were thrown overboard to get rid of the weight, small though it was.

Frequently I was able to check myself on the course by holding the sun-compass in one hand and steering with the other.

I had time now leisurely to examine the ice pack and eagerly sought signs of life, a polar-bear, a seal, or birds flying, but could see none.

On one occasion, as I turned to look over the side, my arm struck some object in my left breast pocket. It was filled with good-luck pieces!

I am not superstitious, I believe. No explorer, however, can go off without such articles. Among my trinkets was a religious medal put there by a friend. It belonged to his fiancée and he firmly believed it would get me through. There was also a tiny horseshoe made by a famous blacksmith. Attached to the pocket was a little coin taken by Peary, pinned to his shirt, on his trip to the North Pole.

When Bennett had finished pouring and figuring the gasoline consumption, he took the wheel again. I went back to the incessant navigating. So much did I sight down on the dazzling snow that I had a slight attack of snow blindness. But I need not have suffered, as I had brought along the proper kind of amber goggles.

Twice during the next two hours I relieved Bennett at the wheel. When I took it the fourth time, he smiled as he went aft. "I would rather have Floyd with me," I thought, "than any other man in the world."

We were now getting into areas never before viewed by mortal eye. The feelings of an explorer superseded the aviator's. I became conscious of that extraordinary exhilaration which comes from looking into virgin territory. At that moment I felt repaid for all our toil.

At the end of this unknown area lay our goal, somewhere beyond the shimmering horizon. We were opening unexplored regions at the rate of nearly 10,000 square miles an hour, and were experiencing the incomparable satisfaction of searching for new land. Once, for a moment, I mistook a distant, vague, low-lying cloud formation for the white peaks of a far-away land.

I had a momentary sensation of great triumph. If I could explain the feeling I had at this time, the much-asked question would be answered: "What is this Arctic craze so many men get?"

The sun was still shining brightly. Surely fate was good to us, for without the sun our quest of the Pole would have been hopeless.

To the right, somewhere, the rays of the midnight sun shone down on the scenes of Nansen's heroic struggles to reach the goal that we were approaching with the ease of an eagle at the rate of nearly 100 miles an hour. To our left, lay Peary's oft-traveled trail.

When I went back to my navigating, I compared the magnetic compass with the sun-compass and found that the westerly error in the former had nearly doubled since reaching the edge of the ice pack, where it had been eleven degrees westerly.

When our calculations showed us to be about an hour from the Pole, I noticed through the cabin window a bad leak in the oil tank of the starboard motor. Bennett confirmed my fears. He wrote: "That motor will stop."

Bennett then suggested that we try a landing to fix the leak. But I had seen too many expeditions fail by landing.

We decided to keep on for the Pole. We would be in no worse fix should we come down near the Pole than we would be if we had a forced landing where we were.

When I took to the wheel again I kept my eyes glued on that oil leak and the oil-pressure indicator. Should the pressure drop, we would lose the motor immediately. It fascinated me. There was no doubt in my mind that the oil pressure would drop any moment. But the prize was actually in sight. We could not turn back.

At 9.02 a.m., May 9, 1926, Greenwich civil time, our calculations showed us to be at the Pole! The dream of a lifetime had at last been realized.

We headed to the right to take two confirming sights of the sun, then turned and took two more.

After that we made some moving and still pictures, then went on for several miles in the direction we had come, and made another larger circle to be sure to take in the Pole. We thus made a non-stop flight around the world in a very few minutes. In doing that we lost a whole day in time and of course when we completed the circle we gained that day back again.

Time and direction became topsy-turvy at the Pole. When crossing it on the same straight line we were going north one instant and south the next! No matter how the wind strikes you at the North Pole it must be travelling north and however you turn your head you must be looking south and our job was to get back to the small island of Spitzbergen which lay somewhere south of us!

There were two great questions that confronted us now. Were we exactly where we thought we were? If not – and could we be absolutely certain? – we would miss Spitzbergen. And even if we were on a straight course, would that engine stop? It seemed certain that it would.

As we flew there at the top of the world, we saluted the gallant, indomitable spirit of Peary and verified his report in every detail.

Below us was a great, eternally frozen, snow-covered

ocean, broken into ice fields or cakes of various sizes and shapes, the boundaries of which were the ridges formed by the great pressure of one cake upon another. This showed a constant ice movement and indicated the non-proximity of land. Here and there, instead of a pressing together of the ice fields, there was a separation, leaving a water-lead which had been recently frozen over and showing green and greenish-blue against the white of the snow. On some of the cakes were ice hummocks and rough masses of jumbled snow and ice.

At 9.15 a.m. we headed for Spitzbergen, having abandoned the plan to return via Cape Morris Jesup on account of the oil leak.

But, to our astonishment, a miracle was happening. That motor was still running. It is a hundred to one shot that a leaky engine such as ours means a motor stoppage. It is generally an oil lead that breaks. We afterward found out the leak was caused by a rivet jarring out of its hole, and when the oil got down to the level of the hole it stopped leaking. Flight Engineer Noville had put an extra amount of oil in an extra tank.

The reaction of having accomplished our mission, together with the narcotic effect of the motors, made us drowsy when we were steering. I dozed off once at the wheel and had to relieve Bennett several times because of his sleepiness.

I quote from my impressions cabled to the United States on our return to Kings Bay:

The wind began to freshen and change direction soon after we left the Pole, and soon we were making over 100 miles an hour.

The elements were surely smiling that day on us, two insignificant specks of mortality flying there over that great, vast, white area in a small plane with only one companion, speechless and deaf from the motors, just a dot in the centre of 10,000 square miles of visible desolation.

We felt no larger than a pinpoint and as lonely as the tomb; as remote and detached as a star.

Here, in another world, far from the herds of people, the smallnesses of life fell from our shoulders. What wonder that we felt no great emotion of achievement or fear of death that lay stretched beneath us, but instead, impersonal, disembodied. On, on we went. It seemed forever onward.

Our great speed had the effect of quickening our mental processes, so that a minute appeared as many minutes, and I realized fully then that time is only a relative thing. An instant can be an age, an age an instant.

We were aiming for Grey Point, Spitzbergen, and finally when we saw it dead ahead, we knew that we had been able to keep on our course! That we were exactly where we had thought we were!

It was a wonderful relief not to have to navigate any more. We came into Kings Bay flying at about 4,000 feet. The tiny village was a welcome sight, but not so much so as the good old *Chantier* that looked so small beneath. I could see the steam from her welcoming and, I knew, joyous whistle.

It seemed but a few moments until we were in the arms of our comrades, who carried us with wild joy down the snow runway they had worked so hard to make.

Among the first to meet us had been Captain Amundsen and Lincoln Ellsworth, two good sports.

TSANGPO GORGE

Frank Kingdon-Ward

Frank Kingdon-Ward (1885–1958) was born in Britain. A plant collector, his botanizing trips took him to China, Tibet, Thailand, Burma and other remote corners. His publications include The Land of the Blue Poppy *and* In Farthest Burma. *The journey through the Tsangpo Gorge, Tibet, that Kingdon-Ward recounts below took place in 1926.*

The name of Tibet is instinct with the spirit of the land, a spirit aloof and mysterious, brooding over the vast, white roof-top of the world in an icy silence broken by the blare of trumpets or the heavy throbbing of drums from some dim temple, or the crash of mighty waters as the lost rivers break their way through the greatest mountain range in the world to the unseen sea.

There are two Tibets. There is the Chang Tang, the plateau country, including the lake region and the upper courses of the great rivers, and there is the little-known, or unknown, gorge country, seamed by the middle courses of these rivers, where they change direction to the south and force the barrier-ranges on their way to India and China . . . Tibet possesses the largest unexplored areas in the world and one of the richest mountain floras; and it was to collect and bring to England specimens and seeds of Tibetan plants, as well as to add to geographers' knowledge of the country, that I set out from Bengal, accompanied by Lord Cawdor, on a journey to the Gorge of the Tsangpo itself.

We expected to be lost to civilization for a year, and in addition to our tents, equipment, scientific instruments, and personal belongings, we had to take with us all our money in silver rupees. We travelled via Sikkim, and in Gangtok received our passports for Tibet, which had been specially obtained for us direct from Lhasa. For two days we rode our ponies through the wonderland of the Sikkim forest, and then crossed the Nathu La (14,500 feet) and entered Tibet. Leaving Yatung, we began the sharp ascent to the Tibetan plateau. The valley of the Ammo Chu was as pleasant as England in May. Steep grass-slopes glowed honey-yellow in the mild sunshine, or glimmered with the lilac shadow of *Primula denticulata*. Barberry bushes shone red as Chinese lacquer against the turquoise sky, and silver tails of willows glistened on the half-fledged twigs. But when we entered the rhododendron-juniper forest bleak winter shut us in like night, nor did we see again the face of spring till we reached the Tsangpo a month later . . .

In the Tsangpo valley the villagers plant crab, walnut and peach trees, and the terraces were covered with a thick scrub of rose, potentilla and cotoneaster. There were occasional birch trees.

We usually marched from ten to four, with a midday luncheon halt. As we had to cut our baggage to a minimum, we lived on the country as much as possible, buying eggs and chickens, yak milk, yak or goat meat, and *tsamba* – roast barley flour. We carried a small supply of tinned foods, and such provisions as cocoa, chocolate, coffee, and Quaker Oats. Birthdays, special achievements, or chance meetings were celebrated by breaking into our small store of luxuries.

We crossed the Lung La, lifted heavenward between two snow peaks, and, in driving snow and gathering darkness . . . we came to the monastery of Chokorchye. Sitting by a huge charcoal fire and drinking buttered tea, one degree less hot than the charcoal, we forgot the storm. Next day we pushed on to Tsegyu, and by night reached Gyatsa Dzong . . . Beyond this the river looked to be twisted sharply, but it did not change its character. It still wound slowly along – like our transport! We had a dozen girls carrying the overflow of bundles which were not strapped on our oxen or little stubborn ponies. Round Gyantse the ladies stretch their hair over frames of wood and wire, projecting some eight inches at the sides and decorated with coloured beads. Our female porters were small and very strong in build, and, to enhance their attractions (we thought unsuccessfully), they covered their faces with black varnish – in contrast to the shades affected by Western womanhood.

We came to the village of Trungsasho, birthplace of the then Dalai Lama, and here we met his sister, taking her ponies to water. She still lived her old life as a peasant, unaltered by the knowledge that her brother was ruler of all Tibet and venerated by millions of believers in other lands . . .

Transport troubles increased. According to the custom of the country, we had to change transport at each village; and when the villages lie close together, you are lucky if you change only four times in the day. Ponies were badly broken and often bolted, strewing the track with the wreckage of packing-cases and boxes which contained our worldly all. However, we were near Tsela Dzong, where we planned to make our first halt. Firewood and pine torches were plentiful – and local provisions also. We saw peas and beans occasionally – a great luxury – and we could always procure small and strong-flavoured onions. The main fruit crops are walnuts and peaches. The peaches are sun-dried on the roofs of the houses – and

that, as Cawdor said, is "a sound investment, for, sucked
conscientiously, a sun-dried peach lasts a long time . . ."

Soon after our arrival at Tsela, we called on the
Dzongpon, but found his manager, with whom we exchanged presents and arranged for the delivery of our
mails. His Tibetan mastiffs almost broke their chains in a
dutiful attempt to accomplish our deaths. Luckily the
chains stood the strain. Besides these mastiffs they breed a
Tibetan poodle, which is something like a Pekingese, but
longer in the leg and shorter-coated. He is black, and may
have a small, white patch on the chest. There are pariahs
here, as everywhere in Asia, and – a feature often found in
hill countries – many of them are wall-eyed.

Tibetans are not, by English standards, "kind to animals", in the sense that they do not make a cult of them;
but they are not unkind. Simply they live hard lives
themselves, and expect their animals to follow their example and take stoically what comes next. We saw here
nothing of the "Oriental cruelty" of which one hears so
much in the West. We did see one criminal, a thief who
was condemned to wear leg-irons for life, and passed on
from *dzong* to *dzong* as a Horrible Warning. He was
clanking cheerfully about his work when we saw him.

We now decided to leave Tsela Dzong, and make our
permanent base at Tumbatse, in the upper valley of the
Rong Chu. We went down the Tsangpo in skin boats to
Luding, and then up the Temo Valley till we saw above us
Temo Gompa, raised heavenward on a hill between two
racing streams. So in the golden evening we rode through
the narrow street, past silent, quiet-moving Lamas, and
were made welcome at the guest house.

The *Depa* of Temo was a young man, "easy to look at"
as the Americans say, with native courtesy and a cosmo-
politan urbanity. He had visited India, and said that he
had learned of many of the material benefits of Western
civilization. He had certainly learned of one, for he had
brought back an awe-inspiring collection of firearms. He

dressed in Chinese style: jacket of imperial yellow silk, black plush boots, and a hat with a scarlet mandarin tassel.

We constituted Temo our rationing base for the season. After leaving Tsetang we made the horrible discovery that we had forgotten the curry powder – a serious matter in a country where cooking does not rank as one of the arts, and raw materials are sometimes questionable. However, we summoned up our courage, and sampled the *masala* which they make in Kongbo of dried fruits and chips of bark and wood and seeds, pounded in a mortar with a stone. We found it excellent.

In early June we left Temo Gompa and crossed the Temo La. We were now on the range which runs northward to the Nambu La, and divides the Gyamda River to the west from the Rong Chu. I climbed the peak opposite Tumbatse, 16,008 feet. The night was bitter and the dawn mist-blinded, but in the last precious hour of evening I saw one of those sights which never quite leave one throughout life – the setting sun firing the great snowbergs of the Salween Divide.

Beyond the Temo La we reached the rhododendron moorland, which was later awash with the sea-foam flowers of an aromatic-leafed "Anthopogon" and the pinks and purples of other dwarf alpine rhododendrons. By mid-June three alpine poppies flowered. One was the lovely azure *Meconopsis simplicifolia* – the true colour, as originally shown in the *Botanical Magazine*. Later a dingy violet form, said to be perennial, reached England. Not till Major F. R. Bailey sent home in 1913 seed of a rich blue form, collected in the Eastern Himalaya, did we recover the true *M. simplicifolia*, under the name of Bailey's variety. Ours from the Temo La was a fragrant form; but this must not be confused with *Meconopsis Baileyi*, which I brought back and which has done very well in English parks and gardens.

Other lovely poppies from this region were *M. impedita*, with small gold and violet silken flowers, twenty or

more to a cluster, and a beautiful yellow-flowered species
covered with silky, honey-coloured hairs. This aspiring
plant grew only between 15,000 and 17,000 feet. I collected a very fine barberry with jet black stems and coral
fruits. In the autumn its flame-red and old gold foliage is
very beautiful . . .

In June the open boggy places are flushed with the rose
of *Primula tibetica*; in September its small capsules fill
with gold-dust seed. Edging a stream I found a lovely
"Sibirica" iris, violet coloured, with a cobweb of gold
spun over the falls. We returned to Tumbatse at the
beginning of July, and there I collected . . . another plant
which has taken kindly to English gardens (especially
when wet and shady) – the giant cowslip, *Primula Flor-
indae*. When conditions suit it this plant sends up flower-
stalks four feet high, bearing a hundred flowers in a
cluster . . .

Rope bridges supply one of the more doubtful joys of a
traveller's life in the gorge country. They are of various
types. A common one hereabouts consists of two cables of
twisted bamboo, some five inches thick. These are tied to
trees above the river on either bank, and on them rides a
yoke-shaped wooden carrier with a two-foot span,
notched on each side to hold the safety-rope in place.
The ordinary mortal attaches himself to this carrier, with
his arms free for hauling, and courageously but ungrace-
fully pulls himself across. Superior persons (we, thank
heaven, were superior persons) are literally tied hand and
foot to two carriers, and pulled across by slow jerks which
shake every tooth in the head and rack every nerve in the
body . . .

There was trouble at Drukla, which had formerly been
an important monastery housing 800 monks. Wars with
the Pobas and the Chinese had wasted the neighbourhood, and the strength of Drukla dwindled to 130. Now
the enemy within the gates – the very old enemy of man –
had been active; 60 monks had been discovered in the

error of their ways, and the Commissioner had ordered immediate expulsion. This would leave the monastery a mere shell. We felt sympathy for the *Labrang Lama*, but, on looking at the sixty delinquents, we also felt sympathy for the world without, upon which they were suddenly to be released in force.

At Napo Dzong we were guests in the house of a magnate of the first water. The windows of the room where we supped were fitted with glass, protected without by wire netting and embellished within by curtains. The paved yard was bright with flowers like an English cottage garden – stocks, asters, hollyhocks. The *Dzongpon* had visited Calcutta and returned with a tin of Sutton's seeds, which provided all this display. The apartments allotted to us were furnished in the Chinese style, with chairs, tables, and a carved and curtained bedstead fit for an Empress. There was also a painted prayer-drum in a pagoda . . .

We sent home seeds of 250 species, many travelling in thermos flasks for protection against the violent changes of temperature through which they had to pass.

At Pe we saw three Lopas, the Tibetan name for the most savage of the Assam jungle tribes. These dwarfs had small animal eyes, bulging foreheads, and projecting muzzles which called to mind the Neanderthal man. They are evidently the people we call Abors. They were un-friendly, spoke no Tibetan, and wore next to no clothes; but they carried 80-lb loads over tracks that would kill a white man, and crossed the Doshong La almost naked in deep snow, and in the teeth of the awful interstellar wind which eternally scours the Tibetan uplands.

The *Depa* at Pe gave an entertainment for us, and by the smoky light of burning pine-chips we watched a Tibetan dance, stamped out to the accompaniment of a weird and wonderful song, without tune or rhythm. After this a *Monba*, a tall, good-looking fellow, sang one of the slow, sad songs of his own jungle. Even the

Pobas gave a "turn", though they were very drunk by
that time . . .

Some time after this we saw the sun glitter on the snow
peaks of the Trans-Himalayan range, the first of the three
great barriers which still separated us from India. We
pressed on now, making short marches and short halts. At
Tating we had the exciting experience of losing the trail
(and ourselves) for two hours, on a 15,000-foot plateau,
during a winter's night. And at Dengshu I myself was ill
and passed into a strange stupor, in which my mind was
active, but my body nearly unconscious. I was glad that it
lasted only for a day.

When we reached Tsona we were worn out, bloodshot,
and frost-bitten – and here we met further transport
difficulty. However, on 9 January transport of a sort
was found for us, and we reached the Po La, in Monyul,
and stood at last upon the third barrier. Behind us the
plateau lay, dead and shrouded. No sound of bird or
beast, no crack of twig or stir of leaf, could be heard,
only the eternal fierce call of the wind in that unearthly
emptiness. Below us, dark and full of promise, the forest
began – the forest full of life and loveliness, through
which our road lay to the flowery plains of Hindustan.

DHOW SAFARI

Michael McRae

Michael McRae is a contributing editor for Outside *magazine. He lives in Oregon.*

The coast of Kenya differs so markedly from the interior that it seems a foreign land – a place that is in Africa but not entirely of Africa. Author V.S. Naipaul draws this distinction in *A Bend in the River*. "It was an Arab-Indian-Persian-Portuguese place," explains Naipaul's narrator, Salim, about a fictitious coastal city where he grew up, "and we who lived there were really people of the Indian Ocean. True Africa was at our back."

My wife and I lived in Kenya for half a year but did not get around to seeing the coast until our sojourn was almost over. I cherish the time we squandered on safari, spending whole weeks traversing the Masai Mara game reserve during the wildebeest migration, or buzzing formations of pink flamingos while flying up the Rift Valley. But for pure exoticism, very little we did in true Africa compares with the adventure of boarding an Arab dhow at Mombasa and riding the trade winds north to Lamu Island.

If I had to choose one symbol for the coast, it would be a dhow, one with its delta-shaped lateen sail billowing in the soft Indian Ocean breezes. These sturdy vessels have been sailing to and from the coast for more than a thousand years, ever since Arab traders first arrived and intermarried with the indigenous Bantus, giving rise to the Swahili culture (*swahili* means "coastal" in Arabic). Sailing in from the east, the dhows imported salt, dates, roofing tiles, dried fish, and Islam; on the return voyage, they took away gold, ivory, coffee, slaves, and once, in 1415, a giraffe sent by the people of Malindi as a gift to the emperor of China.

Fifty years ago, the old harbor at Mombasa, Kenya's principal port, would have been crowded with several hundred dhows – Arab *booms* and *sambuks*, Indian *barigs* and *dhangis*, African *jahazis* and *mashuas*, and half a dozen other hull configurations. Though their numbers are declining, the big oceangoing dhows still blow in from distant lands, riding the monsoon south from December through March and returning home when the winds shift direction from April to October. During the peak of the dhow season, a parade of boats can be seen passing off-shore, though most now are the smaller *jahazis*, which conduct intracoastal trade from Somalia to Tanzania.

One of these cargo haulers bears the name *Tusitiri* carved on her teak bow and stern. Sixty-five feet from stem to stern, she was built by hand by master boatmen in the village of Matondani on Lamu Island. Her lyrical name can be translated in either of two ways: as a prayer to Allah for protection, or as a pact among conspirators to conceal a secret – say, a crew carrying a cargo of contra-band ivory beneath a load of building materials and cornmeal.

So far as our contact in Mombasa could tell, though, the *Tusitiri*'s owner and captain, Omar Mohamed Salim, was a devout and honest man who traded only in legal goods. On a voyage from Mombasa to Lamu one recent October, for example, her cargo manifest listed soft drinks, salt, biscuits, bottled gas, cornmeal – and my wife and me.

Arranging passage on the *Tusitiri* had taken some doing, not least because we were living in Nairobi, some 250 miles from the Indian Ocean. Also, for reasons of liability, dhow captains are generally reluctant to accept passengers, especially Westerners. To overcome these difficulties, we had enlisted the help of Omari Bwana, the director of the Fort Jesus Museum near the old harbor. Each day, walking to the imposing sixteenth-century Portuguese garrison, he would inquire at the harbor on our behalf. When Omar Salim agreed to take us on, Omari Bwana notified us by telephone. That same day we took the overnight train to Mombasa.

The *Tusitiri* carried a crew of sixteen. We boarded her one night at 10:00 and found them all fast asleep on deck. Scattered about in full-length sleeping sacks plaited of palm fronds, the bodies were indistinguishable in the darkness from the plaited deck matting, and I tripped over several men while tiptoeing back to the quarterdeck. There were no cabins below, only 80 tons of cargo. Captain Salim, a rotund man with a shaved head, stopped snoring and sat up long enough to give my wife a gaudy red pillow of satin and lace: we were honored guests.

Ali, the apprentice seaman who had guided us aboard, showed us a spot to sleep, explaining that the captain planned to get underway as soon as the full moon rose. We spread out our sleeping bags and laid down, but the stench seeping up from the bilge was so putrid that we both gagged. Sitting up with our noses in the faint breeze, we fell into a fitful slumber, jerking awake whenever we slumped over into the malodorous layer of bilge fumes.

By 4:00 a.m., the brilliant moon was perched atop the mast. Captain Salim arose and took the helm, sitting Buddha-like on his sea chest. Without command, the crew took up the halyards and prepared to raise the yard, which was longer than the boat itself and ungodly heavy. The work began when the eldest crewman launched into a chant that began, "Ali Baba . . . Oh, Mama. Ali Baba . . .

Oh, Papa." Between each verse of this ancient song, the
crew heaved mightily, raising the yard a few inches, then
groaned a refrain, "*Ya fatiha*," which is the opening of
the Koran and a prayer for the dead.

In ten minutes, the yard had ascended the stout mast,
and the sail was unfurled with a great *whump*. Slowly,
silently, we began to drift away from the dock with the
moon lighting our way. Just then the haunting cry of a
muezzin echoed over the still harbor, summoning the
faithful to prayer, and the sail caught a puff of wind,
pulling us toward the mouth of the harbor.

Thus did the voyage of the *Tusitiri* begin – in much the
same manner, I imagined, as the voyage of Sindbad
setting off in search of adventure.

Soon after the sun appeared on the horizon, the slight
wind died, and with it our progress. By 9:00 we were
becalmed, drifting like Sindbad in the doldrums. The
rigging creaked, the boat pitched, the captain sat on his
sea chest, shirtless and with his big belly straining his
kikoy, the brightly colored sarong that is standard dress
on the coast. (Even we were wearing them.) The sun was
blazing, and it quickly turned my toes into ten little
cocktail sausages, all pink and swollen. We sought relief
in the shade of the sail, but by mid-morning there was no
escape. I marked our progress against the closely spaced
beachfront hotels we passed: one hour, two hotels. It was
going to be a long day.

When the sun was directly overhead, the men rigged an
awning over the quarterdeck, but the bilge fumes, now
rising in the heat, were a bad tradeoff for shade. Instead,
we took to the dinghy lashed amidships next to the mast
and claimed it as our stateroom. We made a nest with our
sleeping bags and covered ourselves with sheets we had
brought along. Lunch was announced: *ugali*, a sticky
porridge of cornmeal served communally on one battered
aluminum platter, and hunks of dried fish sliced off of

what looked like a dead bat. We nibbled at the porridge (also called *posho*) and, for dessert, reciprocated with oranges and cheese we had purchased in Mombasa. Dinner was more *posho*, this time with a fiery tomato relish.

That day we sailed – drifted, really – until two hours after dark. Navigating by the stars, Captain Salim put in at a cove north of Malindi and dropped anchor within sight of a brightly lit off-shore satellite-tracking station, which looked straight out of a James Bond movie. "Men who fly rockets live there," explained Ali. "We will stay here for the night because there are dangerous rocks ahead. The navy can also stop us and ask a lot of questions. We are afraid of them."

Ali was the only English speaker aboard, but he was an engaging raconteur. We talked into the night, of stars and satellites and friendly spirits. Ali's grandfather from Matondani was a witch doctor who spoke to giants in his dreams. "They tell him what will happen and help him when he is in danger," said Ali. He showed us constellations and pointed out key stars that Captain Salim had taught him to recognize as navigational guides. Later, having retired to our dinghy, I drifted off while studying the Milky Way, trying to imagine what the grandfather's giants looked like.

When the moon rose again, the men chanted the ponderous yard back up the mast, and we set sail in a fresh breeze. The wind stayed strong all day, and as we pushed up the coast Ali narrated the passing of the landmarks: the dangerous rocks at the mouth of the Tana River, a whirlpool, a beach where elephants come down to bathe at sundown. Periodically, the men would kneel facing Mecca to offer prayers. The sun was searing, the day endlessly long. A mound of *ugali* the size of a ski slope was passed around for lunch, but the heat and fetid bilge had killed our appetites. We lay under our sheets in a stupor.

Finally Lamu appeared on the horizon. Ali and his young pals became more boisterous the nearer we got, cocking their embroidered caps at rakish angles, like American sailors on leave, and poking each other in the ribs. The tomfoolery ended as we entered the harbor channel and the first mate barked out orders.

Our arrival in Lamu town brought a dozen hustlers spilling out of its maze of narrow lanes onto the quay, each vying loudly to become our guide. But the mate would have none of it and chased them off. We paid our fare to Captain Salim – 300 shillings, about $21 – and, waving farewell, boarded another smaller dhow, a motorized water taxi named *Radhina*. On the hull next to its name, the owner had added the words BEST AND CHEAP.

Lamu has remained largely unchanged for centuries and, for the most part, seemed delightfully oblivious to tourism. As we chugged up the waterfront, we passed a row of dazzling white Arab-style houses built of coral blocks. Many featured columned facades and the ornately carved entryways for which the island is famous. Donkey carts were the only vehicles in evidence – the island has but one car, the district commissioner's – and pedestrians on the esplanade dressed according to tradition: women in black *buibui*, men in *kikoys* or long white robes.

After about two miles we reached the sleepy fishing village of Shela and our hotel. Built by Arab craftsmen as a private residence in the 1930s, it had been converted into a small, quiet resort, with a staff of forty-five for the fifty guests. Beyond its white-walled gardens there were miles of empty beach and an endless ocean view toward Mecca.

Early the next morning, I awoke to the sound of the muezzin at the Shela mosque. Lying under the diaphanous cocoon of a mosquito bed, with the ceiling fan whispering above and palm fronds stirring outside, I rejoiced for the previous day's wind, which had delivered us from the doldrums to a kind of paradise. Indeed, *Peponi*, the hotel's name, like that of the *Tusitiri*, could be translated in two ways: as paradise or breeze. To a couple of burned-out voyagers who had been becalmed off the coast of Kenya, inhaling bilge fumes and broiling under the equatorial sun, the two meanings seemed as synonymous to me as they must have been to Sindbad.

CONQUERING HALF DOME

Don George

Don George is the travel editor of Salon.

Sometimes we know a journey will be a grand adventure –
the three-week expedition I made a few springs ago along
Pakistan's avalanche-laden Karakoram Highway to enchanted Hunza comes to mind. Other times we know it
will be a little one – on a business trip to Paris this January
I was content with stumbling onto a wonderful ancient
restaurant and a precious new park I'd never known
about.

But sometimes our trips surprise us.

I recently returned from a five-day family excursion to
Yosemite. It was supposed to be a little camping lark, but
it turned out to be a much grander – and much more
terrifying – adventure than I'd ever imagined.

The trip seemed innocent enough: Our plan was to
drive to Yosemite on a Saturday, spend the next three
days camping and hiking to the top of Half Dome, then
hike back to our car and drive home on the fifth day. This
would require three days of four to six hours of hiking.
The only moderately troublesome part would be the final
ascent of Half Dome, that iconic granite thumb that juts

almost 9,000 feet over the meadows and waterfalls and lesser crags of California's Yosemite Valley. But I had seen pictures of the cable-framed walkway that leads to the top of the mountain, and it didn't look too difficult. My wife and I felt confident that our 8-year-old son and 12-year-old daughter could handle it.

So off we went. We made the winding drive from the San Francisco Bay Area to Yosemite National Park in about four hours. It was a splendid day, all cotton-candy clouds against a county-fair sky. Eating carrots and apple slices in the car, we sped through the suburbs and into parched golden hills, and before we knew it we were off the main highway and passing hand-painted signs advertising red onions, fresh-picked tomatoes, almonds, peaches and nectarines. Our eyes lingered on the weather-beaten stands, where we could see shiny red mounds of tomatoes and green mountains of watermelons, but we pressed on.

We reached Yosemite as the sun was setting, picked up our trail permit, pitched our tent, cooked a quick camp supper and went to bed.

Our plan was to get up early, hike more than halfway up – to the highest source of water on the Half Dome trail – and camp, thereby minimizing the distance we would have to cover the next day before making our assault on the peak. If you're young and strong, or old and foolhardy, you can hike from Yosemite Valley to the top of Half Dome and back in a day. In previous trips to Yosemite we had met people who had done just that; they would leave at daybreak and plan to get back around dusk. But we wanted to take it easy on ourselves. We also had built in an extra day so that if for any reason we couldn't make Half Dome the first time, we would have a second chance, so we weren't in any hurry.

The next day took longer than we had planned – as it invariably does. By the time we had gotten the kids rousted and had packed up our tents and ground covers and cooking gear, it was about 10 a.m and the sun was high and hot in the sky.

We set off along the John Muir Trail, winding into the rocks and pines. The first section of this trail is still a little like Disneyland, and you pass people in flip-flops and even occasionally high heels, sweating and puffing and swigging fresh-off-the-supermarket-shelf bottles of Crystal Geyser.

After about a half hour's stroll you reach a picturesque bridge with a fantastic foaming view of the Merced River cascading over the rocks – and a neat wooden bathroom and a water fountain that is the last source of water that doesn't have to be filtered. The flip-flops and high heels turn back with a grateful sigh at this point, and the few people you do pass hereafter on the trail exchange friendly nods and greetings and the smug satisfaction of getting into the real Yosemite.

Then you walk and you walk and you walk, stepping heavily over rocks, kicking up clouds of dirt that settle on your legs and socks and boots. Occasionally you'll be cooled by a shower of water trickling from high rocks right onto the trail, or by a breeze blowing unexpectedly when you turn a corner. But for the most part you step and mop your brow and swat at mosquitoes in the patches of shade and take swigs of water, careful to roll the water in your mouth as your long-ago football coach taught you, until you're surprised by a dazzling quilt of purple flowers, or a tumbling far-off torrent shining white and silver and blue in the sun, and you stop and munch slowly on Balance bars and dried apples and nectarines and notice how the sunlight waterfalls through the branches of the trees.

After four hours we reached the halfway point at Little Yosemite Valley. It's a popular camping spot with loosely demarcated camping areas – framed by fallen tree trunks with rock-outlined fire circles and tree stumps for tables and stools – plus a resident ranger, an outhouse and easily accessible water in the form of the Merced River fast-flowing by. We hadn't really prepared for the trip physically, and were already grimy and sweaty and exhausted. On top of that, we had received conflicting information about where exactly the last source of water on the trail would be, so rather than press further up, we decided to stop there for the night. Tomorrow we would rise early and climb Half Dome.

We had planned to get up at 6 and be on the trail by 8. Again, reality intruded, and we got up at 8 and set out for Half Dome around 9:30. This was not wise. We had never hiked this trail before and didn't know how long it would take or what obstacles it would present; besides that, we'd been told that the best time to climb Half Dome is the morning, since clouds tend to come in by the afternoon. Weather changes quickly in the mountains, and you don't want to be anywhere near the summit when the clouds come in, rangers had said. The mountain is a magnet for lightning. All Half Dome hikers are explicitly told that if they see rain clouds on the horizon, they shouldn't attempt the ascent. Lightning strikes the dome at least once every month – and at least a few careless people every year. Even the cables that run up the final 800 feet of the slope are lightning magnets.

So we wound up through the trees as fast as we could. We passed through deep-shadowed, pine-needled stretches of forest path like places in a fairy tale, and we emerged onto sun-blasted stretches of rock that offered amazing views of the surrounding peaks – and of Half Dome towering precipitously into the sky.

We reached the base of Half Dome, after a final, extremely arduous half-hour zigzag trek up a series of massive steps cut out of the stone, at about 1 p.m. Clouds were massing to the east and to the west, but we pressed on. A motley pile of gloves left by previous climbers lay at the spot where the cable walkway began. We chose gloves we liked, grabbed hold of the cables and began to haul ourselves up.

This is when our little lark turned into a grand adventure.

In the pictures we had seen before the trip, the cable route didn't look all that daunting. Basically, they showed a gangplank-like walkway with thick steel cables running along either side that stretched up the slope of the mountain. In the pictures, hikers with day-packs strode confidently up the slope as if they were out for a Sunday stroll.

Somehow the pictures hadn't prepared me for the reality. The cables are set about four feet off the ground and are about three feet apart. As a further aid to climbers, wooden planks connected to the posts that support the cables are set across the mountain-path at an interval of about every four to five feet. This is not as comforting as it sounds.

I'd read before the trip that the path slopes up at an angle of about 60 degrees. In my mind I had pictured that angle and had mentally traced a line along the living room wall. That doesn't seem too steep, I had said to myself.

Beware estimates made in the comfort of your living room. From the plushness of my couch, with a soothing cup of steaming tea in my hand, 60 degrees hadn't seemed too steep – but in the sheer, slippery, life-on-the-line wildness of Yosemite, it seemed real steep. I looked at the cables, and I looked at the sloping pate of the mountain – and I thought, "This is a really stupid way to die."

"Why," I continued, "am I consciously choosing to risk my life like this? What's the point? All it would take would be one slip, a hand loosened from the cables." I could already see myself sliding down the face of Half Dome, grabbing frantically at the smooth surface, thudding-scraping-bumping along the rock until, if I was really lucky, I managed to grab a bloody finger-stub handhold on the rock face or, if I wasn't really lucky, I just slipped off the face of the rock, with all the assembled climbers gasping and screaming and my wife and kids yelling not knowing what to do, how to prevent my fall, and then it would be a brief free-fall flight before bone-crushing oblivion. Hopefully, I thought, I will pass out before contact and die relatively peacefully.

All this flashed through my mind as I stood at the base of the cables. "What are we waiting for?" my daughter asked impatiently.

"We're waiting until we grow wings," I wanted to say.

But she was ready – ah, youth, that hath no fear – and began to scramble up the slope. And then my wife went. And then my son started – a little apprehensively, being 8 years old and all. But he was on his way. None of them seemed to understand that what we were doing was inherently suicidal!

Still, they were gone, and there really was nothing to do but grab hold of the cables and start to pull myself up this suddenly stupid and hateful mountain.

The whole thing seemed so absurd – dying to prove what point? Hadn't I evolved beyond this kind of macho risk-taking decades ago?

Somehow the fact that all kinds of people, from base-ball-capped teens to silver-haired seniors, had scrambled up that day and were now headed down the very walkway I was staring up, and that numerous others were perched on the face of the mountain in mid-ascent a dozen yards above me, scrambling up even as I quaked – somehow this was of no comfort.

I was scared. I wasn't exactly convinced I was going to die – I thought I probably had a chance of making it alive – but I felt I was consciously subjecting myself to an experience that could really kill me. This was my idea of a vacation? Whatever happened to a full-service beach resort and little cocktails with bright paper parasols?

But so we started. My first few steps were leaden. My hiking boots kept slipping; my arms, which hadn't done anything all day, suddenly felt dead-tired and couldn't haul up the dead weight of my body. In a classic case of self-fulfilling prophecy, I kept slipping and sliding, just as I thought I would. I was utterly miserable.

One thing you should never do – or at least one thing I should never do – when climbing Half Dome is look around at the view. The view is what can kill you. You stop and brush your brow with your sleeve and your eyes steal a look to the left and whoa! It's a long, long way down. Your view drops right off the side of the cliff to green trees the size of matchsticks and postage-stamp meadows. You don't want to see this and you definitely don't want to think about it. I swayed and held onto the cables and stayed frozen, letting other climbers brush by me, until the dizziness and the wave-swells in my stomach stopped. My mouth was drier than I could ever remember it being before. My arms ached.

After about 15 wooden planks, my son and I paused. My wife Kuniko looked down from a perch a few posts ahead. "How are you feeling, Jeremy? Do you want to keep going, or do you want to stop?"

"Say you want to stop, Jeremy," I prayed. "For the love of God, tell her you want to stop!"

He was undecided. I was probably green in the face. "How are you doing, honey?" Kuniko asked, concern creasing her face.

"I don't know," I said.

We looked around and saw bulbous black clouds blowing swiftly in. "Maybe we should head down," Kuniko said.

"Yes! Yes!" a little voice inside me said.

"I want to keep going!" Jenny said.

"No, I think we should head down," Kuniko said.

"I think so, too," I said, whining with as much authority as I could muster. "I don't like the look of those clouds."

So, much to Jenny's loud disappointment, we slid down

– which was almost as terrifying as hauling up, except that now your body was helping gravity pull you to your death.

At one point I really did completely slip – my feet just went out from under me, I landed with a sacroiliac-smacking thud and before I knew what was happening I began to slide down the face of the mountain. Luckily I managed to stomp the sole of one boot squarely against the iron post that supported the cable, thus stopping my fall. Mortality had never seemed nearer.

I lay on the side of the mountain for a few minutes, trying to slow my heart, waiting for my arms to stop shaking.

"Are you all right?" people asked as they stepped gingerly by me.

Then I said to myself, "Just go down slowly, one by one," and I did. And suddenly I was at the bottom, stepping off the last plank onto level rock, and I was sitting down and sluggishly taking off my gloves and Jenny was asking, "Dad, are you OK?"

The hike back to camp seemed about 10 times longer than the morning's walk. My head was black-clouded with doubts and fears about attempting the climb again the next day. What a stupid way to die, I kept thinking.

But at the same time I felt that I had to do it. The kids were going to do it, everyone was doing it – I couldn't say, "Gee, I think I'll just stay down here and watch."

So even though I knew I was putting my life unnecessarily at risk, I also knew I had to make the climb.

I tossed and turned for hours that night, thinking about that blasted slippery-slope cable walkway. I knew it was virtually all mental, that I was psyching myself into failure. It didn't matter. I couldn't magically find the switch in my mind.

After a fractured sleep we woke up and retraced our path of the previous day. I wish I could say that everything had changed, that I had come to peace with the idea of climbing Half Dome and had found a deep pool of confidence in myself, but I hadn't. I had made up my mind to climb Half Dome, but I was fundamentally unsettled about it all.

Still, everything seemed a little more propitious this time. We got an earlier start and so we were passed by only a handful of day-hikers, which felt good. The sky was a broad expanse of blue, with only a few puffs of white here and there. I was hiking strongly, and we covered the same territory in about an hour less than the previous day. We reached the arduous rocksteps at about 10:30 and were at the glove-heaped base of Half Dome by 11:00. We paused to take some deep swigs of water and eat an energy bar, and then we were ready.

Jeremy and Jenny set off first, fearlessly. Kuniko and I had decided that I would go up next, so that if I slipped, she might be able to help me. I swapped the thick leather gloves I had used the day before for lighter cloth gloves that permitted more feeling in my fingers. That seemed to help some.

I knew it was all mental, but that knowledge wasn't helping much. It was still terrifying. But this time I thought: If you just focus on each step, you'll be OK. Don't think about the slope to the left or the right. Don't think about what's beneath you or how much more you still have to go. Just focus on each step, step by step.

I took my first step and pulled myself up by the cables. Took another step and did the same. Took another step and I was at the first wooden plank.

I repeated the process, planting my foot slowly, making sure it was secure on the rock face before using my arms, then pulling myself up to make the next step. Three steps and I had reached plank No. 2.

It seemed easier than yesterday.

Gradually my body relaxed. The tension left my arms and they didn't ache. The fear left my legs and they were more flexible; I was finding secure sole-holds in the rock. I didn't slip, and I was learning to focus my breathing and energy in discrete spurts of arm-pulling.

The trick, I thought, is to restrict the world to the small plot of rock in front of me and the cables on either side, to extend my arm about 10 inches up the cable, like this, grab tight hold of it, secure my grip, like this, say "OK, now!" and pull – ugh! and up! – and then pause a while to catch my breath and coil my energy, and then repeat the process, hauling myself up, step by step.

I reached the point where we had stopped the day before and dimly recorded that it had been much easier so far. If I could just focus on each rung.

I kept pulling myself up, foothold then handhold, plank by plank. At one point, with a quick glance up, I realized that Jenny and Jeremy, who seemed to have sprinted up the slope, had disappeared. They were already running freely around the broad summit. Somewhere inside me, I registered the fact that I was going to make it, too.

There were still a few tricky places – places where a two-foot fissure appeared between the part of the slope-trail I was on and the slope where the trail continued. Here I had to simultaneously pull myself over the displacement and up the slope, a doubly difficult and slippery task.

But by focusing precisely on what I was doing – plant the foot there, make sure it's secure, OK, now pull yourself up on the cable, move your other foot forward, pull yourself up again – I was able to make it without slipping.

There was one particularly steep step where I felt my arms begin to falter and in mid-stride I felt my body begin to sway backward, as if my arms weren't going to be able to pull my body up. Death flickered in my brain and in a millisecond I thought, "You've GOT to pull yourself up" and the adrenaline zapped through my arms like lightning and I forced myself – brain and arms pulling together – to the next rung. The prospect of death had glimmered, but it hadn't paralyzed me as the day before.

After about 25 minutes I reached the point where the

summit begins to taper off and the angle eases. Another ten wooden planks and the end of the ascent was in sight.

I almost ran the last few steps, so exhilarated to have made it to the top. Jenny and Jeremy saw me from their post at the peak and came jumping over the summit. We gave each other big bear hugs.

"You made it, Dad!" they said.

In another few minutes Kuniko came to the top, grinning widely.

We explored the summit, took in the extraordinary 360-degree panorama of snow-capped peaks, piney slopes, glistening waterfalls and green meadows far below.

And we felt on top of the world.

We shared a celebratory chocolate bar I had stuffed in my pocket, and after a half hour snapping photos and walking to the extreme compass points of the peak, we heard thunder to the east and saw black clouds massing, moving with deceptive speed our way.

We shared a huge family hug and set off.

Jenny and Jeremy fairly skipped down the slope – or at least that's the way it seemed to me. I slipped and slid – three times I slowly let myself down on the seat of my pants from one rung to another – but never lost control and within about a half hour I was standing again on level rock, tossing my gloves into the heap, my heart pounding wildly and my head splitting-spinning with the triumph.

I had done it! I had overcome all those fear-boulders that we throw up in front of ourselves, that keep us from doing the things we are capable of doing.

We had climbed Half Dome, and from now on, whenever we looked at that stunning granite jut from afar, we would have the joyful and astounding knowledge that we had once stood on that very peak, looking down on the whole world around us. We had conquered the slippery slope of Half Dome, and we would have much to celebrate that night.

It seemed symbolic of so many things in life, and I was

just beginning to enjoy the light-footed walk back to camp and to feel the success suffuse my body from the top of my head to the tips of my fingers and toes, when Jeremy turned to me and said, "Dad, can we do this again next year?"

ROAD TRIP

Hunter S. Thompson

Hunter S. Thompson was born in 1939 in Louisville, Kentucky. His books include Fear and Loathing in Las Vegas *and* The Great Shark Hunt.

We were somewhere around Barstow on the edge of the desert when the drugs began to take hold. I remember saying something like "I feel a bit lightheaded; maybe you should drive . . ." And suddenly there was a terrible roar all around us and the sky was full of what looked like huge bats, all swooping and screeching and diving around the car, which was going about a hundred miles an hour with the top down to Las Vegas. And a voice was screaming: "Holy Jesus! What are these goddamn animals?"

Then it was quiet again. My attorney had taken his shirt off and was pouring beer on his chest, to facilitate the tanning process. "What the hell are you yelling about?" he muttered, staring up at the sun with his eyes closed and covered with wraparound Spanish sunglasses. "Never mind," I said. "It's your turn to drive." I hit the brakes and aimed the Great Red Shark toward the shoulder of the highway. No point mentioning those bats, I thought. The poor bastard will see them soon enough.

It was almost noon, and we still had more than a hundred miles to go. They would be tough miles. Very soon, I knew, we would both be completely twisted. But there was no going back, and no time to rest. We would have to ride it out. Press registration for the fabulous Mint 400 was already underway, and we had to get there by four to claim our sound-proof suite. A fashionable sporting magazine in New York had taken care of the reservations, along with this huge red Chevy convertible we'd just rented off a lot on the Sunset Strip . . . and I was, after all, a professional journalist; so I had an obligation to *cover the story*, for good or ill.

The sporting editors had also given me $300 in cash, most of which was already spent on extremely dangerous drugs. The trunk of the car looked like a mobile police narcotics lab. We had two bags of grass, seventy-five pellets of mescaline, five sheets of high-powered blotter acid, a salt shaker half full of cocaine, and a whole galaxy of multi-colored uppers, downers, screamers, laughers . . . and also a quart of tequila, a quart of rum, a case of Budweiser, a pint of raw ether and two dozen amyls.

All this had been rounded up the night before, in a frenzy of high-speed driving all over Los Angeles County – from Topanga to Watts, we picked up everything we could get our hands on. Not that we *needed* all that for the trip, but once you get locked into a serious drug collection, the tendency is to push it as far as you can.

The only thing that really worried me was the ether. There is nothing in the world more helpless and irresponsible and depraved than a man in the depths of an ether binge. And I knew we'd get into that rotten stuff pretty soon. Probably at the next gas station. We had sampled almost everything else, and now – yes, it was time for a long snort of ether. And then do the next hundred miles in a horrible, slobbering sort of spastic stupor. The only way to keep alert on ether is to do up a lot of amyls –

not all at once, but steadily, just enough to maintain the focus at ninety miles an hour through Barstow.

"Man, this is the way to travel," said my attorney. He leaned over to turn the volume up on the radio, humming along with the rhythm section and kind of moaning the words: "One toke over the line, Sweet Jesus . . . One toke over the line . . ."

One toke? You poor fool! Wait till you see those goddamn bats. I could barely hear the radio . . . slumped over on the far side of the seat, grappling with a tape recorder turned all the way up on "Sympathy for the Devil." That was the only tape we had, so we played it constantly, over and over, as a kind of demented counterpoint to the radio. And also to maintain our rhythm on the road. A constant speed is good for gas mileage – and for some reason that seemed important at the time. Indeed. On a trip like this one *must* be careful about gas consumption. Avoid those quick bursts of acceleration that drag blood to the back of the brain.

My attorney saw the hitchhiker long before I did. "Let's give this boy a lift," he said, and before I could mount any argument he was stopped and this poor Okie kid was running up to the car with a big grin on his face, saying, "Hot damn! I never rode in a convertible before!"

"Is that right?" I said. "Well, I guess you're about ready, eh?"

The kid nodded eagerly as we roared off.

"We're your friends," said my attorney. "We're not like the others."

O Christ, I thought, he's gone around the bend. "No more of that talk," I said sharply. "Or I'll put the leeches on you." He grinned, seeming to understand. Luckily, the noise in the car was so awful – between the wind and the radio and the tape machine – that the kid in the back seat couldn't hear a word we were saying. Or could he?

How long can we *maintain?* I wondered. How long before one of us starts raving and jabbering at this boy?

What will he think then? This same lonely desert was the last known home of the Manson family. Will he make that grim connection when my attorney starts screaming about bats and huge manta rays coming down on the car? If so – well, we'll just have to cut his head off and bury him somewhere. Because it goes without saying that we can't turn him loose. He'll report us at once to some kind of outback Nazi law enforcement agency, and they'll run us down like dogs.

Jesus! Did I *say* that? Or just think it? Was I talking? Did they hear me? I glanced over at my attorney, but he seemed oblivious – watching the road, driving our Great Red Shark along at a hundred and ten or so. There was no sound from the back seat.

Maybe I'd better have a chat with this boy, I thought. Perhaps if I *explain* things, he'll rest easy.

Of course. I leaned around in the seat and gave him a fine big smile . . . admiring the shape of his skull.

"By the way," I said. "There's one thing you should probably understand."

He stared at me, not blinking. Was he gritting his teeth?

"Can you *hear* me?" I yelled.

He nodded.

"That's good," I said. "Because I want you to know that we're on our way to Las Vegas to find the American Dream." I smiled. "That's why we rented this car. It was the only way to do it. Can you grasp that?"

He nodded again, but his eyes were nervous.

"I want you to have all the background," I said. "Because this is a very ominous assignment – with overtones of extreme personal danger . . . Hell, I forgot all about this beer; you want one?"

He shook his head.

"How about some ether?" I said.

"What?"

"Never mind. Let's get right to the heart of this thing. You see, about twenty-four hours ago we were sitting in the Polo Lounge of the Beverly Hills Hotel – in the patio section, of course – and we were just sitting there under a palm tree when this uniformed dwarf came up to me with a pink telephone and said, 'This must be the call you've been waiting for all this time, sir.' "

I laughed and ripped open a beer can that foamed all over the back seat while I kept talking. "And you know? He was right! I'd been *expecting* that call, but I didn't know who it would come from. Do you follow me?"

The boy's face was a mask of pure fear and bewilderment.

I blundered on: "I want you to understand that this man at the wheel is my *attorney*! He's not just some dingbat I found on the Strip. Shit, *look* at him! He doesn't look like you or me, right? That's because he's a foreigner. I think he's probably Samoan. But it doesn't matter, does it? Are you prejudiced?"

"Oh, hell *no*!" he blurted.

"I didn't think so," I said. "Because in spite of his race, this man is extremely valuable to me." I glanced over at my attorney, but his mind was somewhere else.

I whacked the back of the driver's seat with my fist. "This is *important*, goddamnit! This is a *true story*!" The car swerved sickeningly, then straightened out. "Keep your hands off my fucking neck!" my attorney screamed. The kid in the back looked like he was ready to jump right out of the car and take his chances.

THE RIDE TO ARFAJA

T.E. Lawrence

Thomas Edward Lawrence was born in Wales in 1888. He is primarily remembered as a guerrilla fighter but his campaign in the Syrian Desert 1917–19 was half made up of travels. To escape from his identity as "Lawrence of Arabia" he changed his name in 1927 to Shaw. He died eight years later in a motorcycle accident.
From Seven Pillars of Wisdom:

Our business was to reach Arfaja alive.

So we wisely marched on, over monotonous, glittering sand; and over those worse stretches, "Giaan", of polished mud, nearly as white and smooth as laid paper, and often whole miles square. They blazed back the sun into our faces with glassy vigour, so we rode with its light raining direct arrows upon our heads, and its reflection glancing up from the ground through our inadequate eyelids. It was not a steady pressure, but a pain ebbing and flowing; at one time piling itself up and up till we nearly swooned; and then falling away coolly, in a moment of false shadow like a black web crossing the retina: these gave us a moment's breathing space to store new capacity for suffering, like the struggles to the surface of a drowning man . . .

Only Gasim was not there: they thought him among the Howeitat, for his surliness offended the laughing soldiery and kept him commonly with the Beduin, who were more of his kidney.

There was no one behind, so I rode forward wishing to see how his camel was: and at last found it, riderless, being led by one of the Howeitat. His saddle-bags were on it, and his rifle and his food, but he himself nowhere; gradually it dawned on us that the miserable man was lost. This was a dreadful business, for in the haze and mirage the caravan could not be seen two miles, and on the iron ground it made no tracks: afoot he would never overtake us.

Everyone had marched on, thinking him elswhere in our loose line; but much time had passed and it was nearly midday, so he must be miles back. His loaded camel was proof that he had not been forgotten asleep at our night halt. The Ageyl ventured that perhaps he had dozed in the saddle and fallen, stunning or killing himself: or perhaps someone of the party had borne him a grudge. Anyway they did not know. He was an ill-natured stranger, no charge on any of them, and they did not greatly care.

True: but it was true also that Mohammed, his country-man and fellow, who was technically his road-companion, knew nothing of the desert, had a foundered camel, and could not turn back for him.

If I sent him, it would be murder. That shifted the difficulty to my shoulders. The Howeitat, who would have helped, were away in the mirage out of sight, hunting or scouting. Ibn Dgheithir's Ageyl were so clannish that they would not put themselves about except for one another. Besides Gasim was my man: and upon me lay the responsibility of him.

I looked weakly at my trudging men, and wondered for a moment if I could change with one, sending him back on my camel to the rescue. My shirking the duty would be understood, because I was a foreigner: but that was precisely the plea I did not dare set up, while I yet presumed to help these Arabs in their own revolt. It was hard, anyway, for a stranger to influence another people's national movement, and doubly hard for a Christian and a sedentary person to sway Moslem nomads. I should make it impossible for myself if I claimed, simultaneously, the privileges of both societies.

So, without saying anything, I turned my unwilling camel round, and forced her, grunting and moaning for her camel friends, back past the long line of men, and past the baggage into the emptiness behind. My temper was very unheroic, for I was furious with my other servants, with my own play-acting as a Beduin, and most of all with Gasim, a gap-toothed, grumbling fellow, skrimshank in all our marches, bad-tempered, suspicious, brutal, a man whose engagement I regretted, and of whom I had promised to rid myself as soon as we reached a discharging-place. It seemed absurd that I should peril my weight in the Arab adventure for a single worthless man . . .

I had ridden about an hour and a half, easily, for the following breeze had let me wipe the crust from my red eyes and look forward almost without pain, when I saw a figure, or large bush, or at least something black ahead of me. The shifting mirage disguised height or distance; but this thing seemed moving, a little east of our course. On chance I turned my camel's head that way, and in a few minutes saw that it was Gasim. When I called he stood confusedly; I rode up and saw that he was nearly blinded and silly, standing there with his arms held out to me, and his black mouth gaping open. The Ageyl had put our last water in my skin, and this he spilled madly over his face and breast, in haste to drink. He stopped babbling, and began to wail out his sorrows. I sat him, pillion, on the camel's rump; then stirred her up and mounted.

At our turn the beast seemed relieved, and moved forward freely. I set an exact compass course, so exact that often I found our old tracks, as little spurts of paler sand scattered over the brown-black flint. In spite of our double weight the camel began to stride out, and at times she even put her head down and for a few paces developed that fast and most comfortable shuffle to which the best animals, while young, were broken by skilled riders. This proof of reserve spirit in her rejoiced me, as did the little time lost in search.

Gasim was moaning impressively about the pain and terror of his thirst: I told him to stop; but he went on, and began to sit loosely; until at each step of the camel he bumped down on her hinder quarters with a crash, which, like his crying, spurred her to greater pace. There was danger in this, for we might easily founder her so. Again I told him to stop, and when he only screamed louder, hit him and swore that for another sound I would throw him off. The threat, to which my general rage gave colour, worked. After it he clung on grimly without sound.

Not four miles had passed when again I saw a black bubble, lunging and swaying in the mirage ahead. It split into three, and swelled. I wondered if they were enemy. A minute later the haze unrolled with the disconcerting suddenness of illusion; and it was Auda with two of Nasir's men come back to look for me. I yelled jests and scoffs at them for abandoning a friend in the desert. Auda pulled his beard and grumbled that had he been present I would never have gone back. Gasim was transferred with insults to a better rider's saddle-pad, and we ambled forward together.

Auda pointed to the wretched hunched-up figure and denounced me, "For that thing, not worth a camel's price . . ." I interrupted him with "Not worth a half-crown, Auda", and he, delighted in his simple mind, rode near Gasim, and struck him sharply, trying to make him repeat, like a parrot, his price. Gasim bared his broken teeth in a grin of rage, and afterwards sulked on. In another hour we were on the heels of the baggage camels, and as we passed up the inquisitive line of our caravan,

Auda repeated my joke to each pair, perhaps forty times in all, till I had seen to the full its feebleness.

Gasim explained that he had dismounted to ease nature, and had missed the party afterwards in the dark: but, obviously, he had gone to sleep, where he dismounted, with the fatigue of our slow, hot journeying. We rejoined Nasir and Nesib in the van. Nesib was vexed with me, for perilling the lives of Auda and myself on a whim. It was clear to him that I reckoned they would come back for me. Nasir was shocked at his ungenerous outlook, and Auda was glad to rub into a townsman the paradox of tribe and city; the collective responsibility and group-brotherhood of the desert, contrasted with the isolation and competitive living of the crowded districts . . .

So we agreed to camp for the night where we were, and to make beacon fires for the slave of Nuri Shaalan, who like Gasim, had disappeared from our caravan to-day.

We were not greatly perturbed about him. He knew the country and his camel was under him. It might be that he had intentionally taken the direct way to Jauf, Nuri's capital, to earn the reward of first news that we came with gifts. However it was, he did not come that night, nor next day; and when, months after, I asked Nuri of him, he replied that his dried body had lately been found, lying beside his unplundered camel far out in the wilderness. He must have lost himself in the sand-haze and wandered till his camel broke down; and there died of thirst and heat. Not a long death – even for the very strongest a second day in summer was all – but very painful; for thirst was an active malady; a fear and panic which tore at the brain and reduced the bravest man to a stumbling babbling maniac in an hour or two: and then the sun killed him . . .

Each morning, between eight and ten, a little group of blood mares under an assortment of imperfect saddlery would come to our camping place, and on them Nasir, Nesib, Zeki and I would mount, and with perhaps a dozen of our men on foot would move solemnly across the valley by the sandy paths between the bushes. Our horses were led by our servants, since it would be immodest to ride free or fast. So eventually we would reach the tent which was to be our feast-hall for that time; each family claiming us in turn, and bitterly offended if Zaal, the adjudicator, preferred one out of just order.

As we arrived, the dogs would rush out at us, and be driven off by onlookers – always a crowd had collected round the chosen tent – and we stepped in under the ropes to its guest half, made very large for the occasion and carefully dressed with its wall-curtain on the sunny side to give us the shade. The bashful host would murmur and vanish again out of sight. The tribal rugs, lurid red things from Beyrout, were ready for us, arranged down the partition curtain, along the back wall and across the dropped end, so that we sat down on three sides of an open dusty space. We might be fifty men in all . . .

Then would follow an awkward pause, which our friends would try to cover, by showing us on its perch the household hawk (when possible a sea-bird taken young on the Red Sea coast) or their watch-cockerel, or their greyhound. Once a tame ibex was dragged in for our admiration: another time an oryx. When these interests were exhausted they would try and find a small talk to distract us from the household noises, and from noticing the urgent whispered cookery-directions wafted through the dividing curtain with a powerful smell of boiled fat and drifts of tasty meat-smoke.

After a silence the host or a deputy would come forward and whisper "Black or white?" an invitation for us to choose coffee or tea. Nasir would always answer "Black", and the slave would be beckoned forward with the beaked coffee-pot in one hand, and three or four clinking cups of white ware in the other. He would dash a few drops of coffee into the uppermost cup, and proffer it to Nasir; then pour the second for me, and the third for Nesib; and pause while we turned the cups about in our hands, and sucked them carefully, to get appreciatively from them the last richest drop.

As soon as they were empty his hand was stretched to clap them noisily one above the other, and toss them out with a lesser flourish for the next guest in order, and so on round the assembly till all had drunk. Then back to Nasir again. This second cup would be tastier than the first, partly because the pot was yielding deeper from the brew, partly because of the heel-taps of so many previous drinkers present in the cups; whilst the third and fourth rounds, if the serving of the meat delayed so long, would be of surprising flavour.

However, at last, two men came staggering through the thrilled crowd, carrying the rice and meat on a tinned copper tray or shallow bath, five feet across, set like a great brazier on a foot. In the tribe there was only this one food-bowl of the size, and an incised inscription ran round it in florid Arabic characters: "To the glory of God, and in trust of mercy at the last, the property of His poor suppliant, Auda abu Tayi." It was borrowed by the host who was to entertain us for the time; and, since my urgent brain and body made me wakeful, from my blankets in the first light I would see the dish going across country, and by marking down its goal would know where we were to feed that day.

The bowl was now brim-full, ringed round its edge by white rice in an embankment a foot wide and six inches deep, filled with legs and ribs of mutton till they toppled over. It needed two or three victims to make in the centre a dressed pyramid of meat such as honour prescribed. The centre-pieces were the boiled, upturned heads, propped on their severed stumps of necks, so that the ears, brown like old leaves, flapped out on the rice surface. The jaws gaped emptily upward, pulled open to show the hollow throat with the tongue, still pink, clinging to the lower teeth; and the long incisors whitely crowned the pile, very prominent above the nostrils' pricking hair and the lips which sneered away blackly from them.

This load was set down on the soil of the cleared space between us, where it steamed hotly, while a procession of minor helpers bore small cauldrons and copper vats in which the cooking had been done. From them, with much-bruised bowls of enamelled iron, they ladled out over the main dish all the inside and outside of the sheep; little bits of yellow intestine, the white tail-cushion of fat, brown muscles and meat and bristly skin, all swimming in the liquid butter and grease of the seething. The bystanders watched anxiously, muttering satisfactions when a very juicy scrap plopped out.

The fat was scalding. Every now and then a man would drop his baler with an exclamation, and plunge his burnt fingers, not reluctantly, in his mouth to cool them: but they persevered till at last their scooping rang loudly on the bottoms of the pots; and, with a gesture of triumph, they fished out the intact livers from their hiding place in the gravy and topped the yawning jaws with them.

Two raised each smaller cauldron and tilted it, letting the liquid splash down upon the meat till the rice-crater was full, and the loose grains at the edge swam in the abundance: and yet they poured, till, amid cries of astonishment from us, it was running over, and a little pool congealing in the dust. That was the final touch of splendour, and the host called us to come and eat.

We feigned a deafness, as manners demanded: at last we heard him, and looked surprised at one another, each urging his fellow to move first; till Nasir rose coyly, and after him we all came forward to sink on one knee round the tray, wedging in and cuddling up till the twenty-two for whom there was barely space were grouped around the food. We turned back our right sleeves to the elbow, and, taking lead from Nasir with a low "In the name of God the merciful, the loving-kind", we dipped together.

The first dip, for me, at least, was always cautious, since

the liquid fat was so hot that my unaccustomed fingers could seldom bear it: and so I would toy with an exposed and cooling lump of meat till others' excavations had drained my rice-segment. We would knead between the fingers (not soiling the palm), neat balls of rice and fat and liver and meat cemented by gentle pressure, and project them by leverage of the thumb from the crooked fore-finger into the mouth. With the right trick and the right construction the little lump held together and came clean off the hand; but when surplus butter and odd fragments clung, cooling, to the fingers, they had to be licked care-fully to make the next effort slip easier away.

As the meat pile wore down (nobody really cared about rice: flesh was the luxury) one of the chief Howeitat eating with us would draw his dagger, silver hilted, set with turquoise, a signed masterpiece of Mohammed ibn Zari, of Jauf, and would cut criss-cross from the larger bones long diamonds of meat easily torn up between the fingers; for it was necessarily boiled very tender, since all had to be disposed of with the right hand which alone was honour-able.

Our host stood by the circle, encouraging the appetite with pious ejaculations. At top speed we twisted, tore, cut and stuffed: never speaking, since conversation would insult a meal's quality, though it was proper to smile thanks when an intimate guest passed a select fragment, or when Mohammed el Dheilan gravely handed over a huge barren bone with a blessing. On such occasions I would return the compliment with some hideous impossible lump of guts, a flippancy which rejoiced the Howeitat, but which the gracious, aristocratic Nasir saw with dis-approval.

At length some of us were nearly filled, and began to play and pick; glancing sideways at the rest till they too grew slow, and at last ceased eating, elbow on knee, the hand hanging down from the wrist over the tray edge to drip, while the fat, butter and scattered grains of rice cooled into a stiff white grease which gummed the fingers together. When all had stopped, Nasir meaningly cleared his throat, and we rose up together in haste with an explosive "God requite it you, O host", to group ourselves outside among the tent-ropes while the next twenty guests inherited our leaving.

Those of us who were nice would go to the end of the tent where the flap of the roof-cloth, beyond the last poles, drooped down as an end curtain; and on this clan handkerchief (whose coarse goat-hair mesh was pliant and glossy with much use) would scrape the thickest of the fat from the hands. Then we would make back to our seats, and re-take them sighingly; while the slaves, leaving aside their portion, the skulls of the sheep, would come round our rank with a wooden bowl of water, and a coffee-cup as dipper, to splash over our fingers, while we rubbed them with the tribal soap-cake.

Meantime the second and third sittings by the dish were having their turn, and then there would be one more cup of coffee, or a glass of syrup-like tea; and at last the horses would be brought and we would slip out to them, and mount, with a quiet blessing to the hosts as we passed by. When our backs were turned the children would run in disorder upon the ravaged dish, tear our gnawed bones from one another, and escape into the open with valuable fragments to be devoured in security behind some distant bush: while the watchdogs of all the camp prowled round snapping, and the master of the tent fed the choicest offal to his greyhound.

AVALANCHE

George Mallory

George Leigh Mallory was born in England in 1886. He took part in all three of the Everest expeditions of the 1920s. It was Mallory who famously explained the desire to climb the mountain: "Because it's there." The incident below is from 1922. Mallory, along with his climbing companion Andrew Irvine, died in a summit bid on Everest in 1924. Whether or not they succeeded and died on the way down is uncertain. Mallory's body was found in 1999 almost perfectly preserved.

It was already evident that whatever we were to do would now have to wait for the weather. Though the Lama at the Rongbuk Monastery had told us that the monsoon was usually to be expected about 10 June, and we knew that it was late last year, the signs of its approach were gathering every day. Mount Everest could rarely be seen after 9 or 10 a.m. until the clouds cleared away in the evening; and a storm approaching from the West Rongbuk Glacier would generally sweep down the valley in the afternoon. Though we came to despise this blustering phenomenon – for nothing worse came of it than light hail or snow, either at our camp or higher – we should want much fairer days for climbing, and each storm threatened to be the beginning of something far more serious. However, we planned to be on the spot to take any chance that offered. The signs were even more ominous than usual as Finch and I walked up to Camp I on the afternoon of 3 June; we could hardly feel optimistic; and it was soon apparent that, far from having recovered his strength, my companion was quite unfit for another big expedition. We walked slowly and frequently halted; it was painful to see what efforts it cost him to make any progress. However, he persisted in coming on.

We had not long disposed ourselves comfortably within the four square walls of our "sangar", always a pleasant change from the sloping sides of a tent, when snow began to fall. Released at last by the west wind which had held it back, the monsoon was free to work its will, and we soon understood that the great change of weather had now come. Fine, glistening particles were driven by the wind through the chinks in our walls, to be drifted on the floor or on our coverings where we lay during the night; and as morning grew the snow still fell as thickly as ever. Finch wisely decided to go back, and we charged him with a message to General Bruce, saying that we saw no reason at present to alter our plans. With the whole day to spend confined and inactive we had plenty of time to consider what we ought to do under these conditions. We went over well-worn arguments once more. It would have been an obvious and easy course, for which no one could reproach us, to have said simply: The monsoon has come; this is the end of the climbing season; it is time to go home. But the case, we felt, was not yet hopeless. The monsoon is too variable and uncertain to be so easily admitted as the final arbiter. There might yet be good prospects ahead of us. It was not unreasonable to expect an interval of fine weather after the first heavy snow, and with eight or ten fair days a third attempt might still be made. In any case, to retire now if the smallest chance

remained to us would be an unworthy end to the expedition. We need not run our heads into obvious danger; but
rather than be stopped by a general estimate of conditions
we would prefer to retire before some definite risk that we
were not prepared to take or simply failed to overcome the
difficulties.

After a second night of unremitting snowfall the weather on the morning of 5 June improved and we decided to
go on. Low and heavy clouds were still flowing down the
East Rongbuk Glacier, but precipitation ceased at an early
hour and the sky brightened to the west. It was surprising,
after all we had seen of the flakes passing our door, that no
great amount of snow was lying on the stones about our
camp. But the snow had come on a warm current and
melted or evaporated, so that after all the depth was no
more than 6 inches at this elevation (17,500 ft). Even on
the glacier we went up a long way before noticing a
perceptible increase of depth. We passed Camp II, not
requiring to halt at this stage, and were well up towards
Camp III before the fresh snow became a serious im-
pediment. It was still snowing up here, though not very
heavily; there was nothing to cheer the grey scene; the
clinging snow about our feet was so wet that even the best
of our boots were soaked through, and the last two hours
up to Camp III were tiresome enough. Nor was it a
cheering camp when we reached it. The tents had been
struck for the safety of the poles, but not packed up. We
found them now half-full of snow and ice. The stores were
all buried; everything that we wanted had first to be dug
out.

The snow up here was so much deeper that we anxiously discussed the possibility of going farther. With 15
to 18 inches of snow to contend with, not counting drifts,
the labour would be excessive, and until the snow solidified there would be considerable danger at several
points. But the next morning broke fine; we had soon a
clear sky and glorious sunshine; it was the warmest day

that any of us remembered at Camp III; and as we watched the amazing rapidity with which the snow solidified and the rocks began to appear about our camp, our spirits rose. The side of Everest facing us looked white and cold; but we observed a cloud of snow blown from the North Ridge; it would not be long at this rate before it was fit to climb. We had already resolved to use oxygen on the third attempt. It was improbable that we should beat our own record without it, for the strain of previous efforts would count against us, and we had not the time to improve on our organization by putting a second camp above the North Col. Somervell, after Finch's explanation of the mechanical details, felt perfectly confident that he could manage the oxygen apparatus, and all those who had used oxygen were convinced that they went up more easily with its help than they could expect to go without it. Somervell and I intended to profit by the experience. They had discovered that the increased combustion in the body required a larger supply of food; we must arrange for a bountiful provision. Their camp at 25,000 ft had been too low; we would try to establish one now, as we had intended before, at 26,000 ft. And we hoped for a further advantage in going higher than Finch and Bruce had done before using oxygen; whereas they had started using it at 21,000 ft, we intended to go up to our old camp at 25,000 ft without it, perhaps use a cylinder each up to 26,000 ft, and at all events start from that height for the summit with a full supply of four cylinders. If this was not the correct policy as laid down by Professor Dryer, it would at least be a valuable experiment.

Our chief anxiety under these new conditions was to provide for the safety of our porters. We hoped that after fixing our fifth camp at 26,000 ft, at the earliest three days hence, on the fourth day of fine weather the porters might be able to go down by themselves to the North Col in easy conditions; to guard against the danger of concealed crevasses there Crawford would meet them at the foot of the North Ridge to conduct them properly roped to Camp IV. As the supply officer at this camp he would also be able to superintend the descent over the first steep slope of certain porters who would go down from Camp IV without sleeping after carrying up their loads.

But the North Col had first to be reached. With so much new snow to contend with we should hardly get there in one day. If we were to make the most of our chance in the interval of fair weather, we should lose no time in carrying up the loads for some part of the distance. It was decided therefore to begin this work on the following day, 7 June.

In the ascent to the North Col after the recent snowfall we considered that an avalanche was to be feared only in one place, the steep final slope below the shelf. There we could afford to run no risk; we must test the snow and be certain that it was safe before we could cross this slope. Probably we should be obliged to leave our loads below it, having gained, as a result of our day's work, the great advantage of a track. An avalanche might also come down, we thought, on the first steep slope where the ascent began. Here it could do us no harm, and the behaviour of the snow on this slope would be a test of its condition.

The party, Somervell, Crawford and I, with fourteen porters (Wakefield was to be supply officer at Camp III), set out at 8 a.m. In spite of the hard frost of the previous night, the crust was far from bearing our weight; we sank up to our knees in almost every step, and two hours were taken in traversing the snowfield. At 10.15 a.m. Somervell, I, a porter, and Crawford, roped up in that order, began to work up the steep ice-slope, now covered with snow. It was clear that the three of us without loads must take the lead in turns stamping out the tracks for our porters. These men, after their immense efforts on the first and second attempts, had all volunteered to "go high", as they said once more, and everything must be done to ease the terrible work of carrying the loads over the soft snow. No trace was found of our previous tracks, and we were soon arguing as to where exactly they might be as we slanted across the slope. It was remarkable that the snow adhered so well to the ice that we were able to get up without cutting steps. Everything was done by trenching the snow to induce it to come down if it would; every test gave a satisfactory result. Once this crucial place was passed, we plodded on without hesitation. If the snow would not come down where we had formerly encountered steep bare ice, *a fortiori*, above, on the gentler slopes, we had nothing to fear. The thought of an avalanche was dismissed from our minds.

It was necessarily slow work forging our way through the deep snow, but the party was going extraordinarily well, and the porters were evidently determined to get on. Somervell gave us a long lead, and Crawford next, in spite of the handicap of shorter legs, struggled upwards in some of the worst snow we met until I relieved him. I found the effort at each step so great that no method of breathing I had formerly employed was adequate; it was necessary to pause after each lifting movement for a whole series of breaths, rapid at first and gradually slower, before the weight was transferred again to the other foot. About 1.30 p.m. I halted, and the porters, following on three separate ropes, soon came up with the leading party. We should have been glad to stay where we were for a long rest. But the hour was already late, and as Somervell was ready to take the lead again, we decided to push on. We were now about 400 ft below a conspicuous block of ice and 600 ft below Camp IV, still on the gentle slopes of the corridor. Somervell had advanced only 100 ft, rather up the slope than across it, and the last party of porters had barely begun to move up in the steps. The scene was peculiarly bright and windless, and as we rarely spoke, nothing was to be heard but the laboured panting of our lungs. This stillness was suddenly disturbed. We were startled by an ominous sound, sharp, arresting, violent, and yet somehow soft like an explosion of untamped gunpowder. I had never before on a mountainside heard such a sound; but all of us, I imagine, knew instinctively what it meant, as though we had been accustomed to hear it every day of our lives. In a moment I observed the surface of the snow broken and puckered where it had been even for a few yards to the right of me. I took two steps convulsively in this direction with some quick thought of getting nearer to the edge of the danger that threatened us. And then I began to move slowly downwards, inevitably carried on the whole moving surface by a force I was utterly powerless to resist. Somehow I managed to turn out from the slope so as to avoid being pushed headlong and backwards down it. For a second or two I seemed hardly to be in danger as I went quietly sliding down with the snow. Then the rope at my waist tightened and held me back. A wave of snow came over me and I was buried. I supposed that the matter was settled. However, I called to mind experiences related by other parties; and it had been suggested that the best chance of escape in this situation lay in swimming. I thrust out my arms above my head and actually went through some sort of motions of swimming on my back. Beneath the surface of the snow, with nothing to inform the senses of the world outside it, I had no impression of speed after the first acceleration – I struggled in the tumbling snow, unconscious of everything else – until, perhaps only a few seconds later, I knew the pace was easing up. I felt an increasing pressure about my body. I wondered how tightly I should be squeezed, and then the avalanche came to rest.

My arms were free; my legs were near the surface. After a brief struggle, I was standing again, surprised and breathless, in the motionless snow. But the rope was tight at my waist; the porter tied on next me, I supposed, must be deeply buried. To my further surprise, he quickly emerged, unharmed as myself. Somervell and Crawford too, though they had been above me by the rope's length, were now quite close, and soon extricated themselves. We subsequently made out that their experiences had been very similar to mine. But where were the rest? Looking down over the foam of snow, we saw one group of porters some little distance, perhaps 150 ft, below us. Presumably the others must be buried somewhere between us and them, and though no sign of these missing men appeared, we at once prepared to find and dig them out. The porters we saw still stood their ground instead of coming up to help. We soon made out that they were the party who had been immediately behind us, and they were pointing below them. They had travelled farther than us in the avalanche, presumably because they were nearer the centre, where it was moving more rapidly. The other two parties, one of four and one of five men roped together, must have been carried even farther. We could still hope that they were safe. But as we hurried down we soon saw that beneath the place where the four porters were standing was a formidable drop; it was only too plain that the missing men had been swept over it. We had no difficulty in finding a way round this obstacle; in a very short time we were standing under its shadow. The ice-cliff was from forty to sixty feet high in different places; the crevasse at its foot was more or less filled up with avalanche snow. Our fears were soon confirmed. One man was quickly uncovered and found to be still breathing; before long we were certain that he would live. Another whom we dug out near him had been killed by the fall. He and his party appeared to have struck the hard lower lip of the crevasse, and were lying under the snow on or near the edge of it. The four porters who had escaped soon pulled themselves together after the first shock of the accident, and now worked here with Crawford and did everything they could to extricate the other bodies, while Somervell and I went down into the crevasse. A loop of rope which we pulled up convinced us that the other party must be here. It was slow work loosening the snow with the pick or adze of an ice-axe and shovelling it with the hands. But we were able to follow the rope to the bodies. One was dug up lifeless; another was found upside down, and when we uncovered his face Somervell thought he was still breathing. We had the greatest difficulty in extricating this man, so tightly was the snow packed about his limbs; his load, four oxygen cylinders on a steel frame, had to be cut from his back, and eventually he was dragged out. Though buried for about forty minutes, he had survived the fall and the suffocation, and suffered no serious harm. Of the two others in this party of four, we found only one. We had at length to give up a hopeless search with the certain knowledge that the first of them to be swept over the cliff, and the most deeply buried, must long ago be dead. Of the other five, all the bodies were recovered, but only one was alive. The two who had so marvellously escaped were able to walk down to Camp III, and were almost perfectly well next day. The other seven were killed.

TOO CLOSE TO THE ICE

Umberto Nobile

The Italian aviator Umberto Nobile (1885–1978) flew across the North Pole in 1926 with his airship the Norge. *Two years later, Nobile took a new airship to the Arctic, the* Italia, *with the aim of exploring the unknown north of Greenland and from there taking a new route to the North Pole. Among Nobile's crew was the Swedish meteorologist Finn Malmgren.*

From Nobile's My Polar Flights:

Having recognized Cape Bridgmann, we turned back and steered for the Pole, along the 27th meridian W of Greenwich.

At six o'clock, a few miles from Cape Bridgmann, the sky – until then covered with clouds – cleared up.

With the blue sky above, the radiant sun lighting the inside of the cabin, and the wind astern increasing our speed, the journey to the Pole proceeded in joyous excitement. All on board were happy, and contentment shone from every face.

One of the Naval officers stood at the steering-wheel, whilst the other two divided their time untiringly between solar observations and measurements of drift and speed.

Trojani and Cecioni, as usual, manned the elevator-wheel.

Malmgren was standing up, with his spectacles on, to mark on a chart fixed to the wall of the wireless cabin the meteorological data which Biagi, as he intercepted them, came to communicate to us. Pontremoli and Behounek attended imperturbably to their instruments, without troubling in the least about what was going on around them. One would have thought they were working in the quiet of their laboratories.

The three mechanics were at their posts, vigilant and attentive as ever: Pomella in the stern engine-boat, Caratti on the left, and Ciocca on the right. But only the stern engine and one of the side ones were in motion.

Arduino was walking backwards and forwards along the gangway, to supervise the mechanics and check and regulate the consumption of petrol.

Alessandrini, after visiting all the accessible parts of the ship during the first hours of flight to make sure that nothing was wrong, and pulling up the handling-ropes that dangled outside – to prevent their offering an unnecessary resistance to the air and getting coated with ice – had come down into the cabin, some time before, to help Trojani and Cecioni and take a spell at the steering-wheel.

With such a strong wind astern we advanced rapidly towards our desired goal. At 6 p.m. we had reached the 84th parallel; by 10.30 p.m., 88°10'.

The region over which we were flying was unknown to man. It lay between the route of the *Norge*, to the right of us, and that of Peary, to the left. Not a trace of land in sight, although the visibility was exceptional, as we could see clearly up to 60 miles all round.

The height at which we were sailing gradually increased: at 6 p.m. it was 750 ft; at 8 p.m., 1,500; at 10 p.m., 1,650; at 10.30 p.m., 1,800.

I was delighted at such splendid visibility occurring unexpectedly after the 8 hours' fog which had made the first part of our voyage so trying. But the strong wind, although it helped us on our way to the Pole, made me regretfully consider that I should have to give up the descent we had planned.

Meanwhile I watched Malmgren at work. He was now tracing the curves of two cyclonic areas which apparently existed, one above the Arctic Ocean towards the Siberian coast, the other above the Barents Sea.

Which was the best route to follow, after leaving the Pole? This was the problem which had been preoccupying me for some time.

The notion of sailing against a wind as strong as the one at present behind us did not at all appeal to me, especially as I feared it might be accompanied by fog. So I thought that, having reached the Pole, it would be better to fly before the wind to the Siberian coast, or steer for the coast of Canada, where the meteorological bulletins forecast fog, it is true, but with atmospheric calm.

I discussed it with Malmgren, who dissuaded me.

"It would be better to return to King's Bay," he said. "Then we shall be able to complete our programme of scientific research."

I remained undecided. I knew from long experience what a hard – and often intolerable – strain it was to fight for hours against a strong wind, and so instinctively I shrank from it. But Malmgren reassured me.

"No!" he said. "This wind will not last long. When we are on our way back it will drop, after a few hours, and be succeeded by north-west winds."

Eventually I was won over and followed his advice.

The conversation on this subject was resumed, in dramatic circumstances, four days later. On May 27th, on the pack after the catastrophe, Malmgren asked me if I thought that all would have been well had we followed out my idea of reaching the mouth of the Mackenzie. Probably it would, because the airship would have been spared the torment of a prolonged struggle against the wind – but who can tell whether, on this route too, some other peril would not have been lying in wait for us?

At the Pole

Whilst I was talking to Malmgren, we continued to draw rapidly nearer to the Pole.

Towards ten o'clock there was an unexpected change in the sky, which until then had been blue all over. In front of us, an hour or two away, a barrier of cloud over 3,000 ft high rose from the horizon, standing out against the azure of the sky above. With its weird outlines it looked like the walls of some gigantic fortress.

That band of cloud, dark and compact, had a menacing aspect which struck my imagination. "There's no getting through that!" I thought. "We shall be bound to turn back."

At 10.30 we encountered a bank of thick cloud. And as at that moment it did not suit us to lose sight of the sun – height measurements being more than ever necessary – we rose above the fog, to about 2,400 ft.

We were then at 88° 10'. Another 54 miles and we should be at the Pole.

Meanwhile the Naval officers were making their solar observations. We were getting nearer and nearer to the goal, and the excitement on board was growing.

Twenty minutes after midnight, early on May 24th, the officers who were observing the sun with a sextant cried: "We are there!"

The *Italia* was at the Pole.

We had covered 425 miles from Cape Bridgmann at an average speed of 62 m.p.h.

I had the engines slowed down and ordered the helmsman to steer in a circle.

It was impossible, alas! to descend on the pack, but we had a promise to keep: to deposit on the ice of the Pole the Cross entrusted to us by Pius XI, and by its side the

Italian flag. We prepared ourselves in religious silence to
carry out this gesture – so simple and yet so solemn. I
ordered Alessandrini to get ready.

Then I had the engines accelerated once more, to pass
under the fog. It was 12.40. Twenty minutes later we were
in sight of the pack. We went on circling round at a
reduced speed until the preparations were completed. I
had had a large tricolour cloth fastened to the Cross, to
catch the wind and guide it down.

At 1.20 a.m. I leaned out of the cabin and let fall the
Italian flag. Then followed the *gonfalone* of the City of
Milan, and a little medal of the Virgin of the Fire, given me
by the inhabitants of Forli. For the second time our tricolour spread itself over the ice of the Pole. Beside the flag we
dropped the Cross. It was 1.30, and we were about 450 ft up.

At the moment when these rites were completed, I felt a
thrill of pride. Two years after the *Norge* flight we had
come back to the Pole, and this time the bad weather,
from Italy onwards, had made it much more difficult.

Inside the cabin, now that the engines were almost still,
a little gramophone was playing an old folk-song: "The
Bells of San Giusto", bringing back memories, taking us
all of a sudden to Italy, to our homes. We were all moved:
more than one had tears in his eyes. Zappi cried: "Long
live Nobile!" I was grateful to him, as I was to Malmgren,
when he came and said, clasping my hand: "Few men can
say, as we can, that we have been twice to the Pole."

Few men indeed: six Italians and one Swede.

*Thereafter matters went quickly awry. Turning around for
Spitzbergen, the* Italia *encountered fog. To determine their
position, Nobile ordered the airship to descend.*

We were flying between 600 and 900 ft up. The dirigible
was still light, so to keep it at the proper height we had to
hold the nose down.

At 10.30 I again ordered a speed measurement. When

this had been taken I walked to the front of the cabin and looked out of the right-hand porthole, between the steering-wheel and the elevator. To test the height, I dropped a glass ball full of red liquid, and stood there, timing its fall with a stop-watch.

While I was attending to this, I heard Cecioni say excitedly: "We are heavy!"

I turned with a start to look at the instruments.

The ship was right down by the stern, at an angle of 8 degrees to the horizon; nevertheless, we were rapidly falling.

The peril was grave and imminent. A short distance below us stretched the pack. I at once gave the orders which had to be given, the only ones that could save the ship in this emergency – if that was possible: to accelerate the two engines, start the third, and at the same time lift the nose of the dirigible still higher. I hoped by these means to overcome the unexpected heaviness.

Simultaneously, I shouted to Alessandrini to run out on the top of the ship and inspect the stern valves, as I thought gas might be escaping – the only explanation that occurred to me at the moment of this serious and rapid increase in weight.

Meanwhile, the mechanics had carried out my orders. Pomella and Caratti had speeded their engines up to 1,400 revolutions and Ciocca, with surprising promptness, had started his own. The ship began to move faster, and tilted at an angle of 15 or 20 degrees.

The dynamic lift obtained in this way must certainly have represented several hundredweight.

But unfortunately we went on falling. The variometer – on which my eyes were fixed – confirmed it; in fact, we seemed to be dropping even faster.

I realized that there was nothing more to be done. The attempt to combat the increased weight by propulsion had failed . . . A crash was now inevitable; the most we could do was to mitigate its consequences.

I gave the necessary orders: to stop the engines at once, so as to avoid fire breaking out as we crashed; and to drop the ballast-chain. Sending Cecioni to do this, I put Zappi in his place.

It was all that could have been ordered; it was ordered promptly and with absolute calm. The perfect discipline on board was unbroken, so that each man carried out my orders as best he could, in the vertiginous rapidity of the event.

In the meantime the pack was approaching at a fearful speed. I saw that Cecioni was finding it difficult to untie the rope which held the chain. "Hurry up! Hurry up!" I shouted to him. Then noticing that the engine on the left, run by Caratti, was still working, I leaned out of a port-hole on that side, and at the top of my voice – echoed, I think, by one of the officers – repeated the order: "Stop the engine!" At that moment I saw the stern-boat was only a few tens of yards from the pack. I drew back into the cabin.

The recollection of those last terrible instants is very vivid in my memory. I had scarcely had time to reach the spot near the two rudders, between Malmgren and Zappi, when I saw Malmgren fling up the wheel, turning his startled eyes on me. Instinctively I grasped the helm, wondering if it were possible to guide the ship on to a snow-field and so lessen the shock . . . Too late! . . . There was the pack, a few yards below, terribly uneven. The masses of ice grew larger, came nearer and nearer . . . A moment later we crashed.

There was a fearful impact. Something hit me on the head, then I was caught and crushed. Clearly, without any pain, I felt some of my limbs snap. Some object falling from a height knocked me down head foremost. Instinctively I shut my eyes, and with perfect lucidity and coolness formulated the thought: "It's all over!" I almost pronounced the words in my mind.

It was 10.33 on May 25th.

The fearful event had lasted only 2 or 3 minutes!

When I opened my eyes I found myself lying on the ice, in the midst of an appalling pack. I realized at once that others had fallen with me.

I looked up to the sky. Towards my left the dirigible, nose in air, was drifting away before the wind. It was terribly lacerated around the pilot-cabin. Out of it trailed torn strips of fabric, ropes, fragments of metal-work. The left wall of the cabin had remained attached. I noticed a few creases in the envelope.

Upon the side of the crippled, mutilated ship stood out the black letters *Italia*. My eyes remained fixed on them, as if fascinated, until the dirigible merged in the fog and was lost to sight.

It was only then that I felt my injuries. My right leg and arm were broken and throbbing; I had hurt my face and the top of my head, and my chest seemed all upside down with the violence of the shock. I thought my end was near.

Suddenly I heard a voice – Mariano's – asking: "Where is the General?" And I looked around me.

I had never seen such a terrible pack: a formless, contorted jumble of pointed ice-crags, stretching to the horizon.

Two yards away on my right, Malmgren was sitting, and a little farther off lay Cecioni, moaning aloud. Next him was Zappi. The others – Mariano, Behounek, Trojani, Viglieri, and Biagi – were standing up. They appeared unhurt, except for Trojani, whose face was stained by a few patches of blood.

Here and there one could see wreckage – a dreary note of grey against the whiteness of the snow. In front of me a strip of bright red, like blood which had flowed from some enormous wound, showed the spot where we had fallen. It was the liquid from the glass balls.

I was calm. My mind was perfectly clear. But now I was

feeling the seriousness of my injuries – worst of all, a terrible convulsion in my chest. Breathing was a great effort. I thought I had probably sustained some grave internal injury. It seemed that death was very near – that maybe I had only 2 or 3 hours to live.

I was glad of this. It meant that I should not have to watch the despair and slow death-agony of my comrades. What hope was there for them? With no provisions, no tent, no wireless, no sledges – nothing but useless wreckage – they were lost, irremediably lost, in this terrible wilderness of ice.

I turned towards them, looking at them with an infinite sadness at heart. Then I spoke: "Steady, my lads! Keep your spirits up! Don't be cast down by this misfortune." And I added: "Lift your thoughts to God!"

No other words, no other ideas, came to me in those first unforgettable moments when death seemed imminent. But suddenly I was seized by strong emotion. Something rose up from my soul – from the depths of my being: something stronger than the pain of my tortured limbs, stronger than the thought of approaching death. And from my straining breast broke out, loud and impetuous, the cry: "*Viva l'Italia!*"

My comrades cheered.

Beside me on the right Malmgren was still sitting silent in the same place, stroking his right arm. On his face, frowning and ashen pale, a little swollen from his fall, was a look of blank despair. His blue eyes stared fixedly in front of him, as if into the void. Lost in thought, he seemed not even to notice the other men around him.

I had been very fond of this young scientist, ever since we had shared in the *Norge* expedition. And lately my affection for him had grown. He had become my most valued collaborator – the only one to whom I confided my plans, my ideas, my thoughts. I attached a good deal of weight to his judgment and advice. Some days previously we had decided the general lines of our future flight – the bold scheme which, if carried out, would have utilized to the utmost the possibilities afforded by our ship and crew . . . But now all our plans had come to naught.

Wishing to speak to him, I said softly: "Nothing to be done, my dear Malmgren!"

Nothing to be done! . . . A painful confession for men of action!

He looked at me and answered: "Nothing, but die. My arm is broken."

Suddenly he got up. He could not stand erect, for his injured shoulder made him stoop. Once more he turned to me and said in English: "*General, I thank you for the trip . . . I go under the water!*"

So saying, he turned away.

I stopped him: "No, Malmgren! You have no right to do this. We will die when God has decided. We must wait. Please stop here."

I shall never forget the look he turned on me at that moment. He seemed surprised. Perhaps he was struck by the gentle and affectionate seriousness of my tone. For a moment he stood still, as if undecided. Then he sat down again.

The fate of the downed airmen gripped all the Western world. The Polar explorer Roald Amundsen died on a rescue flight to the Italia *crew. Eventually, after four weeks, the Italian airmen were rescued by the Soviet ice-breaker* Krasin.

SNOW FROM THE MOON

Tom Fremantle

Tom Fremantle is an English travel writer, the author of Johnny Ginger's Last Ride *and* The Moonshine Mule, *the latter his account of a 2,700-mile walk from Mexico to Manhattan in 2001. He was accompanied by Browny, a 17-year-old mule.*

On our way to the Louisiana border Browny and I spent a night camping in the Martin Dies national park. Although an idyllic setting it was not an especially happy experience. The BEWARE OF ALLIGATORS sign at the entrance got things off to a bad start. Alligators are fine if your name is Johnny Weissmuller: not if you are a faint-hearted muleteer with a blunt Swiss Army knife. But this was nothing compared with the storm that whipped up soon after dark sending a cascade of magnolia cones and black walnuts raining down on my little tent. To cap it all a park ranger appeared well after midnight and shone a torch through my tent flap. I woke up with a start, brandishing my knife.

"No livestock are allowed in this park," shouted the torch-wielding shadow, battling to be heard against the wind. "Please remove your livestock." *Livestock?* I thought. I have one geriatric mule, not a herd of Long-horn steers.

Considering the wind was howling and I was camping alone on a carpet of pine needles in the middle of a wilderness, I felt the man was being more than a little pedantic. Why couldn't he wait until morning, for heaven's sake? I shouted into the wind about my walk and mentioned that I had got permission to camp here from another ranger earlier in the evening, all of which was true. I also promised I would clear up any mule dung. As we spoke the wind continued to buffet the canvas, threatening to fill out my tent like a spinnaker.

"All right then," bellowed the shadowy ranger. "But all livestock out of here first thing."

The next day Browny and I walked through the community of Jasper. People had been talking about Jasper for the last week. It was a fairly nondescript, rundown sort of town, but in 1998 it had made headlines across the world after the violent lynching of a young black man by a couple of violent racists. James Byrn, Jnr, had been beaten up then chained to the back of a truck before being dragged along a country road at speed. The hateful nature of the murder outraged the community and the world.

The town park had been named in James Byrn's honour. While walking past there I struck up a conversation with Wayne, a friendly black man who worked at a local liquor store. He had tight-fitting dreadlocks and gold-capped teeth.

"The main two murderers were white supremacists from the Houston area," Wayne explained, as we walked through town. "They both got the death penalty. One Jasper man was with them too, but he was only an onlooker. He just got a life sentence. It was pretty horrible, all the stir it caused, especially for the Byrn family."

"Do you think it could happen again?"

"I doubt it," he mused, spitting out an oyster of green tobacco into the dust. "It was a very isolated case. Of course there are still too many rednecks and racists lurking about, but not the sort who would lynch someone. The KKK is largely a spent force now.

"People associate this area with racism but other areas are just as bad," he spat out some more tobacco. "What about those Rodney King riots in Los Angeles? Stuff is brewing all over the place. It was the bad ass nature of the crime here that caused such upset. Jasper is a nice little place on the whole, but now it's going to be remembered for that lynching, the same way Waco is remembered for that crazy cult."

"Have you experienced any racism here?"

"Nothing directly," Wayne replied as he chewed. "But let me tell you something, I wouldn't walk through Texas with no mule. Don't get me wrong, I like what you are doing. It's real interesting. It's OK for a clean-cut white boy like you, but not so OK for a black man like me. Maybe one day, but not yet."

I would have liked to talk more, but Wayne had to get to work. He slapped me on the shoulder. "Watch your back out there, my man," he warned. "America can be a dangerous place whatever your colour."

Two days later Browny and I finally marched over the Louisiana border. We had already clocked up twelve miles that morning, having camped our final night in Texas at a local farmstead.

I was aiming to reach the town of Leesville, meaning a thirty-mile day – the first time Browny had I had tried this. Twenty-seven miles was our record to date. But Browny was champing at the bit, the sun was shining, the crickets chirping and the sky a pure, fresh, cloudless blue. To add to all the glory I saw a turtle cavorting beneath us as we crossed over the Sabine river; for no other reason than its sheer spontaneous beauty I took this as a sign of good luck. Oh, yes, I thought, today my mule and I are unstoppable.

Much as I had enjoyed Texas I liked the fact I was in a new state. I had finally made it through the immense Lone Star, all six hundred miles of it. People still waved and tooted their horns as if in Texas, the pine trees were still as tall as Texas, the people sounded the same too, but I knew I had crossed that precious line and completed another thumbnail of map.

But the one big difference with Texas was that I was no longer hot on Colonel Arthur's trail.

After Houston my ancestor had caught a stagecoach and crossed into Louisiana a hundred miles further north of Leesville than me. He then plied on to Monroe, near to the Arkansas border. It would have meant a huge detour with the mule. However, our paths would soon cross with Arthur again in the historic town of Natchez on the banks of the Mississippi.

Arthur's journey to Monroe does not make for a compelling chapter in his diary. He travels through a landscape "deserted except by women and very old men . . . the land not fertile, but the timber is fine." The most interesting part is when he strikes up a conversation about "the peculiar institution" of slavery in his stagecoach.

Colonel Arthur mentions that his fellow passengers frowned on slavery but considered it a necessary evil to sustain the South's labour intensive cotton harvest. He claims that most Southerners only defended it so fiercely due to the "meddling, coercive conduct of the detested and despised abolitionists".

Although Arthur says his companions admit there are many instances of cruelty to slaves he goes on to write: "But they say a man who is known to ill-treat his Negroes is hated by all the rest of the community. They declare that Yankees make the worst masters when they settle in the South."

On arrival in Monroe he comes across a group of "fifty Yankee deserters" who when asked their reason for leaving their regiment reply: "We enlisted to fight for the Union, and not to liberate slaves."

Arthur points out that many Northerners were bla-
tantly hostile or at least ambivalent towards liberating
slaves. This was perfectly true. He is also right to point
out many Southerners looked after their slaves with a
degree of compassion. What he is never prepared to do,
however, is mention that some Southerners treated their
slaves horribly too. Although he keeps saying how dis-
tasteful slavery is to an Englishman, he never really backs
this up. Rather than conceding that the Union holds the
moral high ground over the issue (Lincoln's Emancipa-
tion Proclamation had just been issued) he makes it sound
as if the Yankees are the only true culprits. Although
clearly an observant and at times sensitive man, Arthur
continues to accept lock, stock and barrel whatever the
Southerners fire at him. Worst of all, he does not once try
to see things from a slave's perspective.

But I am perhaps being hard on Colonel Arthur, who was
writing his diary without the hindsight of history. He was a
twenty-eight-year-old soldier more out for adventure than
on a crusade for the truth. What he writes about best are
battles, soldiers and everyday observances, rather than
about the landscape, the culture or the politics. He was
certainly a far tougher, more practical man than I, able to
cover huge distances and undergo any hardship. Throughout his three-and-half month marathon he shows few signs
of flagging, and remains persistently chipper. The same
could not be said for his wimp of a great great cousin.

Colonel Arthur would have been truly ashamed of me as I
trudged the last two miles into Leesville. Trying to
attempt thirty miles had been a catastrophic error of
judgement. Despite being buoyant and optimistic for
the first twenty-five miles, I was now suffering from shin
cramps. Even more worrying, Browny was also on her last
legs. Her nose was bleeding sporadically and her head
hung very low: both blatant symptoms of what Justin
called "beast burn out".

The good news was that Leesville was in sight. On the map it looked like a little place and I was confident we could pinpoint somewhere to camp. It was already dark. Above us some unfamiliar stars spun around a milk-blue slice of moon.

As we trudged on it concerned me that there was absolutely nobody around. I had passed the usual rash of red brick or corrugated churches, a library, some shops. All was quiet bar Browny's clopping and the faint creak of her saddle straps. We were now in the heart of the town and still not a squeak. I finally saw somebody locking up a shop ahead of us and quickened my pace to reach him. Browny sensed my urgency and fell in line. "Good Brown girl, good girl," I encouraged her as if she was a child.

"Sir, sir," after seven weeks in Texas I had picked up this formality. "Sir, do you know somewhere we can camp for the night?"

The man before us had a big, jowly face and hair the colour of ashes. Considering he had just been accosted by a desperate, bobble-hatted man with a limping mule in a dark, deserted street he stayed remarkably composed. After I explained what we were up to he shook his head slowly, as if watching a tennis rally made up exclusively of high, very slow lobs.

"You know what," he said dreamily. "I can't think of anywhere, no, nowhere at all." *Can't think of anywhere!* I had a huge urge to vigorously shake his jowls.

"All I need is a stretch of grass and somewhere to get water," I stated as patiently as possible. "You are a local, aren't you?" The man looked at me blankly.

"This is the centre of Leesville, isn't it?" I asked softly, a slight whimper now evident in my voice.

"Well, it was," murmured the man, "but it's pretty much dried up these days. The centre is on the outskirts where the malls are. Another couple of miles down that way." He pointed towards a distant highway full of fast-

food restaurants, garages and motels all heralded with
bright signs in primary colours. No, no, *no*! I told myself.

"There is one place with a bit of grass," he suddenly
blurted. "It's called The Redwood Motel, two or three
miles from here. Cheapest in town, no others will let you
in. You'll have to go down a busy road though."

"I can't stay in a motel with a mule," I said petulantly,
my eyes watering in frustration. "God, we've already
walked thirty miles today. Thirty bloody miles."

"Well, that's all I can think of," he replied with a look
of growing anxiety. He clearly wanted to terminate the
conversation right now. "Good luck." He retreated, firing
nervous glances before ducking around a corner.

This is bad, very bad, I told myself. I was even tempted
to doss down in a churchyard but couldn't face unloading
Browny and then possibly being told to move on. I also
needed somewhere I could find water and pasture. Sod it,
I decided, let's try The Redwood.

We struck out down the busiest street Browny and I
had yet confronted. There was no pavement so I walked
across the lawns of local businesses and the forecourts of
garages. It was Friday night, and boozed-up youths made
braying noises as they sped past. Somebody threw an
empty beer can at me but other than a brief sneer I was too
exhausted to respond. Browny was close to collapse. I
stopped on a paltry stretch of grass near a Kentucky Fried
Chicken and fetched her some water. When I got back to
her, she had slumped down. This was the first time I had
seen her do this all trip: even at night she always slept on
her feet.

Browny drank the water. I was happy to see her nose
had stopped bleeding. I took the packs off her and
collapsed down beside her. Families chewing on drum-
sticks and burgers watched us in fascination. This was
horrible. Why was this the centre of Leesville? I asked
myself. Why was the pretty old part of town deserted and
everyone hovering around these soulless glasshouses,

these identical rashes of neon, these fast-food shrines honouring only the Gods of petroleum and sloth.

Oh, in heaven's name, Fremantle, snap out of it. Focus on your own ludicrous mission and let's get this poor beast some pasture. As Dan Aykroyd in Blues Brothers mode might suggest in a situation like this: "It's a mile to The Redwood, we've got a half tank of oats, three mouldy carrots, it's dark and I'm wearing a bobble hat. Hit it."

I levered up Browny and put the bags back on her. She would not stand. I couldn't blame her. I teased her, prodded her gently. "Hey Browny, hey Brown Girl." People say mules are stubborn. Mules aren't stubborn. Ketchup bottle tops are stubborn, children without pocket money are stubborn, King Lear is stubborn. Browny, however, at this moment in time is not stubborn. She is utterly unbudgeable. After over ten minutes of increasingly frenzied tactics, whispering, slapping, cooing, bellowing, she is still tent-pegged into the ground. Just as I am about to give up and burst into tears she launches off, obedient as a lamb. I swear that mule knows me too well. She's got my number, as the veteran skinners say, and can call it any time she wants.

We once again weaved the gauntlet of fast-food forecourts and car showrooms, while serenaded by the howls of passing revellers. Finally we reached our Mecca. The Redwood Motel. It did not look very hopeful. All that was on offer was a concrete car park with no cars and more importantly, no grass. The NO PETS sign above reception wasn't a source of unbridled encouragement either. I was in a very fragile state, somewhere between bursting into hysterical sobs or crazed Vincent Price-like laughter. The man behind the counter was Asian. He had a small, angular face with that serene and immensely rare look of someone who is utterly at peace with the world. It was not to last.

"You want a room?" he asked pleasantly.

"Well, er, I have a mule." I pointed out of the window

to Browny who was tied to a railing and tucking into a bed of marigolds.

My Oriental friend did a double-take of such magnitude he knocked over the reception bell.

"What is that?"

"It's a mule."

I explained what I was doing and the man, whose name I had now discovered was Chin, came outside to inspect Browny.

"Can I touch her?" he asked, laughing.

"Of course."

Chin moved towards her with outstretched fingers, a bit like a man testing an electric fence. Browny sensed his fear, and got a little jumpy herself, backing off. I felt like a salesman who had just lost his deal. *Bitchy mule, sorry amigo, no room in the inn.* But Chin was captivated by Browny despite her standoffish behaviour. He led me through a back gate at the side of the motel and there before me was a vision to thrill Kublai Khan. It was enough to make a man weep. Well, enough to make me weep anyway. Even Colonel Arthur's granite upper lip might have quavered a little after a day like this.

A sward of lush grass studded with fruit trees and wild bamboo stretched out towards a thick, very English-looking hedgerow. There were cages of wild birds: blue and yellow lovebirds, squawking parrots and a couple of macaws. The cages were large enough for the birds to fly. A wind chime tingled in the warm breeze. It was hard to believe just across the road from this was a modern-day heart of darkness. Mr Kurtz and friends gnawing on a Colonel Sanders and Ronald McDonald combo.

Chin told me it would be fine for Browny to graze here for the night and insisted I take a room at a discount rate. I practically kissed him. Together we unloaded Browny. Chin's wife, a talkative, dark-haired lady with a permanent smile brought out some iced tea. I fed Browny handfuls of oats. Chin supplemented this with apples and sugar lumps while I lugged the saddlebags into my room.

Room 3 was the height of luxury. A television with a zapper. Hurrah! An enormous clean-sheeted bed with *two* pillows. Hurrah! And perhaps best of all, a cummerbund of paper stretched over my lavatory seat, proudly announcing IN THE INTEREST OF HYGIENE, as if my butt was the first ever to be parked on it. And there I was thinking I'd had a hard day: no Civil War soldier received such blatant mollycoddling. Thanking all my lucky stars I went back outside. Chin was sitting on a bench beneath his aviary of parrots. He was watching Browny.

I sat next to him and soon his wife bought me out another cup of tea. Chin told me he was from Taiwan and had come to Leesville twenty years ago to run the motel. His wife was from mainland China. She had been born at the outbreak of Mao's Cultural Revolution during which her parents were brutally separated. He said his wife's family were all happy when she moved to America, and married Chin. They were excited that she could start a new life, have a go at the American dream.

"I'm proud to be an American," Chin told me. "But this garden is my little piece of home."

He saw me watching his birds. "Those little silver parrots are called African Greys. Very rare. And that one," he pointed at an enormous black bird cracking a pecan nut with its beak, "that can live up to a hundred years, he'll outdo me. Those little lovebirds are my favourite; they stay devoted to one another all their lives. Sing sweeter than any other birds."

Chin whistled at a white parrot flapping in the nearest cage. It was hanging upside down, its toes throttling the thin bars. "They are beautiful aren't they, all these birds. They are my snow from the moon."

"Snow from the what?" I asked.

"Snow from the moon," Chin replied softly. "It's an expression my father used when I was growing up. Snow from the moon is something that sounds impossible, unachievable. You've never seen snow from the moon, right?"

"No."

"But there are some things that mean so much to us that they can become snow from the moon. For me sitting here with my wife, one of my children on my knee, listening to the lovebirds, it's magic. I've worked so hard for it. It's my snow from the moon.

"Look at you tonight," he said abruptly. "You looked so tired and sad and lonely. Now you are sitting here with me drinking tea. Maybe that's the snow from the moon for someone like you."

Chin took my empty teacup and headed in to join his wife. He told me to stay in the garden longer if I wanted. I walked over to Browny and watched her drinking from her bucket. I thought back to a couple of hours ago when her nose had been bleeding, her legs buckling, my shins smarting, fear in my guts, no idea how to dig us out of it. I was as low as I could have sunk, a roadside wretch. But perhaps it is only when things go spectacularly wrong for us, so wrong we may as well howl at the night, that we can see clearly. Only once outward calamity has been shifted to a sublime, soul-whooping contentment, perhaps it is only then Chin's strange snow reveals itself.

I lay back on a deckchair in the garden. It was late now and the traffic had eased up. After our intense urban experience today it was good to be in this beautiful oasis. I was so at ease here, safe, calm, a fresh breeze on my face. It was as if I could almost sense clouds moving through the night, hear the bamboo breathing, the fruit sweat and the heartbeats of the tiny birds.

I became transfixed by the half moon framed in its aureole of blue light. I watched it for a while and dozed off, a head full of dreams. When I woke Browny was grazing nearby, her face lit up in the moonshine.

THE LOST CITY OF THE INCAS

Hiram Bingham

Hiram Bingham (1876–1956), American explorer and archaeologist, was the discoverer of the Inca ruins at Machu Picchu, in the Peruvian Andes. The date was 24 July 1911.

When Arteaga learned that we were interested in the architectural remains of the Incas, and were looking for the palace of the last Inca, he said there were some very good ruins in this vicinity – in fact, some excellent ones on top of the opposite mountain, called Huayna Picchu, and also on a ridge called Machu Picchu.

The morning of July 24th dawned in a cold drizzle. Arteaga shivered and seemed inclined to stay in his hut. I offered to pay him well if he would show me the ruins. He demurred and said it was too hard a climb for such a wet day. But when he found that I was willing to pay him a *sol* (a Peruvian silver dollar, 50 cents, gold), three or four times the ordinary daily wage in this vicinity, he finally agreed to go. When asked just where the ruins were, he pointed straight up to the top of the mountain. No one supposed that they would be particularly interesting. And no one cared to go with me. Our naturalist said there were "more butterflies near the river!" and he was reasonably certain he could collect some new varieties. Our surgeon said he had to wash his clothes and mend them. Anyhow it was my job to investigate all reports of ruins and try to find the Inca capital.

So, accompanied only by Sergeant Carrasco, I left camp at ten o'clock. After a walk of three quarters of an hour Arteaga left the main road and plunged down through the jungle to the bank of the river. Here there was a primitive bridge which crossed the roaring rapids at its narrowest part, where the stream was forced to flow between two great boulders. The "bridge" was made of half a dozen very slender logs, some of which were not long enough to span the distance between the boulders, but had been spliced and lashed together with vines!

Arteaga and the sergeant took off their shoes and crept gingerly across, using their somewhat prehensile toes to keep from slipping. It was obvious that no one could live for an instant in the icy cold rapids, but would immediately be dashed to pieces against the rocks. I frankly confess that I got down on my hands and knees and crawled across, 6 inches at a time. Even after we reached the other side I could not help wondering what would happen to the "bridge" if a particularly heavy shower should fall in the valley above. A light rain had fallen during the night and the river had risen so that the bridge was already threatened by the foaming rapids. It would not take much more to wash it away entirely. If this should happen during the day it might be very awkward. As a matter of fact, it did happen a few days later and when the next visitors attempted to cross the river at this point they found only one slender log remaining.

Leaving the stream, we now struggled up the bank through dense jungle, and in a few minutes reached the bottom of a very precipitous slope. For an hour and twenty minutes we had a hard climb. A good part of the distance we went on all fours, sometimes holding on by our fingernails. Here and there, a primitive ladder made from the roughly notched trunk of a small tree was placed in such a way as to help one over what might otherwise have proved to be an impassable cliff. In another place the slope was covered with slippery grass where it was hard to find either handholds or footholds. Arteaga groaned and said that there were lots of snakes here. Sergeant Carrasco said nothing but was glad he had good military shoes. The humidity was great. We were in the belt of maximum precipitation in Eastern Peru. The heat was excessive; and I was not in training. There were no ruins or *andenes* of any kind in sight. I began to think my companions had chosen the better part.

Shortly after noon, just as we were completely exhausted, we reached a little grass-covered hut 2,000 feet above the river where several good-natured Indians, pleasantly surprised at our unexpected arrival, welcomed us with dripping gourds full of cool, delicious water. Then they set before us a few cooked sweet potatoes. It seems that two Indian farmers, Richarte and Alvarez, had recently chosen this eagles' nest for their home. They said they had found plenty of terraces here on which to grow their crops. Laughingly they admitted they enjoyed being free from undesirable visitors, officials looking for army "volunteers" or collecting taxes . . .

Without the slightest expectation of finding anything more interesting than the ruins of two or three stone houses such as we had encountered at various places on the road between Ollantaytambo and Torontoy, I finally left the cool shade of the pleasant little hut and climbed further up the ridge and round a slight promontory. Melchor Arteaga had "been there once before", so he decided to rest and gossip with Richarte and Alvarez. They sent a small boy with me as a "guide". The sergeant was in duty bound to follow, but I think he may have been a little curious to see what there was to see.

Hardly had we left the hut and rounded the promontory

than we were confronted with an unexpected sight, a great flight of beautifully constructed stone-faced terraces, perhaps a hundred of them, each hundreds of feet long and 10 feet high. They had been recently rescued from the jungle by the Indians. A veritable forest of large trees which had been growing on them for centuries had been chopped down and partly burned to make a clearing for agricultural purposes. The task was too great for the two Indians so the tree trunks had been allowed to lie as they fell and only the smaller branches removed. But the ancient soil, carefully put in place by the Incas, was still capable of producing rich crops of maize and potatoes.

However, there was nothing to be excited about. Similar flights of well-made terraces are to be seen in the upper Urubamba Valley at Pisac and Ollantaytambo, as well as opposite Torontoy. So we patiently followed the little guide along one of the widest terraces, where there had once been a small conduit, and made our way into an untouched forest beyond. Suddenly I found myself confronted with the walls of ruined houses built of the finest quality of Inca stone work. It was hard to see them for they were partly covered with trees and moss, the growth of centuries, but in the dense shadow, hiding in bamboo thickets and tangled vines, appeared here and there walls of white granite ashlars carefully cut and exquisitely fitted together. We scrambled along through the dense undergrowth, climbing over terrace walls and in bamboo thickets, where our guide found it easier going than I did. Suddenly, without any warning, under a huge overhanging ledge the boy showed me a cave beautifully lined with the finest cut stone. It had evidently been a royal mausoleum. On top of this particular ledge was a semicircular building whose outer wall, gently sloping and slightly curved, bore a striking resemblance to the famous Temple of the Sun in Cuzco. This might also be a temple of the sun. It followed the natural curvature of the rock and was keyed to it by one of the finest examples of masonry I had ever seen. Furthermore it was tied into another beautiful wall, made of very carefully matched ashlars of pure white granite, especially selected for its fine grain. Clearly, it was the work of a master artist. The interior surface of the wall was broken by niches and square stone-pegs. The exterior surface was perfectly simple and unadorned. The lower courses, of particularly large ashlars, gave it a look of solidity. The upper courses, diminishing in size towards the top, lent grace and delicacy to the structure. The flowing lines, the symmetrical arrangement of the ashlars, and the gradual gradation of the courses, combined to produce a wonderful effect, softer and more pleasing than that of the marble temples of the Old World. Owing to the absence of mortar, there were no ugly spaces between the rocks. They might have grown together. On account of the beauty of the white granite this structure surpassed in attractiveness the best Inca walls in Cuzco, which had caused visitors to marvel for four centuries. It seemed like an unbelievable dream. Dimly, I began to realize that this wall and its adjoining semicircular temple over the cave were as fine as the finest stonework in the world.

It fairly took my breath away. What could this place be? Why had no one given us any idea of it? Even Melchor Arteaga was only moderately interested and had no appreciation of the importance of the ruins which Richarte and Alvarez had adopted for their little farm. Perhaps after all this was an isolated small place which had escaped notice because it was inaccessible.

Then the little boy urged us to climb up a steep hill over what seemed to be a flight of stone steps. Surprise followed surprise in bewildering succession. We came to a great stairway of large granite blocks. Then we walked along a path to a clearing where the Indians had planted a small vegetable garden. Suddenly we found ourselves standing in front of the ruins of two of the finest and most interesting structures in ancient America. Made of beautiful white granite, the walls contained blocks of Cyclopean size, higher than a man. The sight held me spellbound.

Each building had only three walls and was entirely open on one side. The principal temple had walls 12 feet high which were lined with exquisitely made niches, five high up at each end, and seven on the back. There were seven courses of ashlars in the end walls. Under the seven rear niches was a rectangular block 14 feet long, possibly a sacrificial altar, but more probably a throne for the mummies of departed Incas, brought out to be worshipped. The building did not look as though it had ever had a roof. The top course of beautifully smooth ashlars was left uncovered so that the sun could be welcomed here by priests and mummies. I could scarcely believe my senses as I examined the larger blocks in the lower course and estimated that they must weigh from ten to fifteen tons each. Would anyone believe what I had found? Fortunately, in this land where accuracy in reporting what one has seen is not a prevailing characteristic of travellers, I had a good camera and the sun was shining.

The principal temple faces the south where there is a small plaza or courtyard. On the east side of the plaza was another amazing structure, the ruins of a temple containing three great windows looking out over the canyon to the rising sun. Like its neighbour, it is unique among Inca ruins. Nothing just like them in design and execution has ever been found. Its three conspicuously large windows, obviously too large to serve any useful purpose, were most beautifully made with the greatest care and solidity. This was clearly a ceremonial edifice of peculiar significance. Nowhere else in Peru, so far as I know, is there a similar structure conspicuous for being "a masonry wall with three windows". It will be remembered that Salcamayhua, the Peruvian who wrote an account of the antiquities of Peru in 1620, said that the first Inca, Manco the Great, ordered "works to be executed at the place of his birth, consisting of a masonry wall with three windows." Was that what I had found? If it was, then this was not the capital of the last Inca but the birthplace of the first. It did not occur to me that it might be both.

THE PRINCE'S CARAVAN

Peter Fleming

*Peter Fleming was born in England in 1907. A sometime
assistant literary editor of the* Spectator, *he participated in
the 1932 expedition to ascertain the fate of Colonel Percy
Fawcett (see pp 351–356), an experience he recounted in*
Brazilian Adventure. *His other travel titles include* News
from Tartary, *an account of his 3,500-mile journey from
Peking to Kashmir, undertaken with the Swiss journalist
Ella Maillart. Fleming died in 1971. He was the brother of
Ian Fleming, the creator of James Bond.*

From News from Tartary:

One night our stuff was still being unloaded from
the camels when we received a summons from the
Prince of Dzun who was travelling in the same direction.
The Prince ought, I am conscious, to be a romantic
figure, a true-blue, boot-and-saddle, hawk-on-wrist
scion of the house of Chinghis Khan, with flashing
eyes and a proud, distant manner and a habit of getting
silhouetted on sky-lines. But God, not Metro-Goldwyn-
Mayer, made the Prince, and I must tell you what I saw,
not what you will be able to see for yourself when
Hollywood gets loose in Tartary.

The Prince's tent, by virtue of a blue design worked on it, stood out a little from the rest; but inside magnificence was neither achieved nor attempted. Dirty felts covered the floor; bundles and boxes were stacked round the perimeter of the tent. Half a dozen men were squatting round a fire of dried dung. They made room for us in the place of honour, which is at the left of the back of the tent as you go in.

The Prince greeted us non-committally; it would have been beneath his dignity to show surprise or curiosity. He reminded me of a cat. At first it was something about the way his eyes moved in his head, about the way he sat and watched you; then later, when I saw him walk, there was something cat-like in his gait as well. He was a young man, probably in his early thirties, though with those people it is hard to judge. He wore a cap lined with squirrel fur, and a voluminous scarlet robe, also fur-lined. He was a man of little ceremony, but, although he received from his followers few outward signs of respect, his writ appeared to run effectively and all the time we travelled with him we were conscious that his will directed the caravan. Exactly what he was prince of – how many people, how much land – we never rightly discovered. The Tsaidam has been studied less, has in fact been visited less, by foreigners than (I should think) any inhabited area of comparable size in Asia. All I know about the tribal organization of the Mongols who live there is that they are divided into four *hoshuns*: Dzun and Barun in the east, Teijinar in the south and west, and Korugu, reputedly the largest, in the north.

Li, our general helpmeet, who had travelled the Tsaidam, on and off, for ten years, spoke Mongol well, and through him we conveyed fumbling courtesies. When the Prince asked where we were going I said "To Teijinar" (which was the next place of importance after the Prince's own head-quarters at Dzunchia); after that, I said, we didn't know – for it would have been indiscreet to talk about getting through to Sinkiang. We had given him our cards, and presently we showed him our various Chinese passports, which neither he nor Li could read but which looked good and had our photographs on them. We were very much on our best behaviour.

At last the time came to produce our gift. It was a small second-hand telescope. I handed it across the fire with a low bow, holding it on the unturned palms of both hands in the approved style. With it went a *katag*, the flimsy light blue ceremonial scarf which must accompany all presents. The Prince had never seen a telescope before (which was just as well, for this one was a gimcrack affair). He and his staff spent some time peering through it, with faces contorted in the effort to keep one eye shut; and at first it appeared that visibility was poor. We were a prey to those misgivings which assail you when you give a child a toy and the toy, in spite of all they told you at the shop, declines to work. But at last somebody got the focus right, and there were grunts of amazement and delight as a distant camel was brought magically nearer. We withdrew from the audience feeling that we had been accepted at court.

That first day, and for several days thereafter, life in the camp was made irksome by sightseers. There was a crowd perpetually round the tent; all our actions, all our belongings, were closely scrutinized – by the Mongols with vacant gravity, by the Chinese with ill-concealed amusement and a magpie curiosity. "How much did this cost, Mr. Fu? (As they called me). How much this cost?" It was laughable to recall that we had brought with us a tiny portable gramophone (and three records) because it would be *so* useful to attract the natives; there were times, at this period, when we would gladly have exchanged the gramophone for its weight in tear-gas bombs.

After our call on the Prince I left Kini to play the two-headed calf alone and went out with the .22 rifle. I had seen a couple of mandarin duck go down behind a little hill opposite the camp, and I followed them up and had a splendid afternoon, crawling about a soggy little valley through which a stream ran. There were a lot of bar-headed geese there; they had never been under fire before and they usually let me get within a hundred yards, crawling in full view. I shot very moderately, but came back to camp with three. I wanted to present one to the Prince, for this, I thought, would be taken as an appropriate and charming gesture; Li only stopped me in the nick of time. Buddhism, as interpreted in these parts, forbids the Mongols the meat of geese, ducks and hares, but allows them antelope and pheasants. To give the goose would have been a frightful solecism.

The Chinese in the party were less scrupulous. They happened to be Moslems, and as such they should have touched no meat which had not died by the knife; but there is a proverb about Chinese Moslems which gives a good idea of their attitude to Koranic law. "Three Moslems are one Moslem; two Moslems are half a Moslem; one Moslem is no Moslem." In other words, the eyes of a man matter more than the eyes of God. So our fellow-travellers contented themselves with cutting the throats of the two dead birds we gave them and began plucking them without a qualm of conscience. We boiled ours – or as much of it as we could get into the pot – and ate it with rice. It was delicious. We felt very Swiss Family Robinson.

We travelled for seventeen days with the Prince of Dzun. Every morning there it wound, stately, methodical, through the bleak and empty land, 250 camels pacing in single file. At the head of it, leading the first string, usually rode an old woman on a white pony, a gnarled and withered crone whose conical fur-brimmed hat enhanced her resemblance to a witch. Scattered along the flanks, outriders to the main column, went forty or fifty horse-men. Both Chinese and Mongols wore Tibetan dress,

which the Mongols, I suppose, originally adopted as a
kind of protective disguise, for they are milder, less
formidable people than the warlike Tibetans. The little
ponies were dwarfed by the bulging sheepskins which
encased their masters. Everyone carried, slung across his
back, an ancient musket or a matchlock with a forked rest,
and a few of the Chinese had repeating carbines, mostly
from the arsenal at Taiyuanfu and all of an extremely
unreliable appearance. Some people wore broadswords as
well.

   Thus we marched. For the first two or three hours it
was always cold, and we would walk to restore the
circulation in our feet. Sooner or later, every day, the
wind got up. It came tearing out of the west and scourged
us without mercy. It was enough to drive you mad. You
could not smoke, you could not speak (for nobody heard
you anyway), and after a time you could not think con-
secutively. The wind was the curse of our life; ubiquitous
and inescapable, it played the same part on the Tibetan
plateau as insects do in the tropical jungle. It did us no
harm (except to chap our faces), but it plagued us and got
on our nerves.

   However, the wind never blew all day, and there were
times when the sun shone and the march was a joy. Men
climbed on lightly loaded camels and went to sleep in
perilous positions. The Mongols and the Chinese ragged
each other and played – with, I always thought, an under-
lying hint of fierce and ancient hatreds – a primitive game
which consisted of lashing your opponent and his horse
with your whip until you or he were put to flight; the
whips were light and the sheepskins gave plenty of protection, but it was a tough game for all that. Sometimes a
hare was sighted and pursued. Sometimes a few of us
would ride on and sit down in the shelter of a hollow to
smoke; the long-stemmed, small-bowled pipes would be
passed from hand to hand, and mine with them if it was
asked for, for I saw no reason to be haughty and exclusive

in this matter! When people know no customs but their own, and when their own customs are few because of the extreme simplicity of their life, it is only courteous to respect those customs when you can. Besides, my pipe was a great marvel to them. They had little acquaintance with wood (many of them would not see a tree again until they went back to the markets on the edge of the plateau) and they were used to pipes with metal bowls; they could not conceive how I could smoke mine without setting fire to it. Mongols, though hopelessly uncommercial, know a good thing when they see it, and they appreciated the pipe in the same way that they appreciated my .22 rifle or my field-glasses.

The hours passed at varying speeds. If it was warm and windless you fell sometimes into a meditation which blotted out a segment of the march, so that when you returned from the far-off things and places that had filled your mind you remembered the country you had passed through hazily, as you remember country in a dream. But if the wind blew no anaesthetic availed; for every yard of every mile you had your wits too much about you, and progress was a slow and wearisome routine.

Towards the end of the seventh hour you began, like everybody else, to watch the Prince, riding his pale horse near the head of the column with three or four followers about him. The moment he wheeled off the trail and dismounted everyone who had a horse put it into a gallop. From all down the mile-long column ponies scurried out across the steppe, their manes and tails streaming, their riders whooping in the headlong race for tent-sites. We always chose one – at his invitation – near the Prince. While we waited for the camels to come up we unsaddled the horses (by no means everyone did this) and hobbled them. Even Greys, my horse, submitted meekly to the hobble, which fastened both hind legs and one foreleg; I never saw a Tibetan pony object to having its legs handled.

Soon the camels arrived, string after string; were claimed and separated; knelt, roaring, to be unloaded. It was a scene of great confusion, yet it resolved itself astonishingly quickly into a neat, placid cluster of tents. All the tents except ours were circular; they were pitched with their backs to the wind, and the loads were stacked in a low rampart under their flaps. Men scattered to collect dung in the wide skirts of their sheepskins; others brought water in big kettles from the stream; and presently the smoke of cooking fires, flattened by the wind, was streaming from the door of every tent. But the Prince, who was a pious man, prayed before he cooked; a low, rhythmic mutter came from inside his tent, and one of his staff walked round and round it, his lips moving mechanically, sprinkling drops of water from a wooden bowl upon the ground.

It was always one of the best moments of the day when we had got our tent pitched and the things stowed inside it, and could plunge in and lie luxuriously on our sleeping bags, out of the wind. Out of the wind; it made such a difference. The air still roared outside and the thin walls bulged in upon us; but we could talk and smoke and rub butter on our chapped and burning faces and feel at peace. Presently there would be tea with red pepper in it and tsamba to abate the gnawing in our bellies. Tsamba is parched barley meal, and can be mistaken, even in a good light, for fine sawdust. You eat it in tea, with butter if you have got butter, or with melted mutton fat if you haven't got butter, or with neither if you have got neither. You fill your shallow wooden bowls with tea, then you let the butter melt in the tea (the butter is usually rancid and has a good cheesy flavour); then you put a handful of tsamba in. At first it floats; then, like a child's castle of sand, its foundations begin to be eaten by the liquid. You coax it with your fingers until it is more or less saturated and has become a paste; this you knead until you have a kind of doughy cake in your hand and the wooden bowl is empty and clean. Your meal is ready.

Tsamba has much to recommend it, and if I were a poet I would write an ode to it. For three months we lived on a diet of tsamba.

We marched usually from 6 a.m. to about 2 p.m., so we had several hours of daylight still before us. After lunch I always went out with the .22, to wander happily along the lake or, when we left the lake, among the hills, recalling with an exile's pleasure many evenings similarly spent elsewhere, and coming back to camp with a goose or a duck or a hare, even the odd antelope, or with nothing at all. But Kini never took the afternoon off, except to photograph, for there was nothing for her to do out of camp. She read or wrote or darned or slept; and whichever she did she was sooner or later interrupted by somebody who wanted medicine. The Mongols seldom bothered us, but any of the Chinese who were ill, or who had once been ill, or thought they might be going to be ill, came regularly. They fell into three classes: those who had nothing the matter with them at all, those who had had something the matter with them for years and years, and those whom we were able to help. The third class was the smallest.

What with my wretched Chinese and their determination to pile on the agony, it took a long time to discover even approximately the nature of their various afflictions. We were at our best with cuts and sores, which Kini disinfected and bandaged with skill and care (she had once done some Red Cross training with a view to becoming a professional ski teacher). Internal complaints were not so easy, but when in doubt we gave castor oil, a policy which scored several medical triumphs and once won us the gratitude of the most important Chinese by curing him of a fearful belly-ache. One nice and unusually intelligent boy had an old abscess in his thigh and wanted us to cut it open; this we declined to do, but Kini worked on it so successfully with fomentations that in the end it was giving him hardly any trouble. At the close of a long day one of the last things you want to do is to attend to stinking sores on unwashed anatomies, but Kini did it cheerfully and took immense trouble over it; all along the road it was she, not I, who did the dirty work.

It was she, for instance, who went out into the cold and saw to the cooking of the evening meal, while I squatted in the warm tent, cleaning the rifle or writing my diary or playing patience on a suitcase, and asking at frequent intervals how soon the food would be ready. When it was, we put the great black pot just inside the tent and Li brought his bowl and we got out our enamel plates and dinner was served: rice or mien or a kind of noodles which we called by its Russian name of *lapsha*, and whatever meat we had in hand. How we ate! We did not speak. We shovelled the food down until the pot was empty and we were distended. It was my misfortune that I had only a teaspoon to shovel with, for three or four larger spoons which we bought in Sining had broken almost on sight; but it is wonderful what you can do with a teaspoon when you are in the mood, and it equalled things up with Kini, who was a slow eater but had the only larger spoon. They were delicious meals.

As soon as we had finished eating we felt sleepy. Washing up was not a very arduous business, for we had only one plate and one mug each; all the same, it was usually omitted. We pulled off the soft sheepskin boots which I had had made at Tangar for use in camp, wriggled into our flea-bags, and covered ourselves with our overcoats. We made pillows of rolled up sweaters on a foundation of boots and field-glasses; Kini's was always very neat, mine was always a lumpy scrabble. Just outside, our horses munched their barley, making a sound as charming and as soporific as the sound of running water or of waves upon a beach. The tiny tent looked very warm and cheerful in the candlelight, and one of us would perhaps grow suddenly talkative, theorizing about the future or reminiscing about the past. But conversation became increasingly one-sided; monosyllables were succeeded by grunts, and grunts by a profound indifferent silence. Whichever of us was talking abandoned soliloquy and blew out the candle.

The wind dropped at night. Outside the iron land froze in silence under the moon. The silver tents were quiet. The watchman moved among them squatly (it was bandit country), like a goblin – thinking what thoughts, suppressing what fears? A wolf barked. A star fell down the tremendous sky. The camp slept.

MOUNT BURNEY

Eric Shipton

The English mountaineer Eric Earle Shipton was born in 1907. His books include Nanda Devi, Blank on the Map, Land of Tempest *and* Upon That Mountain. *He died in 1977.*

Mount Burney is supposed to be an active volcano; if so it is the most southerly in South America and a very isolated one. I had tried to discover something about it, but a search through several geographical libraries revealed only that very little was known; nor did I find anyone in Patagonia who could tell me anything about it. Clearly it had been named after a British naval officer who had sailed with Captain Cook, and had later become a distinguished admiral; though it is most improbable that he himself discovered it. It was mentioned by Captain King of H.M.S. *Adelaide* which accompanied the *Beagle* on her famous voyage through the Fuegan Archipelago; and it is now frequently seen from ships passing through Smyth and Union Channels, which lie close to its western and northern slopes. In 1910 it was reported to be in a state of violent eruption. So far as I could learn, no one had ever penetrated the country surrounding it.

This almost complete ignorance about a familiar landmark is not at all uncommon in that fantastic labyrinth of
channels and islands which stretches for a thousand miles
north from Cape Horn along the Pacific coast of South
America. For, though the channels themselves have been
fairly thoroughly charted, and although the larger ones
are frequented by ships in their passage to and from the
northern ports, most of the country on either side is
uninhabited and a great deal of it, both the islands and
on the mainland, is still unexplored.

With so many fascinating projects clamouring for attention, I had not considered mounting a special expedition to explore the unknown volcano. But there was
something very interesting about it, and I found that
my interest was shared by Cedomir Marangunic, a young
geologist who was with me on my expedition to Tierra del
Fuego in 1962. So, when we returned from there to Punta
Arenas early in March, we decided to spend a couple of
weeks in an attempt to reach Mount Burney.

It stands near the north-west corner of a large block of
country known as the Munos Gamero Peninsula, which is
almost completely surrounded by a maze of waterways.
Indeed it is only connected to the mainland by a tiny neck
of land named Paso del Indio after the strange Alakluf
Indians who spend their nomadic lives wandering about
the channels in search of food, and occasionally carry their
canoes over the isthmus from Obstruction Fjord to Skyring Sound.

The only practicable way of reaching the Peninsula is
by boat; to attempt to do so overland would involve a
journey of many weeks through untrodden and exceedingly rugged country. We decided to approach it from the
east, through Skyring Sound to the Paso del Indio,
making the voyage in the inflatable rubber boat, *Zodiac*,
which we had used on our expedition.

On March 9, we were taken in an Army lorry to
Estancia Skyring, a ranch owned by Mr. Friedli on the

northern shore of Skyring Sound, at the end of the motor
road, 100 miles from Punta Arenas.

Skyring Sound is a large body of salt water, eighty miles
long, connected to the sea by a narrow channel at its
south-western end. Constantly lashed by north-westerly
gales it is nearly always very rough. Though our *Zodiac*
was thoroughly seaworthy, it gave us no protection from
the weather, and the prospect of battling against powerful
head winds and heavy seas in this tiny craft was somewhat
intimidating. We intended to keep close inshore, getting
whatever shelter we could from headlands and bays, along
the northern shore. Unfortunately, there was a long,
mountainous peninsula which jutted right out into the
middle of the Sound, and after rounding this, we would
be exposed for many hours to the full force of the gale.
However, the base of the Peninsula was connected to the
mainland by a low-lying isthmus, only about a mile wide.
Mr. Friedli kindly arranged for three pack horses to be
sent to meet us at that point which would enable us to
transport our boat, outboard motor, and supplies across
the isthmus, thus avoiding the long hazardous voyage
around the Peninsula.

After lunch we went in the lorry for ten miles over
rough forest tracks, accompanied by Mr. Friedli's young
son, Richard, to show us the way. Our progress was so
slow that the *peón* with the unladen horses had no trouble
in keeping up with us. In the late afternoon we reached a
point where the lorry could go no farther, so we carried
our baggage down a steep slope to the shore of a bay,
launched the boat and set sail.

It had been very stormy all day, and though by then the
weather had moderated, as soon as we got out of the
shelter of the bay we were met by a strong head wind and a
boisterous sea. The waves dashed over us and before long
we were soaking wet and very cold. We were not sorry
when, two hours later, in the gathering dusk, we rounded
a rocky headland and saw a wooden cabin standing on a

high bluff above a sheltered bay, where we had arranged to meet the pack horses the following day.

The cabin, the last permanent habitation in Skyring Sound, was occupied by a man called Daniel Lever who lived there all alone. Obviously delighted by our unexpected arrival, he greeted us with great enthusiasm as we landed. It was deliciously hot inside his cabin. We stripped off our sodden garments, and stood warming our naked bodies by the roaring stove, while he busied himself with the preparation of a large stew.

We had been told that Daniel knew more than anyone else about the western reaches of Skyring Sound. He was a tremendous talker, but though he kept up a ceaseless flow of Spanish, my companions found it hard to steer his conversation into fruitful channels. We found in fact that even his knowledge was somewhat vague. The Paso del Indio was little more than a name to him. He had never been there and had no idea what it was like, while he gave us to understand that no one except the Alakluf Indians had ever crossed it. He told us, however, that on one of the many islands beyond the Peninsula, there was a log cabin used by a family who made a living by cutting cypress timber and transporting it during the comparatively calm winter season to the sawmill near the eastern end of the Sound.

I had begun that day with a slight fever, and by now, after becoming thoroughly chilled in the boat, I was feeling far from well. So, as soon as supper was finished, I took my sleeping bag into the second room of the cabin, and dossed down on the floor, well away from the now oppressive heat of the stove. After a restless night, I awoke feeling considerably worse, and decided to spend the day in bed.

When, at noon, the *peón* arrived with the three pack horses, my companion and Daniel set off with them to the narrowest part of the isthmus to transport our baggage across it. Besides the boat and motor, the food and tents, we had brought thirty-five gallons of petrol, and at least two relays would be necessary. It was a wretched day and I lay in my sleeping bag listening to the violent wind and lashing rain outside.

It was almost dark before the others returned, wet and tired, having had a rough time. They had crossed the isthmus with the first relay of loads, but while returning for the second, one of the horses had got stuck in a bog. They had spent several hours trying to extricate it, but eventually had to abandon the attempt so as to get back to the cabin before dark.

The next morning, Daniel produced two of his own horses to help us, and we all set out at nine o'clock. I was still feeling a bit light-headed as we made our way along the shore to the isthmus. It was still blowing hard, but the rain had stopped, and the sun was shining fitfully through ragged banks of racing cloud, which accentuated the wildness of the scene. A large area of the forest had been burnt to make room for grazing land, and the white skeletons of the dead trees thronged, like a multitude of ghosts, around the bay, while beyond stood the gaunt mountains of the Peninsula, where the high crags held patches of snow which had survived the summer.

We packed the boat and motor and the remaining loads on the four horses. By then, the others had found a good route through the woods and swamps of the isthmus and we reached the shore on the other side early in the afternoon. I was anxious to help with the rescue of the unfortunate horse that was still stuck in the bog, but Daniel and the *peón* made it clear that they would prefer to cope with it themselves, so they left us there, with warm good wishes, and started back. Later, we heard that they had managed to rescue the animal by towing it to safety with the other four horses harnessed to a long rope.

While I made a fire of driftwood and brewed tea, Cedomir and Ricardo, the third member of my party, assembled the boat. With the help of one of the tents, they

constructed a snug little cabin, which would accommo-
date one of us at a time, keep our bedding dry and
minimise the shipment of water. By three o'clock all
was ready.

We had some trouble in launching the boat through the
breakers, and keeping her off the shore until we got the
motor started; but we succeeded at the third attempt. We
were now in a deep gulf, and although there was a stiff
breeze blowing, the waves were comparatively small. I
took the helm and Ricardo sat huddled in the cabin; but
soon he began to feel seasick and we changed places.
Although the cabin was very cramped, and I could see
nothing except the view directly astern, I was grateful for
the warmth it afforded, for I was still feeling rather
delicate.

Before we had been going an hour, the motor, which
had behaved perfectly during our expedition to Tierra del
Fuego, suddenly stopped. We managed to get it going
again, but, from then on, we could only keep it running in
fits and starts by judicious manipulation of the choke and
we made very slow progress.

At six-thirty we passed through a narrow straight at the
entrance to the gulf, landed on a beach beyond and
pitched camp on the edge of the dense forest. It was a
good spot, sheltered from the wind and with a stream of
clear water close by. We found, however, from the evidence of tracks through the undergrowth and droppings,
that it was frequented by wild cattle. These creatures can
be dangerous, and Cedomir insisted upon our building a
strong stockade round the camp; but we were not disturbed.

We spent most of the next day trying to locate the
trouble in the motor; but we were not very successful and
when we set off again in the late afternoon, it still needed a
good deal of coaxing to keep it running. However, the
wind had stopped and we made fair progress. At seven-
thirty, as dark was falling, we reached a large island and

ran into a tiny cove on its eastern shore. There we found
an old Alakluf encampment; the remains of a fire and a
circle of withered saplings which had formed the frame-
work of a primitive hut. Two rocky headlands enclosed
the bay, which was fringed with tall trees and flowering
shrubs, crowding so close to the deep clear water that
there was no bank. It was a lovely evening, so still that
even the sea beyond the cove was velvet smooth, silvered
by the light of a half moon.

The next morning, we woke to a fiery dawn, beautiful
but menacing. However, although we were obviously in
for more bad weather before long, it was still perfectly
calm at seven-thirty when we started. We had scarcely
emerged from the cove when the motor started giving
trouble again. This time no amount of manipulating the
choke would keep it running for more than half a minute,
and it looked as if we would have to spend the next few
days rowing back the way we had come.

We had already taken the carburettor to pieces and had
satisfied ourselves that there was no dirt or water in the
petrol. In desperation we dismantled the petrol pump.
None of us knew much about motors, and as the pump
was a complicated piece of mechanism it took us an hour
and a half to reassemble it, having discovered no apparent
fault. Then, with little hope, we pulled the starting cord.
To our incredulous delight the motor started and continued running smoothly.

On an island close to the one where we had camped, we
saw a cabin which was obviously the one Daniel had told
us about. To take advantage of the calm spell we cruised at
full speed, and by eleven o'clock we were approaching the
north-west corner of Skyring Sound.

This consisted of a perfect labyrinth of channels divided and sub-divided by innumerable islands and pro-
montories. However, we had with us a map on a scale of
1 :250,000 (about four miles to the inch) made from some
aerial photographs of the region, and although it con-

tained a number of inaccuracies, it was sufficiently good
to give us some idea of the whereabouts of the Paso del
Indio. Beyond this there was a large and complicated
system of lakes, also shown on the map, which filled a
large part of the interior of the Munos Gamero Peninsula,
and by means of which we hoped to reach within twelve
miles of Mount Burney. So far as I know, no one except
the Alakluf had been to the lakes before.

We threaded our way along one of the narrow channels,
between steep mountains covered right down to the
water's edge with dense vegetation, and at eleven-thirty
we landed on its northern shore. We had expected the
Paso to be a neck of flat land, not more than 200 yards
wide, but we had found no such place. We set off each in a
different direction, to explore the area. After scrambling
over several wooded hills, I reached the top of one from
which I saw down into a fjord stretching away to the
north-west which was obviously part of the lake system.
But I could see no easy way of reaching it, so I returned to
the boat.

Cedomir, however, found a more hopeful route, and we
decided to explore it. We made a depot of petrol and food
for the return journey, which we hid deep in the undergrowth against the most unlikely chance of some Alakluf
passing that way; and then set about the task of carrying
the boat, the motor and the rest of our baggage over the
fjord. By then the rain, which had held off throughout the
morning, was falling steadily and continued to do so for
the rest of the day.

As Cedomir had reported two tarns to be crossed on the
way, we decided to carry the boat over as it was, so that we
could use it to float our gear across them. The boat
without the engine weighed two hundredweight, and
although we lightened it somewhat by removing the floor
boards, it was an awkward thing to carry. First we had to
haul it up a steep ramp, then over a swamp to the first of
the tarns. So it went on until the final descent through

dense forest to the shore of the fjord beyond. It was remarkable that the boat did not become punctured on one of the many jagged tree stumps against which it scraped; but the splinters were so rotten that they failed to pierce the fabric.

The job took us five and a half hours of very hard work, and it was almost dark by the time we had got the last load over to the fjord. As a result we had a rather miserable camp. Though I managed to light a fire, the sodden wood would do nothing but smoulder. We soon abandoned it, crawled into our small tent out of the rain, stripped off our wet clothes, and cooked supper on our Primus. Unlike that of Skyring Sound, the water of the lake was fresh, so that we no longer had to rely upon finding streams.

We awoke the next morning to an enchanting scene. It had stopped raining and the air was still. The clouds covering the sky and hiding the higher mountain tops were bright pink in the sunrise. The trees of the forest, *notafagus, cypress*, and *magnolia*, were of various shades of green; the banks of moss which lined the shores were rich emerald, and here and there were great clusters of red flowering shrubs. This riot of colours was mirrored in the smooth surface of the fjord. Complete silence reigned.

From the resinous wood of a dead cypress, we made an excellent fire, and hung our clothes to dry while we had breakfast, and then assembled the boat. It was nine o'clock before we set sail down the fjord. By then the rain was falling gently, but it was perfectly calm. It was tempting to travel at full speed, but we had used much more petrol than we had expected, punching against the strong head winds and rough seas in the early part of the voyage. So, to conserve our supply, we now ran the motor at half throttle, and cruised along at four knots.

We had to do some careful navigation to find our way through the complicated network of waterways into a long west-bound channel which led to the main lake. It was a fascinating world through which we passed; a world of dense, primaeval forest, growing out of a dark blanket of moss; of rugged cliffs and plunging waterfalls; of a deep mountain that climbed into the clouds, and of little islets which looked like green velvet pin cushions floating on the blue surface of the water. Though it rained for a great deal of the morning, shafts of sunlight were constantly breaking through the clouds to light some part of the scene. Rainbows, too, made a frequent appearance; we must have seen at least a dozen of them in a couple of hours. Some of them were astonishingly brilliant, and some so close that it seemed as though one could reach out and touch them.

Unlike Skyring Sound, where we saw great numbers of wildfowl, such as black-necked swans, steamer duck and cormorants, we rarely saw any on the lakes. Indeed, we saw remarkably little wild life of any sort, which may partly explain the feeling of intense loneliness the place inspired. Despite its beauty and colour, it was not friendly; it seemed aloof, mysterious and rather cruel. Certainly it would be terrible country to get through without a boat.

Shortly before noon, we reached the end of the west-bound channel and emerged into the main lake, which stretched some miles from north to north. The western shore was dominated by a fine conical mountain with several glaciers flowing down its sides.

As soon as we entered the lake, we were hit by a sudden violent storm. It became unpleasantly rough and clouds of spindrift swept over us. We decided to put into a sheltered bay. In my haste to do so, I steered too close to the headland on the near side, and we were nearly blown on to some rocks. For this clumsy piece of helmsmanship, I received a gentle reprimand from Cedomir.

We lit a fire and brewed some tea while we waited for the storm to abate, and a couple of hours later, we set out on the last stage of the voyage. There was a strong headwind, but by running the motor at full speed, we made good headway. We were two miles from our destination when the motor started to fire on only one of its two cylinders. However, by then we had reached comparatively sheltered waters and at five o'clock we ran up a little creek at the northern end of the lake and secured the boat to a grassy bank. Close by, there was a pleasant grove of young notafagus trees, where we pitched camp and lit an enormous fire.

The next day, we took stock of our position. It was now March 15, nearly a week since we had started. The voyage had taken several days longer than we had anticipated. We still had food enough for ten days, and a further three days' supply had been dumped at the Paso del Indio. We estimated that Mount Burney was now about ten miles away to the north-west. Unless the going was much better than we had reason to expect, it would take us all of a week to cover this distance and return. This would leave us six days' food for the voyage back, and as we could expect to have the wind behind us all the way, this should leave us ample margin for unforeseen contingencies.

But we were expected back in Punta Arenas by the 23rd, and it now looked as if we might be nearly a week late. A few weeks before we had caused a great deal of unnecessary concern when we had been reported missing in the Darwin Range, due to our failure to make radio contact with the naval station on Dawson Island, and Cedomir and I did not relish the prospect of a repetition of that situation. So it was with some feelings of guilt that we decided to press on to Mount Burney with a week's food.

To the north our view was blocked by a steep mountain, which was partly covered with snow on its upper part. Two thousand feet up, just beyond the limit of the forest, there was a broad grassy terrace which appeared to extend round to the unseen western side of the mountain and to offer a good route at least for the first two miles. Before reaaching it, we had a long and exhausting struggle through dense forest and tangled undergrowth which covered the steep lower slopes of the mountain. When we had gained the terrace, though we had to cross several deep ravines, the going was easy, and we made our way along it with mounting excitement to see what lay round the corner.

The morning had been fine, but by the middle of the afternoon, the weather had turned bad, and when we reached the corner we were met by a fierce northerly gale and blinding rain. The friendly terrace continued along the western side of the mountain. Presently, on our left, we found ourselves looking down a sheer precipice to a huge lake, some 2,000 feet below. Beyond this we could see through gaps and the driving mist to a range of peaks, some of which were festooned with glaciers. We could not see the far end of the lake but it appeared to curve round the northern side of the mountain we were on.

Though we still had nearly three hours' daylight left, we decided to pitch camp and to make a reconnaissance the following morning. We had some difficulty in finding a spot that was reasonably sheltered from the wind and not too swampy. Our little two-man tent provided cramped quarters for the three of us, particularly as both of my companions were six foot three inches and broad in proportion. But our sleeping bags were dry and we passed a comfortable night.

It froze during the night, and in the morning getting back into our sodden garments was an unpleasant operation. But by then, the rain and wind had stopped and climbing rapidly we soon got warm. In an hour, we reached a prominent northern shoulder of the mountain. By then the sun had come out, and the clouds, which earlier had hidden the surrounding peaks, were fast disappearing. The point we had reached commanded a magnificent view to the east, north, and west.

We were surprised to see another large lake lying at the eastern foot of our mountain, its far end hidden beyond another range. To the north, a wide grass plain stretched into the distance, and beside it to the north-west rose the massive bulk of Mount Burney. Soon the vanishing cloud revealed its highest peaks. We were astonished; for instead of the simple volcanic cone that we had been expecting to find, we saw a splendid mountain, completely sheathed in glacier, with sweeping curves of ice, dominated by a huge white fang.

We started down the northern side of the mountain which descended towards the plain in a series of wide terraces. Each of these seemed to be a little world of its own, enclosed by high cliffs and filled with woods and tarns and green meadows, as warm and fragrant as a summer's day in Devon. It took us two hours to walk through them, and at last we reached the edge of a precipitous slope running down a thousand feet to a deep channel, which connected the two lakes and separated the mountain from the plain.

Narrow though it was, the channel formed a decisive barrier to our further progress. Even if it had been possible, it would have taken far too long to return to the boat and lug it through the forest to either of the great lakes flanking the mountain. But I had no feeling of disappointment at our failure to reach our objective. The journey thus far had been so fascinating, the discoveries of the day so unexpected and so enthralling that there was no room for regret. Moreover we were incredibly lucky to have such a wonderful day for this reconnaissance.

Basking in the sun on a grassy ledge and gazing out over the splendid panorama of mountains and lakes, Cedomir and I discussed plans for returning to this exciting place. We agreed that we would require at least a month to make even a rough exploration of Mount Burney and the country surrounding it.

Cedomir formed the opinion that the great northern plain might have been formed by an immense bed of volcanic ash which now filled the valley that had once been occupied by a wide fjord, connecting the lakes with the sea. From its general appearance, we found it hard to believe that Mount Burney was in fact a volcano, but the quantity of pumice that we found lying about, left us in no doubt that there was a volcano somewhere in the vicinity.

We started back at one o'clock. Twenty-four hours later, we arrived back at the creek where we had left the boat. The fine spell had ended and the weather was stormy, with a strong wind blowing from the north. After lunch, we started to prepare for the return journey. Ricardo cut down a small cypress, and with this, a climbing rope, and a tent, he rigged up a sail, while Cedomir tried to doctor the motor. The trouble this time was with one of the plugs. Unfortunately, though we had a spare one, we had lost our screw spanner, probably during the struggle across the Paso, and we could not change it. However, we had found that by holding the terminal a minute distance from the top of the plug, the spark was transmitted. After many abortive attempts, Cedomir succeeded in tying the lead in this position. It was an insecure arrangement which caused us anxiety in the storms we encountered during the next few days.

We set off at three-thirty. The sail was most effective, and once beyond the shelter of the surrounding mountains, we stopped the motor and ran before the wind at six knots, steering with a couple of oars. Once we encountered the channels, however, we lost the wind and had to start the motor again. With the petrol we saved, we could now afford to cruise at full speed, and at seven fifty-five, as night was falling, we reached the Paso del Indio. An hour before the weather had begun to look increasingly threatening. We had no sooner secured the boat and pitched the tent than the storm broke with torrential rain and a mighty wind which continued throughout the night.

The crossing of the Paso del Indio took us all the next morning. This time we deflated the boat and carried it in a pack frame. It was a very heavy load for one man, but it saved time, and was certainly less hard on the boat than hauling it through the forest. Except for a few showers, it had stopped raining. But the wind now showed no sign of abating and it was evident that we were in for a rough time on Skyring Sound.

My companions cut down another cypress and made a new mast, and when this and the sail had been rigged, we set off again in the middle of the afternoon. While we were still in the network of channels leading from the Paso, we were in calm water, but as soon as we reached the open water beyond, we met the full force of the north wind and a heavy sea.

We had intended to steer south-east, over a wide stretch of open water to the head of the great peninsula. But the waves were so intimidating that we decided to take a longer course to the east to the group of islands we had passed through on the outward journey. Even so, we had a long way to go across the line of the waves before we gained their protection. But the boat behaved splendidly. It was so buoyant that it rose to the waves like a cork, and only occasionally did one of the bigger waves break over the side. Even so, what with these and the frequent squalls of swirling spindrift we shipped a good deal of water, and were kept busy bailing. With the wind abeam, our make-shift sail was useless, so we took it down.

Soon after six we landed in a little bay on the island where the woodcutter's cabin was situated. We were not at all sorry to get ashore and the prospect of shelter was more than welcome, for by then, it was raining hard and the storm was increasing in violence. The cabin itself was locked, but we found lodging in a dilapidated shed near-by, which had four stout log walls and a roof. Inside was a varied collection of objects, such as old clothing, strings of dried mussels, and otter skins, and also an ample supply of firewood. There was also a stove made of a rusty oil-drum and a length of piping which served as a chimney.

We lost no time in lighting a fire; before long the stove became red hot and, having stripped off our wet clothes, we sat naked in a temperature of some 90°F. Another unwonted luxury was a cabbage, which we had found growing near the cabin, and which made a welcome addition to our evening stew. The place was inhabited by a small colony of cats, which had apparently resented our intrusion, but soon changed their minds when they found what we had to offer. Their scraggy appearance made it clear that they found life on the island hard to sustain.

The fury of the storm continued to mount and we were deliciously aware of our good fortune in having found such a snug billet, though we often expected to be bereft of our roof. However, though it leaked, it clung on manfully. The noise of the wind and the rain was so loud that we had to shout to make ourselves heard, but in spite of that, we slept for eleven hours.

When we awoke, though it had stopped raining, the wind was as strong as ever. Obviously we could not put out to sea in such conditions. After breakfast, I climbed to the top of a small hill which commanded a view over the island. It was an impressive sight. The sea was white with flying spume and the channel between me and the next island looked like a cataract.

However, at two o'clock, the wind dropped and the water in the channels became calm, so we decided to start, having paid for our night's lodging by leaving a supply of tea and sugar in the cabin. It turned out to be only a temporary lull. We had been going barely an hour, and had got past the island into the open sea, west of the Peninsula, when the wind regained some of its old force. It had veered towards the north-west.

We were now steering for Punta Laura, the southern-most cape of the Peninsula, which we could see in the far distance to the S.S.E. The sea was thus in our starboard quarter, and we were making some leeway; so we had to keep well out from the coast to avoid being driven on to the shore. We could have taken refuge in one of the bays on the Peninsula and waited for the weather to moderate, but storms in this part of the world can often go on for weeks, and now we were at sea we thought that we might as well try to get round our "Cape Horn" as we called Punta Laura. These Zodiac boats have been tested in extremely heavy seas at home, and I have been assured both by the makers and by the Royal Marines who use them, that it is virtually impossible to capsize them, particularly with a reasonable amount of ballast aboard. Also they can be filled with water without it having much effect on their buoyancy. So providing we had sufficient sea room, there was little danger. The only cause for worry was the possibility of the motor ceasing to function; for our makeshift sail gave us little room for manœuvre, and suitable landing places along the coast were few and far between.

Nonetheless, it was an exciting voyage, and for a landsman like me, not a little alarming. We would race along on the crest of a breaking wave as though on a surf board. Usually, we would then overshoot the wave and plunge down into the deep trough beyond, bouncing like a rubber ball, while the swirling spindrift flew overhead. To port the cloud-capped mountains loomed above us; to starboard we could see nothing but the storm-tossed sea.

By six o'clock we were racing past the sheer cliffs of Punta Laura, a splendid sight with the waves dashing against them; and it was a blissful moment when we shot round the sharp point to the calm water beyond. Half a mile further we entered a deep wooded bay where we landed. We had some difficulty in finding fresh water, but at length we came across a stagnant pool in the forest, and though the water was the colour of tea, it tasted sweet. It was a delightful spot, completely sheltered from the wind by the tall forest, with banks of fuchsia in full bloom along the rocky shore. Its charm was certainly enhanced by our feeling of elation and relief at having got around "Cape Horn" in such wild weather.

The next morning we resumed our voyage, going down the east coast of the Peninsula. It was blowing as hard as ever, but we were now on the lee side, and could keep in the comparatively calm water close to the shore. Soon after noon we had reached Daniel's cabin near the base of the Peninsula, where we were greeted with great warmth. He had another visitor with him who turned out to be the owner of the cabin on the island. They plied us with questions about our journey into the unknown country beyond the Paso del Indio.

After lunch, we set out on the last leg of the voyage. We were soon beyond the shelter of the Peninsula where we found the wind had not diminished at all since the day before. But it was now dead astern and with our sail hoisted and the motor running at full throttle, we skimmed over the waves like a steamer duck. Half way along the coast, a narrow spit ran several miles out to sea, and it was separated by a narrow strait from an island called Isla Juan. The strait was marked on our map, but as the island overlapped the spit on the western side, we could not see it until we were within fifty yards of the shore; then we made a right-angled turn and shot through the narrow strait at great speed. The water beyond the spit was a curious sight, for though it was quite calm, it was white with spray whipped off the surface by the wind.

The only other hazard beyond was an ugly reef of rocks at the last headland; to clear them we had to beat far out to sea, and at six o'clock, we ran the *Zodiac* on to the beach in front of Estancia Skyring.

Stiff with wet and cold, we made our way to the Friedli house where we were given a wonderful welcome and cherished with all the luxuries of a highly civilised home.

Though the trip had been inconclusive, we were more than satisfied. We had travelled far into unknown territory; we had crossed the mysterious Paso del Indio; we had discovered an entirely new lake system, and all this in two short weeks.

The following summer, before starting on my new expedition to Tierra del Fuego, I returned to Skyring with John Earle and Jack Ewer to continue the exploration of the area. This time we allowed ourselves a month for the job. We succeded in carrying the *Zodiac* through into the lake system that had stopped us before, and we reached the great plain. This we found to be largely composed of swamp, but we managed to cross it to Mount Burney where we spent a fortnight exploring. But the weather was appalling, and though we made a journey right round the mountain, almost continuous storms gave us no opportunity of climbing it.

Though it is certainly a volcano, we found no evidence of recent activity.

DESPERATE STRAITS

Frederick A. Cook

*Dr Frederick Albert Cook was born in New York State in
1865. He began his career as an Arctic explorer as the
surgeon on Robert E. Peary's 1891 expedition to Greenland.
In 1908 Cook claimed to be the first man to reach the North
Pole, although both Peary (see pp. 391–395) and an in-
vestigative committee set up by Copenhagen University
disputed his claim; Cook wrote* My Attainment of the Pole
in justification. He died in 1940.

The stormy sea rose with heavy swells. Oceanward, the
waves leaped against the horizon tumultuously. Pursuing
our vain search for food along the southern side of Jones
Sound, early in September, we had been obliged to skirt
rocky coves and shelves of land on which we might seek
shelter should harm come to the fragile craft in which we
braved the ocean storms and the spears of unseen ice
beneath water.

We had shaped crude weapons. We were prepared to
attack game. We were starving; yet land and sea had been
barren of any living thing.

Our situation was desperate. In our course it was often
necessary, as now, to paddle from the near refuge of low-

lying shores, and to pass precipitous cliffs and leaping glaciers which stepped threateningly into the sea. Along these were no projecting surfaces, and we passed them always with bated anxiety. A sudden storm or a mishap at such a time would have meant death in the frigid sea. And now, grim and suffering with hunger, we clung madly to life.

Passing a glacier which rose hundreds of feet out of the green sea, heavy waves rolled furiously from the distant ocean. Huge bergs rose and fell against the far-away horizon like Titan ships hurled to destruction. The waves dashed against the emerald walls of the smooth icy Gibraltar with a thunderous noise. We rose and fell in the frail canvas boat, butting the waves, our hearts each time sinking.

Suddenly something white and glittering pierced the bottom of the boat! It was the tusk of a walrus, gleaming and dangerous. Before we could grasp the situation he had disappeared, and water gushed into our craft. It was the first walrus we had seen for several weeks. An impulse, mad under the circumstances, rose in our hearts to give him chase. It was the instinctive call of the hungering body for food. But each second the water rose higher; each minute was imminent with danger. Instinctively Ah-we-lah pressed to the floor of the boat and jammed his knee into the hole, thus partly shutting off the jetting, leaping inrush. He looked mutely to me for orders. The glacier offered no stopping place. Looking about with mad eagerness, I saw, seaward, only a few hundred yards away, a small pan of drift-ice. With the desire for life in our arms, we pushed toward it with all our might. Before the boat was pulled to its slippery landing, several inches of water flooded the bottom. Once upon it, leaping in the waves, we breathed with panting relief. With a piece of boot the hole was patched. Although we should have preferred to wait to give the walrus a wide berth, the increasing swell of the stormy sea, and a seaward drift forced us away from the dangerous ice cliffs.

Launching the boat into the rough waters, we pulled for land. A triangle of four miles had to be made before our fears could be set at rest. A school of walrus followed us in the rocking waters for at least half of the distance. Finally, upon the crest of a white-capped wave, we were lifted to firm land. Drawing the boat after us, we ran out of reach of the hungry waves, and sank to the grass, desperate, despairing, utterly fatigued, but safe.

Now followed a long run of famine luck. We searched land and sea for a bird or a fish. In the boat we skirted a barren coast, sleeping on rocks without shelter and quenching our thirst by glacial liquid till the stomach collapsed. The indifferent stage of starvation was at hand when we pulled into a nameless bay, carried the boat on a grassy bench, and packed ourselves in it for a sleep that might be our last.

We were awakened by the glad sound of distant walrus calls. Through the glasses, a group was located far off shore, on the middle pack. Our hearts began to thump. A stream of blood came with a rush to our heads. Our bodies were fired with a life that had been foreign to us for many moons. No famished wolf ever responded to a call more rapidly than we did. Quickly we dropped the boat into the water with the implements, and pushed from the famine shores with teeth set for red meat.

The day was beautiful, and the sun from the west poured a wealth of golden light. Only an occasional ripple disturbed the glassy blue through which the boat crept. The pack was about five miles northward. In our eagerness to reach it, the distance seemed spread to leagues. There was not a square of ice for miles about which could have been sought for refuge in case of an attack. But this did not disturb us now. We were blinded to everything except the dictates of our palates.

As we advanced, our tactics were definitely arranged. The animals were on a low pan, which seemed to be loosely run into the main pack. We aimed for a little cut of ice open to the leeward, where we hoped to land and creep up behind hummocks. The splash of our paddles was lost in the noise of the grinding ice and the bellowing of walrus calls.

So excited were the Eskimos that they could hardly pull an oar. It was the first shout of the wilderness which we had heard in many months. We were lean enough to appreciate its import. The boat finally shot up on the ice, and we scattered among the ice blocks for favorable positions. Everything was in our favor. We did not for a moment entertain a thought of failure, although in reality, with the implements at hand, our project was tantamount to attacking an elephant with pocket knives.

We came together behind an unusually high icy spire only a few hundred yards from the herd. Ten huge animals were lazily stretched out in the warm sun. A few lively babies tormented their sleeping mothers. There was a splendid line of hummocks, behind which we could advance under cover. With a firm grip on harpoon and line, we started. Suddenly E-tuk-i-shook shouted. "Nan-nook!" (Bear.)

We halted. Our implements were no match for a bear. But we were too hungry to retreat. The bear paid no attention to us. His nose was set for something more to his liking. Slowly but deliberately, he crept up to the snoring herd while we watched with a mad, envious anger welling up within us. Our position was helpless. His long neck reached out, the glistening fangs closed, and a young walrus struggled in the air. All of the creatures woke, but too late to give battle. With dismay and rage, the walruses sank into the water, and the bear slunk off to a safe distance, where he sat down to a comfortable meal. We were not of sufficient importance to interest either the bear or the disturbed herd of giants.

Our limbs were limp when we returned to the boat. The sunny glitter of the waters was now darkened by the gloom of danger from enraged animals. We crossed to the barren shores in a circuitous route, where pieces of ice for refuge were always within reach.

On land, the night was cheerless and cold. We were not in a mood for sleep. In a lagoon we discovered moving things. After a little study of their vague darts they proved to be fish. A diligent search under stones brought out a few handfuls of tiny finny creatures. With gratitude I saw that here was an evening meal. Seizing them, we ate the wriggling things raw. Cooking was impossible, for we had neither oil nor wood.

On the next day the sun at noon burned with a real fire – not the sham light without heat which had kept day and night in perpetual glitter for several weeks. Not a breath of air disturbed the blue glitter of the sea. Ice was scattered everywhere. The central pack was farther away, but on it rested several suspicious black marks. Through the glasses we made these out to be groups of walruses. They were evidently sound asleep for we heard no calls. They were also so distributed that there was a hunt both for bear and man without interference.

We ventured out with a savage desire sharpened by a taste of raw fish. As we advanced several other groups were noted in the water. They gave us much trouble. They did not seem ill-tempered, but dangerously inquisitive. Our boat was dark in color and not much larger than the body of a full-sized bull. To them, I presume, it resembled a companion in distress or asleep. A sight of the boat challenged their curiosity, and they neared us with the playful intention of testing with their tusks the hardness of the canvas. We had experienced such love taps before, however, with but a narrow escape from drowning, and we had no desire for further walrus courtship.

Fortunately, we could maintain a speed almost equal to theirs, and we also found scattered ice-pans, about which we could linger while their curiosity was being satisfied by the splash of an occasional stone.

From the iceberg we studied the various groups of

walruses for the one best situated for our primitive methods of attack. We also searched for meddlesome bears.
None was detected. Altogether we counted more than a
hundred grunting, snorting creatures arranged in black
hills along a line of low ice. There were no hummocks or
pressure lifts, under cover of which we might advance to
within the short range required for our harpoons. All of
the walrus-encumbered pans were adrift and discon-
nected from the main pack. Conflicting currents gave
each group a slightly different motion. We studied this
movement for a little while.

We hoped, if possible, to make our attack from the ice.
With the security of a solid footing, there was no danger
and there was a greater certainty of success. But the speed
of the ice on this day did not permit such an advantage.
We must risk a water attack. This is not an unusual
method of the Eskimo, but he follows it with a kayak, a
harpoon and line fitted with a float and a drag for the end
of his line. Our equipment was only a makeshift, and
could not be handled in the same way.

Here was food in massive heaps. We had had no breakfast and no full meal for many weeks. Something must be
done. The general drift was eastward, but the walrus pans
drifted slightly faster than the main pack. Along the pack
were several high points, projecting a considerable distance seaward. We took our position in the canvas boat
behind one of these floating capes, and awaited the drift of
the sleeping monsters.

Their movement was slow enough to give us plenty
of time to arrange our battle tactics. The most vital part
of the equipment was the line. If it were lost, we could
not hope to survive the winter. It could not be replaced,
and without it we could not hope to cope with the life of
the sea, or even that of the land. The line was a new,
strong sealskin rawhide of ample length, which had
been reserved for just such an emergency. Attached
to the harpoon, with the float properly adjusted, it is

seldom lost, for the float moves and permits no sudden strain.

To safeguard the line, a pan was selected only a few yards in diameter. This was arranged to do the duty of a float and a drag. With the knife two holes were cut, and into these the line was fastened near its center. The harpoon end was taken into the boat, the other end was coiled and left in a position where it could be easily picked from the boat later. Three important purposes were secured by this arrangement – the line was relieved of a sudden strain; if it broke, only half would be lost; and the unused end would serve as a binder to other ice when the chase neared its end.

Now the harpoon was set to the shaft, and the bow of our little twelve-foot boat cleared for action. Peeping over the wall of ice, we saw the black-littered pans slowly coming toward us. Our excitement rose to shouting point. But our nerves were under the discipline of famine. The pan, it was evident, would go by us at a distance of about fifty feet.

The first group of walruses were allowed to pass. They proved to be a herd of twenty-one mammoth creatures, and, entirely aside from the danger of attack, their unanimous plunge would have raised a sea that must have swamped us.

On the next pan were but three spots. At a distance we persuaded ourselves that they were small – for we had no ambition for formidable attacks. One thousand pounds of meat would have been sufficient for us. They proved, however, to be the largest bulls of the lot. As they neared the point, the hickory oars of the boat were gripped – and out we shot. They all rose to meet us, displaying the glitter of ivory tusks from little heads against huge wrinkled necks. They grunted and snorted viciously – but the speed of the boat did not slacken. E-tuk-i-shook rose. With a savage thrust he sank the harpoon into a yielding neck.

The walruses tumbled over themselves and sank into the water on the opposite side of the pan. We pushed upon the vacated floe without leaving the boat, taking the risk of ice puncture rather than walrus thumps. The short line came up with a snap. The ice-pan began to plough the sea. It moved landward. What luck! I wondered if the walrus would tow us and its carcass ashore. We longed to encourage the homing movement, but we dared not venture out. Other animals had awakened to the battle call, and now the sea began to seethe and boil with enraged, leaping red-eyed monsters.

The float took a zigzag course in the offing. We watched the movement with a good deal of anxiety. Our next meal and our last grip of life were at stake. For the time being nothing could be done.

The three animals remained together, two pushing the wounded one along and holding it up during breathing spells. In their excitement they either lost their bearings or deliberately determined to attack. Now three ugly snouts pointed at us. This was greatly to our advantage, for on ice we were masters of the situation.

Taking inconspicuous positions, we awaited the assault. The Eskimos had lances, I an Alpine axe. The walruses dove and came on like torpedo boats, rising almost under our noses, with a noise that made us dodge. In a second two lances sank into the harpooned strugglers. The water was thrashed. Down again went the three. The lances were jerked back by return lines, and in another moment we were ready for another assault from the other side. But they dashed on, and pulled the float-floe, on which we had been, against the one on which we stood, with a crushing blow.

Here was our first chance to secure the unused end of the line, fastened on the other floe. Ah-we-lah jumped to the floe and tossed me the line. The spiked shaft of the ice-axe was driven in the ice and the line fixed to it, so now the two floes were held together. Our stage of action was enlarged, and we had the advantage of being towed by the animals we fought.

Here was the quiet sport of the fisherman and the savage excitement of the battle-field run together in a new chase. The struggle was prolonged in successive stages. Time passed swiftly. In six hours, during which the sun had swept a quarter of the circle, the twin floes were jerked through the water with the rush of a gunboat. The jerking line attached to our enraged pilots sent a thrill of life which made our hearts jump. The lances were thrown, the line was shortened, a cannonade of ice blocks was kept up, but the animal gave no signs of weakening. Seeing that we could not inflict dangerous wounds, our tactics were changed to a kind of siege, and we aimed not to permit the animal its breathing spells.

The line did not begin to slacken until midnight. The battle had been on for almost twelve hours. But we did not feel the strain of action, nor did our chronic hunger seriously disturb us. Bits of ice quenched our thirst and the chill of night kept us from sweating. With each rise of the beast for breath now, the line slackened. Gently it was hauled in and secured. Then a rain of ice blocks, hurled in rapid succession, drove the spouting animals down. Soon the line was short enough to deliver the lance in the captured walrus at close range. The wounded animal was now less troublesome, but the others tore about under us like submarine boats, and at the most unexpected moments would shoot up with a wild rush.

We did not attempt to attack them, however. All our attention was directed to the end of the line. The lance was driven with every opportunity. It seldom missed, but the action was more like spurs to a horse, changing an intended attack upon us to a desperate plunge into the deep, and depriving the walrus of oxygen.

Finally, after a series of spasmodic encounters which lasted fifteen hours, the enraged snout turned blue, the fiery eyes blackened, and victory was ours – not as the result of the knife alone, not in a square fight of brute force, but by the superior cunning of the human animal under the stimulus of hunger.

During all this time we had been drifting. Now, as the battle ended, we were not far from a point about three miles south of our camp. Plenty of safe pack-ice was near. A primitive pulley was arranged by passing the line through slits in the walrus' nose and holes in the ice. The great carcass, weighing perhaps three thousand pounds, was drawn onto the ice and divided into portable pieces. Before the sun poured its morning beams over the ice, all had been securely taken ashore.

With ample blubber, a camp fire was now made between two rocks by using moss to serve as a wick. Soon, pot after pot of savory meat was voraciously consumed. We ate with a mad, vulgar, insatiable hunger. We spoke little. Between gulps, the huge heap of meat and blubber was cached under heavy rocks, and secured – so we thought, from bears, wolves and foxes.

When eating was no longer possible, sleeping dens were arranged in the little boat, and in it, like other gluttonous animals after an engorgement, we closed our eyes to a digestive sleep. For the time, at least, we had fathomed the depths of gastronomic content, and were at ease with ourselves and with a bitter world of inhuman strife.

At the end of about fifteen hours, a stir about our camp suddenly woke us. We saw a huge bear nosing about our fireplace. We had left there a walrus joint, weighing about one hundred pounds, for our next meal. We jumped up, all of us, at once, shouting and making a pretended rush. The bear took up the meat in his forepaws and walked off, manlike, on two legs, with a threatening grunt. His movement was slow and cautious, and his grip on the meat was secure. Occasionally he veered about, with a beckoning turn of the head, and a challenging call. But we did not accept the challenge. After moving away about three hundred yards on the sea-ice, he calmly sat down and devoured our prospective meal.

With lances, bows, arrows, and stones in hand, we next crossed a low hill, beyond which was located our precious cache of meat. Here, to our chagrin, we saw two other bears, with heads down and paws busily digging about the cache. We were not fitted for a hand-to-hand encounter. Still, our lives were equally at stake, whether we attacked or failed to attack. Some defense must be made. With a shout and a fiendish rush, we attracted the busy brutes' attention. They raised their heads, turned, and to our delight and relief, grudgingly walked off seaward on the moving ice. Each had a big piece of our meat with him.

Advancing to the cache, we found it absolutely depleted. Many other bears had been there. The snow and the sand was trampled down with innumerable bear tracks. Our splendid cache of the day previous was entirely lost. We could have wept with rage and disappointment. One thing we were made to realize, and that was that life here was now to be a struggle with the bears for supremacy. With little ammunition, we were not at all able to engage in bear fights. So, baffled, and unable to resent our robbery, starvation again confronting us, we packed our few belongings and moved westward over Braebugten Bay to Cape Sparbo.

BUSH MAN

Laurens van der Post

Laurens van der Post was born in Africa in 1906. After service in World War II he undertook several expeditions to little-known parts of Africa, including to the Kalahari in search of the "Wild Bushmen", the original inhabitants of South Africa, which became the subject of his book The Lost World of the Kalahari. *His other books include* Venture to the Interior, The Heart of the Hunter *and* The Seed and the Sower. *Sir Laurens van der Post died in 1996.*

From The Lost World of the Kalahari:

We had clearly come to the highest and most solid part of the swamp. Much as I would have liked to go on to Maun by water, I was not over-disappointed. We were through the outer defences, across the last moat, and within the inmost keep of this formidable stronghold of ancient life. If there were River Bushmen still to be found in organized entities it would be here among the sparkling islands rising now everywhere out of the burning water. Behind screens of elegant reeds and sedges and fringes of palms, their dense bush and gleaming crown of lofty wood stood out resolutely in the blue.

"Do you think there could be any people there?" I

asked our guide. I did not mention Bushmen specifically, because I had become daily more superstitious about too direct an approach in so indirect a world.

"Sometimes, perhaps two, perhaps three," he said, gravely dubious, knowing what I meant.

"Where do you think would be the best shade to rest for a while then, and perhaps find a buck or two to shoot before we go home?" I went on, pressing him no further.

At that a look of new life came into his eyes and a low laugh broke from him. He jumped into the water, swung the makorro round so fast without warning that Long-axe was nearly thrown off his balance, climbed quickly in and raced across to the north where a long slope of yellow winter grass went slowly up from green reeds to clumps of dense black high wood. So slight were all gradients in the swamp that we had to disembark a hundred yards from the edge of the lagoon and wade ankle-deep ashore, leaving the makorros caught in the reeds. Instinctively no one spoke but conveyed their meaning by signs. The water was so hot it almost burned my cooler ankles and at the first touch of the fiery island earth I put on my boots. How still the island was! And yet I had an odd feeling that some kind of vibration was running there through the shining air, as if somewhere within these black woods a powerful dynamo was running to charge the lonely place with electricity. My companions seemed aware of it too, for as I took my gun from Comfort to move off towards the clumps of wood, the paddlers, each with a long throwing spear in hand, began hotly disputing with one another as to who should lead the way.

"What's the matter?" I whispered to Comfort.

"They're afraid of buffalo, *Moren*," he said. "No one likes being in the lead when there might be buffalo about."

Tired of the dispute, Long-axe turned his broad shoulders disdainfully on the others and, with a superb look of scorn on his broad, open young face, walked to the front. But I held him back and called the guide.

"This is your place," I commanded him in a whisper. "You are the guide. You go ahead and I'll follow immediately behind you."

He looked as if he would still demur but he was at heart a fair person and the justice, as much as the note of command, compelled him. Perhaps I should have paused a moment then to let the turmoil of the dispute subside within him. However, I let him walk straight on, his long spear in hand, but not looking about him as attentively as he should have done. I followed, with Comfort next and the paddlers in single file behind him.

We walked thus for about a quarter of a mile. All the while I felt increasingly uneasy and aware of the odd vibration and crackle of electricity charging the shining element of the high noonday air. Carefully as I looked around me I saw no fresh spoor of any kind, and I am certain none of the others did or they would have warned me. None the less because of my growing uneasiness I was about to halt our small procession, when it happened.

We were in a round, hollow depression up to our chins in yellow grass and approaching the centre of the island. All around us were dense copses of black trees sealed with shadow and invariably wearing a feather of palm in their peaked caps. Suddenly the guide slapped his neck loudly with the flat of his hand. I myself felt the unmistakable stab of a tsetse fly on my own neck and thought: "If there's fly here, buffalo can't be far away."

At that precise moment the copses all around us burst apart and buffalo, who had been within, sleeping, came hurtling through their crackling sides with arched necks, thundering hooves, and flying tails, all with the ease and speed of massed acrobats breaking hoops of paper to tumble into the arena for the finale of some great circus.

The guide dropped his spear, instantly fell flat on his

stomach and wriggled away into the grass. So did the paddlers. Comfort stood his ground only long enough to call out to me hoarsely: "Master, throw your gun away. Let's crawl on our hands and knees and pretend to be animals nibbling the grass. It's our only chance."

However, I stood my ground because, in some strange way, now that my uneasiness was explained I was not afraid. Perhaps I knew, too, it would be useless to run. But whatever the reason, I remember only a kind of exultation at witnessing so truly wild and privileged a sight. Automatically I slammed a cartridge into the breech of my gun and held it ready on my arm while the copses all round me went on exploding and the ground began to shake and tremble under my feet. For one minute it looked as if some buffalo, coming up from behind me, were going to run me down. But at the last minute they divided and passed not ten yards on either side of me. From all points and at every moment, their number was added to until the yellow grass and the glade far beyond ran black with buffalo, as if a bottle of indian ink had been split over it. They took to the channel ahead in a solid black lump, like a ship being launched, throwing up a mighty splash of white water over the reeds before they vanished round a curve of the main wood. I thought with strange regret, "They have gone", and stood turning over in my exalted senses the tumultuous impression of their black hooves slinging clay at the blue; bowed Mithraic heads and purple horns cleaving grass and reeds and spray of thorn like the prows of dark ships of the Odyssey on the sea of a long Homeric summer; deep eyes so intent with the inner vision driving them that they went by me unseeingly.

Suddenly there was another crackle of paper wood behind me. A smaller copse burst open and the greatest bull I have ever seen came charging straight at me.

The paddlers and Comfort, who were all miraculously reappearing, formed a kind of Greek chorus round me,

shouting over and over again: "Shoot, Master! Shoot,
Father! Shoot, Chief of Chiefs! It's the lone one! It's the
lone bull!"

Yet again I held my fire, though for a different reason,
and such a fantastic one that I must apologize for it in
advance. When my paddlers shouted "Shoot!" I knew
they were right. Here, even if safety did not seem to
command it, was a chance to ensure our supply of food for
days to come. But all my life I have dreamed about one
particular buffalo. Much as I love the lion, elephant,
kudu, and eland, the animal closest to the earth and with
most of the quintessence of Africa in its being is for me the
buffalo of the serene marble brow. Ever since I have been
a small boy I have dreamed of one particular buffalo above
all buffaloes. I will not enlarge on all the fantastic situa-
tions in which my dreaming mind has encountered him,
and the great and little-known stretches of the continent
in which my eyes have, for years, sought him with a
growing hunger. All that matters is that unless absolutely
forced to, I could not shoot on this occasion because here,
at last, was the buffalo of my dreams. He took shape as a
lone bull charging at me, the purple noonday light billowing like silk around him. He came straight at me, so close
that at last, reluctantly, I was about to put my gun to my
shoulder and shoot.

For the second time my companions vanished. Then
the buffalo abruptly swerved aside, and charged by me so
close that his smell, the lost smell of the devout animal age
before man, went acid in my nose.

I stood there watching him vanish like a man seeing his
manhood in the field die down before him, thinking:
"Only one thing saved me. I was not afraid. Because of
that I belonged to them and the overall purpose of the
day. In their magnetic deeps they knew it. But afraid, no
gun or friend on earth could have saved me."

I came to, trembling all over with the fear of what
would have happened if I had been afraid, to hear the

guide, sufficiently relieved to find himself alive to be mockingly reproachful of me, saying: "There was meat there you know, Master, for many days." His voice sounded as if he were far away and not rising out of the grass near me. I gave no answer but walked over to where the others were uttering cries of astonishment over the spoor of the lone bull.

"Look!" Comfort exclaimed, pointing to the puncture in the clay behind each of the rear hoof-prints. "Look how deep his after-claws have pierced the clay!"

The buffalo, once he has stunned his enemies with head and horn, likes to give them the *coup de grâce* with the pointed dagger he carries in a leather sheath at the heels of his hind legs. But none of us had ever seen after-claws so long as these.

"Auck!" Long-axe said, shaking his head and his voice gentle as a woman's with wonder. "He must be the Chief of their Chiefs!"

But Samutchoso was looking more at me, not the spoor. In the same tone of awe that he had used the evening before when I shot the lechwe, he said quietly, certain of his meaning: "He knew you, Master. He recognized you and knowing you turned aside."

After that we tried to rest in the nearest shadows but the shade-loving tsetse fly soon drove us out to seek relief in the hot sun. I made no attempt to hunt because I was certain the alarm raised by the buffalo would have stampeded the game for many miles around. In fact we were hardly back in the open when a baboon, now thoroughly on the alert, spotted us and broadcast a loud warning to the bush below him. Instead we did a complete circuit of the island to look for signs of human occupation. We found none except, well above flood-water level, the remains of three ancient makorros, unlike our paddlers' of flat-bottomed design, slowly rotted and rotting in the grass.

"Massarwa! Bushmen!" Samutchoso, who seemed

more aware of my main purpose than the others, explained unbidden as he came to stand sharing my absorption beside me.

All this time I noticed that the nerves of my companions had been sorely tried by the encounter with the buffalo. Whenever a baboon frantically rattled a palm in the silence, or a foraging party of indefatigable termites dropped a dry limb from a dead tree to crash in the bush below, they started violently and appeared ready to run. They followed me into the dark main wood with reluctance, and sought the daylight beyond with the eagerness of a vivid apprehension. Their relief when we rounded the circle where we had left the makorros among the motionless rushes, and started back for camp, made them chant with joy as they bent down to take up their paddles. However, I lay on my back in the bottom of the craft, looking deeply up into the blue channel of the sky framed between the trembling reed tips above me, with my heart and mind still so much in the scene with the buffalo that I had no room even for the negative answer implicit in the rotting Bushman dug-outs on the island. I felt that the encounter had for a moment made me immediate, and had, all too briefly, closed a dark time-gap in myself. With out twentieth-century selves we have forgotten the importance of being truly and openly primitive. We have forgotten the art of our legitimate beginnings. We no longer know how to close the gap between the far past and the immediate present in ourselves. We need primitive nature, the First Man in ourselves, it seems, as the lungs need air and the body food and water; yet we can only achieve it by a slinking often shameful, back-door entrance. I thought finally that of all the nostalgias that haunt the human heart the greatest of them all, for me, is an everlasting longing to bring what is youngest home to what is oldest, in us all.

ACKNOWLEDGEMENTS

The editor has made every effort to secure the requisite permission to reprint copyrighted material in this volume. In case of any omissions or errors, please contact the editor c/o the Publishers.

"The Worst Journey in the World", from *The Worst Journey in the World*, Apsley Cherry-Garrard, Picador, 1994. Copyright © Angela Mathias 1922, 1965.

"Beauty and the Badlands", from *Sierra* magazine, March/April 2000. Reprinted by permission of the Sierra Club.

"In Trouble Again", from *In Trouble Again: A Journey Between the Orinoco and the Amazon*. Redmond O'Hanlon, Hamish Hamilton, 1988. Copyright © 1988 Redmond O'Hanlon.

"Crossing the Empty Quarter" from "The First Crossing of the Great South Arabia Desert". *Explorers All*, Sir Percy Sykes (ed.), George Newnes Ltd, 1938.

"Walkabout" from *Feet of Clay*, Ffyona Campbell, Orion, 1999. Copyright © 1991 Ffyona Campbell.

"West with the Night" from *West with the Night*, Beryl Markham, Virago, 1984, Copyright © 1942 Beryl Markham.

"The Crossing" from *Danziger's Travels*, Nick Danziger, Paladin, 1988. Copyright © 1987 Nick Danziger. Reprinted by permission of HarperCollins Publishers.

"Heart of Darkness", from *East Along the Equator*, Helen Winternitz, Sceptre, 1989. Copyright © 1987 Helen Winternitz.

"The Brendan Voyage" from *The Brendan Voyage*, Tim Severin, Arrow Books, 1979. Copyright © 1978 Tim Severin.

"Den of Thieves" from *Children of Kali*, Kevin Rushby, Constable & Robinson, 2002. Copyright © 2002 Kevin Rushby.

"Across the Syrian Desert" from *The Letters of Gertrude Bell*, ed. Lady Bell, Benn, 1930.

"A Long Climb in the Hindu Kush" from *A Short Walk in the Hindu Kush*, Eric Newby, Secker & Warburg, 1958. Copyright © 1958 Eric Newby. Reprinted by permission of HarperCollins.

"Ice Bird" from *Ice Bird*, David Lewis, Collins, 1976. Copyright © 1975 David Lewis.

"River of Doubt" from *Through the Brazilian Wilderness*, Theodore Roosevelt, John Murray, 1914.

"Sledge-Tracks" from *The People of the Polar North*, Knud Rasmussen, Kegan, Paul, Trench, Trubner, 1908.

"The Reef" from *The Kon-Tiki Expedition*, Thor Heyerdahl, Penguin, 1963. Copyright © 1950 Thor Heyerdahl. Reprinted by permission of HarperCollins.

"Flight to Apia" from Ernest K. Gann's *The Flying Circus*. Ernest K. Gann. Hodder & Stoughton, 1976.

"In Patagonia" from *Chasing Che*, Patrick Symmes, Robinson, 2001. Copyright © 2000 Patrick Symmes.

"Romancing the Stone" from *The Wild Calling*. Quentin Chester, New Holland, 1998. Copyright © 1998 Quentin Chester.

"American Horseman" from *Tschiffeley's Ride*. A. F. Tschiffeley, Heinemann, 1933.

"In Chief Yali's Shoes" from *Pass the Butterworms*. Tim Cahill, Black Swan, 2004. Copyright © 1997 Tim Cahill.

"Kampala Halt" from *The World Commuter*, Christopher Portway, Summersdale, 2001. Copyright © 2001 Christopher Portway.

"In a Lost Valley" from *Explorers Remember*, ed. Odette Tchernine, Jarrolds, 1967. Copyright © 1967 Ralph Izzard.

"Open Boat" from *Shackleton's Boat Journey*, F. A. Worsley, 1999. Copyright © The Estate of F.A. Worsley.

"Across South Georgia" from *South: The Endurance Expedition*, Ernest Shackleton, Penguin, 2002.

"Travels with Pegasus" from *Travels with Pegasus*, Christina Dodwell, Sceptre, 1989. Copyright © 1989 Christina Dodwell.

"Victim of Ramadan" from the *Spectator*, 13 September 1980. Copyright © 1980 Shiva Naipaul.

"The Haunt of the Anaconda" from *Exploration Fawcett*, ed. Brian Fawcett, Hutchinson, 1953.

"Into the Belly of Bolivia" from *Outside*, June 2001. Copyright © 2001 Kent Black and *Outside* magazine.

"In Disguise to Everest" from *Through Tibet to Everest*, J.B.L. Noel, Edward Arnold & Co., 1927.

"Farthest North" from *The North Pole*, Robert E. Peary, Frederick A. Stokes, 1910.

"Wings over the Pole" from *Skyward*, Richard Evelyn Bird, G.P. Putnam's Sons, 1928. Copyright © 1928 The Estate of Richard Evelyn Byrd.

"Tsangpo Gorge" from *Explorers All*, Sir Percy Sykes (ed.), George Newnes Ltd, 1938.

"Dhow Safari" from *Continental Drifter*, Michael McRae, Lyons & Burford, 1993. Copyright © 1993 Michael J. McRae.

"Conquering Half Dome" from *Salon*, 31 July 1999, Copyright © Salon 1999.

"Road Trip" from *Fear and Loathing in Las Vegas*, Hunter S. Thompson, Flamingo, 1986. Copyright © 1971 Hunter S. Thompson. Reprinted by permission of HarperCollins.

"The Ride to Arfaja" from *The Essential T.E. Lawrence*, ed. David Garnett, Penguin, 1951.

"Avalanche" from *The Assault on Mount Everest*, Brigadier-General Hon. C.G. Bruce et al, Edward Arnold, 1923.

"Too Close to the Ice" from *My Polar Flights*, Umberto Nobile, Muller, 1961.

"Snow from the Moon" from *The Moonshine Mule*, Tom Fremantle, Robinson, 2003. Copyright © 2003 Tom Fremantle.

"The Lost City of the Incas" from *Lost City of the Incas*, Hiram Bingham, Phoenix House, 1951. Reprinted by permission of the Orion Publishing Group.

"The Prince's Caravan" from *News from Tartary*, Peter Fleming, Futura, 1980.

"Mount Burney" (originally "Volcano of Patagonia") from *Explorers Remember*, ed. Odette Tchernine, Jarrolds, 1967. Copyright © 1967 Eric Shipton.

"Desperate Straits" from *My Attainment of the Pole*, *Frederick A. Cook*, Frederick A. Cook, Polar Publications, 1911.

"Bush Man" from *The Lost World of the Kalahari*, Laurens van der Post, Penguin, 1962. Copyright © 1958 Laurens van der Post.

Other titles available from Robinson Publishing

The Mammoth Book of Endurance & Adventure
Ed. Jon E. Lewis   **£7.99** [ ]
Inspired by Sir Ernest Shackleton's 1914–15 escape from the bitter clutches of
Antarctica, this vast collection of over 30 accounts of true-life adventures,
spanning the years from 1800 to the end of the twentieth century, is by turns
exhilarating, harrowing and tragic.

The Mammoth Book of Heroes   Ed. Jon E. Lewis   **£7.99** [ ]
True courage is one of the most highly valued attributes of humanity, honoured
in the historical record from ancient times to present. Gathered together in this
volume are over 70 accounts, many of them in the words of those who were there
– from the experiences of Florence Nightingale to the unflinching protestors
killed in Tiananmen Square.

The Mammoth Book of Journalism   Ed. Jon E. Lewis   **£7.99** [ ]
Every day newspapers both record and influence the course of history. From
social documentaries like Charles Dickens's harrowing description of the Ragged
School in 1852 to war reports such as John F. Burns's account of the Taliban
insurrection in Afghanistan in 1997, what is written in the world's papers makes
waves that affect us all.

Robinson books are available from all good bookshops or direct from the publisher.
Just tick the titles you want to order and fill in the form below.

TBS Direct
Colchester Road, Frating Green, Colchester, Essex CO7 7DW
Tel: +44 (0) 1206 255777
Fax: +44 (0) 1206 255914
Email: sales@tbs-ltd.co.uk

UK/BFPO customers please allow £1.00 for p&p for the first book, plus 50p for
the second, plus 30p for each additional book up to a maximum charge of £3.00.
Overseas customers (inc. Ireland), please allow £2.00 for the first book, plus
£1.00 for the second, plus 50p for each additional book.

Please send me the titles ticked above.

NAME (Block letters). . . . .

ADDRESS . . . .

. . . .

POSTCODE . . . .

I enclose a cheque/PO (payable to TBS Direct) for . . . .

I wish to pay by Switch/Credit card

Number . . . .

Card Expiry Date . . . .

Switch Issue Number . . . .

Other titles available from Robinson Publishing

The Mammoth Book of On the Road
             Ed. Maxim Jakubowski and M. Christian   £7.99 [ ]
The lure of the open road is freedom and travel more exciting than the arrival.
Included in this wide-ranging collection are excerpts from classics such as
Kerouac's *On the Road* as well as little known gems by J.G. Ballard, Michael
Moorcock and John Kessel.

The Mammoth Book of Travel in Dangerous Places
                         Ed. John Keay   £6.99 [ ]
Explorers were once the premier celebrities of their day capturing the world's
headlines. John Keay, editor of the *Royal Geographical Society's History of
World Exploration*, has selected the original first-hand narratives of many of
these heroes, including Ross and Franklin's experiences in the Arctic, Huc's
account of the "Forbidden City" of Lhasa and the last poignant accounts of
Wills in Australia and Scott in Antarctica.

The Mammoth Book of War Correspondents
                         Ed. Jon E. Lewis   £7.99 [ ]
If the words of untutored soldiers offer the most heartfelt communication of the
experience of war, the war correspondents give the most lucid and complex
picture of its origin and nature. Starting with William Howard Russell's reports
from the Crimea – the birth of war reportage – many of the major conflicts of the
modern era are covered, including John Pilger on the last days of Saigon and
Eric Schmitt on Scud-hunting in the Gulf.

*Robinson books are available from all good bookshops or direct from the publisher.
Just tick the titles you want to order and fill in the form below.*

TBS Direct
Colchester Road, Frating Green, Colchester, Essex CO7 7DW
Tel: +44 (0) 1206 255777
Fax: +44 (0) 1206 255914
Email: sales@tbs-ltd.co.uk

UK/BFPO customers please allow £1.00 for p&p for the first book, plus 50p for
the second, plus 30p for each additional book up to a maximum charge of £3.00.
Overseas customers (inc. Ireland), please allow £2.00 for the first book, plus
£1.00 for the second, plus 50p for each additional book.

Please send me the titles ticked above.

NAME (Block letters). . . . .

ADDRESS . . . .

. . . .

POSTCODE . . . .

I enclose a cheque/PO (payable to TBS Direct) for . . . .

I wish to pay by Switch/Credit card

Number . . . .

Card Expiry Date . . . .

Switch Issue Number . . . .